THE
Wine Atlas
OF CANADA

TONY ASPLER

THE
Wine Atlas
OF CANADA

AN ANGEL EDITION
for

RANDOM HOUSE CANADA

Library and Archives Canada Cataloguing in Publication

Aspler, Tony, 1939-
The wine atlas of Canada / Tony Aspler.

Includes bibliographical references and index.
ISBN-10: 0-679-31334-6
ISBN-13: 978-0-679-31334-2

1. Wine districts–Canada–Guidebooks.   2. Wine districts–Canada–Maps.
3. Wineries–Canada–Guidebooks.   4. Vintners–Canada.
5. Wine and wine making–Canada.   6. Wine industry–Canada–History.   I. Title.

TP559.C3A863 2006   663'.2'00971   C2006-900862-0

Printed and bound in Singapore
10 9 8 7 6 5 4 3 2 1

OPENING SPREAD: Vineyard at Vignoble de la Chapelle Ste. Agnès, Eastern Townships, Quebec.
OPPOSITE: Plantings at Naramata Bench, Okanagan Valley, British Columbia.
FOLLOWING PAGE: Inniskillin Wine's Donald Ziraldo picking Icewine grapes, Niagara
Peninsula, Ontario. FOREWORD SPREAD: Pre-flowering Cabernet Franc vines.

To Canada's winegrowers
and winemakers, all God's children
with hands stained purple

CONTENTS

CHAPTER ONE

The Wine Industry in Canada

CHAPTER TWO

British Columbia

ACKNOWLEDGEMENTS

My apologies if this section reads like an Oscar speech, but I have many people to thank for their contribution to *The Wine Atlas of Canada*. This enterprise has been some years in the making. Since my first book on Canadian wines, *Vintage Canada*, was published in 1982, I have been following the industry both as critic and as evangelist. I have always believed that Canadians could make great wine that would express the soil and climate of our many regions. Now I am convinced of it. *Vintage Canada* has gone through four editions over the years. Then, in 2000, I wrote *Canadian Wine for Dummies* with Barbara Leslie, to bring the information up to date. These books, it now appears, have been a warm-up for this volume.

Every self-respecting wine region has an atlas that shows not only where the wineries are relative to each other but gives information about the soils, the climate, the technologies, and, above all, the people and the sense of place where the grapes are grown and the wines are made. With the exponential growth in the number of wineries across the country, it is no longer possible to keep up with all the activity: the opening of new facilities, the planting of new vineyards, the introduction of new varietals, the movement of winemakers, the acquisitions, mergers, and expansions, and, of course, the wines from each new vintage. I have had to rely on the advice and expertise of many individuals and agencies across Canada.

In each province I have had the privilege of working with dedicated wine lovers whose knowledge and time I have shamefully exploited. They have patiently answered my questions, corrected my mistakes, and accompanied me on this long and sometimes arduous journey.

I would like to thank Steve Elphick, the best wine photographer in Canada, who, with his assistant (and wife), Paula, accompanied me on my travels across the country to all regions. Steve's images capture the beauty of the land and the commitment of the winemakers to their art and craft.

In British Columbia, Dave Gamble, publisher of *Canadian Grapes to Wine* magazine, has been an indispensable and generous source of information on that province's wine industry. Peggy Athans and her staff at the British Columbia Wine Institute were most helpful in providing statistics and facilitating travel. Pat Bowen at the Summerland Research Station gave me invaluable insights into the soils and microclimates of the Okanagan. Finally, to my winewriter/author colleague John Schreiner a debt of gratitude for keeping me abreast of all the latest developments in the province—right up until press time.

In Ontario, I thank Tony Shaw at Brock University for sharing with me his learned research papers on the soils and climate of Ontario's wine regions. Larry Patterson, who rejoices in the name "Little Fat Wino," was an enthusiastic booster of this project and pointed me to winegrowers outside the designated appellations and many of the personalities who will eventually become Canada's new winegrowers. Debra Marshall squired me around Prince Edward County; her pride in her region and her affection for her fellow winegrowers were infectious. Laurie Macdonald, director of the VQA Ontario, and Linda Franklin and Linda Watts at the Wine Council of Ontario never failed to come up with the information I needed to complete my research and to encourage me along the way.

Dr. Chris Naugler, author and winegrower, was my "Deep Palate" in Nova Scotia: he gave me the background I needed to know about Nova Scotia's wineries and their history through our frequent emails and discussions. I would also like to thank my wine-writer colleague Sean Wood, who read and proofed the chapter on his home province, and Hans Christian Jost, who drove my wife, Deborah, and me around Nova Scotia to see all his competitors before showing us his winery under construction in the Gaspereau Valley.

In Quebec I shall be eternally grateful to Alain and Mariette Breault, who took time out of their lives as grape propagators to show Steve and me the wineries of Quebec. On our two trips to "la belle province," Alain drove us on marathon tours to almost every facility in the province, stopping to point out vineyards that were planted with his vine stocks.

I would like to thank my agent, Dean Cooke, who believed in this project from its start. My thanks to Anne Collins at Random House Canada, who embraced the idea, and to Sara Angel at Angel Editions, who kept my nose and palate to the grindstone to ensure that such a complex publishing project would come out as it has. I am grateful to Claire Dawson and Underline Studio for creating this book's design and its maps. My thanks too to Sarah Davies and Rosemary Shipton, whose editing skills improved the manuscript immeasurably, to researchers Amy Hick and Amber Austin, and to my colleague Dean Tudor, whose eagle eye corrected the errors and inconsistencies in my final manuscript. And my deepest appreciation to Deborah, who not only helped with the research but buoyed me up when faced with the daunting challenges of deadlines and computer failures. And then there was Pinot, our Wheaten terrier, who licked my face when I needed it.

Finally, I would like to thank the winemakers across Canada who took the time to respond to my questionnaires and to be interviewed either on site, by phone, or by email. I have tried to include every winery in Canada here, but there comes a point when you have to say "That's it." This atlas would never have been published if I had waited until every Canadian who was poised to open a winery did so. But I am eagerly anticipating future visits to all of the regions to explore the creative efforts of these proudly Canadian winemakers. Cheers!

FOREWORD

There was a time when those of us who know something about the vineyards of Canada felt we had a handle on what was happening across the country. Suddenly there are more winemakers than an outsider could possibly know. And the details of what works best, and where, have taken on the complexity of a great tapestry.

A wine atlas places us wherever we want to be in this world rich in individual experiment and established patterns. There are particular wines I follow every year, but there is also the excitement of discovering the new. It isn't surprising that Tony Aspler has set about producing this atlas. He has the historical experience and the memory, but he is also perpetually curious about the new.

Any analysis of the Canadian wine-producing world reveals just how central the creation of the Vintners Quality Alliance has been to its success. Do not delude yourself in the foggy world of international wine promotion. The most famous European systems are dysfunctional as quality control systems, and they won't help you figure out the difference between great, good, and awful wines. You have to buy the wine and taste it to find out, or rely on a recommendation. The VQA, in contrast, although flawed, is a true quality-control system, and it should tell you something about an unopened bottle.

As for what we are producing in Canada, my own experience leads me to a remarkable revelation: we are often among the best in the world, particularly where the standards are toughest. Great and good Pinot Noir is one of the hardest wines to produce. We are now in that tiny handful of countries that can do it. Riesling is for many the queen of white wines, a severe grape that resists the doctoring of Chardonnay and a wine that, when well made, has a long, complex life. We are now in a tiny group of the best producers.

And then there is sparkling wine, of which there is so much around the world and so little of it drinkable, in spite of vast amounts of publicity. It is now clear that Canada has an almost natural climate and geography for high-quality sparkling wine.

But wine producing is about more than famous, mainstream varieties. It is also about minor grapes, strange microclimates, and wines that are not great but interesting in particular conditions with particular foods.

Tony Aspler places all this detail in a context that makes sense. From famous Icewines and Cabernet Francs to unknown areas with curious grape varieties, he lays out the remarkable reality of Canada's vineyards and their products.

My hope is that this book will encourage more people to incorporate the world of wine into part of their own reality, by taking the atlas and discovering first-hand the geography, the winemakers, and all the other details that make Canada's wines among the best in the world.

John Ralston Saul
TORONTO, NOVEMBER 2005

HOW TO USE THIS BOOK

The Wine Atlas of Canada is your ready reference guide to wineries across the country, giving you details of where they are, how to contact them, and who owns them, as well as information on what you will find when you arrive and what to sample or buy when you get there. I have tried to be as complete and up to date as possible, but the Canadian wine industry is anything but static. I beg your indulgence if a winemaker has moved on or a winery has been sold or you can't find the wines I recommend. Where information has not been available, I have used the term n/a (not available).

This book is designed to give basic information so you can plan your wine tour before you leave home. Remember that many wineries are small, family-run operations and can staff their tasting rooms only on weekends. I strongly advise you to phone ahead if you plan on visiting during weekdays or in the off-season months of November to April. I have also suggested other interesting visits in the vicinity or sights worth experiencing, and noted what not to miss. If you're touring for a day, a few days, or a week, I offer suggestions on which wineries are of special interest and how much time you might spend there.

Each winery entry lists name, address, telephone number, and website. Where there is no website, an email address is provided. There are symbols that accompany every winery entry. Here is an overview of what they mean:

A GUIDE TO WINERY VISITS

Winery size: Rather than quote the number of cases a winery produces, which is very fluid, depending on the year, I have divided them up into three categories by size, each with its own symbol: SMALL: up to 10,000 cases, MEDIUM: 10,000–20,000 cases, LARGE: above 20,000 cases.

Tastings: The opportunity to taste the wines is essentially the reason you visit wineries in the first place (not to admire their bottling lines). Most wineries have tasting rooms where you can sample their products. The usual limit is four tastes per person. Some wineries offer complimentary tasting; others have a small charge they may refund with a purchase of a bottle. In many cases where sampling is without charge, you will be asked to pay for the more expensive specialty wines, such as Icewine.

Restaurant: More and more wineries are opening restaurants. They vary from fine dining to bistro food to cheese plates on the patio. Full-service restaurants are named, and I've included their telephone numbers for reservations.

Accommodation: If you want to sleep in a vineyard, so to speak, look for those wineries that offer accommodation. Rooms vary from luxurious spas to B&Bs with rustic cabins. These are usually fully booked during the summer season, so reserve ahead to avoid disappointment.

�֎

Picnic area: Many of the wineries provide places where you can lunch outdoors or on covered patios, ranging from the rustic to the opulent. Some of these areas are licensed and others are not. Many of the wineries, especially in British Columbia, are in the process of applying for licences, so I recommend that you phone ahead and inquire if they serve wine in their picnic area. However, you cannot bring your own wine to these areas.

👤

Public tours: Most wineries offer tours. Some are highly organized, with dedicated personnel to show you around and explain the operation. The majority, however, rely on the winemakers and their assistants to do the job, so conducted tours may not always be available. Some wineries have self-guided tours, with signage to direct you through the proper sequence of winemaking events, from the delivery of the grapes at the crush pad to the final product in their shop. A small percentage of wineries charge for their tours, but most offer them free. If you are travelling in a group, it is advisable to phone ahead and reserve your day and time.

HELPFUL INFORMATION ABOUT SERVICES

The following symbols indicate limitations that might apply to any of the above services, whether there is a charge, if it is necessary to make an appointment, or if the services are available only to groups.

$ Charge   **)** By Appointment   **ɢ** Groups Only

A WORD ON WINERY INFORMATION

Year founded: The year I have cited is the opening of the winery, not when the vineyard was planted.

Founders: The names of the founders may, if the property has been sold, be different from the current proprietors. In these cases, the present owners' names will appear in the winery's profile.

Winemakers: Now this listing is trickier because winemakers are like chefs and tend to move around a lot. I have noted the names of the winemakers at the time of writing. If they have moved on, I hope it is to a more profitable position.

Grape varieties: This category lists the varieties the winery has planted in its own vineyard. In some cases, you will find that I recommend wines not grown by the winery but made from grapes purchased from other growers.

Recommended wines: The wines I have chosen to recommend are those for which the winery has a proven track record, or, in the case of new wineries, those I have tasted from the barrel that augur well for the future. Where I have been unable to taste the products of a given winery, I have noted them as "not tasted."

A NOTE ON THE MAPS

The maps included throughout the book are intended as guides only. I have included maps that highlight the winegrowing regions of the world and of each province, as well as maps that illustrate the relative placement of operating wineries in each region.

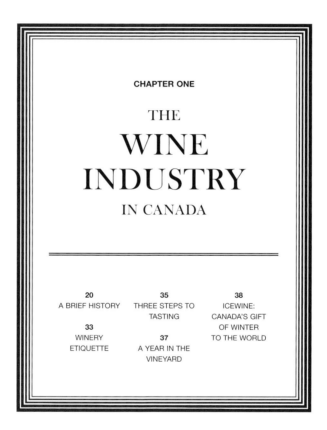

CHAPTER ONE

THE
WINE
INDUSTRY
IN CANADA

THE WINE INDUSTRY IN CANADA
A BRIEF HISTORY

Winemaking in Canada dates from early European settlement in this country. It's a history we share with all Commonwealth countries whose territories are located between latitudes 30° and 50° both north and south of the equator—the zone where wine grapes can survive and flourish. As in Australia, South Africa, and New Zealand, our grandparents' palates were influenced by the British predilection for port and sherry, and wines from the 1800s to the Second World War mimicked those products. They were sweet and powerful, with alcohol volumes of 20 percent or more. The mid-twentieth century saw a veritable revolution in taste for wine. When Canadian servicemen and women returned from the battlefields after the Second World War, they remembered the wines they had tasted in Europe. And, with the waves of European immigration to Canada after the late 1940s, the desire for such wines meshed with the knowledge of how to produce them.

There was a problem, though: the Horticultural Research Institute in Ontario and the Summerland Agricultural Research Station in British Columbia considered it folly to try to grow the noble vinifera grape varieties that make the great wines of Bordeaux, Burgundy, and the Rhine. These grape vines, the experts advised, were too delicate to survive the rigours of a Canadian winter. So the industry in both provinces played it safe by planting the unkillable native North American labrusca varieties (Concord, Niagara) along with sturdy, early ripening hybrids such as Seyval Blanc and Maréchal Foch. The wineries, in a calculated move to copy the wines of Europe, labelled their bottles with pictures resembling German castles or French châteaux and called them Claret, Burgundy, and Hock. On liquor board shelves they might have looked European, but in the glass they tasted anything but.

In the span of one generation the Canadian wine industry has changed beyond recognition. Today our wineries are winning gold medals in international competitions not only for their Icewine but for Chardonnay, Riesling, Cabernet blends, and Pinot Noir. At the 2004 San Francisco International Wine Competition, Jackson-Triggs' Okanagan winemaker Bruce Nicholson was awarded the prestigious André Tchelistcheff Winemaker of the Year award for excellence in a single line of wines. A total of 964 wineries from twenty-one countries and twenty-five US states had entered the competition. What has caused this sea change in Canadian wines? Basically, there are four factors: global free trade, the switch in grapes from native labrusca varieties to world-class vinifera varieties, the introduction of the VQA quality-control system, and the explosion in viticultural expertise in the country.

The watershed year was 1988 and free trade with the United States. The Free Trade Agreement included a ruling, under the General Agreement on

PREVIOUS SPREAD: Vineyard in Prince Edward County.
OPPOSITE: Grapes being loaded into a crushing and de-stemming machine, Inniskillin Wines, Ontario.

Harvesting grapes in the Niagara Peninsula.

Tariffs and Trade, that phased out the tariffs on imported wines that had hitherto protected the local industry. Wineries in Ontario and British Columbia would now have to compete with the wines of the world on an equal playing field. (The nascent wine regions of Quebec and Nova Scotia were not yet on the radar.)

Until then, provincial governments had given guarantees to grape growers that their crops would be sold to wineries at negotiated prices; the grapes rejected by winemakers would be purchased by the government for distillation into industrial alcohol. There was no incentive for growers to move from hybrids to the vinifera varieties. A few dedicated growers, such as John Marynissen and Bill Lenko in Ontario, however, had proved they could grow and sustain Cabernet Sauvignon and Chardonnay in a marginal climate, so long as they used the right viticultural practices.

With the abolition of trade barriers, the industry

CANADIAN OAK

Wine barrels made from Canadian oak, in the traditional Bordeaux 225 litre format, were first used by the Niagara Peninsula winery Lailey Vineyard for their 2001 Chardonnay. The oak came from a forest in Ancaster, Ontario, and was coopered in the United States.

The concept of using Canadian oak for Canadian wine was the brainchild of Hamilton physician, amateur winemaker, and woodworker Dr. Jim Hedges. While hiking through a forest in Brant County, Ontario, the idea occurred to him that Canadian white oak, a species similar to the American *Quercus alba* that is widely used by the world's wineries, could also be pressed into service. With his colleague Mike Risk, a professor of biology and geology at McMaster University who shares both his hobbies of winemaking and woodworking, he formed a company to research, produce, and market barrels made of Canadian oak. The wood is harvested and seasoned in Ontario, then shipped to A&K Cooperage in Higbee, Missouri, to be coopered into barrels.

Canadian oak, because it grows in a colder climate, is tighter grained than American oak and gives a distinctively different flavour to the wine. "At the outset," says Hedges, "we were happily surprised to discover that Canadian oak barrels smelled different from either American or French oak barrels. The Canadian oak seemed to impart a flavour similar to French oak, but with different overtones." Subjected to solid-state NMR spectra–generated chemical analysis, Canadian oak was found to be very similar to American oak in structure, though there were strong differences in the range of compounds that give that distinctive vanilla note to wines. Canadian vanillan phenolics are similar to those extracted from oak grown in the forests of France's Massif Central.

In addition to their Chardonnay, Lailey Vineyard has also used Canadian oak for its barrel-aged Pinot Noir, Cabernet Sauvignon, Cabernet Franc, and Vidal Icewine. "What we find most exciting about Canadian oak," says winemaker Derek Barnett, "is how elegantly it complements the flavours of the grapes grown in the same climate. The oak character is integrated with the wine from a very early stage in the barrel, and the flavours are charmingly subtle and pervasive." Other Ontario wineries that have been using Canadian oak barrels include Malivoire, Featherstone, Daniel Lenko, Marynissen, and Thirty Bench. In British Columbia, Burrowing Owl, Golden Mile, Hillside, and Orofino have been trying out Canadian oak.

Ontario may not be the only region in Canada that can supply oak barrels to winemakers. Petite Rivière Vineyards in Nova Scotia has experimented with local oak barrels but is not using them commercially as yet.

gave a collective shudder, convinced it was doomed. The vintners' response to this gloom-and-doom scenario was to look at their vineyards and decide they had a massive culling to do. Ontario reduced its vineyards from 24,000 to 17,000 acres, and British Columbians were even more draconian, pulling out more than two-thirds of the vineyards and leaving a mere thousand acres of vines in the ground. The growers began to plant the traditional European varieties that would prove to be the phoenix for the

Stone wall sculpture at Vignoble de la Chapelle Ste. Agnès, Cantons-de-l'Est, Quebec. OPPOSITE: Cherry blossoms in May, Vineland, Ontario.

gives some idea when he quotes the Russian-born American winemaker Alexander Brailow in his *History of Wine in America from the Beginnings to Prohibition* (1989): "People have tried to compare the smell and taste to things they know. In Russia, for instance, they say that the grape Isabella, which is grown extensively in Crimea for red wine, smells like bedbugs. It all depends on the association and personal taste."

These pull-out programs in Ontario and British Columbia meant that future vineyards would be planted to vinifera varieties—the ones the consumer wanted. The same year as free trade, the Vintners Quality Alliance was introduced in Ontario, an appellation system requiring that its wines be 100 percent grown in designated viticultural areas. The regulations stipulated minimum sugar levels for grapes and the varieties that could be used for wine. And, most important, all wines had to be blind tasted for typicity and quality by an independent panel. In 1990, the VQA system was instituted in British Columbia as well.

From the early years, winemaking in Canada had been the preoccupation of passionate amateurs. Farmers and basement hobbyists whose skills were sufficient to make decent wine opened commercial wineries at the urging of friends. They may have taken courses in winemaking or followed the instruction of European relatives, but they had no experience of winemaking in other countries. Growers knew little of trellising techniques used around the world to maximize ripening, and many thought that dropping fruit to concentrate the flavours was a crime against nature. (This procedure is called a "green harvest" when a number of bunches are cut off the vine in August to concentrate the flavours of those that remain. The dropped fruit is left on the ground as fertilizer.) With the advent of the VQA, the more established wineries began to recruit winemakers from other parts of the world who could bring a different experience to working with Ontario and BC fruit. They also sent their own assistant winemakers to do harvests abroad. Today the tally of winemakers from Europe and other New World regions who bring their expertise to Canadian wineries is impressive.

renascent Canadian wine industry, along with preferred hybrids such as Baco Noir and Vidal. It was exactly the right response.

That same year, the *Wine Content Act* in Ontario was revised and labrusca varieties were banned from table wines (they could still be used for "pop" wines such as Baby Duck and for faux sherry and port). Anyone who has ever tasted Concord grape juice will be familiar with the aroma and taste of labrusca grapes. The marker is a chemical called methyl anthranilate, which, when fermented, gives varieties such as Niagara and Isabella a smell that the wine community calls "foxy." It's a difficult smell to define—and I have never been close enough to a fox to confirm this descriptor. But Thomas Pinney

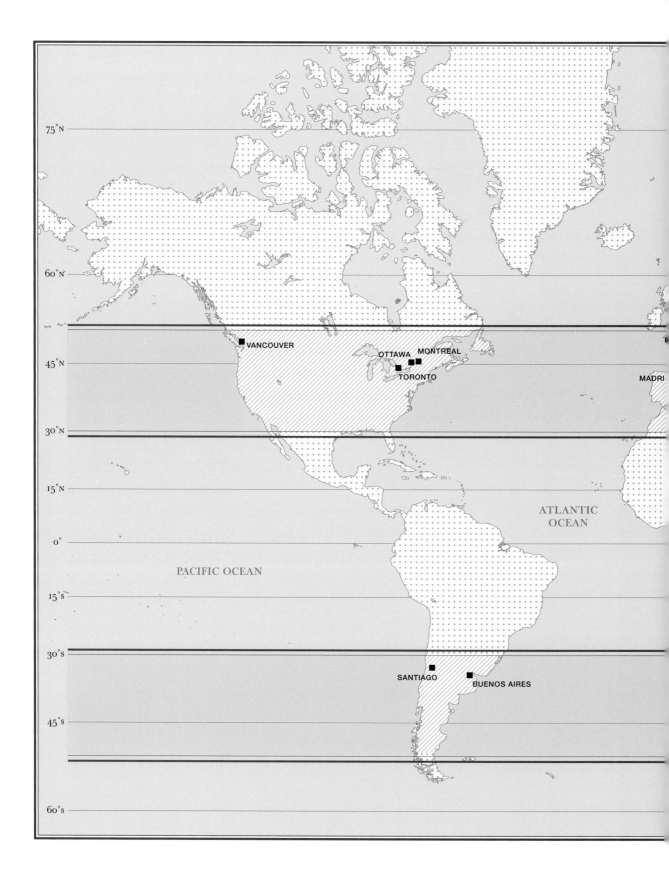

75°N

60°N

45°N   VANCOUVER   OTTAWA   MONTREAL

                          TORONTO   MADRI

30°N

15°N

                                                                   ATLANTIC
                                                                    OCEAN

0°

PACIFIC OCEAN

15°S

30°S

                               SANTIAGO
                                      BUENOS AIRES

45°S

60°S

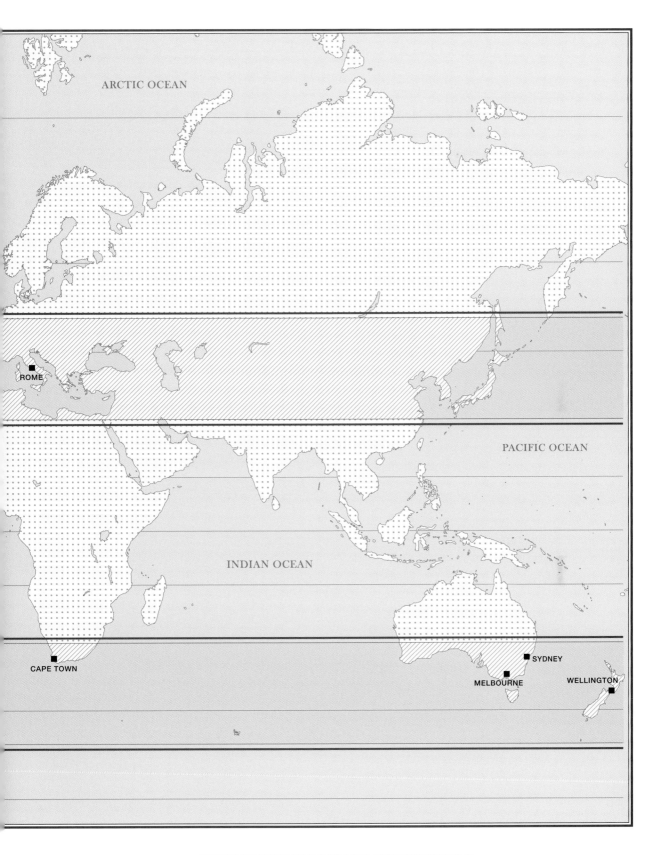

ARCTIC OCEAN

ROME

PACIFIC OCEAN

INDIAN OCEAN

CAPE TOWN

SYDNEY

MELBOURNE

WELLINGTON

WINEGROWING REGIONS OF THE WORLD

Wine grapes flourish in two bands across the globe between
the 30th and 50th parallels north and south of the equator.

CANADIAN WINE FESTIVALS

Alberta

WINEFEST CALGARY: SAIT Campus Centre, February www.winefestcalgary.com

TASTE OF CALGARY: early August www.tasteofcalgary.com

ROCKY MOUNTAIN WINE & FOOD FESTIVAL: Calgary: mid-October; Edmonton: early November www.rockymountainwine.com

British Columbia

OKANAGAN SPRING WINE FESTIVAL: early May www.owfs.com

OKANAGAN SUMMER WINE FESTIVAL: early to mid-August www.owfs.com

OKANAGAN FALL WINE FESTIVAL: late September to early October www.owfs.com

OKANAGAN ANNUAL PEOPLE'S CHOICE AWARDS, KELOWNA: late September www.owfs.com

OKANAGAN ICEWINE FESTIVAL: mid-January www.owfs.com

GALIANO WINE FESTIVAL: mid-August www.galianoisland.com

TOFINO FOOD & WINE FESTIVAL: early June www.tofinofoodandwinefestival.com

VANCOUVER PLAYHOUSE INTERNATIONAL WINE FESTIVAL: early March www.playhousewinefest.com

VANCOUVER ISLAND VINTNERS VIVA WINE FESTIVAL: end August, early September www.islandwineries.ca

Manitoba

WINNIPEG WINE FESTIVAL: early May www.winnipegwinefestival.com

New Brunswick

MONCTON: late October, early November www.wineexpo.ca

Ontario

CUVÉE: May www.cuvee.ca

ONTARIO WINE AWARDS: April www.ontariowineawards.ca

NIAGARA NEW VINTAGE FESTIVAL: early June www.niagarawinefestival.com

NIAGARA WINE FESTIVAL: mid-September www.niagarawinefestival.com

NIAGARA ICEWINE FESTIVAL: January www.niagarawinefestival.com

FIESTA BUCKHORN: July www.fiestabuckhorn.com

TORONTO SANTÉ: Bloor-Yorkville Wine Festival, early May www.santewinefestival.net

SOUTHWESTERN ONTARIO'S VINTNERS ASSOCIATION ANNUAL NEW VINTAGE TASTING www.swovintners.com

OTTAWA WINE & FOOD SHOW: early November www.playerexpo.com/WineShow

GOURMET FOOD & WINE EXPO: mid-November www.foodandwineshow.ca

TORONTO WINE & CHEESE SHOW: March www.towineandcheese.com

Prince Edward Island

PRINCE EDWARD ISLAND WINE FESTIVAL: June www.gov.pe.ca

Quebec

FESTIVAL DES VINS: Parc Masson, mid-August www.ile-des-moulins.qc.ca

WEST ISLAND WINE FESTIVAL: Pierrefonds, mid-September www.westislandwinefestival.com

GRAPE HARVEST FESTIVAL: Magog, early September www.fetedesvendanges.com

In British Columbia the natural tendency is to look south of the border, rather than east to the rest of Canada. Vintners here tend to model their wines on California and Washington State, although there is still a lingering German influence with grapes such as Bacchus, Ehrenfelser, Kerner, Ortega, and Schönburger. Because of its large European immigrant population, Ontario has modelled its wine styles on France, Italy, and Germany.

Given its geography, British Columbia is more like Chile, a vertical wine region stretching from Salmon Arm in the north, where Recline Ridge and Granite Creek are located, to Mission Hill's southernmost vineyard that marks the US border. The range in temperature and rainfall is enormous. The town of Oliver, the self-styled Wine Capital of Canada, boasts 318 days with temperatures over 18° Celsius; Cowichan Bay on Vancouver Island has a mere fifty-two days over that mark. Thus, the island and the northern Okanagan feature early ripening hybrids, while Oliver and the Osoyoos region (Canada's only pocket desert) can ripen Bordeaux varieties such as Cabernet Sauvignon and Merlot and the Rhône variety Syrah. The cool Fraser Valley and the even more marginal Vancouver Island rely heavily on Okanagan fruit to supplement their own.

Ontario, by contrast, is a horizontal region with an even climate in the three designated VQA regions—Niagara Peninsula, Lake Erie North Shore, and Pelee Island. The emerging Prince Edward County, soon to join the VQA, is as challenging a growing region in which to ripen grapes as Nova Scotia and Quebec. Yet often it's the marginal growing regions that produce the world's great wines—Burgundy and the Mosel, for instance.

All in all, the future for the wine industries in Ontario and British Columbia is rosy. Canadian Icewine, in a mere fifteen years since Inniskillin won the Prix d'honneur trophy for its Vidal Icewine 1989 at Vinexpo 1991, has become an icon wine around the world.

While Canada will never be a major wine-exporting country like Australia or Chile, we can produce red and white table wines of great quality for which, I predict, the demand will grow within

TIMING YOUR WINERY VISITS

SUMMER: If you're interested in getting acquainted with the vines before you sample the wines, this is the best time to go. Many of the wineries have guided tours that take you into the vineyards to show you how they grow grapes and protect the vines during the winter months. Be prepared to deal with traffic, both pedestrian and vehicular.

FALL: Harvest time seems to be the favourite period for most wine tourists, especially when the leaves are changing colour. Keep in mind that this is the busiest season for the winemakers and they won't have time to discuss the merits of their wines with you. If you plan to visit with a group, phone ahead and alert the winery personnel. And make sure to check up on their parking facilities, given the crowds of visitors in September and October.

WINTER: If you don't mind driving in snow, you can catch the wineries in mid-winter harvesting their grapes for Icewine, or the cider makers in Quebec gathering frozen apples for Ice Cider. Call ahead to find out when the wineries intend to pick, as harvest dates vary from year to year. You might even find yourself co-opted into helping to pick.

SPRING: The snow may still be on the ground, but it's maple syrup time and you will have the opportunity to visit and taste at the many sugar bushes and *cabanes à sucre* as well. The vines begin to sprout only in May, so don't expect to see much in the vineyards or inside the wineries, unless you're fascinated with bottling lines at work.

USEFUL WINE WEBSITES

National/General

Official Wines of Canada:
www.winesofcanada.com
Canadian Vintners Association:
www.canadianvintners.com
A forum for discussion of Canadian wines:
www.canwine.com
In-depth information about Canadian and
American wineries:
www.appellationamerica.com
Dean Tudor's complete listing of the
world's wine websites:
www.ryerson.ca/~dtudor/wine.htm

British Columbia

BC Wine Institute:
www.winebc.com
Okanagan Wine Festival Society:
www.owfs.com
Hidden Wineries of BC:
www.winegrowers.bc.ca
The Wine Islands:
www.islandwineries.ca
Touring Okanagan:
www.tourcanada.com/winetour.htm

Ontario

Wine Council of Ontario:
www.winesofontario.org
Grape Growers of Ontario:
www.grapegrowersofontario.com
Ontario Icewine:
www.Icewineniagara.net
Southwestern Ontario Vintners
Association:
www.ontariograpes.com
VQA Ontario:
www.vqaontario.com
Larry Paterson's informative site on
growing wine grapes:
www.littlefatwino.com
Prince Edward County Wine Growers
Association:
www.pecountywines.ca
Prince Edward County:
www.thecounty.ca/wine/
Niagara Grape & Wine Festivals:
www.grapeandwine.com

Quebec

Association of Winemakers:
www.vignerons-du-quebec.com
Faith Stewart's personal Quebec
winery guide:
www3.sympatico.ca/rogersjw

USEFUL CANADIAN WINE PUBLICATIONS

Tidings Magazine subscription/newsstands www.tidingsmag.com
The Harvest Table Southeastern Ontario, subscription, email theharvesttable@primus.ca
Vines Magazine subscription/newsstands www.vinesmag.com
Wine Access Magazine subscription/newsstands www.wineaccess.ca
Canadian Grapes to Wine Magazine subscription www.trailspublishing.com
BC Wine Trails subscription www.winetrails.ca
The Wine Regions of Ontario free www.wro.ca

Gaspereau Vineyards, Gaspereau Valley, Nova Scotia.

our own borders in the very near future. The next generation of Canadians, who were born after the introduction of the VQA in 1988 and have no taste memory of the desultory products of the 1970s and early 1980s, will have nothing but a positive response to the wines that are grown in their own backyard. They will be the proud advocates of the Canadian wine industry and will discuss Canadian vintages and winemakers as their parents did those of France, Italy, Germany, and other New World regions.

As exporters, our wineries will always be niche players because we do not have the economies of scale that make our wines attractive for British supermarkets or American wine shops. We have, however, shown the world how good our sweet wines are—Icewine and Late Harvest wines—and they will continue to be our major contribution to the world's wine lovers. But one area of great potential has yet to be exploited. Like the Champagne region in France, we have in our cool-climate growing regions the ability to produce the high-acid grapes for sparkling wines. There's but one question: Is there a market for Canadian bubbly among Canadians? As soon as the consuming public shows an interest in this particular category, the wineries will take on the expensive and labour-intensive task of producing sparkling wines by the champagne method. I, for one, can't wait for that to happen. In anticipation, I raise a glass to you, gentle reader, and hope that this journey in words and pictures through the vineyards and wineries of Canada will make you want to see it all for yourself.

VQA
CANADA'S APPELLATION

The Vintners Quality Alliance (VQA) is Canada's wine appellation. Currently, the VQA symbol adorns bottles of BC and Ontario wine that are produced according to its set of regulations. Quebec and Nova Scotia are negotiating with Ontario and British Columbia to have their wines under the same quality umbrella, although they are hindered by their use of grapes not sanctioned in the other two wine-growing provinces.

The Vintners Quality Alliance was introduced in 1988 in Ontario (where it is obligatory for wineries to join) and two years later in British Columbia (where it is optional). The VQA recognizes designated grape-growing areas within each province: Ontario's Niagara Peninsula, Pelee Island, and Lake Erie North Shore; British Columbia's Okanagan Valley, Similkameen Valley, Fraser Valley, and Vancouver Island. Other regulations include these points:

- Wines must be made from the classic vinifera varieties (Chardonnay, Riesling, Cabernet Sauvignon, Pinot Noir, etc.) or from preferred hybrids (Vidal, Seyval Blanc, Maréchal Foch, Baco Noir).
- To use the grape name on the label, the wine must contain at least 85 percent of that variety and exhibit its taste character.
- All grapes must have a minimum sugar level at the time of picking. These sugar levels will be higher for vineyard-designated and estate-bottled wines, as well as for Late Harvest wines.
- Labels stating that the wine is "Estate Bottled" must be 100 percent grown on that estate.
- All wines in Ontario are taste tested blind by a panel of experts to ensure authenticity and typicity.

The VQA symbol, found on the capsule of the bottle, is your assurance that the wine is 100 percent grown in the appellation stated on the label. You might think this qualification is axiomatic—that any self-respecting wine region would grow its own grapes—but a fair range of so-called Canadian non-VQA wine is a blend of imported wine with locally grown grapes. Those products that contain bulk wines shipped in from outside the region (usually from Chile or California) are labelled "Cellared in Canada" or "Product of Canada" and can, in extreme cases, such as after the disastrous harvests of 2003 and 2004 in Ontario, contain up to 90 percent off-shore material. Unfortunately, these blends end up in close proximity to local product on store shelves. To ensure you're buying Canadian, look for the VQA logo.

Winery Etiquette

Running a winery and vineyard is a year-round business, but many wineries' tasting rooms are open only during the summer season, from May to October or November. Rather than turning up on the doorstep to find a "Closed" notice on the door, call ahead or check the website for the winery's hours. If you are travelling in a large group, phone ahead and advise the tasting room when you're arriving. The weekends are the busy time and, if you want special treatment as a group, ask if there is a private tasting room. My advice is to avoid visiting wineries on holiday weekends if you want to ask the staff questions. They'll be too busy to spend much time with you.

If you're driving, don't block access to doorways or to your fellow visitors with your car. If you're cycling, make sure you park your bike so that no one will back over it. Many wineries now have bike racks.

You will be greeted with open arms as long as you are there to sample the wines and not to party. Most wineries don't charge for a sample pour and will be happy to serve you up to four selections. You may have to pay for their specialty wines, such as Icewine. It is *de rigueur* for professional wine tasters to spit, so don't be afraid to follow this custom. Spittoons and dump buckets are provided, but make sure your aim is true. And don't feel you have to finish each sample. You won't offend the tasting-room staff if you dump the sample after one sip. Keep your opinion to yourself and move on.

Don't start with Icewine and then try to taste a Sauvignon Blanc, because the initial sweetness will make the wine that follows taste sour. Begin with the dry white wines, move to the dry red wines, and finish with the Late Harvest and dessert wines.

If you're on a guided tour, don't carry on a conversation with your friends/partner/strangers while your guide is explaining the winemaking process.

Château des Charmes' 25th anniversary party, St. Davids, Ontario.

And don't monopolize the guide's attention by asking too many questions. Others may have questions, too. Avoid touching anything to see if it's working or if it's full (knocking on barrels or tanks), and keep your eyes open for hoses or anything else that's lying around. Be sure to close doors after you: wines have to be kept at a cool temperature.

Sign the guest book. This way you can receive information about the winery's upcoming events. Tour the wine store and pick up some wine. You will find a much better selection here—older vintages, small lots, experimental wines—than you will find at any liquor store or even the winery's off-premise stores. There is an old joke: How do you make a small fortune in the wine business? Answer: Start with a large one. Remember, wineries are in business to make money. To show your gratitude for a tour and tasting, pick up a bottle or two of your favourite wines on the way out.

Three Steps to Tasting

Wine appeals to all five senses: sight, smell, taste, touch, and hearing. But it's mainly the first three you use when judging the quality of a wine, and in that order as well. The first sensory response you have is to the colour of the wine, then to the smell as you lift the glass to your nose, and, finally, to the taste.

Step 1: *Sight.* Hold the glass against a white background or a good source of light. The wine should look clean and bright. Study the colour and tilt the glass so you can see the rim where the wine touches the glass. Young wines hold their colour to the rim; older wines begin to fade at the edge. White wines start life as white as water and gain a golden colour with age. Red wines begin as a deep purple and lose colour over time. Browning edges in a red wine are a warning sign and suggest age or oxidation. A browning of the yellow of white wine suggests

The restaurant at Peller Estates Winery,
Niagara-on-the-Lake, Ontario.

THE RESTAURANT RITUAL

A little T-shirt philosophy: life's too short to drink bad wine. So don't be bashful about going through the ritual of pre-tasting a wine you've ordered in a restaurant. The waiter has presented your selected bottle to you. Read the label and confirm it's what you ordered. Check that the vintage year is correct. When assessing a wine, you start by being negative—you're looking for faults. If you find none, you can start praising the wine's virtues. Here's the drill.

The waiter pulls the cork and hands it to you. Good signs: the cork is firm and smells of the wine. Bad signs: the cork smells bad (cork taint); the cork is hard as oak because it's dried out (air could get into the bottle and oxidize it); the cork's entire length is stained (wine has come into contact with air); the cork is spongy and wets your fingers (again, air could have got in and oxidized the wine).

The waiter pours you one ounce of wine. Study its colour; swirl the glass and sniff; then taste. Does the wine look bright and clear? Does it have a clean bouquet, no off-odours? Does it taste good? Is it at the right temperature? A red wine served too warm will lose its structure and taste soupy (refresh it by sticking the bottle in an ice bucket for ten minutes). A white wine served so cold that it frosts the glass will have little taste (let it warm up in the glass); served at room temperature, it will lose its freshness and length of flavour (ask for the ice bucket). If the wine looks murky and browning or if it smells bad, it will taste bad—send it back.

Sumac Ridge vineyard, Okanagan Valley, British Columbia.

maderization (oxidation that gives a sherry-like flavour to the wine).

Swirl the glass and watch the transparent wet residue on the sides form into tears, or legs, and slide down the glass. This residue is the alcohol in suspension on the side of the glass. The thicker and more slow moving these legs, the higher the alcohol content.

Step 2: *Smell.* Swirl the wine in the glass. This action causes the esters that carry the wine's aromatics to evaporate and rise, and you'll get a more concentrated bouquet. You can tell 75 percent about a wine on your nose. The bouquet will tell you what the wine will taste like; the only thing it won't tell you is how long the wine will linger on your palate.

Look for faults first. Are there any off-odours such as the smell of vinegar (volatile acidity) or prunes (oxidation) or damp basements (corkiness)? The wine, depending on the variety or blend, should generally smell of fruit, flowers, sometimes vegetables (especially Sauvignon Blanc), and it will have the scent of vanilla or coconut, toast, and smoke if aged in oak.

Step 3: *Taste.* Take a sip and let the wine wash over your entire palate. The first sensation you'll notice is the wine's sweetness. (The taste buds that register sweetness are on the tip of the tongue.) As the wine works its way to the back of the mouth you'll experience acidity (a lemon-like flavour) and, in red wines, a slight bitterness caused by tannin, a natural compound found in the skins, pits, and stalks of grapes. Tannin is a preservative that allows red wines to age. Astringent when young, the tannins soften with the years and, eventually, in old wines, will precipitate out as sediment.

Feel the weight of the wine in your mouth. High-alcohol wines, whether red, white, or rosé, will be full bodied and mouth filling. Low-alcohol wines will feel lighter.

Ask yourself if the wine is balanced. A great wine will be seamless: the fruit, acidity, alcohol, oak, and tannin will be in harmony. If the wine is over-acidic, over-oaked, highly tannic, or shy on fruit, it will be unbalanced. You should not be able to pick out one particular element of its composition if the wine is well balanced.

A taster's secret: suck in air when the wine is in your mouth. You'll extract more flavour, just as you get more of the wine's bouquet by swirling it.

A Year in the Vineyard

Winegrowers in Canadian vineyards tend their vines basically the same way that European farmers have done since Roman times. Some things have changed over the centuries: the tractor has replaced the horse-drawn plough, and harvesting machines have taken over the picking in larger enterprises where the land gradient and row spacing permit. Essentially, though, winegrowing is a hands-on business in all its phases, from planting to pruning to picking.

Vines go dormant in winter, but work in the vineyard continues even though there are no leaves or fruit on the vines.

January Traditionally pruning begins on St. Vincent's Day (January 22), to honour the patron saint of bakers, roof-makers, sailors, schoolgirls, and vine-dressers. Growers prune unwanted canes to stimulate new growth and take cuttings for grafting onto root-stock to be planted in the spring of the following year. Icewine is generally harvested in late December into January and sometimes into February, when there are sustained temperatures of −8°C or below.

February Pruning continues, though it must finish well before bud break in April or May so the vines can heal. Otherwise, it's a good time for the overworked grower to go on vacation. You'll find many wineries closed this month.

March If the vines are "hilled," they have to be uncovered. Growers begin to plough to aerate the soil and may also fertilize. They check stakes and trellis wires to ensure they are tight and weight-bearing. They begin to bottle last year's non-oaked red and white wines (oak-aged wines are bottled at the discretion of the winemakers, depending on how much time in barrel they decide the wine needs).

April Growers take measures to eliminate weeds either through herbicides or by ploughing them under. They tie canes to trellis wires before bud break. When the weather is warm enough, late in the month or in May, the sap begins to rise and bud break occurs.

May One-year-old cuttings from the nursery are planted when soil temperatures reach 10°C. The new shoots begin to grow and often have to be contained

COOL-CLIMATE CANADA

Canada has been described as a cool wine-growing region. What exactly does that mean? What is a cool-climate growing region?

One definition is that the mean temperature of the warmest month during the growing season is less than 20°C. In France, growers use 10°C as a base temperature and add up the number of degrees during each day of the growing season when the temperature rises above this level. If the total is less than 1390°, it's a cool region. Ideally, wine growers prefer a long growing season that is not too warm—to allow a slow maturation of the fruit, which produces a good balance of sugar and acid, and so provides a richly flavoured wine with a lingering finish. A hot growing season builds up sugars, but, without cool nights, the acidity level will be low and the resulting wine will lack structure, tasting soft and flabby.

by the use of catch wires. Growers worry about a spring frost at this time of year because it could destroy the fruiting buds. They begin spraying against oidium and downy mildew.

June Flowering occurs in mid to late June and lasts about ten days if temperatures are constant around 18–20°C. Growers tie down shoots and spray the vines against insects and rot. In roughly one hundred days the grapes will be ready for harvesting.

July In this time of vigorous growth, workers thin leaves by hand to expose the fruit to sunlight as the berries form. Some growers may thin their crop to get lower yields and so concentrate the flavours of the remaining grape bunches. They also do occasional spraying when required.

August In this month what the French call *veraison* occurs—the berries begin to look like real grapes and change colour from red to purple in red varieties or from green to translucent in white. Workers continue to weed but stop spraying. Vines left for Icewine and Late Harvest wines are netted against the birds.

September Growers check sugar levels in the grapes for physiological ripeness, and early ripening varieties such as hybrids are ready for harvesting. Growers want to pick the fruit as ripe as possible to ensure a good extraction and sufficient potential alcohol. The crush pads are busy this month with the arrival of grapes at the weigh scale. Bottling of some red wines begins.

October Harvesting of late ripening varieties continues. Once the harvest is completed, usually by the end of the month, the vineyard is often ploughed, especially to force the roots of young vines to penetrate the soil more deeply. Some wineries will use the pomace (grape residue) from their winemaking to spread back on the vineyards as fertilizer. October is one of the busiest months in the cellar, with the crush (breaking the skins so the fermentation starts) and the pressing of the grapes (to extract the juice).

November Growers bank the soil against the base of the vine stocks to protect them from a deep winter freeze. They may also spread any minerals and nutrients that are needed at this time. The onset of colder weather shuts down the vine and it becomes dormant until the spring.

December Workers remove the year's shoots by pruning, but, otherwise, December is a quiet month in the vineyard. Unless an early cold spell demands the harvest of Icewine, growers draw up their holiday wish lists and think of warmer climes.

OPPOSITE: Winter view of the Cave Spring Cellars vineyard from the Bruce Trail, Beamsville, Ontario.

Icewine: Canada's Gift of Winter to the World

Icewine is the one good thing about Canadian winters. Of all the wines made in Canada, the one the world knows best is Icewine. Within fifteen years this sweet dessert wine has become an international celebrity, an icon product that is as Canadian as the Mounties, Wayne Gretzky, and the maple leaf. In 2005 Inniskillin Icewine was the top-selling wine product in all duty-free stores around the world, beating out champagne. Whenever it is entered in competitions anywhere on the planet, Icewine walks off with the medals. It appears on the exclusive wine lists of the world's best restaurants, and you can now buy it in India, Taiwan, Hong Kong, Beijing, New York City, London, Rome, and Paris. It's the luxury gift that everyone loves to give and to receive. And like all desirable luxury goods, it is being counterfeited on an unprecedented scale in Southeast Asia. The majority of the phony products end up on wine shelves in Pacific Rim countries. After the United States, Taiwan is Canada's largest market for Icewine. According to Ted Lipman, executive director of the Canadian Trade Office in Taipei, "About 50 percent of what claims to be Icewine in Taiwan is fake."

Not only are Canadian vintners losing revenue—because the faux product sells for a lot less than the genuine article—but the quality of the knockoffs is harming the reputation of the wine. Ontario's Pillitteri Estates is one of the world's largest exporters of Icewine, with nearly 75 percent of its production going to Asian markets. Its exasperated proprietor, Charlie Pillitteri, says, "Imitation is the highest form of flattery, but people are making Icewine in their garage and selling it in China. It's ridiculous."

The counterfeiters try to make the label and the package look like a VQA product, but their sense of geography sometimes leaves much to be desired. William Ross, president of the Canadian Vintners Association, points out: "You have counterfeit Icewine bottles with 'Chilliwacko, Ontario,' instead of Chilliwack, British Columbia, or 'Elixir of the Gods, Torontow,' with a picture of Whistler, BC, in

Riesling Icewine grapes, Beamsville, Ontario.

TOP TEN
EXPORT MARKETS FOR
CANADIAN ICEWINE

1 Taiwan
2 Singapore
3 United States
4 Japan
5 South Korea
6 Hong Kong
7 China
8 Belgium
9 Malaysia
10 France

ICEWINE EXPORTS BY PROVINCE (PERCENT)

Ontario 82
British Columbia 16
Quebec 1

(STATISTICS CANADA, AUGUST, 2005)

the background and maple leaves festooned all over."

When I was in China in 2002 I saw several fake Icewines on the shelves of Guangzhou wine stores. The couple I got to taste were disgusting—sickly sweet, without structure, and tasting of labrusca grapes and pear juice.

CCOVI, the Cool Climate Oenological and Viticultural Institute at Brock University in St. Catharines, Ontario, the VQA, and the Liquor Control Board of Ontario are all working to solve the problem. CCOVI is concentrating on the sensory aspect of the product by taste testing, while the LCBO has come up with a sophisticated chemical analysis to determine if the wine was grown in Ontario and contains the right balance of fruit sugars and alcohol to comply with VQA regulations. "We look at a number of variables," says Dr. George Soleas, vice-president of the LCBO's Quality Assurance Department. "First, the package. If it doesn't say 'VQA' on it, we know that potentially this could be a contraband product. Then we look at the

WHAT MAKES CANADIAN ICEWINE SO EXPENSIVE?

The average price of Canadian Icewine is $45–$60 a half-bottle. Unlike German Eiswein, it is rarely bottled in a 750 millilitre format. To make it more affordable, many producers package the wine in 200 millilitre bottles and even in miniatures of 50 millilitres, sufficient to satisfy the sugar cravings of a couple after dinner.

Farmers have to gamble when they grow grapes for Icewine and harvest them, and that's what makes it so costly:

- The amount of juice from frozen grapes is 80 to 90 percent less than winemakers would normally get if pressing for a dry Riesling or Vidal table wine.
- Under normal harvest conditions, a tonne of grapes will yield about 650 litres of juice; for Icewine, the harvest can be as low as 100 litres per tonne.
- Farmers always risk losing their crop to hungry birds that still find ways to pick the berries through the netting.
- The necessity of netting the vines to protect the fruit is an additional cost.
- The longer the fruit hangs on the vine, the more susceptible it is to rot and storm damage.
- Finally, rarity, perceived value, and image also contribute to the pricing structure.

liquid. We smell and taste it, and that's an indication whether the product is authentic. But, most important, we look at the chemistry."

The LCBO has also developed a test that determines whether the alcohol in the wine came from grapes that were processed the same way as a legitimate Icewine and whether there were additions of high-fructose corn syrup, concentrate, pear juice, or synthetic alcohol.

The Canadian consumer, however, does not have to worry about counterfeit Icewine. If the bottle in the wine store bears a VQA seal, it will be the genuine article.

The kudos for having produced the first Icewine in Canada goes to Walter Hainle, a former textile salesman from Hamburg who immigrated to British Columbia in 1970. In 1973 Hainle made about 40 litres of Icewine from frozen grapes he had purchased from a local grower in the Okanagan Valley, a tradition he continued until his death in 1995. When he opened his own winery in 1988, one of the first products on the shelf was the 1978 vintage of Okanagan Riesling Icewine.

It was not the vinifera Riesling as we know it but Okanagan Riesling, a rather insipid grape of dubious origin that was widely planted in the 1960s and 1970s and has virtually disappeared from the Okanagan since the BC pull-out program of 1989. The very first attempts at producing Icewine on a

TOP CANADIAN ICEWINE PRODUCERS

Ontario
Cave Spring Cellars
Château des Charmes
Daniel Lenko
Henry of Pelham
Hillebrand
Inniskillin
Jackson-Triggs
Konzelmann Estate
Pillitteri
Reif Estate

Nova Scotia
Jost

British Columbia
Gray Monk
Hawthorne Mountain
Inniskillin Okanagan
Jackson-Triggs
Lang Vineyard
Mission Hill
Paradise Ranch
Quails' Gate
Sumac Ridge
Summerhill Estate

Quebec
Clos Saragnat
Chapelle Ste. Agnès
Clos le Pinnacle
Clos Saint-Denis
Vergers Lafrance

commercial basis in Ontario were sabotaged by bird and man. In 1983 Inniskillin lost its entire crop to the birds the day before picking was scheduled. That same year winemaker Walter Strehn at Pelee Island Vineyards had taken the precaution of netting his vines to protect them from the feathered frenzy, because his vineyard was in the direct flight path of migrating birds from the Point Pelee sanctuary. Some persistent blue jays, however, managed to break through his nets and were trapped in the mesh. A passing bird fancier reported him to the Ministry

of Natural Resources and officials descended on the vineyard and tore off the netting. Strehn not only lost $25,000 worth of Riesling and Vidal grapes to the rapacious flock but was charged with trapping birds out of season and using the dried grapes as bait! Happily, the case was dropped and, with the grapes that were left, Strehn managed to make fifty cases of Vidal Icewine 1983, which he labelled in the German designation as Beerenauslese Eiswein. He sold the wine to the LCBO, which set a retail price of $12.50 a half-bottle. The consuming public was not familiar with this wine style and bought very little, so the LCBO returned the majority of bottles and demanded a refund. Pelee Island found a more willing market in the United States, where the product sold for $100 a bottle. The LCBO then begged to have it back!

Given its price, Icewine is a highly lucrative product for Canadian wineries. Joseph DeMaria in Ontario and James Stewart in British Columbia share the distinction of being the world's only wine producers who specialize in the production of Icewine. Stewart, who has made Icewine from eight different varieties, sold his Paradise Ranch vineyard in Naramata, BC, to Mission Hill, but continues to make the product from bought-in grapes. DeMaria, a Toronto hairdresser by trade, owns Royal DeMaria, a 25-acre vineyard in Vineland, Ontario, where he produces Icewine from twelve different grape varieties, including Merlot, Gamay, and a Meritage blend of Cabernet Sauvignon, Merlot, and Cabernet Franc. His 2002 vintage should go in the Guinness Book of Records as most expensive Icewine in the world, at $5,000 a 375 millilitre bottle. (As the product sold through, DeMaria put up the price of the remaining bottles.)

De Maria and Stewart are two of some ninety wine producers across Canada—from Nova Scotia to British Columbia—who make Icewine from vine-frozen grapes. The sheer number of producers puts Canada at the top of the international Icewine

Harvesting Icewine grapes in the Niagara Peninsula.

league in terms of volume. If we can't do it in the frozen north, however, who can?

Icewine is made by allowing the grapes to hang on the vine until they freeze naturally. Since the juice is rich in sugar, the temperature has to drop well below freezing and stay there long enough for the bunches to be harvested and pressed while still in their frozen state. A thaw will cause the ice to melt and the water will dilute the sugars and acids, rendering the juice at harvest below the minimum sugar level of 35 Brix.

A grape berry contains roughly 80 percent water and, if the berries are frozen solid and then pressed, the water will remain in the skins as shards of ice, allowing small amounts of concentrated juice to flow out. All the elements of the juice are concentrated, including flavour, sugar, and acidity. The juice from Icewine grapes is about one-fifth the amount you would normally get if you pressed unfrozen grapes. To put it another way, a vine will normally produce sufficient grapes to make a bottle of wine; but frozen grapes would produce only one glass of Icewine. Under Canadian wine law, grapes designated for Icewine cannot be picked until the mercury drops to at least minus 8°C (17° Fahrenheit) for a sustained period of time to allow the berries to freeze, although colder temperatures make for a better-quality Icewine. The harvesting of Icewine is truly an act of masochism for the pickers because it's usually done in the early morning hours before the sun is up. From personal experience, the wind whipping across a vineyard at those temperatures can make you feel like Scott of the Antarctic. Fermenting the sugar-rich juice in wine can take months, and special hard-working yeast is required. The final alcohol level can vary from 9 percent to 13 percent depending on how much residual sugar is left in the wine.

Canada prides itself on being able to produce Icewine consistently every year, unlike Germany and Austria, where it is a periodic thing. However, the

Winter apples, Île d'Orleans, Quebec.

QUEBEC'S WINTER WINE: ICE CIDER

Quebec makes almost as much cider as it does wine. It's a cottage industry whose history goes back to the first settlers in the province from Normandy and Brittany in the seventeenth century. Those early pioneers brought cider with them but soon found that the conditions around Montérégie were ideal for growing apples. As a result, cider-making has been a venerable and venerated occupation in Quebec. Today, the range of styles is impressive—from dry to sweet and sparkling to fortified. But none is more cherished than Ice Cider.

Of all Quebec's wines, Ice Cider is perhaps the one that will become an international icon product—just as Icewine has become for Ontario, British Columbia, and Nova Scotia. What is Ice Cider? Think of Icewine and replace the frozen grapes with frozen apple juice. You get the same honeyed sweetness and racy acidity in Ice Cider as you do in Icewine. But it tastes of apples, of course, rather than the more concentrated peach and tropical fruit flavours found in Icewine.

While grapes for Icewine have to be frozen naturally on the vine as stipulated by the VQA, the apples for Ice Cider can either be picked after the first autumn frost or left to freeze on the tree and then harvested and pressed. There are two schools of thought here. At La Face Cachée de la Pomme, Quebec's leading *cidrerie*, both styles of Ice Cider are made: Neige, by freezing the pressed juice—a process that separates out much of the water in the juice as ice, which, when removed, leaves a highly concentrated, syrupy liquid ready to be fermented; and Frimas, by pressing frozen apples that have been left to hang until winter's end. The product label tells you which technique was used.

As with Icewine, regulations prohibit the use of industrial freezers for either the apples or the extracted juice. According to the Association des cidriculteurs artisans du Québec, the natural sugar in the juice to be fermented must measure at least 310 grams per litre and no other sweetener can be added. Nor can the producer add alcohol if it is to be sold as Ice Cider. Fermentation can take as long as seven months or more. After fermentation, the residual sugar in the wine must be at least 150 grams per litre, with an alcohol level between 9 percent and 13 percent depending on the style produced. It can take as much as 7 kilograms of apples to make one 500 millilitre bottle of Ice Cider.

Winter view of Vineland Estates vineyard, Vineland, Ontario.

VQA REGULATIONS FOR ICEWINE

- The grapes for Icewine must be frozen naturally on the vine (not artificially in commercial freezers).
- Juice before fermentation must have a minimum sugar reading of 32 Brix degrees or higher.
- After pressing, the juice in the tank must measure at least 35 Brix degrees.
- Residual sugar in the finished wine must be at least 125 grams per litre.
- No sugar can be added to the fermentation to boost the alcohol level.
- All wines labelled as Icewine must be produced by VQA-registered growers and winemakers.
- The harvest for Icewine grapes must start after November 15 when the temperature drops below –8°C. Before harvesting, the producer must verify in writing, by specified form, the following:
  - the temperatures at the time of each individual harvest;
  - the acreage and tonnage of each given crop;
  - the measured Brix level of each must;
  - the harvesting date and time of day; and
  - the winery's Icewine pressing capacity.

2001 vintage gave Canadian winemakers a real scare. Global warming or a freak of nature produced a balmy winter with no snow to speak of, let alone freezing temperatures. Usually the Icewine harvest starts in early December and is finished by January. For the 1997 "El Nino" vintage in Ontario, Peller Estates did not harvest its crop until March 11, 1998, and its 2001 vintage of Cabernet Franc Icewine was on the vine until March 4. The Peller vineyards are very close to Lake Ontario, a large body of water that acts like a hot-water bottle, giving off its summer-stored heat in winter, ameliorating the air temperature as the wind blows off the lake over the vineyards. The lake factor, combined with a warm winter, conspired to create a very late Icewine harvest, making for some very nervous wine producers.

Canadian Icewine first gained global attention at Vinexpo in 1991. Donald Ziraldo, co-founder of Inniskillin Wines, entered his Vidal Icewine 1989 in the biennial wine fair's Challenge internationale du vin competition in Bordeaux. His wine won the Grand prix d'honneur, one of only nineteen such awards for the 4,100 wines submitted by forty countries. The effect was immediate both at home and abroad. Winemakers in Ontario and British Columbia began to set aside portions of their vineyards for netting to produce Icewine, and overseas buyers began to take an interest in the product. Canadian Icewine became an instant cult wine, selling for up to $250 a half-bottle in Japan, Taiwan, and Hong Kong. Far East consumers have a sweet tooth when it comes to appreciating wine.

Although Icewine accounts for only 6 percent of the total Canadian wine production, it is the industry's most celebrated wine. Australia has Shiraz; New Zealand, Sauvignon Blanc; Argentina, Malbec; Chile, Carmenère; Austria, Grüner Veltliner;

California, Zinfandel; and Canada, Icewine. Donald Triggs, CEO of Vincor International, Canada's largest winery and the fifteenth-largest winery in the world, says: "Icewine is the ambassador of our industry. When we move into new markets we start selling Icewine first, then we feed our other products in on the back of Icewine's success." Vincor itself produces and sells more Icewine than any other company in the world and has approximately 40 percent of the Canadian Icewine market.

In April 2004, after several years of lobbying by federal and provincial governments, the European Commission finally allowed Canadian Icewine into its markets. That is just what the industry needed, as more and more Canadian wineries get into the lucrative Icewine business. But for all its popularity abroad, the industry cannot survive on Icewine alone.

I have tasted Icewines from four provinces, made from a range of grape varieties, but my preference is for the two originals—Vidal and Riesling from my home province of Ontario—with my ultimate vote going to Riesling because it has a better acid structure and balance and is not as sweet. Riesling will also cellar longer than Vidal, lasting about fifteen years compared to Vidal's ten.

Of the red grape varieties, Cabernet Franc makes the best Icewine; it's not as sweet as Vidal or Riesling, but has interesting strawberry and cran-

CANADIAN WINE LIBRARY

In the basement of Inniskillin Hall, the CCOVI centre at Brock University, is a state-of-the-art, atmosphere-controlled cellar designed by Toronto architect Tony Manzini. Built at a cost of $400,000, it can house 43,000 bottles.

The concept of creating a permanent, revolving collection of the finest Canadian VQA wines judged age-worthy by the directors of the Canadian Wine Library was first discussed by winemaker Ann Sperling of Malivoire, consultant Peter Gamble, Dr. David Bergen, and CCOVI directors in December 1996. This non-profit organization, run by volunteers from the wine industry, the LCBO, the wine press, and academia, was incorporated two years later. The purpose of the collection is to give winemakers and students a reference as to how Canadian wines develop in the bottle and to show vintage variation and stylistic changes.

Every spring, the library's board of directors holds an annual blind tasting to select new entries to the cellar. Once a wine is accepted, the winery is requested to submit two cases of the wine in question. All wines in the collection are held for a minimum of three years following the vintage date (or longer if specified by the winery) and then released for tasting to wine professionals.

One part of the cellar, the Vinoteque, is used to store research wines (unique bottlings, flawed wines, etc.) for educational use by CCOVI faculty members and students, as well as wines made by the students themselves.

berry flavours. Icewine has been used as a dosage (sweetening) in sparkling wine (Peller Estate's Crystalle) and a grappa (Magnotta), and it has been added to brandy (Kittling Ridge). However, its best use, other than to end a meal, is as a sparkling wine.

A well-chilled Icewine makes an excellent aperitif, or serve it with aged Canadian raw-milk Cheddar, blue cheeses, foie gras, or fruit-based desserts.

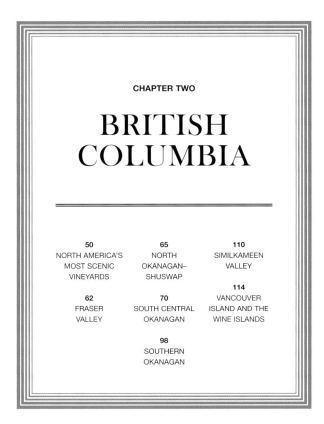

CHAPTER TWO

BRITISH COLUMBIA

As an Ontarian, it grieves me to admit that British Columbia has the most beautiful winescape in Canada. The hills and mountains that enclose the Okanagan and Similkameen valleys offer vistas of incredible beauty, none more spectacular than the Naramata Bench, with vineyards that seem to float above the blue waters of the lake like a green eiderdown. The Fraser Valley reminds me of Western Australia, with its farms and trees, while Vancouver Island, its remarkable vineyards tucked into forest clearings, is a delight to discover.

I wonder if Father Charles Pandosy saw a wine future for this land of forests and mountains in 1859, when he created the first non-native settlement on the banks of L'Anse au Sable (Mission Creek). Today it bears the postal address of 3685 Benvoulin Drive, Kelowna. Some time in the early 1860s, Pandosy planted a vineyard to supply his Oblate mission and the settlement with wine and, in the process, he became the father of the BC wine industry.

More than any other institution, the Catholic Church is responsible for today's flourishing wine industry around the world. The monks of Europe kept the vineyards alive during the Dark Ages, and their missionaries carried vine cuttings along with

PREVIOUS SPREAD: Blue Mountain Vineyard and Cellars.
BELOW: King Vineyards, Naramata Bench.

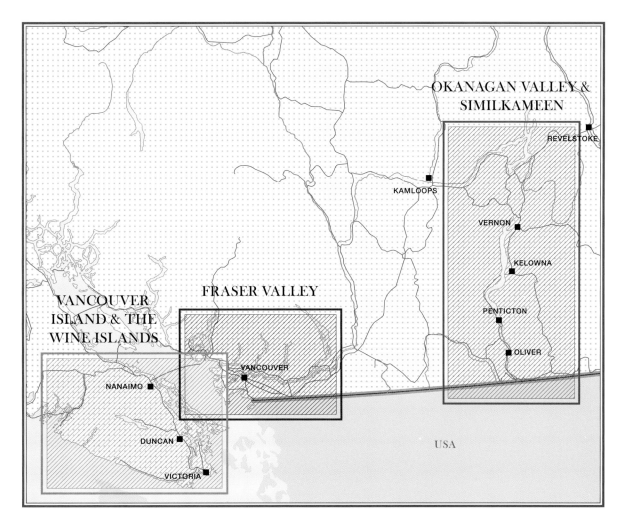

THE WINE REGIONS OF BRITISH COLUMBIA

their Bibles when they established religious settlements in the New World. Wine was needed to celebrate mass, and, wherever priests set down roots, they planted vines. The situation in British Columbia was no exception.

But the farmers who followed the example of Father Pandosy were more interested in fruit crops such as apples, peaches, and apricots than in grapes. Although there were experimental plantings as early as 1905, the first commercial vineyard in the province was planted by W.J. Wilcox only in 1920, some 88 kilometres north of Kelowna at Salmon Arm—not the most promising place to start, as it is the most northerly limit of winegrowing in the province. This small plot yielded such grape varieties as Concord, Niagara, Delaware, and Agawam, for eating rather than fermenting. Six years later a grower named

Jim Creighton planted a small vineyard in Penticton, an area that would ultimately prove to be one of the best sites for grape growing along the shores of Lake Okanagan.

The first wines in British Columbia were not made from grapes but from loganberries that flourished on the Saanich Peninsula of Vancouver Island. These beverages, made by the Growers' Wine Company, bore names such as Slinger's Logan and Logana. Only a few intrepid souls turned their attentions to wine grapes. Charles Casorso of Kelowna (the grandfather of winemaker Ann Sperling) was a pioneer winegrower who planted a vineyard on a 35-acre property at Rutland, near Kelowna, in 1925. The following year a farmer by the name of Jesse Willard Hughes, encouraged by Hungarian oenologist Dr. Eugene Rittich, bought a 45-acre vineyard in Kelowna, near the Pandosy mission, and planted vines that had been locally propagated. Hughes also purchased a 20-acre site east of Kelowna on Black Mountain. The larger vineyard in Kelowna prospered to such an extent that, four years later, wines made from these grapes were vinified at the Growers' Wine Company in Victoria. Encouraged by his success, Hughes expanded his Kelowna vineyard to 300 acres, but the experiment at Black Mountain proved a disaster when the vines were wiped out by winterkill (frost).

In 1930, when Rittich was hired as the winemaker for the Growers' Wine Company, a freak of nature gave the fledging industry the boost it needed. Successive abundant harvests of apples caused a glut on the market, and many farmers were forced to tear out their orchards and plant grapes instead. Growers' was paying $100 a tonne for grapes (compared to $65 a tonne in Ontario), while apples were left rotting under the trees. "A cent a pound or on the ground," was the farmers' anguished cry. "A dollar a box or on the rocks."

Then, at the height of the Depression in 1932, an immigrant Italian winemaker named Giuseppe Ghezzi came to Kelowna with the idea of creating a winery expressly to use the worthless apple crop.

Summerland Research Station in Summerland.

The same idea had also occurred to local hardware-store owner William Andrew Cecil Bennett, who discussed just such a possibility with his neighbour on Kelowna's main street, an Italian grocer named Pasquale "Cap" Capozzi. Both men were teetotallers, but they joined with Ghezzi to form a company called Domestic Wines and By-Products that would manufacture not only wines but a gamut of products including "apple cider, brandy, alcohol, spirits of all kinds, fruit juices, soft drinks, fruit concentrates, jelly, jams, pickles, vinegar, tomato paste, tomato catsup, tomato juice and by-products of every kind."

Bennett and Capozzi set about raising money to finance their new operation. At a time when soup kitchens meant more to the public than wineries, they began selling shares in the company for one dollar. They raised $4,500 and, although they were under-capitalized, they bought fermenting tanks and other equipment to begin this multifaceted business. In September 1932 they took up residence in an old rented building on Kelowna's Smith Avenue. The following year they hired Ghezzi's son Carlo as winemaker to complete their staff of eight employees. The debonair Giuseppe Ghezzi stayed long enough to set up the winery before emigrating to California, where he established a sparkling-wine plant.

Domestic Wines and By-Products' initial production included four apple-based wines—Okay Red, Okay Clear, Okay Port, and Okay Champagne. But the products were far from "okay." Even the company's official history records show that the wines were "a bitter disappointment." Many bottles refermented on liquor store shelves and had to be thrown out. Liquor stores were reluctant to stock the ill-famed domestic wines, and people were reluctant to buy them. "Sales in the company's first full year of operation were a disaster, amounting to a mere few thousand dollars."

After three years of ineffectual competition against the genuine wines of the Growers' Company, Bennett and Capozzi realized that BC consumers did not want apple wines. They switched to grapes bought in California for their ripeness and sugar levels, superior to the grapes grown locally. Soon other companies such as Growers' and the Victoria Wineries on Vancouver Island also bought grapes from California, perpetuating the fiction of making domestic wines by using whatever local grapes were available—a practice that still persists.

With the change in product, the former apple winery needed a change in name. In 1936 the directors chose a phonetic spelling of the Indian place name where the company was located: Calona Wines Limited. Okay Clear apple wine became Calona Clear grape wine, a white semi-sweet product whose label read ominously, "When Fully Mature: About 28% Proof Spirit."

In 1940 W.A.C. Bennett left Calona Wines to pursue a career in politics. One year later he was elected to the BC Legislative Assembly, and he sold his shares to Capozzi. When Bennett became premier of the province in 1952, he took a serious look at the wine industry he had helped to create. If the wineries were to sell their products through the government-controlled liquor stores, he argued, they should do their part in promoting the grape-growing industry. In 1960 the BC government passed a law stating that wines vinified in the province had to contain a minimum percentage of locally grown grapes. Because only 585 acres were under vines in the Okanagan Valley, that figure was set at 25 percent. To encourage the planting of new vineyards, the Liquor Board stated that the quota would rise to 50 percent in 1962, and 65 percent by 1965.

In the early 1960s, farmers in the Okanagan Valley began planting French and American hybrids (Okanagan Riesling, De Chaunac, Maréchal Foch, Verdelet, Rougeon, Chelois, and Baco Noir) and, within four years, the total acreage had risen by 400 percent. In 1961 Andrew Peller, aged fifty-seven and already a successful brewer and icemaker in Ontario, built a spanking new winery for Andrés at Port Moody. Six years later a company called Southern Okanagan Wines of Penticton opened for business, but it soon changed its name to Casabello. At the same time, the beautifully situated Mission Hill Winery was built on a ridge overlooking Okanagan Lake at Westbank. This facility was acquired in 1969 by the ebullient construction king and brewer Ben Ginter, who promptly renamed it with characteristic flamboyance (if little understanding of consumer sophistication) Uncle Ben's Gourmet Wines. He also put a portrait of himself on his labels. Among the products Ginter was to market were such pop wines as Fuddle Duck and Hot Goose.

From 1974 to 1979, growers turned their attention to grape varieties imported from California and Washington. Experimental plantings of Cabernet Sauvignon, Merlot, Chenin Blanc, Gewurztraminer, White and Grey Riesling, Semillon, and Chardonnay were evaluated at eighteen sites throughout the Okanagan. In 1975, on the advice of Germany's renowned grape researcher Dr. Helmut Becker, George Heiss, the founder of Gray Monk

THE BECKER PROJECT

The BC wine industry owes a great debt of gratitude to Dr. Helmut Becker, the world-renowned oenologist and grape researcher who headed the Geisenheim Research Institute in the Rheingau, Germany. In 1976 Becker visited the Okanagan and convinced George Heiss of Gray Monk and others that their region could grow European vinifera grapes (as opposed to the hybrids that were planted at the time). It was just a question of selecting the right varieties to survive the winter, planting them in suitable sites, employing the right trellising techniques, and not overcropping. Geisenheim's own research plots were basically on the same latitude as the central and northern parts of the Okanagan, so Becker sent over a variety of cuttings that he considered could be grown there. The infant vines were planted in 1978 at Gray Monk and at the Summerland Research Station. The eight-year trial ended with a selection of vinifera vines that could ripen in the Okanagan's growing season. Among these vines were Gewurztraminer, Pinot Blanc, and Pinot Gris—three white varieties, now planted widely throughout the valley, that produce some of the best wines in the province. George Heiss claims that Auxerrois topped all the varieties tested for growing characteristics and the quality of the wine made from it; however, the difficulty of getting Auxerrois plant material made it less popular among growers.

Pre-harvest grapes in a Naramata vineyard.

Winery, brought in Auxerrois, Pinot Gris, and Gewurztraminer vines from France to plant in his Okanagan Centre vineyard.

Looking south to the Napa and Sonoma valleys of California, the BC government realized there was great tourist potential for a thriving wine industry in the beautiful Okanagan Valley. After years of bureaucratic foot-shuffling, the politicians finally agreed to the creation of cottage or estate wineries—the first in the field was Claremont. In 1979 Bob Claremont took over a facility built by Marion John, who had planted vineyards on a steep slope

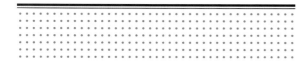

VIRTUAL WINERIES

A virtual winery is a new phenomenon on the BC wine scene—a winery that you can't visit because it has no bricks and mortar. It is only a label. Under wine regulations in British Columbia, a winemaker is permitted to piggy-back on a colleague's licence and to make wine and bottle it in that facility. Most virtual vintners sell their wine through the host's shop or through private retail outlets, mail order, or the Internet. There are also a few virtual wineries that have a tasting room and store, such as Desert Hills, but no winemaking facility.

DESERT HILLS ESTATE WINERY
30480—71 STREET (BLACK SAGE ROAD), OLIVER, BC V0H 1T0
(250) 498-1040, WWW.DESERTHILLS.CA

PARADISE RANCH WINES CORP.
SUITE 901—525 SEYMOUR STREET, VANCOUVER, BC V6B 3H7
(604) 683-6040, WWW.ICEWINES.COM

SANDHILL WINES
C/O CALONA VINEYARDS, 1125 RICHTER STREET, KELOWNA, BC V1Y 2K6
(250) 762-9144; 1-888-246-4472, WWW.SANDHILLWINES.CA

just north of Peachland nineteen years earlier. John's first wines were made and bottled at Mission Hill Winery, but Claremont, who had worked as a winemaker at Calona as well as at Jordan's Ontario plant, set up a crusher, fermentation tanks, and a bottling line and began to vinify British Columbia's first estate-bottled wines in 1979.

The BC Liquor Control and Licensing Branch, not knowing how to deal with the novel enterprise, hastily introduced regulations that both encouraged and inhibited the new winery. To be an estate winery, the company had to cultivate 20 acres of vines and could make a maximum of only 30,000 gallons of wine (later increased to 40,000 gallons). All the grapes used in the wine had to be grown in the province, and 50 percent of these grapes had to come from Claremont's own vineyards. The winery was allowed to open a retail store on its premises and could sell directly to licensees without having to pay the government's mark-up. Claremont could sell two products through the specialty liquor stores, but they would carry the provincial mark-up of 15 percent. (Today the provincial mark-up is 117 percent.)

Within the next three years, Claremont was joined by five other small producers in the Okanagan: Sumac Ridge, Vinitera (which went into receivership in 1982), Uniacke Cellars (now CedarCreek), Gray Monk, and, in the spring of 1983, Divino Wines in Oliver. In those early days there was a camaraderie among the operators of these small wineries, and they helped each other out when they could by sharing facilities and equipment, such as hand-labelling machines, or by storing each other's wines. They were the pioneers of a new phase in British Columbia's growing wine industry. Today the industry is more corporate and highly competitive. Pioneers like Harry McWatters of Sumac Ridge remember the old days with nostalgia. There is still amiable cooperation among the small wineries,

Harvesting Maréchal Foch at House of Rose Vineyard.

78

FIELD 6
BLOCK 2
MERLOT
CLONE 181
SO4
2003

which exchange equipment, partner in Icewine pressing, and assist each other with bottling. The industry as a whole came to the aid of St. Hubertus, which lost its winery in the great Kelowna fire of 2003.

Meanwhile, Uncle Ben's Gourmet Wines, suffering the consequences of marketing dubious wines, fell afoul of the banks and re-emerged briefly under the name of Golden Valley Wines. However, its reincarnation did not help its balance sheet and, thanks to union animosity following troubles at Ginter's Red Deer Brewery, Ginter was forced to sell out. In 1981 he sold to Anthony von Mandl's Mark Anthony Group, a successful Vancouver-based firm of wine importers. The new owner immediately restored the original name of Mission Hill and began a massive reorganization.

The last commercial winery to open in British Columbia was Brights, which built a spectacular modern winery in 1981 on Inkameep Indian Band land to ferment grapes grown on the band's adjacent Inkameep Vineyard. The building alone cost $2 million and was funded by development money from the provincial and federal governments. Bright's invested $3.5 million in equipment for the new facility. In 1994 Brights merged with Cartier-Inniskillin to form Vincor International, and, for economies of scale, the company enlarged this facility for its combined winemaking operations.

After the extensive vinifera replanting that followed the 1988–89 pull-out program (a government-sponsored effort to make the industry competitive following the Free Trade Agreement), there was a lull while the new vines came into production. For the wine consumer, the impact became apparent in 1993, when many of the vines from the new plantings began to augment the established white Germanic viniferas. Additional volumes of familiar Riesling, Gewurztraminer, and Ehrenfelser were joined by Pinot Blanc, Pinot Gris, and Chardonnay. On the red vinifera side, existing Pinot Noir and small quantities of Merlot and Cabernet suddenly blossomed into appreciable releases of these premium varietals at an increasing number of wineries, including Gehringer Brothers, Gray Monk, and Sumac Ridge.

Essentially, 1993 marked the turning point for the BC wine industry. Consumers responded to the new-found quality with increasing purchases of VQA wines, spurring additional plantings in the province. But some structure was needed to categorize the growing number of wineries.

Up until 1998, British Columbia liquor control regulations divided the wine industry into three categories: major, estate, and farm wineries.

- Farm wineries had to have a minimum of 4 acres of vines and were limited to producing 10,000 gallons of wine from BC grapes. Their wines had to be sold from their own store on the property or directly to restaurants.
- Estate wineries were required to have at least 20 acres of vines and were limited to 40,000 gallons of wine made from BC grapes. Their wines had to be sold through their own wine shop, licensed outlets, or British Columbia Liquor Distribution Branch (BCLDB) stores.

OPPOSITE: End row marker at Quails' Gate Estate Winery indicates grape variety. BELOW: Wine propaganda, BC style.

- Major wineries were not required to own their own vineyards and could produce provincial VQA wines as well as blended imported wines. Major wineries had access to the full range of liquor outlets.

In 1998, in consultation with all the players, the BC government simplified matters by establishing a new licensing policy that, in effect, created only one winery licence for all wineries—a similar system to the one in Ontario.

The most dramatic development in the BC industry came in 1997, when Anthony von Mandl announced that Mission Hill Wines was planting a new 225-acre vineyard across the lake from Osoyoos at the southern end of the Okanagan Valley, on the US border. This vineyard, in addition to other extensive cooperative vineyard projects in the south of the valley, laid the foundation for Mission Hill to begin replacing imported wines with BC-grown VQA wines for its varietal releases.

This move was soon followed by Calona Wines, in close cooperation with the extensive Burrowing Owl Vineyards, also in the Southern Okanagan. Andrés Wines announced a 65-acre joint vineyard venture with a local landowner in the neighbouring Similkameen Valley to the west, but an even more important step was taken by Vincor International in 1998. Vincor planted 130 acres of new vineyards at the northeast corner of Osoyoos Lake, on land leased from the Osoyoos Indian Band. A further 370 acres was planted in 1999, and the site has the potential to be Canada's most extensive premium vineyard, with up to 2,000 acres of planting possible by 2007.

How does British Columbia's wine industry compare to that of Ontario? Climatically the two regions are very different. In European terms, British Columbia is more like the northern Rhône, and Ontario more like Burgundy. The northern Rhône has no difficulty ripening its fruit, while the cooler, variable weather in Burgundy is a challenge for its winemakers.

David Lawrason, the editor of *Wine Access* magazine and founder of the Canadian Wine Awards, has pitted both provinces' wines against each other

Osoyoos Lake and Bench vineyards.

in his annual competition. Comparing the two regions, he says: "The obvious difference is the consistency of fruit ripeness in both the whites and the reds of BC and more consistency from vintage to vintage because of the hot summers they have. The other distinguishing factor I get from the southern reds is the quality of their tannins. There's a really gritty, desert-like texture to them, not hard, green, austere tannins. I think the Pinot Blancs and Pinot Gris have nice peachy notes and obvious fruit."

Certainly the reds from the Southern Okanagan (Osoyoos and Oliver) have more alcohol and more

fruit extract and weight than their Ontario counter-parts. They are more Washington and California in style than they are European.

Ontario wines tend to have higher acids and more delicacy. The future challenge for BC's winemakers is to strive for more elegance and finesse in their wines rather than producing blockbuster reds and highly extracted whites that are often difficult to match with food. Vincor's red wine Osoyoos Larose, made in the elegant, well-balanced Bordeaux style, should be the model for other producers to emu-late. And, like Ontario, British Columbia should concentrate more on blending both reds and whites. The White Meritage (a Sauvignon/Semillon blend) produced by Jackson-Triggs and Sumac Ridge are two of the best whites made in Canada. I would put these two wines up against white Bordeaux any day of the week.

Ultimately, the test of a great wine is how it stands up at the dinner table, matched with food. I believe that both British Columbia and Ontario can produce wines that would grace the tables of the finest restaurants of the world. What we are seeing today is only the beginning.

Fraser Valley

British Columbia's Fraser Valley, while not without its challenges, is proving to be a viable grape-growing region that now accounts for 1.3 percent of the province's 5,500 acres of grapevines. The high ridges, with their sandy loam and red clay soils that offer good drainage and sun exposure, lend themselves to grape growing. Summers are generally sunny and warm and provide enough heat to ripen suitable grape varieties dependably, while, in the winter, the sea-level climate virtually eliminates any danger of freezing damage.

One of the challenges to grape growing is the moderate coastal humidity. Growers combat it with carefully pruned canopies opened to air circulation through basal leaf thinning as well as by judicious spraying for mildew. Grape varieties that do well here include Bacchus, Madeleine Angevine, Madeleine Sylvaner, Ortega, Gewurztraminer, Chardonnay, and Pinot Noir.

A major benefit for these wineries is their proximity to the greater Vancouver area. There are now nine wineries in the Fraser Valley/Lower Mainland area, three of them fruit wineries. Four of the wineries with vineyards and one fruit winery are located within a short distance of each other in Langley and Abbotsford, while two wineries operate cellars and wine shops in the greater Vancouver area. The other two fruit wineries are located to the south, in Delta.

The Fraser Valley has the potential to host more vineyard and winery operations. Building on the success and experience of the trail-blazing Domaine de Chaberton, recently established winery operations have shown that quality grapes can be grown successfully in a number of varieties and are capable of producing award-winning wines. This success depends on many factors, including careful selection of site, varieties that grow and express themselves well in the terroir, and skillful and industrious viticultural practices.

This valley is the place for those who love the outdoors, whether it's cruising on the river or strolling through Campbell Valley Park. Gardeners will want to visit the Tuscan Farm Gardens in Langley, with its annual Lavender Fair and a B&B that makes you feel you're in Tuscany. Aspiring architects will be intrigued with the International Sandcastle Competition on the beach at Harrison Lake in the fall. And, of course, Vancouver is only a short drive away.

TOURING WINERIES
in the Fraser Valley

As the agricultural centre of the province, the Fraser Valley is home to a lot of orchards, berry fields, and pasture land. It's flat for the most part, so there are more wineries making fruit wines than grape wines. The proximity to Vancouver makes it an easy day trip.

SINGLE DAY: Two wineries are not to be missed here, Domaine de Chaberton and Township 7. At Domaine de Chaberton you can stop for lunch and enjoy the patio, if the weather permits, or eat indoors. Township 7 has only a few wines to offer, but their quality makes a stop essential here.

WEEKEND: Spend the first day at fruit wineries, beginning with Blossom Winery in Richmond, then go to Westham Island Estate, Wellbrook, and end with the Fort Wine Company. The next day visit the wineries—Lotusland (browse the store for their funky labels), Glenugie (for a little Scottish culture and some good Gamay and Pinot Noir), Township 7, and Domaine de Chaberton.

Blossom Winery

5491 MINORU BOULEVARD, RICHMOND, BC V6X 2B1 (604) 232-9839
WWW.BLOSSOMWINERY.COM

YEAR FOUNDED: 2000 **FOUNDER:** John Chang **WINEMAKER:** John Chang **GRAPE VARIETIES:** (red) Cabernet Sauvignon, Cabernet Franc, Merlot; (white) Riesling **RECOMMENDED WINES:** Two Left Feet, Late Harvest Riesling, Cabernet Franc Icewine

John Chang credits his grandmother for his entry into the wine business in Canada two years after he emigrated here in 1999. He had watched her making fruit wines in the family farmhouse in Taiwan.

Chang's own urban fruit winery, based in downtown Richmond, specializes in raspberry and blueberry wine, fruit he purchases from local farms. He also buys in grapes from the Okanagan to make Late Harvest Riesling and Icewines as well as a dry Meritage blend called Two

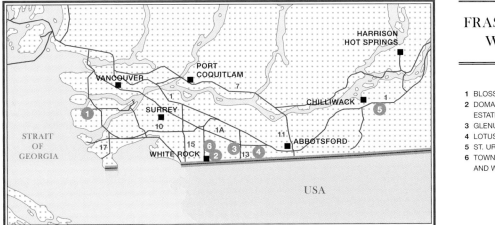

Left Feet. A unique product is his three-in-one stackable bottle that features Late Harvest Riesling, Raspberry, and Blueberry wines, each with its own stopper.

Domaine de Chaberton Estate Winery

1064–216TH STREET, LANGLEY, BC V2Z 1R3 (604) 530-1736; 1-800-332-9463
FAX: (604) 533-9687 WWW.DOMAINEDECHABERTON.COM

YEAR FOUNDED: 1991 **FOUNDERS:** Claude and Ingeborg Violet
WINEMAKER: Elias Phiniotis **GRAPE VARIETIES:** (white) Madeleine
Angevine, Madeleine Sylvaner, Bacchus, Ortega, Chardonnay
RECOMMENDED WINES: Gewurztraminer, Bacchus, Optima, Syrah

In 1980, when Claude and Ingeborg Violet decided to make British Columbia their home, John Harper helped them to find a vineyard site in the Fraser Valley. They chose a raspberry farm south of Langley amid horse and dairy farms. Claude's father had once owned a winery in Tarragona, Spain, and a vineyard and orchard near Montpellier called Domaine de Chaberton. Claude and German-born Inge chose the Fraser Valley, rather than the Okanagan, because it was nearer their potential market in Vancouver. Their success is yet another example of rugged individualism triumphing over accepted wisdom, because everyone told them it was impossible to grow grapes in the Fraser Valley. They grow only white varieties, sourcing their reds from a grower on Black Sage Road in the Southern Okanagan. The winery is a cluster of dazzling white buildings, including a French bistro (great bistro cooking here) and a cedar-panelled Quonset hut that houses the barrel room. After fourteen years, the Violets decided to retire in 2005. They sold the winery to Anthony Cheng and Eugene Kwan, but will stay for a year to ensure a smooth transition of ownership. Depending on the weather, you can dine indoors or outdoors within sight of the beautifully groomed vineyard.

Glenugie Winery

3033–232ND STREET, LANGLEY, BC V2Z 3A8 (604) 539-9463; 1-866-233-9463
WWW.GLENUGIEWINERY.COM

YEAR FOUNDED: 2002 **FOUNDERS:** Gary and Christina Tayler
WINEMAKERS: Gary Tayler, Elias Phiniotis (consultant) **GRAPE
VARIETIES:** (red) Pinot Noir, Gamay Noir; (white) Pinot Blanc,
Chardonnay **RECOMMENDED WINES:** Unoaked Chardonnay, Gamay
Noir, Limited Edition Pinot Noir

The Scottish tartan of the Campbell of Argyll clan on Glenugie labels is a reminder of the family heritage. Christina Tayler's grandmother owned a farm called Glenugie in Longside, Scotland. The 7,777-square-foot winery is modelled after a Scottish fortress, executed in brick with massive wooden doors and hedged around with Scottish heather. The Scottish association is reinforced by the crests of the Campbell, McGregor, Grant, and Galloway clans of family members that decorate the winery's tasting room. Like the owners of many of the other small estate wineries in cooler regions of the province, Gary Tayler uses plastic tenting over his vines in the 5-acre vineyard (planted in 1997) to advance bud break in the spring and give him an earlier harvest date. The organically farmed vineyard is planted to Pinot Noir—a consuming passion of Tayler—while other varieties are brought in from the Okanagan. If it's chilly outside, you can sample your wine by the fireplace in the winery.

Lotusland Vineyards

28450–16TH AVENUE (KING ROAD), ABBOTSFORD, BC V4X 1V1 (604) 857-4188
WWW.LOTUSLANDVINEYARDS.COM

YEAR FOUNDED: 2002 **FOUNDERS:** David and Liz Avery **WINEMAKER:** David Avery **GRAPE VARIETIES:** (red) Pinot Noir, Gamay, Pinot Meunier, Cabernet Franc, Zweigelt; (white) Pinot Gris, Gewurztraminer, Riesling, Siegerrebe, Chardonnay **RECOMMENDED WINE:** Merlot

A radical makeover in 2003 by designer Bernie Hadley-Beauregard, who masterminded the image for Blasted Church, has changed the winery formerly known as A'Very Fine Winery (punning on the proprietors' name, Avery) to Lotusland Vineyards. David Avery maintains an organic vineyard and runs a rustic, countrified boutique. The imaginative labels feature photos of places and people, including prominent Canadians who live in Vancouver, such as former prime minister Kim Campbell, snowboard gold medallist Ross Rebagliati, and architect Arthur Erickson.

St. Urban Winery

47189 BAILEY ROAD, CHILLIWACK, BC V2R 4S8 (604) 858-7652
STURBAN@TELUS.NET

YEAR FOUNDED: 2002 **FOUNDERS:** Paul and Kathie Kompauer
WINEMAKER: Paul Kompauer **GRAPE VARIETIES:** (red) Agria, Gamay Noir, Pinot Noir, Zweigelt; (white) Kerner, Madeleine Angevine, Ortega, Siegerrebe **RECOMMENDED WINES:** Siegerrebe, oak-aged Turan

Paul Kompauer comes from Slovakia, where his family has been making wine for seven generations. He says that he made his first vintage at the age of twelve, and that it was drinkable, too! Kompauer immigrated to Canada when the former Czechoslovakia was invaded by the Russians in 1976, and he finished his civil engineering studies here. The urge to make wine never left him and, in 2001, he purchased a thriving 7-acre vineyard in Chilliwack. He called his winery after St. Urban of Langres, the patron saint of grape growers. The winery is located in restored old barns that had been used for dairy farming in the 1950s. The original farmhouse has been renovated to include ceramics from Modra, in

Corey Coleman of Township 7 Vineyards and Winery.

Slovakia, and a turn-of-the-century wine press. The front entrance has been painted to resemble a Moravian wine cellar in the town of Cejc. You'll find several images of St. Urban around the tasting room and shop, including one painted on slate by local artist Glenda Mantle.

Township 7 Vineyards and Winery

21152–16TH AVENUE, LANGLEY, BC V2Z 1K3 (604) 532-1766
WWW.TOWNSHIP7.COM
NARAMATA WINERY: 1450 MCMILLAN AVENUE, PENTICTON, BC V24 8T4

YEAR FOUNDED: 2001 (Naramata 2004) **FOUNDER:** Corey and Gwen Coleman **WINEMAKERS:** Corey Coleman, Brad Cooper **GRAPE VARIETIES:** (red) Merlot, Syrah, Cabernet Sauvignon; (white) Chardonnay, Sauvignon Blanc **RECOMMENDED WINES:** Chardonnay, Merlot Reserve, Syrah

Corey Coleman made sparkling wine at Blue Mountain and worked the crush at both Hawthorne Mountain and Tinhorn Creek before purchasing the 5-acre site in the Fraser Valley with its sixty-year-old horse barn. His wife, Gwen, learned the marketing side of the operation as a consultant to a number of Okanagan wineries. The couple made an early splash with gold medals in two national competitions. They also purchase grapes from three vineyards in the Southern Okanagan. In 2004 they opened a second winery, a no-frills facility on the Naramata Bench outside Penticton, to vinify the fruit from the 7-acre vineyard they own there. A sparkling wine called Seven Stars has been added to Township 7's small but impressive portfolio. In 2005 Brad Cooper, formerly at Stag's Hollow, joined the winemaking team. You may not be delighted by the facilities in either the Fraser Valley or the Okanagan, but the wines are terrific.

North Okanagan–Shuswap (See map on page 66)

While the North Okanagan and Shuswap area is the most recent interior wine district to develop in British Columbia, some of the earliest experiments in BC grape growing took place in 1905 in Salmon Arm. Recent plantings in the township of Tappen, west of Salmon Arm, have helped to increase the grape acreage north of Vernon to close to 100 acres.

You will experience cooler weather as you advance up the Okanagan Valley to the Shuswap region around Salmon Arm, not far off the 51st parallel (the most northerly latitude for grape growing). The climate of this region is dramatically different from that of the southern desert zone around Oliver and Osoyoos, only a two-hour drive away. The greener surroundings are due to more generous annual precipitation levels as well as to more moderate temperatures.

Here richly forested mountains covered with fir, hemlock, tamarack, and cedar slope down to meadowed valleys, rivers, and lakes. The heat summations are lower than in the southern valley, but blisteringly hot summer days still contrast with swiftly cooling night temperatures to produce stunningly crisp and clean wines from Siegerrebe, Madeleine Angevine, and Ortega grapes, as well as hardy red hybrids led by Maréchal Foch.

There are now six wineries in this region, one each in Vernon, Armstrong, and Salmon Arm, and three in the Tappen area, all benefiting from their proximity to the Vancouver–Alberta traffic on the nearby Trans-Canada Highway. As with parts of the lower Okanagan Valley, soils range from post-glacial sediments to glacial meltwater deposits and unsorted glacial till. Though varying greatly, the areas lending themselves to grape growing generally benefit from favourable soil conditions with good nutrient content and drainage. Irrigation is a necessity as far north as Vernon, and, while it is always a benefit to be able to augment rainfall, the Shuswap area vineyards generally do not require it.

The most northerly vineyards in the district push the wine-growing envelope to the practical limit for the varieties they grow. Happily, these grapes often make some of the most flavourful wines, such as Recline Ridge's Pinot Meunier, Larch Hills "Mad Angie" (Madeleine Angevine), and Granite Creek's Select Late Harvest Ehrenfelser.

Many of these same characteristics also apply to the Columbia River Valley south of Trail in the Kootenays, where Columbia Garden has been operating for three years growing similar varieties to North Okanagan–Shuswap as well as the better-known Pinot Noir, Gewurztraminer, and Auxerrois.

This former gold-mining area, now a major fruit-farming centre, is rich in historic sites and artifacts. The Revelstoke Railway Museum, the Haney House Salmon Arm Museum, the Haney Heritage House and Park (featuring buildings dating back to 1911), and the O'Keefe Historical Ranch (founded in 1867), with its old cowboy guns and gear, give a practical insight into the rugged pioneer life of this northern sector.

TOURING WINERIES
in North Okanagan–Shuswap

SINGLE DAY: There are only five wineries between Vernon and Salmon Arm, so you could visit all of them in a day trip. But that would give you no opportunity to see the other local attractions. For a quick visit, take in the two most northerly wineries in the province—Recline Ridge and Granite Creek. At Recline Ridge, ask Mike Smith to explain why his winery looks as if it belongs in Japan.

WEEKEND: Allow yourself a leisurely tour of Recline Ridge and Granite Creek (you'll have to leave the Pemberton Valley Vineyard & Inn, a twenty-minute drive to Whistler Mountain, for another day because it's not on your route). Spend the night in Vernon at the Castle on the Mountain B&B, with its panoramic view of lakes and mountains. On the second day, visit Hunting Hawk Vineyards in Spallumcheen. Owners Russ and Marni Niles have opened a second vineyard on the 64-acre O'Keefe Ranch, a remarkable heritage site with the historic O'Keefe home, a clapboard church, and a general store. Try to make it there for the Cornelius O'Keefe Days and Cowboy Festival, two days of rodeos and cowboy theatre at the end of July, and other cowboy-inspired events during the summer and fall seasons. A good reason to brave the hill up to Larch Hills is to taste "Mad Angie" (made from the variety Madeleine Angevine) atop BC's highest vineyard.

OKANAGAN VALLEY & SIMILKAMEEN VALLEY WINERIES

NORTH OKANAGAN–SHUSWAP
1 BELLA VISTA VINEYARDS
2 GRANITE CREEK ESTATE WINES
3 HUNTING HAWK VINEYARDS
4 LARCH HILLS WINERY
5 PEMBERTON VALLEY VINEYARD
   AND INN
6 RECLINE RIDGE VINEYARDS
   AND WINERY

SIMILKAMEEN VALLEY
7 CROWSNEST VINEYARDS
8 HERDER WINERY & VINEYARDS
9 OROFINO VINEYARDS
10 ST. LASZLO VINEYARDS
    ESTATE WINERY
11 THE SEVEN STONES WINERY

SOUTH CENTRAL OKANAGAN
12 ADORA ESTATE WINERY
13 ARROWLEAF CELLARS
14 BLASTED CHURCH VINEYARDS
15 BLUE MOUNTAIN VINEYARD
    AND CELLARS
16 CALONA VINEYARDS
17 CEDARCREEK ESTATE WINERY
18 D'ANGELO ESTATE WINERY
19 D'ASOLO VINEYARDS WINERY
20 DIRTY LAUNDRY VINEYARD
21 GRAY MONK ESTATE WINERY
22 GREATA RANCH VINEYARDS
23 HAINLE VINEYARDS ESTATE
    WINERY AND DEEP CREEK
    WINE ESTATE
24 HAWTHORNE MOUNTAIN
    VINEYARDS
25 HILLSIDE ESTATE
26 HOUSE OF ROSE VINEYARD
27 KETTLE VALLEY WINERY
28 LA FRENZ ESTATE WINERY
29 LAKE BREEZE VINEYARDS
30 LANG VINEYARDS
31 LAUGHING STOCK VINEYARDS
32 LITTLE STRAW VINEYARDS
33 MISSION HILL FAMILY ESTATE
34 MT. BOUCHERIE ESTATE WINERY
35 NICHOL VINEYARD FARM
    WINERY
36 NOBLE RIDGE VINEYARD
    AND WINERY
37 PENTÂGE WINES
38 POPLAR GROVE WINERY
39 QUAILS' GATE ESTATE WINERY
40 RED ROOSTER WINERY
41 ST. HUBERTUS ESTATE WINERY

42 SANDHILL WINES
43 SONORAN ESTATE WINERY
44 STAG'S HOLLOW WINERY
    AND VINEYARD
45 STONEHILL ESTATE WINERY
46 SUMAC RIDGE ESTATE WINERY
47 SUMMERHILL PYRAMID WINERY
48 SUMMERLAND CELLARS
    ESTATE WINERY
49 TANTALUS VINEYARDS
50 THERAPY VINEYARDS
51 THORNHAVEN ESTATES WINERY
52 WILD GOOSE VINEYARDS
    & WINERY

SOUTHERN OKANAGAN
53 BLACK HILLS ESTATE
54 BURROWING OWL ESTATE
    WINERY
55 CARRIAGE HOUSE WINES
56 DESERT HILLS ESTATE WINERY
57 DOMAINE COMBRET ESTATE
    WINERY
58 FAIRVIEW CELLARS
59 GEHRINGER BROTHERS
    ESTATE WINERY
60 GOLDEN BEAVER WINERY
61 GOLDEN MILE CELLARS
62 HESTER CREEK ESTATE WINERY

63 INNISKILLIN OKANAGAN
    VINEYARDS
64 JACKSON-TRIGGS OKANAGAN
    CELLARS
65 NK'MIP CELLARS
66 OSOYOOS LAROSE VINEYARD
67 SILVER SAGE WINERY
68 TINHORN CREEK VINEYARDS

Recline Ridge's Vineyard.

Bella Vista Vineyards
(most likely to be renamed Turtle Mountain Estate Winery)
3111 AGNEW ROAD, VERNON, BC V1H 1A1 (250) 545-0105

YEAR FOUNDED: 1994 **FOUNDER:** Larry Passmore **WINEMAKER:** n/a
GRAPE VARIETIES: (red) Maréchal Foch, Pinot Noir; (white) Auxerrois,
Chardonnay, Gewurztraminer, Pinot Gris **RECOMMENDED WINES:**
not tasted

At the time of writing, this winery has been purchased by
Sid Sidhu, the general manager of the Bella Vista Farm
Market and Orchards in Vernon and a commissioner on
the Agricultural Land Commission. He intends to rename
it Turtle Mountain Estate, though its historical provenance
deserves telling. If Steve Martin ever went into the wine
business, this winery is the kind of enterprise he would
build. Bella Vista Vineyards had its beginnings "very near
the end of a very bad golf game in 1991," according to its
founder, Larry Passmore. He got together a consortium
of professionals who constructed the three-storey winery
themselves one summer as a kind of joint hobby-cum-party
place overlooking the city of Vernon. The partners drifted
away, but Passmore stayed to keep the winery going by
relying on group tours and weddings. Sidhu has replanted
10 acres and is currently negotiating for a winemaker.

Columbia Gardens Vineyard
and Winery
9340 STATION ROAD, TRAIL, BC V1R 4W6 (250) 367-7493 WWW.CGWINERY.COM

YEAR FOUNDED: 2001 **FOUNDERS:** Tom Bryden and Lawrence Wallace
WINEMAKER: Lawrence Wallace **GRAPE VARIETIES:** (red) Pinot Noir,
Maréchal Foch, Merlot; (white) Chardonnay, Gewurztraminer, Auxerrois
RECOMMENDED WINES: Garden Gold, Unoaked Chardonnay, Late
Harvest Pinot Noir

If you're into esoteric vineyards or you happen to be hiking the Dewdney Trail, the mining town of Trail, a.k.a
the City of Silver, holds a special surprise. It was here
that Tom Bryden and his son-in-law Lawrence Wallace

blazed the trail with the first commercial vineyard in the
Kootenay region, a good two hours' drive east of the
Okanagan. In the mid-1990s Wallace planted a small
experimental plot on the 50-acre family farm near the US
border on benchland above the Columbia River, 16 kilometres south of Trail. Over time, Wallace gradually found
the varietals best suited to his soil. No doubt the initial
attraction is the mountain scenery, but the wines here,
mainly fruity blends, have their own appeal.

Granite Creek Estate Wines
2302 SKIMIKIN ROAD, RR 1, SITE 12, COMP 2, TAPPEN, BC V0E 2X0
(250) 835-0049 WWW.GRANITECREEK.CA

YEAR FOUNDED: 2004 **FOUNDERS:** Doug and Mayka Kennedy, Gary
and Heather Kennedy **WINEMAKER:** Gary Strachan **GRAPE VARIETIES:**
(red) Pinot Noir, Merlot, Maréchal Foch; (white) Gewurztraminer,
Ehrenfelser, Pinot Gris, Chardonnay, Ortega, Kerner **RECOMMENDED
WINES:** Ehrenfelser Select Late Harvest, Merlot Fortified Dessert Wine,
Pinot Gris

Together with nearby Recline Ridge, Granite Creek is one
of the most northerly wineries in North America: to put
it in perspective, slightly more northerly than Germany's
Rheingau region. The winery and the tasting room are
housed in log-frame structures with all-wood siding, nestled
in an oasis of trees, ravines, and greenery overlooking the
two smaller portions of the vineyards that slope down to
Granite Creek. Gary Kennedy, an agricultural engineer
and agrologist, and Heather (who makes wine-infused
jellies and jams) are long-time residents of the estate (the
Kennedy family has been farming the region for six generations, and Gary himself since 1959). Their son Doug
and his wife, Mayka, complete the family winery team.
Grapes for the first crush in 2003 came from the
Okanagan Valley, but the 1-acre vineyard in front of the
tasting room, the 1.5-acre vineyard next to the winery,
and a 10-acre site across a small ravine approximately 30
metres on the other side of Granite Creek will soon be
able to supply all their needs. Currently the family is
building a new deck for a tasting room that will jut out
over the ravine.

Hunting Hawk Vineyards
4758 GULCH ROAD, ARMSTRONG, BC V0E 1B4 (250) 546-2164
WWW.HUNTINGHAWKVINEYARDS.COM
O'KEEFE RANCH RESTAURANT, (250) 542-2178)

YEAR FOUNDED: 2001 **FOUNDERS:** Russ and Marni Niles **WINEMAKERS:**
Russ Niles, Gary Strachan **GRAPE VARIETIES:** (red) Maréchal Foch;
(white) Pinot Auxerrois, Perle of C'saba, Ortega **RECOMMENDED WINES:**
Gewurztraminer, White Port Style Dessert Wine

The abundant wildlife that inhabits the Spallumcheen
Valley where this winery is located, 8 kilometres north of

Armstrong, is reflected in Hunting Hawk's labels. The images were painted by Allan Brooks, who lived in Vernon in the early 1900s. Proceeds from the sales of Russ and Marni's wines support the Greater Vernon Museum, which houses a large collection of Brooks's paintings. The Nileses augment the fruit from their own vineyard with contracted growers in Naramata, Okanagan Falls, and Westbank. You can taste their wines either at their home winery or at the heritage O'Keefe Ranch shop, 12 kilometres north of Vernon, where Marni Niles, dressed in pioneer costume on occasion, will pour you samples. Russ Niles has planted a 2-acre vineyard here featuring several cool-climate varieties, and he installed a small winery to give visitors an insight into how wines are made. The ranch is run by a non-profit organization, the Interior Heritage Society. A product unique to Hunting Hawk is a sweet white wine made from Pinot Blanc, called White Port Style Dessert Wine, whose alcohol is built up by the addition of sugar rather than brandy during fermentation. It's best to visit the ranch and taste it there, just for the intriguing historical ambiance.

Larch Hills Winery

110 TIMMS ROAD, SALMON ARM, BC V1E 2W5 (250) 832-0155; 1-877-892-0155
WWW.LARCHHILLSWINERY.COM

YEAR FOUNDED: 1997 **FOUNDERS:** Hans and Hazel Nevrkla
WINEMAKER: Hans Nevrkla **GRAPE VARIETIES:** (red) Agria, Merlot, Pinot
Noir; (white) Ortega, Siegerrebe, Madeleine Angevine, Madeleine
Sylvaner **RECOMMENDED WINES:** Ortega, Siegerrebe, Tamarack Rosé

Larch Hills' facility looks like a Tyrolean cottage, perched above the Trans-Canada Highway up a crazily winding forest road. When Hans and Hazel Nevrkla arrived from Calgary in 1987 (Nevrkla had been teaching winemaking there at a community college), their property was nothing but bush. "Salmon Arm—forget about it, don't do it," was the advice the couple got when they suggested settling there. "We didn't originally intend to plant a vineyard here," Nevrkla confesses. "We thought we'd try some vines because, at the time, the BC government was encouraging new vineyard start-ups and the pull-out of non-vinifera vines by establishing the Farm Gate Winery licence." Through hard work, the Nevrklas carved a steeply raked 7-acre site out of the 73 acres they had purchased. Being so far north, they had to rely on early ripening, winter-hardy Germanic varieties such as Ortega, Siegerrebe, and the French crossing Madeleine Angevine—which they market under the creative name of "Mad Angie." They purchase their red varieties from a grower in Westbank. This winery is a stop for the adventurous or for those who collect wines with off-beat names. In 2005 Hans and Hazel Nevrkla decided to retire and sold the winery to Hazel and Jack Manser, who previously ran a dairy farm in Alberta. Hans will continue to make the wines until the 2007 vintage.

Pemberton Valley Vineyard and Inn

1427 COLLINS ROAD, PEMBERTON, BC V0N 2L0 (604) 894-5857; 1-877-444-5857
WWW.WHISTLERWINE.COM

YEAR FOUNDED: 1998 **FOUNDER:** Patrick Bradner **WINEMAKER:** Patrick
Bradner **GRAPE VARIETIES:** (red) Maréchal Foch; (white) Pinot Gris,
Chardonnay **RECOMMENDED WINES:** Maréchal Foch, Pinot Gris

In 1987 Patrick Bradner, a former real estate agent, bought a 5-acre property in the Pemberton Valley, 32 kilometres north of Whistler, BC's premier ski resort. Pemberton Valley is known by the locals as "Spud Valley" because of its seed potatoes, but it seems it can also support grape vines. With his wife, Heather, Bradner created a 6,000-

LEFT: Hans Nevrkla of Larch Hills Winery. ABOVE: Michael Smith of Recline Ridge Vineyards and Winery.

Recline Ridge Vineyards and Winery

2640 KIMIKIN ROAD, TAPPEN, BC V0E 2X0 (250) 835-2212
WWW.RECLINE-RIDGE.BC.CA

YEAR FOUNDED: 1998 **FOUNDERS:** Michael and Susan Smith
WINEMAKER: Michael Smith **GRAPE VARIETIES:** (red) Maréchal Foch;
(white) Ortega, Optima, Siegerrebe, Madeleine Angevine, Sylvaner
RECOMMENDED WINES: Maréchal Foch, Pinot Meunier, Ortega,
Siegerrebe, Perle (dessert wine)

square-foot dovetail square-log home that features three B&B suites (open all year round and with daily maid service) against a magnificent backdrop of mountains that are perfect for a winter getaway. Each beautifully appointed suite is named for a wine—Bordeaux, Burgundy, and Champagne. Curiously, Bordeaux is furnished with Mexican pieces. (Three more rooms are to be added in 2006.) Sheep graze in the front field, while the chickens roost in the back. Dog lovers will have the opportunity to meet the resident brown Labradors, Scarlet and Barkley. Like so many Canadian vintners, Bradner started off as a home winemaker. His initial vineyard, established in 1997, is slowly being replanted to varieties that will do better in this northern exposure. Stop by the Pemberton Museum to check out the gold-rush exhibition as well as some original settler homes dating back to the late nineteenth century.

The Smiths can claim to be North America's most northerly winery and, as such, they have to contend with the coolest of cool climates. If their post-and-beam, three-storey winery looks Japanese, it's because the building was designed by a local company and shipped, log by log, to a family in Japan. The contents of the container were damaged in high seas, and the whole consignment was returned to the company, where Mike Smith discovered the prefabricated house and had it constructed on his property below Mount Tappen. The Japanese motif is carried through to Recline Ridge's label, which features a stylized ideogram that translates as "to meet, match, or pair"—an ideal sentiment for wine. Winemaking for Mike and Sue Smith started as a hobby back in 1975, and they have confounded the naysayers who predicted they could not grow wine so far north. Given the northerly location, Mike manages to coax lots of flavour from his grapes—as you can see from all the trophies in the tasting room.

South Central Okanagan (See map on page 66)

A few kilometres north of Oliver, the Okanagan Valley narrows at McIntyre Bluff and the lake country begins. While fertile land covers the valley bottom in the southern desert region, here a succession of lakes lines the main valley floor, bordered by high silt banks. It is on these benches that some of the finest vineyards in the province are located. Picture rocky, forested mountains skirted by elevated silt benches that plunge in cliffs several hundred feet high to lakeshore beaches. Numerous small streams cut canyons through the banks, filling Okanagan Lake, which in turn empties into Skaha Lake at Penticton and Vaseaux Lake south of Okanagan Falls.

Geologists believe that an ice plug in the south part of the valley remained after the last glacial age, holding back a large meltwater lake whose shoreline extended along the timberline above Penticton. The glacial meltwaters tended to sort different soil materials primarily by water velocity, with faster-moving water courses depositing coarse sands, gravels, cobbles, and stones while slower-moving water deposited sands, silts, and clays. As a result, there is a broad variation in soil type throughout the valley, particularly in the central valley, where there are rolling benches of lighter sandy soils as well as the clay banks in the Penticton district, which are made up of fine sediments.

While the fertile benches were originally given over to apple, peach, apricot, and cherry orchards, increasing blocks are being planted to grapes. From Okanagan Falls north to Vernon, there are about 1,100 acres of vines, or 20.7 percent of the province's total. The Kelowna and Westbank district, the cradle of the early BC grape industry, still accounts for 11 percent of the total plantings.

The lakes have a moderating influence on the vineyards that surround them, creating a natural defence against winter damage as well as spring and fall frosts. The microclimate allows vines to retain their leaves until late November, so, if needed, ripening can continue right to the end of the growing season.

The combination of suitable soils and warm but moderate conditions makes the benches one of the most award-winning grape-growing districts of the province. You have only to visit the tasting rooms of CedarCreek, Gray Monk, Mission Hill, and Quails' Gate to see the medals and trophies their wines have accumulated. The region produces premium Merlot and Chardonnay, along with vineyard locations where Cabernet Sauvignon, Cabernet Franc, and Syrah are successful. Pinot Noir excels in this terroir, as do Riesling, Pinot Blanc, Pinot Gris, Gewurztraminer, and other varieties.

Make the city of Kelowna, with its ample sandy beach and parklands, your starting point for any tour of South Central Okanagan. From here you can ride on the Kettle Valley Steam Train or go parasailing, wind surfing, or boating. You can just lie on the beach and wait for a sighting of Ogopogo, Lake Okanagan's answer to the Loch Ness monster. Or you can hike through Knox Mountain Park and enjoy immense vistas of the valley, lake, and city skyline.

TOURING WINERIES
in South Central Okanagan

This is the heartland of wine country, the longest-established area and, arguably, the one with the best scenery. Kelowna is the place from which to tour, but here you're dealing with two sides of the lake, with this city as the crossing point. That transit can take time in the summer season, so be patient and plan your time accordingly. SINGLE DAY: If you see nothing else in the valley, don't miss Mission Hill and Quails' Gate—the first for the Greek-inspired architecture, the second for the restaurant and the wine. They are very close to each other, and both have spectacular views from their terraces. Then cross the lake to the east bank, where you'll find five wineries. You won't be able to visit all in a day, but I recommend CedarCreek, the most southerly winery, for its elegant design and award-winning wines, and Summerhill Estate for its extravagant showmanship and the pleasure of sipping sparkling wine on a sunlit patio. WEEKEND: Strike for the town of Summerland on Highway 97 and visit Sumac Ridge to taste the White Meritage. Then head for the Naramata Bench that begins at Penticton. This stretch is my favourite part of BC wine country, both for its beauty and the quality of its wines. Must-see wineries include La Frenz for the view from the new tasting room, Red Rooster for the art and the welcome, and Poplar Grove, because it makes stunning red wines as well as great cheese. If time permits, drop in at Kettle Valley and Nichol Vineyard to taste their red wines. Next day, travel north from Penticton on the west bank and visit Mission Hill, Quails' Gate, CedarCreek, and Summerhill.

Chris and Evelyn Campbell of Blasted Church Vineyards.

Adora Estate Winery

6807 HIGHWAY 97, SUMMERLAND, BC V0H 1Z0 (250) 404-4200
WWW.ADORAWINES.COM

YEAR FOUNDED: 2000 **FOUNDERS:** Reid Jenkins, Kevin Golka, Eric von Krosigk **WINEMAKER:** Tilman Hainle **GRAPE VARIETIES:** (red) Syrah, Merlot, Cabernet Sauvignon, Pinot Noir; (white) Riesling, Pinot Gris, Chardonnay **RECOMMENDED WINES:** Maximus (red blend), Decorus (white blend), Merlot, Elements (Riesling)

Adora sits on a small piece of land between the highway and the lake. The 5,000-square-foot winery building is not the most prepossessing sight—its founding winemaker Eric von Krosigk refers to it as a "plain Jane" facility. It looks like a utilitarian metal-clad warehouse with blue trim, but the winemaking that goes on inside belies its industrial appearance. Everything is state of the art, down to the aluminum catwalks above the tanks and the heating and cooling systems that can be manipulated from anywhere with ease. The emphasis here is on blended wines: the red Maximus comes on like a Châteauneuf-du-Pape, and the white Decorus has the richness of California's Caymus Conundrum. Go to taste, not to look.

Arrowleaf Cellars

1574 CAMP ROAD, LAKE COUNTY, BC V4V 1K1 (250) 766-2992
WWW.ARROWLEAFCELLARS.COM

YEAR FOUNDED: 2001 **FOUNDERS:** Joe, Margrit, and Manuel Zuppiger **WINEMAKER:** Manuel Zuppiger **GRAPE VARIETIES:** (red) Merlot, Zweigelt, Pinot Noir; (white) Bacchus, Auxerrois, Pinot Gris, Gewurztraminer, Vidal **RECOMMENDED WINES:** Zweigelt, Gewurztraminer

Arrowleaf, a family-owned, two-storey winery, is situated above Okanagan Centre, commanding a picture-postcard view of the lake and surrounding vineyards. The bright and airy winery, with its steeply sloped vineyard, takes its name from the arrowleaf balsamroot plants (a.k.a "Okanagan sunflower") that bloom each spring on the hillsides. Winemaker Manuel, the son of the owners, was trained in Switzerland and has made wine in Australia. The wines he makes combine both virtues: Swiss precision and Australian bonhomie. If you lack time, this is a wonderful place to stop for the view and a quick tasting.

Blasted Church Vineyards
(formerly Prpich Hills Vineyards)

378 PARSONS ROAD, RR 1, SITE 32, COMP 67, OKANAGAN FALLS, BC V0H 1R0
(250) 497-1125; 1-877-355-2686 (1-8-SPELLBOUND)
WWW.BLASTEDCHURCH.COM

YEAR FOUNDED: 2002 **FOUNDERS:** Chris and Evelyn Campbell **WINEMAKER:** Kelly Moss **GRAPE VARIETIES:** (red) Merlot, Pinot Noir, Lemberger, Cabernet Sauvignon; (white) Gewurztraminer, Pinot Gris, Chardonnay, Pinot Blanc, Riesling, Ehrenfelser, Optima **RECOMMENDED WINES:** Chardonnay Musqué, Pinot Gris, Hatfield's Fuse (white blend), Gewurztraminer, Lemberger

Who said accountants have no sense of humour? Chris and Evelyn Campbell were formerly accountants in Vancouver. Blasted Church is a media-savvy winery with a wry sense of humour and great marketing flair. Its colourful cartoon-like labels for the early vintages of 2001 and 2002—devised by Vancouver designer Bernie Hadley-Beauregard and executed by Toronto illustrator Monika Melnychuk—tell the story behind the winery's name. In

FRANK SUPERNAK

WINEMAKER, HERO

On November 10, 2002, towards the end of the harvest at Silver Sage Estate, Frank Supernak, age forty-one, tried to save the life of the proprietor, Victor Manola, who had fallen into a fermentation vat. On June 24, 2005, Supernak was posthumously awarded Canada's Medal of Bravery by former Governor General Adrienne Clarkson. The citation read: "Although aware of the danger caused by poisonous carbon dioxide, Mr. Supernak tried to pull his unconscious colleague from the container. When his efforts proved unsuccessful, he jumped into the vat and attempted to rescue his friend by lifting him out to safety. Within seconds, Mr. Supernak also succumbed to the deadly fumes and lack of oxygen and could not be revived."

Frank Supernak was born in Nanaimo in 1961. After receiving his Bachelor of Science degree in microbiology from the University of British Columbia in 1983, Supernak was hired by Brights as a research oenologist. He worked his way up by 1992 to cellar master and then head winemaker. The following year, when Brights and Cartier merged as Vincor, Supernak became head winemaker for Jackson-Triggs and Inniskillin Okanagan wines. In this capacity he was reponsible for the production of many of the group's medal-winning wines.

In 1996, with two partners, Hans Lochbichler and Henry Rathje, Supernak purchased Divino Estate Winery and renamed it Hester Creek. Five months before he died, Supernak was named the winemaker at Blasted Church.

In that tragic accident, the Canadian wine industry lost one of its brightest talents. A man of boundless enthusiasm for wine, Frank Supernak always gave advice freely to amateur winemakers and shared his experience with those wineries that sought him out as a consultant. To honour his memory, the Canadian Vintners Association created the Frank Supernak Memorial Bursary to assist young, up-and-coming winemakers.

1929 a wooden church had to be dismantled from its original mining-encampment site at Fairview and reassembled in Okanagan Falls, 16 miles away. The miners used four sticks of dynamite to loosen the wooden nails that held the rafters together, and the parish priest was given the honour of lighting the fuse. The controlled blast not only loosened the nails but also toppled the steeple. The story of the "destruction" of the church and its resurrection in OK Falls is depicted in a series of the winery's labels, along with other satirical images that poke gentle fun at local wine writers (caricatured on the Pinot Gris 2003 label as members of the church choir—the author included) and have fun with oenological celebrities such as wine guru Robert Parker and *Wine Spectator* publisher Marvin Shanken. The labels are rapidly becoming collectors' items.

Frank Supernak supervised the 2002 vintage. For 2003 the Campbells brought Wilhelm Grobbelaar from South Africa, but visa difficulties prevented his return and, in

Ian and Jane Mavety of Blue Mountain Vineyard and Cellars.

2004, they hired Marcus Ansems, formerly the winemaker for Ontario's Creekside. Ansems is now at Therapy Vineyards, and Howard Soon's talented assistant, Kelly Moss, has taken over the winemaking duties. All its whites and its Lemberger are bottled under screwcaps. Blasted Church has a large portfolio of wines with fun names—The Dam Flood, Blasphemy, and Hatfield's Fuse—a little uneven in quality, but certainly worth trying.

Blue Mountain Vineyard and Cellars

RR 1, SITE 3, COMP 4, OKANAGAN FALLS, BC V0H 1R0 (250) 497-8244
WWW.BLUEMOUNTAINWINERY.COM

YEAR FOUNDED: 1991 **FOUNDERS:** Jane and Ian Mavety **WINEMAKERS:** Ian Mavety, Matt Mavety **GRAPE VARIETIES:** (red) Pinot Noir, Gamay Noir; (white) Pinot Blanc, Pinot Gris, Chardonnay **RECOMMENDED WINES:** Pinot Blanc, Pinot Gris, Chardonnay, Pinot Noir, Gamay, Sparkling

Ian Mavety, a self-taught winemaker, is an industry maverick who produces some of BC's best wines. There's a certain exclusivity about this enterprise, run by Ian, his wife, Jane, and their son, Matt, who studied viticulture and oenology in New Zealand and now farms organically. The wines are available only at the winery—a model of cleanliness and precision—or in select restaurants. There's a joke doing the rounds that the reason the disastrous 2003 fires in the Okanagan didn't reach Blue Mountain's vineyards was because they didn't have an appointment. The view from the access road to the winery is one of the most photographed of BC's panoramas, incorporating granite mountains, pine forests, Vaseaux Lake, and undulating vineyards. The Mavetys produce excellent sparkling wines and two qualities of varietals—Cream label and Striped label (Reserve). The portfolio across the board is top-notch. I would rank Blue Mountain as one best wineries in British Columbia.

Calona Vineyards

1125 RICHTER STREET, KELOWNA, BC V1Y 2K6 (250) 762-3332; 1-888-246-4472
WWW.CALONAVINEYARDS.CA

YEAR FOUNDED: 1932 **FOUNDERS:** Giuseppe Ghezzi, Pasquale Cappozzi, and W.A.C. Bennett **WINEMAKERS:** Howard Soon (master winemaker), Stephanie Leinemann **GRAPE VARIETIES:** (red) Cabernet Franc, Cabernet Sauvignon, Gamay Noir, Merlot, Pinot Noir; (white) Chardonnay, Gewurztraminer, Pinot Blanc, Pinot Gris, Optima, Ehrenfelser, Sovereign Opal **RECOMMENDED WINES:** Pinot Blanc, Artist Series Chardonnay, Artist Series Pinot Noir, Cabernet Franc, Blush, Ehrenfelser Icewine

Calona Vineyards was BC's first commercial winery and today looks rather dated. Established in 1932 to turn an apple glut into an alcoholic beverage, the Richmond-based company managed to survive the Depression and grew to be one of the giants of the industry. Calona's blended wine products, such as Schloss Laderheim and Sommet Rouge and Blanc, dominated the Canadian market during the 1980s. Until the pull-out program of 1988, its products and sales strategies were unashamedly modelled on E. & J. Gallo in California, the world's largest winery at the time. Their major business was in bottling offshore wines. Howard Soon has been the winemaker and the conscience of Calona wines since 1988, when the company made a commitment to produce VQA wines. Seven years earlier, Soon, a biochemist, joined Calona as an assistant winemaker. Today he is something of an elder statesman in the BC wine community as a lecturer and consultant, and he continues to make classy wines. Every fall the winery puts out a call to Canadian artists to submit paintings for its Artist Series. The winning artists receive $500 and are named on the label. Calona has a premium label called Sandhill, which produces single-vineyard wines of high quality. Both Calona and Sandhill are now owned by Andrés.

CedarCreek Estate Winery

5445 LAKESHORE ROAD, KELOWNA, BC V1W 4S5 (250) 764-8866
WWW.CEDARCREEK.BC.CA
RESTAURANT: VINEYARD TERRACE, (250) 764-8866 EXT. 107

YEAR FOUNDED: 1986 **FOUNDER:** Ross Fitzpatrick **WINEMAKER:** Tom DiBello **GRAPE VARIETIES:** CedarCreek: (red) Pinot Noir, Merlot; (white) Chardonnay, Gewurztraminer, Riesling, Pinot Gris; Greata Ranch: (red) Pinot Noir, Merlot; (white) Pinot Blanc, Chardonnay, Gewurztraminer; Desert Ridge: (red) Merlot, Cabernet Sauvignon, Cabernet Franc, Malbec, Petit Verdot **RECOMMENDED WINES:** Pinot Gris, Chardonnay, Ehrenfelser, Merlot, Pinot Noir, Cabernet Sauvignon, Meritage

CedarCreek is one of the most beautiful facilities in the Okanagan; it sits like a gleaming white Mediterranean palace above the eastern shore of the lake, with its garden terrace undulating down to the water. The sloping 48-acre vineyard above the terrace faces Quails' Gate on the other shore. The property used to be called Uniacke Cellars, one

of British Columbia's first estate wineries. Senator Ross Fitzpatrick bought it in 1986 and, six years later, injected $4 million into expanding the facilities and creating a 4,500-square-foot barrel room built into a hill. The winery's style is distinctly Californian: its winemaking has been guided by two California winemakers since 1998—Kevin Willenborg and, more recently, Thomas DiBello, who is making wines of great distinction from Chardonnay, Pinot Noir, Merlot, and the Cabernets. DiBello has the luxury of sourcing from three vineyards, the estate, Greata Ranch, south of Peachland, and the hot (in all senses of the terms) Desert Ridge Vineyard in Osoyoos.

The seminal event in the story of CedarCreek goes back to 1993, when the winemaker, Ann Sperling, won a platinum medal at the Okanagan Wine Festival for her 1992 Merlot Reserve—the first and only time such an award has been made. This triumph initiated CedarCreek's flagship Platinum Reserve series in 1998. The winery offers three levels of quality—Classic, Estate Select, and Platinum

Tom DiBello and Gordon Fitzpatrick of CedarCreek
Estate Winery (OPPOSITE).

Reserve. Greata Ranch Vineyards, formerly BC's largest
apple orchard, acquired by Fitzpatrick in 1994, produced
the first wines under that label in 2000. CedarCreek is a
must-visit winery. Sit on the terrace and sip a cool glass
of Chardonnay.

D'Angelo Estate Winery

947 LOCHORE ROAD, PENTICTON, BC V2A 8V1 (250) 493-1364; 1-866-329-6421
WWW.DANGELOWINERY.COM, VINEYARD VIEW BED AND BREAKFAST,
(250) 493-1364; 1-866-329-6421, RESTAURANT: PLANNED FOR 2006

YEAR FOUNDED: 2005 **FOUNDER:** Salvatore D'Angelo **WINEMAKER:**
Salvatore D'Angelo **GRAPE VARIETIES:** (red) Cabernet Sauvignon,
Cabernet Franc, Merlot, Petite Verdot, Malbec, Pinot Noir, Tempranillo,
Shiraz; (white) Chardonnay, Pinot Gris, Viognier (plus "a few surprises")
RECOMMENDED WINES: not tasted

If Salvatore D'Angelo's Ontario experience is anything to
go by, he will soon be putting his inimitable stamp on the
BC wine scene. Italian-born Sal planted his Lake Erie
North Shore vineyard way back in 1983. Two years later
he began scouting for land in the Okanagan. He did not
find what he was looking for at the price he wanted to
pay until 2001, when he moved out to British Columbia
and purchased 27.5 acres of gorgeous beachfront property
on the Naramata Bench. The vineyard, originally 7 acres,
was planted in 2003, mainly to red grapes with the
Okanagan's first Spanish variety, Tempranillo. Ultimately,
with the help of his son Chris, the vineyard will be
expanded to 22 acres. The property is also home to Sal
and his daughter Stephanie's Vineyard View Bed and
Breakfast, whose five rooms are named for some of the
varieties they grow—Merlot Chalet, Cabernet Franc
Room, Cabernet Sauvignon Room, the Petit Verdot
Suite, and the Malbec Suite. The B&B is conviently situated within walking distance of four Naramata wineries
and just minutes away by car from ten or so others.

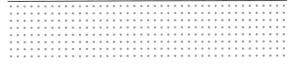

ANN SPERLING'S
WINE HERITAGE

"My first experience of winemaking was when I was eight
years old, helping my grandfather make wine in the basement,"
recalls Ann Sperling. Sperling's family has been making wine
in the Okanagan for five generations, but none of its members
has reached the heights of achievement of this young woman.
In 2004 she was voted Winemaker of the Year at the Ontario
Wine Awards.

After graduating from the University of British Columbia in
1984 with a degree in agriculture, Sperling immediately joined
Andrés Wines. After a seven-year stint at that large commercial
operation, she wanted to make the move to fine winemaking
and was hired by Ross Fitzpatrick as the winemaker for what
was then a small estate, CedarCreek. Her 1992 CedarCreek
Estate Merlot won the first and only Platinum Award granted
by the Okanagan Wine Festival, a triumph now enshrined in
the name of that winery's flagship label. In 1995 Sperling
joined her partner, Peter Gamble, in Ontario. On arrival, she
became winemaking consultant to Culotta (now defunct),
Cilento, and Creekside, before joining Malivoire in 1998.

In 2005 Sperling expanded her consulting business, lending her expertise to Southbrook and Flat Rock in Niagara, as
well as furthering start-up winery projects in Nova Scotia. But
she has not turned her back on British Columbia. Sperling is
involved with her family's Pioneer Country Market in Kelowna.
On that site, she supervised the planting of 2 acres of Pinot
Noir vines.

Sperling plans to make wine under the Sperling Vineyard
label from this vineyard and from the family's 50-acre Pioneer
Ranch Vineyard.

d'Asolo Vineyards Winery & Italian Marketplace

601 WEST BROADWAY AVENUE, SUITE 400, VANCOUVER, BC V5Z 4C2
VINEYARDS: OKANAGAN FALLS AND CAWSTON, BC (604) 871-4329
WWW.ASOLO.CA

YEAR FOUNDED: 2003 **FOUNDER:** Bruce Fuller **WINEMAKER:** Daniel Lagnaz **GRAPE VARIETIES:** (red) Pinot Noir, Merlot; (white) Pinot Gris, Chardonnay **RECOMMENDED WINES:** Isabella Pinot Gris, Franco Merlot, Sophia Chardonnay

D'Asolo Vineyards Winery & Italian Marketplace is phase one of the most ambitious winery project yet undertaken in the Okanagan. Located south of Oliver, Bruce Fuller's company is building an old-world winery in a splendid garden setting. Until the newly planted vineyards reach maturity, the company will buy in grapes from neighbouring ground-crops. Daniel Lagnaz, one of the most awarded winemakers in Canada, is a partner and d'Asolo Vineyards' chief winemaker. He joined Fuller after more than twenty years with Mission Hill.

The Marketplace (Mercato d'Asolo), along with an Italian country kitchen (Cucina d'Asolo), offers a selection of wines, wine-related gift ideas, and specialty Italian and Okanagan foodstuffs. Visitors can picnic in the orchard and play bocce among the apple trees.

Phase two, Il Villaggio d'Asolo, is named after the beautiful town of Asolo in the hills north of Venice. It is conceived as an entire Italian hilltop village on an expansive site overlooking Oliver. This winery is planned as a facility to produce a limited series of northern Italian–style wines from grapes harvested from vineyards surrounding the village. "Il Villaggio d'Asolo," Fuller says, "is designed to be a people-friendly place with two country inns, a wellness centre and spa, a culinary institute, a business management school, upscale shops and restaurants, and a microbrewery."

D'Asolo wines are named for family and friends: Isabella Pinot Grigio for Fuller's grandmother; Franco Merlot for the best man at his wedding, Franco Prevedello, developer and former restaurateur; and Marcello Pinot Nero for winemaker Daniel Lagnaz's brother.

Dirty Laundry Vineyard
(formerly Scherzinger Vineyards)

7311 FISKE STREET, RR 2, SITE 68, COMP 13, SUMMERLAND, BC VOH 1Z0
(250) 494-8815 WWW.DIRTYLAUNDRY.CA

YEAR FOUNDED: 1994 **FOUNDERS:** Edgar and Liz Scherzinger **WINEMAKER:** Ron Watkins **GRAPE VARIETIES:** (red) Pinot Noir; (white) Gewurztraminer, Chardonnay **RECOMMENDED WINES:** Gewurztraminer, Chardonnay, Sweet Caroline (Merlot)

The renamed Scherzinger Vineyards is a concept of Vancouver marketing wizard Bernie Hadley-Beauregard,

who has already recast Prpich Hills as Blasted Church and A'Very Fine Winery as Lotusland. The winery's name refers to a Chinese laundry in Lower Summerland that, according to my colleague Dave Gamble, publisher of *Canadian Grapes to Wine* magazine, "fronted for a bordello in the early 1900s." The new label depicts a flatiron and, in the plume of rising steam, you can make out (if you're looking for them) several subliminal nudes. A far cry from the Old World Bavarian charm of the previous owners! The Scherzinger family tradition of wood carving is evident around the winery. His Bacchus, the god of wine, through whose lips spill water, is still located on the patio. Scherzinger had been growing grapes in Summerland since 1978 on the site of a former cherry orchard, high above the town. His plantings of Gewurztraminer are some of the oldest in the valley, and he has championed vinifera varieties since the 1980s, when others were cautiously planting hybrids. In 2001 the Scherzingers sold the winery to their friends Ron and Cher Watkins, who expanded the wine shop and the patio area before deciding to change the name in 2005.

The extensive patio, shaded from the sun by trellised vines overhead, is a good spot to enjoy a meal of smoked salmon and cheese with the winery's award-winning Chardonnay and Gewurztraminer.

LEFT: Okanagan Lake. ABOVE: George Heiss of Gray Monk Estate Winery.

Gray Monk Estate Winery

1055 CAMP ROAD, OKANAGAN CENTRE, BC V4V 2H4 (250) 766-3168;
1-800-633-4205 WWW.GRAYMONK.COM, THE GRAPEVINE RESTAURANT
(250) 766-3405

YEAR FOUNDED: 1982 **FOUNDERS:** George and Trudy Heiss
WINEMAKERS: George Peter Heiss, Christine Leroux, Roger Wong
GRAPE VARIETIES: (red) Pinot Noir, Merlot, Cabernet Franc; (white)
Pinot Gris, Pinot Auxerrois, Kerner, Pinot Blanc, Gewurztraminer,
Riesling, Ehrenfelser **RECOMMENDED WINES:** Odyssey Pinot Gris, Pinot
Auxerrois, Riesling, Pinot Blanc, Gewurztraminer, Ehrenfelser Late Harvest

George and Trudy Heiss planted their vineyard in 1972 on
a steep slope of the west side of Lake Okanagan—a vista
that reminded them, no doubt, of the Rhineland vineyards
of Trudy's native Germany. Initial plantings were thirty-
three German varieties for experimentation, including
Ruländer (Pinot Gris), known affectionately in Austria,
George's birthplace, as Gray Monk. The winery's first
series of labels featured a cartoon rendition of a bibulous
monk which, thankfully, has been decorously redesigned
to reflect the distinguished wines made here. This
contemporary winery, blindingly white in sunshine, is
magnificently sited in the middle of the 50-acre vineyard,
with an extensive dining terrace that overlooks the lake.

George Jr., who makes an impressive portfolio of twenty-
six wines, spent four years in Germany learning his craft
before returning in 1984 to produce his first Okanagan
vintage. Christine Leroux makes the red wines, the fruit for
which is sourced from the southern end of the valley. I
recommend lunching on the patio with a glass of Gray
Monk's flagship Pinot Gris.

Greata Ranch Vineyards

697 HIGHWAY 97 SOUTH, PEACHLAND, BC V0H 1X9 (250) 767-2768
WWW.CEDARCREEK.BC.CA/GREATARANCH.HTM

YEAR FOUNDED: 2003 **FOUNDER:** Ross Fitzpatrick **WINEMAKER:** Tom
DiBello **GRAPE VARIETIES:** (red) Pinot Noir, Merlot; (white) Pinot Blanc,
Chardonnay, Gewurztraminer **RECOMMENDED WINES:** Pinot Noir,
Chardonnay, Rosé

Greata Ranch, established in 1896 on the west bank of
Lake Okanagan, was once one of the most prolific apple
orchards in the valley. Ross Fitzpatrick, the proprietor of
CedarCreek, purchased the derelict property in 1994 and
planted 40 acres of vines. Buying the property was a
shrewd business decision tinged with nostalgia: Fitzpatrick
recalls that his father used to buy peaches and apples from
the orchard. During the summer season the vineyard terrace, with its delightful view of the lake, offers tapas with
your wine selection (try the Rosé), and the vine-covered
gazebo is an ideal picnic spot. The contemporary ranch-
style wine shop has a stone fireplace that's a welcome sight
in winter months. Architecturally, this is one of the most
impressive wineries in the Okanagan, with its cool, whitewashed Mediterranean look and red-tiled floors.

Hainle Vineyards Estate Winery and Deep Creek Wine Estate

5355 TREPANIER BENCH ROAD, PEACHLAND, BC V0H 1X2
(250) 767-2525; 1-800-767-3109 WWW.HAINLE.COM, RESTAURANT: AMPHORA
BISTRO FOR LUNCHES, (250) 767-2525; FOR GROUP BOOKINGS, (250) 768-1508

YEAR FOUNDED: Hainle Vineyards Estate Winery, 1976; Deep Creek
Wine Estate, 2002 **FOUNDERS:** Walter and Regina Hainle (Hainle
Vineyards Estate Winery), Walter and Rosa Huber (Deep Creek Wine
Estate) **WINEMAKER:** Walter Huber Jr. **GRAPE VARIETIES:** (red) Merlot,
Cabernet Sauvignon, Zweigelt, Pinot Noir, Cabernet Franc, Syrah; (white)
Chardonnay, Pinot Blanc, Gewurztraminer, Riesling, Pinot Gris, Sauvignon
Blanc, Kerner, Johannesburg White Riesling **RECOMMENDED WINES:**
Cabernet Franc, Zweigelt, Pinot Blanc, Gewurztraminer, Chardonnay

Since the 1988 vintage, Tilman Hainle has been making
wine from his own organically grown grapes in this certified organic winery, the first designated in Canada.
Hainle Vineyards was founded that same year, and Hainle's
father, Walter, who had made Canada's first Icewine in
1973, was able to produce enough Icewine to sell in the

winery's shop. Hainle's winemaking style produces high-alcohol, full-flavoured, somewhat austere wines designed for food. You can taste for yourself at the winery's Amphora Bistro under the supervision of Chef Derek Thompson, who has cooked for US president Bill Clinton, British prime minister Margaret Thatcher, rocker Bryan Adams, and other luminaries. The restaurant's balcony on the second floor offers a photogenic view of the lake. In 2002 Walter and Rosa Huber bought Hainle Vineyards, rather than create their own Deep Creek Estate organic winery from the ground up—hence the two names—with Tilman Hainle still consulting on the wines made by Walter Huber Jr. The company's Signature Wine Series is selected by Walter Huber and then submitted to a panel of five sommeliers for their final approval. Tilman Hainle is a Zweigelt specialist, to the point where the winery has issued what it calls the Z-series—blends using Zweigelt—for customers leery of having to pronounce the Z word.

Hawthorne Mountain Vineyards

PO BOX 480, GREEN LAKE ROAD, OKANAGAN FALLS, BC V0H 1R0
(250) 497-8267 WWW.HMVINEYARD.COM, RESTAURANT: HAWTHORNE
MOUNTAIN PATIO, (250) 497-8267

YEAR FOUNDED: 1995 **FOUNDER:** Harry McWatters **WINEMAKER:** Dave Carson **GRAPE VARIETIES:** (red) Merlot, Pinot Noir, Cabernet Franc; (white) Riesling, Chardonnay, Pinot Gris, Gewurztraminer
RECOMMENDED WINES: Hawthorne Mountain Brut, HMV Gold Label Chardonnay, See Ya Later Chardonnay, Pinot Gris, Riesling, Gewurztraminer, Pinot Noir, Cabernet Franc, Ehrenfelser Icewine

Hawthorne Mountain's vineyards are a dramatic sight as you drive south along Skaha Lake—a large carpet of green, 170 acres in all, carved out of the rock and forest at the highest elevation in the province. Wine grapes have been grown here since the early 1960s. Formerly Le Comte winery, the property was purchased in 1995 by Sumac Ridge's Harry McWatters, who changed the name to Hawthorne Mountain. When Vincor acquired Sumac Ridge, Hawthorne Mountain was part of the deal. The tasting room and shop are in the home of the original settler, Major Fraser, and this stone heritage building has a spectacular panoramic view. Dave Carson arrived at Hawthorne Mountain Vineyards as the new winemaker just in time to prepare for the 2003 harvest. He has worked in vineyards since he was eleven years old and, as a boy, he helped to plant at Sumac Ridge Estate and went on to become an assistant winemaker there.

Hawthorne Mountain is the only winery in the world I know of that features a dog cemetery. Several of the Major's faithful companions are buried here, memorialized by the angel-winged dogs on the series of See Ya Later labels. In the same canine spirit, the winery holds Dog Days—an annual open house for dogs and their owners in October; the second day features a pig-roast feast. You can

have your own guided tasting of Hawthorne Mountain's premium wines in the Major Fraser Room for a fee of $10 per person. The vineyard patio offers a menu of deli and BBQ dishes. Don't miss this winery; the drive up the forested mountain is amazing.

Hillside Estate

1350 NARAMATA ROAD, PENTICTON, BC V2A 8T6 (250) 493-6274; 1-888-923-9463
WWW.HILLSIDEESTATE.COM, RESTAURANT: BARREL ROOM BISTRO,
(250) 493-9463

YEAR FOUNDED: 1984 **FOUNDERS:** Vera and Bohumir Klokocka
WINEMAKER: Kelly Symonds **GRAPE VARIETIES:** (red) Merlot, Syrah, Gamay Noir, Cabernet Sauvignon; (white) Chardonnay, Gewurztraminer, Kerner **RECOMMENDED WINES:** Merlot, Chardonnay, Pinot Gris, Gewurztraminer, Muscat Ottonel

In 1984 Vera Klokocka and her husband, Bohumir, began tearing out their apricot orchard to plant Auxerrois and Gamay, followed by Pinot Gris and Muscat Ottonel (the

LEFT: The barn at Hawthorne Mountain Vineyards. ABOVE: The Hillside Estate vineyard.

only winery in the Okanagan Valley to produce this fragrant white wine). Five years later, when the *Farm Gate Winery Act* permitted growers with fewer than 5 acres to sell their products from their back door, the Klokockas opened their winery. Bohumir died in 1994 and, two years later, Vera sold the property to a group from Calgary headed by John Hromyk. The group separated from Hromyk, and Ken Lauzon took over as manager in 1999. The new investors rebuilt the winery as an impressive timber-framed, barnlike building with a striking 22 metre tower, a landmark you can't help but notice as you drive north along the Naramata Road. In 2005 Bill Carpenter, a UC Davis–trained winemaker, and his wife, Cathy, bought out the other shareholders. They are currently reconfiguring the bistro and enlarging both the cellar and the wine shop.

When you enter the 6.7-metre-high cellars carved out from the solid rock of the hillside, you'll realize how appropriately the winery is named. The colourful mosaic depicting Hillside Estate's name at the entrance to the shop has provided the title for the winery's first blend using all five Bordeaux grape varieties—Mosaic. The elegant bistro restaurant has an extensive lunch and dinner menu and is worth a visit. Winemaker Kelly Symonds, who grew up in Abbotsford, joined Hillside Estate winery in February 2003 after graduating from the University of Adelaide's Roseworthy program with a Bachelor of Science in oenology. Symonds's wines show that rich texture that Aussie winemakers can coax from their grapes.

House of Rose Vineyard

2270 GARDNER ROAD, KELOWNA, BC V1P 1E2 (250) 765-0802
WWW.WINTERWINE.COM

YEAR FOUNDED: 1992 **FOUNDER:** Vern Rose **WINEMAKERS:** Vern Rose, Mladen Obradovic **GRAPE VARIETIES:** (red) Maréchal Foch, de Chaunac, Pinot Noir, Merlot; (white) St. Laurent, Lemberger, Chardonnay, Semillon, Verdelet, Okanagan Riesling **RECOMMENDED WINES:** Foch, Semillon

After the BC government's pull-out program of 1989 to make the industry more competitive, Vern Rose stuck with many of his hybrid varieties, including that old workhorse, Okanagan Riesling. Everyone else was ripping out OK Riesling, as it was known, but the bearded Vern, a former schoolteacher given to wearing his signature Tilley hat, stuck with it and still produces a Trocken (dry) wine from half an acre of this coarse, trailer-park grape. Rose's teaching experience shows when he leads visitors around his small, rustic winery and tastes along with them. In 2000 he hired a young winemaker, Mladen Obradovic, who completed his university degree in winemaking in Sarajevo. House of Rose winery is situated in an orchard and, from its windows, you can see mountains on all sides. It's not easy to find this place, but Vern Rose will charm you with his stories and a portfolio of wines larger than wineries five times his size. Try his unique wine—he registered the name Winter Wine—a blend of Verdelet Icewine and aromatic Perle de Zala.

Kettle Valley Winery

2988 HAYMAN ROAD, RR 1, SITE 2, COMP 39, NARAMATA, BC V0H 1N0
(250) 496-5898 WWW.KETTLEVALLEYWINERY.COM

YEAR FOUNDED: 1992 **FOUNDERS:** Robert Ferguson and Tim Watts
WINEMAKERS: Robert Ferguson, Tim Watts **GRAPE VARIETIES:** (red)
Cabernet Sauvignon, Merlot, Shiraz, Malbec, Cabernet Franc, Pinot
Noir, Petit Verdot; (white) Chardonnay, Semillon, Sauvignon Blanc,
Gewurztraminer **RECOMMENDED WINES:** Pinot Gris, Gewurztraminer,
Semillon, Sauvignon Blanc, Pinot Noir, Merlot, Shiraz

Tim Watts and Bob Ferguson made a point of using only
BC grapes when they worked together as amateur winemakers in Vancouver in 1980. They married sisters, Janet
and Colleen, and when Tim moved to the Okanagan and
bought a small property in 1985, the friends began to consider a commercial operation after conducting successful
grape-growing trials. By 1989 the two couples had
acquired 5 acres, and they have slowly bought more land
since. Bob and his wife, Colleen (who runs the tasting
room), joined the Wattses in Naramata in 1992. The four-
some named their winery after the historic railway that
used to run on the east side of Okanagan Lake, and some
of their wines are titled in homage to railway life—Adra
Station, Brakeman's Select, and the dessert wine Derailer.
For a small winery, Kettle Valley makes a significant
number of different wines (twenty-five labels), all of an
admirable quality. It's rewarding to taste here because the
quality is always high.

La Frenz Estate Winery

740 NARAMATA ROAD, PENTICTON, BC V2A 8T5 (250) 492-6690
WWW.LAFRENZWINERY.COM

YEAR FOUNDED: 1999 **FOUNDERS:** Jeff and Niva Martin **WINEMAKER:**
Jeff Martin **GRAPE VARIETIES:** (red) Pinot Noir, Merlot, Shiraz, Cabernet
Sauvignon; (white) Semillon, Chardonnay, Viognier, Muscat
RECOMMENDED WINES: Chardonnay, Semillon, Viognier, Alexandria
(Muscat blend), Shiraz

Australian Jeff Martin used to be McWilliams's chief red
winemaker before he came to Canada in 1994. He made
his reputation at Quails' Gate with his bold Pinot Noirs
and Chardonnays before opening his own small winery
on the Naramata Bench near Penticton. The winery is
named after his grandfather, who was born in Schleswig-
Holstein. His new, Aussie-styled tasting room, with its
shaded pergola and floor-to-ceiling windows, is set in a
sea of vines and offers a fabulous view from the patio
across the lake towards Summerland and Peachland—a
landscape that used to grace the old Canadian $100 bill.
Martin's portfolio is equally strong in both red and white
wines, and, not surprisingly, he makes a Shiraz. The best
reason for visiting here, besides the gorgeous view, is to
sample later vintages of the wines that were selected to

Robert Ferguson and Tim Watts of Kettle Valley Winery.
RIGHT: Lang Vineyards.

be served to Queen Elizabeth II at a banquet during
Alberta's centennial celebrations in 2005—La Frenz 2002
Merlot and 2003 Chardonnay.

Lake Breeze Vineyards

PO BOX 9, 930 SAMMET ROAD, NARAMATA, BC V0H 1N0 (250) 496-5659
WWW.LAKEBREEZEWINERY.CA, RESTAURANT: MAHDINA'S AT LAKE BREEZE,
(250) 496-5619, ACCOMMODATION: THE WINEMAKER'S COTTAGE, THE ARTIST'S
VIEW COTTAGE, (250) 496-5659

YEAR FOUNDED: 1996 **FOUNDERS:** Paul and Verena Moser
WINEMAKER: Garron Elmes **GRAPE VARIETIES:** (red) Merlot, Pinot Noir,
Pinotage, Cabernet Franc; (white) Pinot Blanc, Semillon,
Gewurztraminer, Ehrenfelser, Chardonnay, Morio Muscat
RECOMMENDED WINES: Pinot Blanc, Chardonnay, Semillon, Ehrenfelser

Winemaker Garron Elmes, a South African, has been
with Lake Breeze since its inception in 1996. The original
owner, Paul Moser, was a South African businessman
who immigrated to British Columbia. Moser sold the
winery to Wayne and Joanne Finn, who in turn sold it
to Barbara and Drew McIntyre, Tracey Balland, and
Gary Reynolds in 2001.

The small, whitewashed winery, which looks as though
it was transported from the Cape, is beautifully sited on
the Naramata Bench overlooking Okanagan Lake, 12
kilometres north of Penticton. True to his heritage, Elmes
made the first Pinotage in British Columbia (the only other
winery to grow South Africa's signature grape is Thetis
Island Vineyards), and he does a great job with his white

wines, especially Semillon. Mahdina's serves great Mediterranean dishes. The two guest cottages are set in the lower and upper vineyards overlooking the lake, and the Artist's View has a wraparound deck. The cottages come with the caveat that you might get woken early by a tractor, but, after all, it is a working farm.

Lang Vineyards

2493 GAMMON ROAD, NARAMATA, BC V0H 1N0 (250) 496-5987
WWW.LANGVINEYARDS.COM

YEAR FOUNDED: 1990 **FOUNDERS:** Guenther and Kristina Lang
WINEMAKER: Bernhard Schirrmeister **GRAPE VARIETIES:** (red) Pinot
Noir, Pinot Meunier, Merlot, Maréchal Foch; (white) Riesling,
Gewurztraminer, Auxerrois, Viognier **RECOMMENDED WINES:** Riesling
Reserve, Soaring Eagle Chardonnay, Pinot Gris, Maréchal Foch, Merlot
Icewine, Riesling Icewine

Situated high up on the Naramata Bench, the brick-built Lang winery, with its cobbled patio, has a commanding view of the surrounding scenery. When the Langs emigrated from Germany in 1980 they had no background in winegrowing (Guenther Lang worked as a financial manager for Mercedes-Benz in Stuttgart). Five years later their vineyard was selling grapes to Mission Hill. Lang was in the vanguard of a small group that was lobbying the BC government to issue the first farm-gate winery licences. His success in procuring one in 1990 encouraged others, and he can look back with satisfaction today on the growth of the industry he helped to create. Lang

Vineyards produces a range of dessert wines, including a red and a white wine version of Original Canadian Maple Wine—wines made with the addition of maple syrup from Eastern Canada—packaged in half-bottles. In 2005 the winery and 9.5 acres of vineyard were purchased by Keith and Lynn Holman, who also own Stonehull, Mistral, and Spiller Estate wineries in Penticton. Lang has been contracted to stay on as general manager.

Laughing Stock Vineyards

1548 NARAMATA ROAD, PENTICTON, BC VZA 8T7 (250) 493-VINO (8466)
WWW.LAUGHINGSTOCK.CA

YEAR FOUNDED: 2003 **FOUNDERS:** David and Cynthia Enns
WINEMAKERS: Ian Sutherland, David Enns **GRAPE VARIETIES:** (red)
Merlot, Cabernet Sauvignon, Cabernet Franc, Malbec, Petit Verdot
RECOMMENDED WINE: Portfolio

Laughing Stock is a double pun relating to David and Cynthia Enns's financial background. They gave up the investment business in Vancouver, trading financial stocks on the Vancouver exchange, for growing vine stocks on a 5-acre site on the Okanagan's Naramata Bench—a crazy gamble that could, they confess, make them fit the winery name in the eyes of their former colleagues. With Ian Sutherland from Poplar Grove as their winemaker/consultant, they are certainly hedging their bets. The financial premise is carried over to their labels (which look like stock quotes) and to the name of their signature

Bordeaux-style red—Portfolio. A blended white is also planned. Their gravity-feed winery, with its barrel cellar, was built into the hillside and opened in 2005. The Ennses buy in their Chardonnay from growers in the Oliver area. There's lots of potential for this place to become a favourite among the arbitragers.

Little Straw Vineyards
(formerly Slamka Cellars)

2815 OURTOLAND ROAD, KELOWNA, BC V1Z 2H7 (250) 769-0404
WWW.LITTLESTRAW.BC.CA

YEAR FOUNDED: 1996 **FOUNDERS:** Peter, Richard, and Tim Slamka
WINEMAKER: Peter Slamka **GRAPE VARIETIES:** (red) Pinot Noir, Merlot, Maréchal Foch, Lemberger; (white) Sauvignon Blanc, Riesling, Auxerrois, Gewurztraminer, Siegerrebe, Schönburger **RECOMMENDED WINES:**
Sauvignon Blanc, Old Vines Auxerrois, Auxerrois Icewine, Pinot Noir

The Slamka family winery has been growing grapes in the Okanagan for more than thirty-five years. Their vineyards climb the lower slopes of Mt. Boucherie, with good exposure to the sun. Joe Slamka, a machinist when he arrived in Canada in 1948, was the first grower to plant Auxerrois, an Alsace variety that has become the family's signature wine. His son Peter is the winemaker now. The original winery the family built in 1996 had a stunning view of Okanagan Lake and the surrounding vineyards and orchards, but they outgrew it and, in 2004, had it torn down to double its size. They now have two storeys, with a mezzanine that overlooks the tasting room. The winery's former name will disappear from the labels soon in favour of the English translation of the family's Slovakian name—"Little Straw." Make a short, sweet trip here to taste the Auxerrois.

Mission Hill Family Estate Winery

1730 MISSION HILL ROAD, WESTBANK, BC V4T 2E4 (250) 768-7611
WWW.MISSIONHILLWINERY.COM, RESTAURANT: TERRACE, (250) 768-6470

YEAR FOUNDED: 1981 **FOUNDER:** Anthony von Mandl **WINEMAKER:**
John Simes **GRAPE VARIETIES:** (red) Pinot Noir, Cabernet Franc, Merlot, Cabernet Sauvignon, Syrah; (white) Pinot Blanc, Pinot Gris, Sauvignon Blanc, Riesling Chardonnay, Semillon, Vidal **RECOMMENDED WINES:**
(Five Vineyards label) Pinot Blanc, Pinot Grigio; (Reserve label) Chardonnay, Pinot Gris, Late Harvest Riesling; (Select Lot Collection) Semillon, Merlot, Syrah, Oculus, Chardonnay Icewine

Anthony von Mandl had a dream. He wanted to make Mission Hill Family Estate Winery a beacon to the world for the wines of British Columbia. Perched on top of a hill above the town of Westbank in a spectacular setting overlooking Lake Okanagan, the winery he bought in 1981 was unashamedly patterned on what Robert Mondavi created in the Napa Valley. The style of the original Mission Hill, with its eighteenth-century antiques, tiled

floors, and whitewashed walls, was reminiscent of the Mondavi model, as was von Mandl's penchant for associating his enterprise with cultural events, including support for the Vancouver Symphony Orchestra.

To improve the quality of Mission Hill wines in the early 1990s, von Mandl hired a New Zealander, John Simes, who was Montana Wines' chief winemaker. Simes rewarded his boss's gamble by winning the Avery Trophy at the International Wine and Spirit Competition in London in 1994 for the best Chardonnay in the world, with his Grand Reserve Chardonnay 1992. Once the wines improved, von Mandl turned his sights on the winery.

Anthony, as his staff calls him, owns a beverage alcohol importing company called Mark Anthony Brands, and the success of its sales of Corona beer and Mike's Hard Lemonade in Canada helped finance a complete makeover of the Mission Hill winery. He showed his confidence in the future of the British Columbia wine industry by investing $35 million in rebuilding his winery and purchasing new vineyards.

The result is astonishing. The totally renovated property is one of the most extraordinary wine facilities I have seen anywhere on my wine travels, complete with a collection of ancient glassware, a Léger carpet, and a Chagall-inspired wall hanging. If Dionysus, the god of wine, dreamed of a cathedral to celebrate the fermented grape, he could happily take residence here.

The most dramatic feature, which can be seen and heard for miles around, is the slender twelve-storey bell tower, whose four bells, commissioned by von Mandl and

Anthony Von Mandl of Mission Hill Family Estate Winery.
RIGHT: The winery's entrance and bell tower.

Alex Nichol of Nichol Vineyard Farm Winery.

cast in France, chime every quarter of the hour—much to the chagrin of some of his neighbours. The bells pealed for the first time on December 11, 2000—the day Mission Hill picked its Chardonnay Icewine 2000.

You access the winery under a large concrete arch (similar to the hacienda style of Mondavi's facade) that frames the tower and the winery buildings. The feeling evoked is not dissimilar to entering a Greek temple, with its solitude, its sense of calm, the elegant proportions of the buildings, and the open green spaces.

Von Mandl hired Seattle architect Tom Kundig to transform the Mission Hill Winery. When Kundig first visited the site, he remembers being overwhelmed by its natural beauty, recognizing intuitively that anything he did would be secondary to the landscape itself. The results are one of the architectural wonders of the wine world. Equally dramatic below ground as it is above, Mission Hill boasts a magnificent crypt-like barrel-aging cellar that extends in a gigantic L-shape under the winery. It had to

be blasted out of the rock face, much of which has been left exposed, a subtle contrast to the smoothness of the concrete arches and buttresses. The visitor can look down on the cellar through an "oculus"—a large lens-like piece of glass set in a well outside that directs the only natural light to the cellar below. And Oculus is the name Anthony von Mandl gave to his flagship red wine, a Bordeaux blend of Cabernet Sauvignon, Merlot, and Cabernet Franc.

Mission Hill produces three quality levels of wine—labelled Five Vineyards, Reserve, and the top-notch Select Lot Collection. You can spend a whole day here, strolling the grounds, visiting the museum, the immaculate cellar, and the well-stocked wine boutique, and tasting wines in the library; you can also participate in culinary workshops with resident chef Michael Allemeir or take a wine seminar before dining at the al fresco Terrace Restaurant. Check the website for concerts and performances at Mission Hill's amphitheatre.

Mt. Boucherie Estate Winery

829 DOUGLAS ROAD, KELOWNA, BC V1Z 1N9 (250) 769-8803: 1-877-684-2748
WWW.MTBOUCHERIE.BC.CA

YEAR FOUNDED: 2000 **FOUNDERS:** Nirmal, Sarwan, and Kal Gidda
WINEMAKERS: Graham Pierce, Robert Thilicke **GRAPE VARIETIES:** (red)
Merlot, Gamay, Cabernet Franc; (white) Pinot Gris, Gewurztraminer,
Semillon, Chardonnay, Riesling **RECOMMENDED WINES:** Estate
Gewurztraminer, Pinot Gris, Riesling, Summit Reserve Chardonnay

Originally from the Punjab in India, the Gidda family
has grown wine grapes since 1968. They also have the
distinction of having the largest family-owned holding of
vineyards in British Columbia. They own three sites—80
acres near Cawston in the Similkameen Valley, 40 acres
in Okanagan Falls, and 55 acres in the Westbank area—
from which they produce their estate wines. They operate out of a large, 20,000-square-foot stone-faced facility
with a stunning view from the base of Mt. Boucherie
across the lake. The brothers have recently added to their
portfolio (now up to twenty wines) a sparkling wine made
by the champagne method called Mt. Boucherie Brut,
one of only a handful of this labour-intensive product
made in British Columbia. The consumer-friendly tasting
room/gift shop here is bright and airy, and a new picnic
area has recently been opened. Bring your own food or
order a plate of appetizers.

Nichol Vineyard Farm Winery

1285 SMETHURST ROAD, NARAMATA, BC V0H 1N0 (250) 496-5962
WWW.NICHOLVINEYARD.COM

YEAR FOUNDED: 1993 **FOUNDERS:** Kathleen and Alex Nichol
WINEMAKER: Alex Nichol **GRAPE VARIETIES:** (red) Syrah, Cabernet
Franc, St. Laurent, Pinot Noir; (white) Pinot Gris **RECOMMENDED**
WINES: Syrah, Cabernet Franc, Pinot Noir, Pinot Gris

To Alex Nichol, a former double bassist with the
Vancouver Symphony, goes the credit for producing the
Okanagan's first Syrah—a warm-weather grape that was
initially thought impossible to grow in the Okanagan.
This Rhône variety has become the flagship wine for his
boutique winery, nestled below the granite cliffs of the
Kettle Valley Railway. The 91.4 metre rock face of these
cliffs reflects sunlight back onto the 4.5 acres of vines,
holds the summer heat during the fall, and allows the red
varieties to ripen well in his vineyard. A sprinkler system
alleviates the heat in the dog days of summer. Nichol's
wines are intense and concentrated in their flavours, and
they are very hard to acquire because they generally sell
out on release. Nichol's latest wine, with a musical motif,
is Capriccio, a blend of Pinot Noir and Gamay—what
the Burgundians would call *Passe-toutgrains*. The winery
itself is no more than a large shack, but the quality of

ERIC VON KROSIGK
BC'S FLYING WINEMAKER

Eric von Krosigk is the busiest
winemaker in Canada. He has
consulted to more wineries than
you could shake a corkscrew
at. Von Krosigk was born in
1962 in Vernon, BC, into a
farming family; his grandfather
was an orchardist and his father,
Buko von Krosigk, a dairy
farmer and brewer who founded
Okanagan Spring Brewery in
1985. While still a teenager, von
Krosigk knew that he wanted to
grow grapes and make wine,
so he wrote to Germany seeking
an apprenticeship opportunity. In the interim he studied science at Okanagan College.

In 1983, at the age of twenty-one, von Krosigk left for
Germany, where he worked for the next three years at a
grape research station and at two family wineries in the
Mosel Valley. Finishing his apprenticeship as a vintner, he
enrolled in beverage engineering at the University of
Geisenheim and began six years on the *Amtliche Prüfnummer*
commission (the official German quality-tasting panel that
gives a coded AP number to every bottle of wine). It was during his time in Germany that von Krosigk developed a special
interest in sparkling wines. He returned to Canada in 1991
and founded Summerhill Estate Winery in partnership with
Stephen and Wendy Cipes. Summerhill was the first Canadian
winery to specialize in sparkling wines. Having established
Summerhill's reputation for these wines, Eric von Krosigk
looked for further challenges. He saw great potential at
LeComte Estate Winery (now Hawthorne Mountain Vineyards),
which he joined as winemaker and general manager in 1994.

In September 1997 von Krosigk left the winery to start his
own company, EVK Winery Consulting Inc. He helps fledgling
wineries make their mark in a highly competitive industry. As
consultant to different wineries and vineyards in British
Columbia, he spends much of his life on the road, driving
between Summerland, Penticton, Vancouver Island, and
Saturna Island.

Eric von Krosigk has displayed his winemaking talents at
Pinot Reach, Red Rooster, Hillside Estate, Saturna Island
Vineyards, Godfrey-Brownell, Victoria Estate (now Church &
State), Carriage House, Hester Creek, Echo Valley Vineyards,
Marley Farm, Morning Bay Vineyards, and Adora. He also
owns the small sparkling-wine house Summerland Cellars.

wine produced here is exceptionally high. If you want to buy Nichol wines, you'll have to visit the farm or dine well in Vancouver's top restaurants. In 2005 the Nichols decided to retire and sold the winery to Ross Hackworth, a vice-president of a Vancouver-based paper company.

Noble Ridge Vineyard & Winery

2320 OLIVER RANCH ROAD, OKANAGAN FALLS, BC V0H 1R0 (250) 497-7945
WWW.NOBLERIDGE.COM

YEAR FOUNDED: 2005 **FOUNDERS:** Jim and Leslie D'Andrea
WINEMAKER: Michael Bartier **GRAPE VARIETIES:** (red) Pinot Noir, Cabernet Sauvignon, Merlot; (white) Chardonnay, Pinot Gris
RECOMMENDED WINES: Pinot Noir, Meritage, Chardonnay

A three-month backpacking sabbatical through Europe with three children in 1998 convinced Calgary lawyer Jim D'Andrea that he wanted to own a vineyard. After searching for a suitable site in France, Ontario, and British Columbia, the couple found the 24-acre property they were looking for in Okanagan Falls in February 2001. Jim D'Andrea maintains his law practice while his wife, Leslie, a former health administrator, manages the vineyard and the winery. Courses in viticulture at UBC's Okanagan College and sommelier certification courses will enable Leslie to assist their current winemaker, Michael Bartier, who also makes first-rate Chardonnay for Golden Mile Cellars. Noble Ridge's single-storey, high-ceilinged wine shop (incorporating such Frank Lloyd Wright features as large overhanging eaves and rockwork on the lower portion of the exterior walls) has French doors that lead out to a verandah. From here and the adjacent grassy picnic area, you will enjoy a spectacular panorama of the valley, Vaseaux Lake, and McIntyre Bluff. And you're not far from a perennial stopping site for me—Tickleberry's ice cream shop in Okanagan Falls.

Peller Estates (Andrés Wines)

1125 RICHTER STREET, KELOWNA, BC V1Y 2K6 (250) 762-9144; 1-888-246-4472
WWW.ANDRESWINES.COM

YEAR FOUNDED: 1961 **FOUNDER:** Andrew Peller **WINEMAKERS:** Howard Soon, Karen Gillis **GRAPE VARIETIES:** (red) Gamay, Pinot Noir, Chancellor, Merlot, Cabernet Sauvignon, Cabernet Franc, Shiraz; (white) Chardonnay, Pinot Gris, Pinot Blanc, Sauvignon Blanc, Riesling, Gewurztraminer, Scheurebe, Müller-Thurgau, Vidal, Ehrenfelser
RECOMMENDED WINES: Private Reserve Chardonnay, Private Reserve Merlot, Private Reserve Pinot Gris, Trinity Icewine

Andrés Wines began operating in Vancouver's western suburb of Port Moody in 1961. Although the commercial heart shifted many years ago to the plant in Winona, Ontario, the Port Moody facility is the historic soul of the company. The winery was built on Vintner Street when

Andrew Peller could not purchase a winery at the price he wanted in the Okanagan. The original winemaker, Wallace Pohl, and the equipment came from California. Early bottlings used California grapes, which increased their price in the marketplace compared with wines from other BC wineries. The public equated the expense with higher quality and bought Andrés' products to such a degree that Peller expanded quickly into other provinces. Between 1962 and 1974 Andrés opened bottling facilities in Nova Scotia and Alberta, followed by Quebec and Manitoba, and then a winery in Ontario. The growth took its toll on the founder's health, and Peller died in 1994. His son, Dr. Joe Peller, gave up his medical practice to run the company, and now his grandson John is at the helm. In the 1970s, following advice from Dr. Helmut Becker of the Geisenheim Institute, Andrés developed 300 acres of French hybrid and vinifera vines in Inkameep Vineyards, on Indian land near Oliver. Andrés made a commitment to VQA wines in British Columbia, with 95 percent of its contracted vineyards' acreage planted in vinifera vines.

In 1997 the company, along with Roger Hol, invested in the 70-acre Rocky Ridge Vineyard, in the Similkameen Valley. In 2005 the Andrés company purchased Calona Vineyards, the Sandhill label, and Red Rooster.

LEFT: The view of the vineyards at Poplar Grove Winery. ABOVE: Poplar Grove's winemaker and proprietor Ian Sutherland.

Pentâge Wines

440 LAKESIDE ROAD, PENTICTON, BC V2A 8W3 (250) 493-4008
WWW.PENTAGE.COM

YEAR FOUNDED: 2000 **FOUNDERS:** Paul Gardner and Julie Rennie
WINEMAKER: Paul Gardner **GRAPE VARIETIES:** (red) Merlot, Gamay, Syrah, Cabernet Sauvignon, Cabernet Franc; (white) Sauvignon Blanc, Gewurztraminer **RECOMMENDED WINES:** Sauvignon Blanc, Syrah

Paul Gardner, a marine engineer, started making wine as a hobby, as an extension of his love of different wines. He named his winery Pentâge, a reference to the five red varieties he planted on the property. Paul Gardner and Julie Rennie's custom-built winery is beautifully sited on an elevated plateau below the Skaha Bluffs on the east side of Skaha Lake, south of Penticton. The steeply raked 6.5-acre Vista Ridge vineyard was originally part of a vast apricot orchard. The couple's winery, a 2,200-square-foot metal-clad building panelled inside with red fir, is larger than it looks from below, nestling into a rocky outcrop in the vineyard. The new barrel cellar is 4,500 square feet, with natural rock sides. The newly constructed wine shop on a bench below the vineyard and winery offers some good photo ops of Skaha Lake, but the best view of the valley is from a rock bluff to the

south of the existing building on the property. Gardner's father, Norman, owns an adjacent vineyard, which supplies the winery with its Pinot Gris. Check out the ancient pictographs of deer and a horse and rider on the rock cliff at the base of the property.

Poplar Grove Winery

1060 POPLAR GROVE ROAD, PENTICTON, BC V2A 8T6 (250) 492-4575
WWW.POPLARGROVE.CA

YEAR FOUNDED: 1997 **FOUNDERS:** Ian and Gitta Sutherland
WINEMAKER: Ian Sutherland **GRAPE VARIETIES:** (red) Merlot, Cabernet Franc; (white) Pinot Gris **RECOMMENDED WINES:** Benchmark Cabernet Franc, Benchmark Merlot, Reserve (Merlot/Cabernet Franc blend), Pinot Gris

Ian Sutherland is a Bordeaux fan. This preference led him to plant only Merlot and Cabernet Franc imported from Bordeaux in the 10-acre vineyard he and his ex-wife, Gitta, created when they chopped down the apple orchard on the property they purchased in 1993. Sutherland's first red-blend vintage 1995, released in 1997, won a gold medal at the Okanagan Wine Festival that year. The meticulously manicured vineyard that undulates over the Naramata Bench towards the lake has been captured on canvas by Victoria artist Christine Reimer and now graces Poplar Grove's labels. Ian Sutherland makes some of BC's best wines. He is in the process of building a new winery and expanding the cheese-making operation—Sutherland claims this to be the only winery in North America that produces both wine and cheese. He picked up the recipes from an artisanal cheese producer while he was winemaking in Australia in the mid-1990s. Stop by, taste the cheeses, drink the wine. Both are delicious.

Quails' Gate Estate Winery

3303 BOUCHERIE ROAD, KELOWNA, BC V1Z 2H3 (250) 769-4451;
1-800-420-9463 (WINE) WWW.QUAILSGATE.COM, RESTAURANT: OLD VINES
PATIO RESTAURANT, (250) 769-4441

YEAR FOUNDED: 1989 **FOUNDER:** Ben R. Stewart **WINEMAKER:** Grant Stanley **GRAPE VARIETIES:** (red) Pinot Noir, Cabernet Sauvignon, Merlot, Gamay, Maréchal Foch; (white) Chardonnay, Chasselas, Pinot Blanc, Gewurztraminer, Chenin Blanc, Riesling, Sauvignon Blanc, Optima **RECOMMENDED WINES:** (Limited Release label) Riesling, Gewurztraminer, Old Vine Foch; (Family Reserve label) Chardonnay, Pinot Noir, Gamay Noir, Riesling, Chenin Blanc; Riesling Icewine

Quails' Gate has a tradition, it seems, of hiring "down under" winemakers, beginning with Jeff Martin, who now owns La Frenz. Martin created the winery's bold Burgundian style of Pinot Noir and Chardonnay and the curiosity Old Vine Foch—a grape dismissed by most growers. Jeff was followed by another Australian, Peter

Draper, who died young in 1999. Ashley Hooper, a third Aussie, took over for three years before returning home. The current winemaker, Grant Stanley, trained in New Zealand at Ata Rangi.

The contemporary winery contrasts with the nineteenth-century settler's cabin that functions as the wine shop, but Quails' Gate has set out on a $4.5 million winery enhancement plan "to improve the quality of the wine as well as the visitor experience." The plans involve building a 10,000-square-foot storage and bottling facility and a wine shop large enough to hold cooking classes and wine seminars. The Old Vines Patio Restaurant, known for its great food, was renovated and expanded in 2005 to be an all-year destination. Quails' Gate's 79 acres of vineyard, first established in 1956, run down almost to the edge of Lake Okanagan and slope up to encroaching housing developments on the hills above that surround the immaculately kept vineyard. Ben Stewart has stopped the march of construction by densely planting Pinot Noir, Chardonnay, Merlot, and Cabernet Sauvignon. Quails' Gate also owns 20 acres next to Osoyoos Larose in the Southern Okanagan. In 2004 Quails' Gate was awarded British Columbia Winery of the Year by the American magazine *Wine Press Northwest*. It's a good place to dine and to taste the award-winning Limited Edition and Family Reserve wines.

Red Rooster Winery

891 NARAMATA ROAD, PENTICTON, BC V2A 8T5 (250) 492-2424
WWW.REDROOSTERWINERY.COM, RESTAURANT: (250) 492-2424

YEAR FOUNDED: 1997 **FOUNDERS:** Beat and Prudence Mahrer
WINEMAKER: Richard Kanazawa **GRAPE VARIETIES:** (red) Merlot, Cabernet Franc, Cabernet Sauvignon, Maréchal Foch, Pinot Noir; (white) Pinot Blanc, Pinot Gris, Chardonnay, Gewurztraminer
RECOMMENDED WINES: Pinot Blanc, Pinot Gris, Blanc de Noir, Gewurztraminer, Chardonnay Icewine

In 1990 the Mahrers emigrated from Switzerland, sold their fitness club in Basel, and purchased a Naramata apple orchard, which they promptly tore out and planted to vines. Their first vintage was 1997. "Entertain them and they will come" would be a good description of what happened to Red Rooster—the winery that grew. "We love people and we love to entertain and share our excitement about grape growing and winemaking," says Prudence. So popular did Red Rooster become both for its award-winning wines and the hosts' congenial hospitality that the couple needed more space to welcome visitors and to make wine. They purchased land just outside Penticton and built a spanking-new facility of impressive size (30,000 square feet), which opened in 2004. The cathedral-like winery building, with its green lawns, a vast "wishing fountain," and a shady patio around the wine shop, has made it a great tourist destination. The most recent

Grant Stanley (TOP) and Ben Stewart (ABOVE), of Quails' Gate Estate Winery. RIGHT: The winery's tasting room.

attraction, acquired in June 2005, is the controversial sculpture "The Baggage Handler," by local artist Michael Hermesh. The 2 metre piece, depicting Frank, a naked man carrying a suitcase, caused an uproar when it was displayed at Penticton's Marina Way traffic roundabout in February 2005. First the city council gave the statue a modesty plate, following complaints from some of its citizens, and then vandals took matters into their own hands when they knocked the figure off its pedestal and dismembered it. Frank, his manhood restored, now stands in Red Rooster's tasting room, still clutching his baggage. The Mahrers even produced a wine in homage—Cabernet Frank 2004—featuring the artwork on the label.

The Mahrers are great supporters of local artists, whose works they display at the wine shop. In August the winery holds its annual one-day Bohemian Wine Festival, where artists, sculptors, and potters show how they create their works, followed by a silent auction. In September 2005 Red Rooster was purchased by Andrés.

St. Hubertus Estate Winery

5225 LAKESHORE ROAD, KELOWNA, BC V1W 4J1 (250) 764-7888;
1-800-989-9463 (WINE) WWW.ST-HUBERTUS.BC.CA

YEAR FOUNDED: 1991 FOUNDERS: Andy and Leo Gebert WINEMAKER:
Christine Leroux GRAPE VARIETIES: (red) Pinot Noir, Chambourcin,
Maréchal Foch, Gamay Noir, Pinot Meunier; (white) Gewurztraminer,
Pinot Blanc, Riesling, Chasselas RECOMMENDED WINES: Reserve Dry
Riesling, Reserve Pinot Blanc, Gamay Noir

If you go to St. Hubertus's website, you'll see dramatic photos of the Okanagan Mountain Park fire that destroyed the winery and Leo Gebert's home in August 2003. The winery was back in business within a matter of days, thanks to the family's legendary Swiss efficiency and their neighbours' supply of grapes and facilities. Andy Gebert describes the architectural style of the new 15,000-square-foot winery as a château with a tower, "a cross between

Tuscany and Provence." The Geberts' winegrowing heritage dates back to 1864, when the patriarch, Josef Mauranius Gebert, planted his vineyard in the Swiss town of Uznach (now a subdivision where the family home, "Hubertusklause," was built in 1961). The Swiss influence still persists here, because 3 acres of Leo's 26-acre vineyard is planted to Chasselas, the predominant white variety in Switzerland (Andy's neighbouring vineyard is 51 acres). Both vineyards, now farmed organically, were originally planted in 1928 by J.W. Hughes on one of the steepest slopes in the Okanagan—so steep that a former owner was crushed when his tractor rolled over on him. Only a few of the heritage vines still exist, including an ancient table-grape variety, Himrod, planted outside the tasting room. Unique perhaps in the wine world is the studio, with its collection of some 2,000 rubber art stamps created by Andy Gebert's wife, Susanne, who offers a variety of stamping courses.

Sandhill Wines

C/O CALONA VINEYARDS, 1125 RICHTER STREET, KELOWNA, BC V1Y 2K6
(250) 762-9144; 1-888-246-4472 WWW.SANDHILLWINES.CA

YEAR FOUNDED: 1999 FOUNDER: Howard Soon WINEMAKER: Howard
Soon GRAPE VARIETIES: (red) Cabernet Franc, Gamay Noir, Cabernet
Sauvignon, Merlot, Petit Verdot, Malbec, Sangiovese, Syrah, Barbera;
(white) Chardonnay, Pinot Blanc, Pinot Gris, Sauvignon Blanc
RECOMMENDED WINES: Pinot Blanc, Pinot Gris, Chardonnay, Syrah,
Cabernet Franc

Sandhill is currently a virtual label that allows Howard Soon, the highly talented winemaker at Calona, to select the best fruit from three vineyards designated by name (Burrowing Owl, Osprey Ridge, and Phantom Creek). The concept was first put into practice in 1997 to take advantage of the grapes from the Burrowing Owl Vineyards, where a separate winery is now planned on site. Soon also has a Small Lots label for small batches of promising new varietals, such as Barbera, Malbec, Syrah, Petit Verdot, and Viognier. The Sandhill brand is now owned by Andrés.

Sonoran Estate Winery

21606 HIGHWAY 97 NORTH, SUMMERLAND, BC V0H 1Z0 (250) 494-9323
SONORAN@SHAW.CA WWW.SONORANESTATE.COM, ACCOMMODATION:
WINDMILL B&B, (250) 494-9302

YEAR FOUNDED: 2004 FOUNDERS: Arjan, Ada, and Adrian Smits
WINEMAKERS: Gary Strachan (consultant), Adrian Smits (assistant
winemaker) GRAPE VARIETIES: (red) Merlot, Pinot Noir; (white)
Gewurztraminer, Pinot Gris, Riesling, Chardonnay RECOMMENDED
WINES: Riesling, Desert Morning (Riesling and Oriensteiner), Merlot

Sonoran Estate is named after the desert area that stretches from Mexico to British Columbia. Arjan and Ada

Smits's property, with its landmark windmill (an artifact that speaks to their Dutch heritage), sweeps steeply down to the lakeshore. It offers a spectacular view to the Naramata Bench and the mountains beyond, both for visitors and for those who stay in their four-room B&B across the lake. The grounds around the buildings have been beautifully landscaped by Arjan, a horticulturalist who grew flowers commercially in Ontario and British Columbia before getting into the wine business. The first wines from the 5-acre vineyard in 2003 were unoaked and fruit-forward in style. The welcome here is very friendly, and Arjan has been known to bring into the tasting room a few tank samples of yet-to-be-bottled wines for visitors enthusiastic about his wines.

Stag's Hollow Winery and Vineyard

4870 CHUTE LAKE ROAD, KELOWNA, BC V1W 4M3 (250) 497-6162;
1-877-746-5569 WWW.STAGSHOLLOWWINERY.COM

YEAR FOUNDED: 1996 FOUNDERS: Larry Gerelus and Linda Pruegger
WINEMAKER: Larry Gerelus GRAPE VARIETIES: (red) Merlot, Pinot Noir;
(white) Chardonnay, Sauvignon Blanc, Vidal RECOMMENDED WINES:
Sauvignon Blanc, Renaissance Merlot, Renaissance Pinot Noir,
Tragically Vidal

By his own admission, Larry Gerelus has been making wine since he was "very, very young." A taste of Okanagan wines back in 1981 ignited his interest in winemaking while he was working in the petroleum industry in Calgary, along with his wife, Linda. Ten years later he began looking for suitable vineyard land.

In 1992 Gerelus purchased a 10-acre vineyard, tore out the Chasselas and most of the Vidal planted there, and replaced them with Merlot, Pinot Noir, Chardonnay, and Sauvignon Blanc. A trip to Australia inspired him to design a winery with a wrap-around verandah, which was finished in 1995, the year of his first vintage.

The building, with its steeply raked roof, set in densely planted, sloping vineyards, is beautifully sited between two high ridges in the Okanagan Falls area, a short walk from his neighbour Wild Goose Vineyards. The scenery doesn't get much wilder than it is here, with roller-coaster hills, evergreen forests, and mountains of granite. With the hybrid Vidal virtually disappearing from the valley, Stag's Hollow keeps this neglected variety alive with an off-dry wine called "Tragically Vidal." "People came on bended knees begging us not to pull it out," says Gerelus. This winery is located in a nature reserve, and the wildlife takes its toll on the vineyard. Stags and other creatures feast on the grapes, and the vines have to be netted against the birds as well. If you want to see how hard winemakers work to get great results from difficult terrain, stop at Stag's Hollow.

Stonehill Estate Winery
(formerly Benchland Vineyards)

170 UPPER BENCH ROAD SOUTH, PENTICTON, BC V2A 8T1 (250) 770-1733
WWW.BENCHLANDWINES.CA, ACCOMMODATION: SPILLER'S CORNER B&B,
(250) 490-4162; 1-800-610-3794

YEAR FOUNDED: 2000 FOUNDER: Klaus Stadler WINEMAKER: Craig
Larson GRAPE VARIETIES: (red) Pinot Noir, Cabernet Sauvignon,
Zweigelt, Lemberger; (white) Pinot Blanc, Chardonnay, Riesling
RECOMMENDED WINES: Riesling, Mephisto

Munich-born Klaus Stadler, a brewmaster and distiller who came to Canada in 1997, created this winery on a 9-acre apple orchard a few minutes' drive from Penticton. He called his winery, which commands a great view across the lake, Benchland Vineyards because of its location at the entrance to the Naramata Bench. Stadler planted the first Zweigelt in British Columbia, and he blended it with Lemberger and Cabernet Sauvignon to make a wine he called Mephisto. When he decided to return to Germany in 2004 he sold the winery to Keith and Lynn Holman, who changed the name to Stonehill Estate. The Holmans also own Spiller Estate, which includes extensive orchards, a fruit winery, and a four-bedroom B&B. The couple recently opened Mistral Estate Winery next door to Stonehill. Craig Larson makes the wines for both wineries.

LEFT: Sumac Ridge Estate's vineyard. ABOVE: Sumac Chardonnay grapes await the crusher.

Sumac Ridge Estate Winery

PO BOX 307, 17403 HIGHWAY 97 NORTH, SUMMERLAND, BC V0H 1Z0
(250) 494-0451 WWW.SUMACRIDGE.COM, RESTAURANT: CELLAR DOOR
BISTRO, (250) 494-0451

YEAR FOUNDED: 1979 **FOUNDERS:** Harry McWatters and Lloyd Schmidt
WINEMAKER: Mark Wendenburg **GRAPE VARIETIES:** (red) Merlot,
Cabernet Sauvignon, Cabernet Franc, Carmenère; (white) Chardonnay,
Pinot Blanc, Sauvignon Blanc, Gewurztraminer **RECOMMENDED WINES:**
Pinnacle; Black Sage Vineyard: Chardonnay, Gewurztraminer, Cabernet
Sauvignon, Meritage, White Meritage, Blanc de Noir, Steller's Jay Brut,
Pinot Blanc Icewine

You have to love a winery that began life as a nine-hole
golf course! Harry McWatters and vineyardist Lloyd
Schmidt were colleagues at Casabello in 1979 when they
hatched a plan to start a small estate winery. They purchased the golf course on Highway 97 just north of
Summerland and planted 5 acres of Riesling and
Gewurztraminer. The clubhouse became the winery tasting room, then the winery itself, before the enterprise
took over the entire building from the golfers. (The golf
course is now an independent operation.) The partnership between McWatters and Schmidt ended in 1985. Two
other partners followed, but McWatters remained the
ever-visible and highly articulate face of Sumac Ridge.

HARRY MCWATTERS
THE CONSCIENCE OF THE BC WINE INDUSTRY

Harry McWatters is a big man
in every respect. Much of the
credit for the flourishing state
of British Columbia's wine
scene must go to his talent
for marketing, combined with
boundless energy and pas-
sionate commitment to the
wines of the province. In 2003
his contribution was recog-
nized when he was awarded the Order of British Columbia for
his services to the wine industry.

McWatters was born in Toronto in 1944, where his family
lived in an Italian neighbourhood. "Whenever we went to dinner," he recalls, laughing, "I was always given wine with some
7-Up in it. And guests always brought wine to our house. It
was part of my life." In 1955 his father transferred to Vancouver,
and, from the age of sixteen, Harry was making wine from
local fruit other than grapes, mainly blackberries. "By the
time I was eighteen I was making wines that I could actually
drink. By the time I was twenty I was making wines that others
dared to drink. Wine was a hobby."

When Casabello Wines in Penticton started in 1968, one of
the directors, Evans Lougheed, approached Harry McWatters
because of his demonstrated interest in wine. He was twenty-
nine. Casabello had long-term contracts with Washington and
California growers because the company was permitted to
buy in outside grapes once it had used its regulated BC tonnage. Casabello's most prestigious red at the time was
Canadian Burgundy, made from locally grown Pinot Noir,
Maréchal Foch, and Carignane, with a Gamay Beaujolais clone
grown in Washington. "It was a pretty respectable product,"
McWatters remembers. "For its day it was certainly one of
the better wines to be found in the market. We priced it at
$2.35. I had competitors calling, saying: 'Harry, what are you
doing, pricing your wine at over $2? You've got a lot of guts.'
That was the first wine in British Columbia to have a cork. I've
watched the evolution from introducing cork to watching it
probably fade out in my lifetime."

In 1979 McWatters teamed up with Casabello's vineyard
manager Lloyd Schmidt to buy a 38-acre site north of
Summerland with an operating nine-hole golf course on it.
They called the enterprise Sumac Ridge. The clubhouse was
first used as a tasting room and then converted into the winery
building in 1981. Under McWatters' watchful eye, Sumac
Ridge, now part of Vincor, continues to be one of British
Columbia's best wineries in terms of quality throughout the
large portfolio.

However, beyond his own winery, Harry McWatters has played the same role in British Columbia that Donald Ziraldo played in Ontario—a one-man promotion machine for the local industry while battling with his colleagues over VQA regulations and Wine Council membership. In 2000 McWatters sold Sumac Ridge and his other winery, Hawthorne Mountain, to Vincor, but he remains at the helm, with his daughter Christa Lee doing the marketing. Under the terms of the sale, McWatters kept 75 acres of the Black Sage Vineyard in the southern Okanagan.

The winery has expanded over the years and now resembles a condominium complex at an expensive ski resort. The elegant tasting rooms on the upper floor can accommodate large groups, including wedding receptions.

Sumac Ridge's portfolio is broad, with twenty-two wines produced in three price categories—Cellar Selection, Black Sage Vineyards, and ultra-premium red wines such as Pinnacle. Sumac Ridge was the first Canadian wine to employ the California term Meritage on its labels. The white Meritage is one of the best wines made in Canada. This winery has the distinction of having the first planting in Canada of Chile's signature grape, Carmenère. Take time to sit in on a tutored tasting in the Founder's Room upstairs above the wine shop. There's a lot of history at Sumac Ridge, and the quality of its wines across the range is impressive. Don't miss it as you drive along Highway 97.

Summerhill Pyramid Winery

4870 CHUTE LAKE ROAD, KELOWNA, BC K1W 4M3 (250) 764-8000; 1-800-667-3538 WWW.SUMMERHILL.BC.CA, RESTAURANT: FORSTER'S AT SUMMERHILL SUNSET BISTRO, (250) 764-8000, ACCOMMODATION: JUDY'S B&B, 1-888-763-63730 OR 1-800-667-3538

🍷 🍴 🛏 ✿ 🧍

YEAR FOUNDED: 1991 **FOUNDER:** Stephen Cipes **WINEMAKER:** James Cambridge **GRAPE VARIETIES**: (red) Pinot Noir, Merlot, Baco Noir; (white) Riesling, Chardonnay, Ehrenfelser **RECOMMENDED WINES:** Platinum Series Cabernet Sauvignon, Enchanted Vines "Solus" Foch, Platinum Series Pinot Gris, Cipes Brut

Stephen Cipes is the P.T. Barnum of the BC wine industry. An expatriate New York real estate developer, his showmanship is evident in the huge sparkling wine bottle that appears to float above a giant champagne flute on the winery terrace. With no visible means of support, it pours its bubbling wine but never empties—an apt metaphor, perhaps, for Cipes' enthusiasm and energy when it comes to his winery. Set behind and slightly above the winery is a model replica of Cheops' great pyramid at Giza. The structure, at 8 percent of the original's size, is the most recognized icon in the Okanagan and the second such pyramid to be built at Summerhill. Its presence on the property is an ongoing scientific experiment that Cipes has heralded as an overwhelming success. On my last visit he invited a group of wine writers to hold hands

OPPOSITE: Chardonnay grapes at Summerhill Winery.
ABOVE: Entrance at Summerhill.

under the pyramid's apex to feel its power. All I felt was someone else's clammy fingers!

On the terrace overlooking the vineyard and the lake is the winery's Peace Park, a half-submerged globe surrounded by flowers and a pole that reads "May Peace Prevail on Earth" in sixteen languages. All of these imaginative elements make Summerhill's claim to be the most visited winery in British Columbia more than plausible. According to Cipes, 300,000 wine-loving tourists visit Summerhill every year. The winery also boasts the largest certified organic vineyard in the province.

In 2003 Stephen Cipes, true to his spiritual leanings, introduced a series of organic wines under the Enchanted Vines label. A back label for the sparking wine dosed with Icewine, Inspiration Methode Traditionelle 1997, reads: "Blessed by Shaman Chelsea Wise, Inspiration is the elixir for nurturing our creativity. It is the rising of our passion to meet the balance of our wisdom. Inspiration has been infused with the power to unfold the seed of our potential."

The Summerhill experience is not to be missed for Cipes' showmanship and his delightful sparkling wines. Try a glass as you enjoy the view from the terrace.

Summerland Cellars Estate Winery

11612 MORROW AVENUE, SUMMERLAND, BC V0H 1Z0 (250) 494-5421
EVONKROS@VIP.NET

YEAR FOUNDED: 1999 **FOUNDER:** Eric von Krosigk **WINEMAKER:** Eric von Krosigk **GRAPE VARIETIES:** (red) Pinot Noir; (white) Riesling, Muscat Ottenel, Kerner **RECOMMENDED WINES:** Sparkling Muscat, Sparkling Riesling

Somehow the hyper-busy consultant Eric von Krosigk has found the time to open his own winery to produce what he loves most—sparkling wines. His experience with this labour-intensive wine is impressive. He worked on a research program for Sumac Ridge in 1988–89 and has made champagne-style wines for Hester Creek, Summerhill, Hawthorne Mountain, Pinot Reach, Red Rooster, Hillside, Saturna Island, Victoria Estate (now Church & State), and Marley Farm. His tiny winery is a 1,100-square-foot single-storey facility painted in the same yellow you see throughout southern France; the tasting room is tacked onto one side of it. From a 7-acre vineyard

THE PYRAMID GOSPEL ACCORDING TO STEPHEN CIPES

PROPRIETOR OF SUMMERHILL ESTATE

"There is a definite and profound effect on liquids placed in the sacred geometry," writes Stephen Cipes. "Three years of conclusive taste test comparisons in the 1988 pyramid led to the building of our new pyramid in 1997 that is a four-storey high, 3,249-square-foot replica of Egypt's Great Pyramid. Now all our wines are pyramid aged…Every day at 2 o'clock, for three years, we toured the smaller pyramid with the general public. We did taste comparisons of the same wine, bottled on the same day, and served at the same temperature. One was stored in the pyramid for 30–90 days and the other was never put in the pyramid. The results were overwhelming. The tasters chose the pyramid-aged wine almost unanimously as being smoother and having a better aroma! These experiments boosted our convictions that, indeed, a precisely constructed pyramid becomes a chamber for the 'clarification' of liquids. For instance, a bad tasting wine, or juice, would become more foul tasting. The chamber seems to bring out flaws as well as exaggerating the best qualities. We humans are made mostly of liquid and seem to be affected by the chamber as well. We can actually feel our own 'life force energy' strengthen within the pyramid!

"Many experiments have been documented in replica pyramids. For instance, it is well established that rather than rotting, milk turns to yogurt, meat petrifies and razor blades will become sharper in the pyramid (this has been patented). A timed photography experiment, conducted outdoors in an open frame pyramid, revealed that a plant growing inside the pyramid grew in a clockwise motion, while a twin sister plant nearby, but not in a pyramid, grew 'helter skelter.'"

he makes a series of vibrant sparkling wines from Muscat Ottonel, Riesling, Chardonnay, Pinot Noir, and a blend of Chardonnay and Pinot Noir. Von Krosigk makes the wines in traditional champagne style. The still wine has yeast and sugar added to it, and then it is sealed with a crown cap. The yeast converts the sugar to alcohol and carbon dioxide gas. The dead yeast cells are sticky and cloud the wine, so they have to be removed by a process called "riddling." The bottles are placed in A-frames, where they are shaken and tilted in a motion similar to squeezing oranges. The sticky dead yeast cells settle on the crown cap. The neck of the bottle is then frozen in a brine solution and, when its opened, the pressure of the gas drives out a plug of ice containing the debris. The clean bottle is then topped up and dressed with its cork and wire muzzle.

Tantalus Vineyards
(formerly Pinot Reach Cellars)

1670 DEHART ROAD, KELOWNA, BC V1W 4N6 (250) 764-0078
WWW.TANTALUS.CA

YEAR FOUNDED: Pinot Reach, 1996; Tantalus, 2005 **FOUNDER:** Susan Dulik **WINEMAKER:** Matt Holmes **GRAPE VARIETIES:** (red) Pinot Noir, Pinot Meunier; (white) Riesling, Chardonnay **RECOMMENDED WINES:** Old Vine Riesling Brut, Bacchus, Optima, Gewurztraminer

The Dulik family farmed this property for over 70 years and planted Riesling as early as 1978. In 1997 Susan Dulik opened a small winery on the property with the intention of focusing on the Pinot family of grapes. But her winemaker, Roger Wong, made such a string of award-winning Rieslings that this grape became their signature wine. In 2004 the winery was sold to Eric Savics, a Vancouver stockbroker, and Eira Thomas, a geologist. Roger Wong, who is also a cider master and a former civil servant, presided over the transition when the winery was purchased and has now moved on to Gray Monk. The new owners changed the name to Tantalus Vineyards and have upgraded and expanded the facility with new equipment and cooperage. They hired the Australian winemaker Matt Holmes in 2005.

Therapy Vineyards

910 DEBECK ROAD, NARAMATA, BC V0H 1N0 (250) 496-5217
WWW.THERAPYVINEYARDS.COM, ACCOMMODATION: EIGHT-ROOM THERAPY GUESTHOUSE B&B, (250) 496-5217

YEAR FOUNDED: 2005 **FOUNDERS:** John McBean and Glenn Fawcett **WINEMAKER:** Marcus Ansems **GRAPE VARIETIES:** (red) Merlot, Maréchal Foch; (white) Pinot Gris, Gewurztraminer, Chardonnay **RECOMMENDED WINES:** Pinot Noir, Pinot Gris

Every wine lover knows that wine is great therapy and, as if to drive home the point, the labels of this newly

constituted winery are Rorschach ink-blot tests. It was originally opened by Beat and Prudence Mahrer in 1997 as Red Rooster Winery, but the couple found it was not large enough for the traffic they were generating. So they moved and built a larger facility just outside Penticton. The 12-acre property (9.5 acres of vineyard) was bought by John McBean, a former area secretary for the Opimian Society (a national wine-buying cooperative), and Glenn Fawcett, a Calgary-based businessman whose company, Vinequest, runs wine tours. They had the foresight to hire the highly experienced Australian winemaker Marcus Ansems. "This site is going to be great for Merlot," says Ansems, "and for Pinot Gris." The Napa-esque bungalow-style winery, painted dark green with wood-panel finishing, has been completely refitted and expanded. The landscaped patio adjacent to the vineyard affords a stunning view of orchards and vineyards and a lake vista across to Summerland.

LEFT: Black Widow Vineyard, where grapes for Wild Goose wines are grown. ABOVE: Brothers Roland and Hagen Kruger of Wild Goose Vineyards & Winery.

orchards, vineyards, and mountains while you practise the pronunciation of Gewurztraminer (G'vertz-tram-eener). In 2005 Dennis Fraser sold the winery to his cousins Jack and Jan Fraser, whose children, Cortney and Jason, are also involved in the operation. The wines do well in local and national competitions, so a visit is a reward if you first take the heart-pounding drive up scenic Giant's Head Mountain.

Wild Goose Vineyards & Winery

2145 SUN VALLEY WAY, OKANAGAN FALLS, BC V0H 1R0 (250) 497-8919
WWW.WILDGOOSEWINERY.COM

YEAR FOUNDED: 1990 **FOUNDERS:** Adolf, Hagen, and Roland Kruger
WINEMAKER: Hagen Kruger **GRAPE VARIETIES:** (red) Merlot, Pinot Noir,
Maréchal Foch; (white) Gewurztraminer, Riesling, Pinot Gris, Pinot
Blanc **RECOMMENDED WINES:** Gewurztraminer, Stoney Slope Riesling,
Pinot Gris, Merlot

Brothers Roland and Hagen Kruger continue the work their father, Adolf, started in 1990 when he received BC's second farm-gate winery licence. The family had to clear the slopes of brush and rocks in order to plant their first vines in 1983. The original tasting room was a basement room under the house that has now been converted into the lab. "We don't see ourselves as a destination winery," says Hagen Kruger. "We just want to make the best wines we can." Somewhat off the beaten track but within walking distance of Stag's Hollow, Wild Goose has a folksy, welcoming style: children get fruit juice samples while their parents taste the wines—as do teetotallers in need of refreshment from the heat of the day. The Wild Goose white wines are well worth tasting. The family also operates a one-bedroom guest cottage in Oliver at the Mystic River Vineyard site.

Thornhaven Estates Winery

6816 ANDREW AVENUE, SUMMERLAND, BC V0H 1Z0 (250) 494-7778
WWW.THORNHAVEN.COM

YEAR FOUNDED: 1999 **FOUNDERS:** Dennis, Pam, Alex, and Shawny
Fraser **WINEMAKERS:** Jason Fraser, Christine Leroux (consultant)
GRAPE VARIETIES: (red) Pinot Noir, Pinot Meunier; (white)
Gewurztraminer, Chardonnay, Sauvignon Blanc **RECOMMENDED WINES:**
Pinot Meunier, Barrel Reserve Pinot Noir, Gewurztraminer

This compact, gravity-flow winery, designed in Santa Fe style, sits on the slopes of Little Giant's Head Mountain and looks down on its 8.5-acre vineyard. From its expansive patio you get a great view of Okanagan Lake to the east, the surrounding orchards, and the Ponderosa pine–covered hills. Local art adorns the walls, and the wine shop also sells artifacts created by local artisans. The courtyard patio is an ideal spot to take in the lake,

Southern Okanagan (See map on page 66)

For the tourist, the main interest here is the diversity of wineries. The town of Oliver, which styles itself the "Wine Capital of Canada," is 25 kilometres north of the US border. A favourite summer spot for water sports, golf, and sightseeing, it has BC's densest concentration of wineries, ranging from the mighty Vincor International to the tiny Carriage House Vineyard. The Golden Mile south of Oliver is arguably the finest red-wine growing terroir in the country.

The Okanagan Valley extends only about 200 kilometres north of the US border, but it includes a range of climatic districts that accommodates several distinct viticultural areas. A dramatic example is the Southern Okanagan and the neighbouring Similkameen Valley to the west, which together make up Canada's only pocket desert. There is still evidence of the original desert in the Similkameen and in isolated patches between Oliver and Osoyoos, where sagebrush, creosote bush, and cactus harbour burrowing owls, rattlesnakes, and even a few scorpions. If you plan to walk in the vineyards, make sure you don't wear open-toed shoes; you might encounter a rattler—as Donald Triggs did the first time he set foot in the Nk'Mip Vineyard in Osoyoos.

A major irrigation program in the early 1900s augmented the 8 inches (203 mm) of annual rainfall and transformed the entire floor of the southern valley into a lush green field of crops and orchards. In the 1970s, grape growers recognized the potential of the elevated benches along the valley sides, and today they hold the highest concentration of vineyards in British Columbia.

The southern vineyards account for 60 percent of the province's 5,500 acres of vinifera grapevines. Cabernet Sauvignon and other Bordeaux varieties reign, together with Syrah, Viognier, Semillon, and even blocks of Sangiovese, Barbera, and Zinfandel. While the benches on the east side of the valley consist of deep sand, the western bench between Osoyoos and Oliver, the Golden Mile, has a more rocky makeup. Whereas the climate of the rest of the Okanagan to the north is moderated by valley lakes, the Southern Okanagan and Similkameen valley bottoms are both lined by rivers—a feature that produces some interesting viticultural effects. While the summer days can be blistering, the nights cool off quickly and help retain desirable acid levels. The Southern Okanagan is undoubtedly the best red-wine growing region in Canada if your taste is for bold, fruit-driven, California-style wines.

Summertime temperatures here are often the hottest in Canada, and highs over 40° Celsius are not unusual. In both the Similkameen and the Southern Okanagan, grape growing begins at the US border. The more heavily planted Southern Okanagan benches continue from Osoyoos, literally on the border, to north of Oliver, where the towering McIntyre Bluff constricts the valley and defines the northern extent of this unique desert viticultural region. With its dry heat during the day and its cold nights to build up acidity, this area is red-wine country par excellence, producing our best Bordeaux varieties and Syrah.

TOURING WINERIES in the Southern Okanagan

The area between Oliver and Osoyoos, a distance of 22 kilometres, is the most costly vineyard real estate in the province and the most densely populated with wineries. The compact nature of this region of the Okanagan makes wine touring very easy, but be sure to have water in the car, because the summer heat can be intense.

SINGLE DAY: The concentration of vineyards allows you to pop in and taste at several wineries, but I highly recommend two. Burrowing Owl makes consistently fine products that have become cult wines: they are hard to get if you don't buy them here, and besides, their restaurant is the best in the Okanagan. Nk'Mip Cellars is operated by the Osoyoos Indian Band, along with the neighbouring desert interpretive and heritage centre. If time permits, add in Tinhorn Creek, Gehringer Brothers, Inniskillin, and Golden Mile Cellars. Black Hills habitually sells out its three richly flavoured wines in the spring and will probably be closed in the summer and fall seasons. If you happen to be passing and it has wine to sell, buy it.

WEEKEND: A good base for a weekend of wine touring in this area is the Southwind Winecountry Inn in Oliver. On day one, take in the wineries north of Oliver at Okanagan Falls: Blue Mountain (be sure to call to tell them you're coming), Hawthorne Mountain (for its scenic vista and dog cemetery), Blasted Church (if you have a sense of humour and enjoy whimsical labels), and Wild Goose and its neighbour Stag's Hollow (for well-made wines in unpretentious settings). On day two, concentrate on those wineries south of Oliver (see the suggestions above for single-day tours).

Burrowing Owl Estate Winery.

Black Hills Estate

30880 BLACK SAGE ROAD, RR 1, SITE 52, COMP 22, OLIVER, BC V0H 1T0
(250) 498-0666 WWW.BLACKHILLSWINERY.COM

YEAR FOUNDED: 1999 **FOUNDERS:** Bob and Senka Tennant, Peter and Sue McCarrell **WINEMAKER:** Senka Tennant **GRAPE VARIETIES:** (red) Cabernet Sauvignon, Merlot, Cabernet Franc, Pinot Noir; (white) Sauvignon Blanc **RECOMMENDED WINES:** Alibi, Nota Bene, Sequentia

The tiny winery is housed in a Quonset hut that looks like an overturned rowboat beached on the sunburnt hills of the Black Sage Bench. Before becoming a winery, the hut was used to build demolition derby cars. The tasting room is a bench in front of the barrels—and a blessed escape from the summer heat outside. The winery may be small and produce only three wines—enough for a complete dinner party—but each is a gem: the Bordeaux-inspired white Alibi (Sauvignon and Semillon), the red-blend Nota Bene, and the dessert wine Sequentia. Senka Tennant's richly flavoured and beautifully balanced wines sell out very quickly, and your best chance to buy them is to get on the mailing list through their website.

Burrowing Owl Estate Winery

RR 1, SITE 52, COMP 20, OLIVER, BC V0H 1T0 (250) 498-0620; 1-877-498-0620
WWW.BOVWINE.CA, RESTAURANT: THE SONORA ROOM, (250) 498-2602

YEAR FOUNDED: 1997 **FOUNDER:** Jim Wyse **WINEMAKER:** Steve Wyse **GRAPE VARIETIES:** (red) Pinot Noir, Merlot, Cabernet Franc, Cabernet Sauvignon, Syrah; (white) Pinot Gris, Chardonnay **RECOMMENDED WINES:** Syrah, Merlot, Meritage, Cabernet Franc, Chardonnay

This southwestern style, gravity-flow winery, constructed in 1998, is set in a sea of vines overlooking Osoyoos Lake at its northern end. If you climb up to the square tower above the building, there's a walkway that rewards you with a spectacular 360-degree vista of the vineyards, granite cliffs, and the lake.

The building was originally designed as a 12,000-case facility, but such is the demand for Burrowing Owl wines that they now produce 20,000 cases. Owner Jim Wyse wants to increase production to 30,000 cases and is currently building more cellar space under the car park. He also plans a ten-unit inn with a wine lounge and its own cellar, to open in 2006. The 115-acre vineyard was planted

Welcome to

DESERT WINE COUNTRY

it all starts here !

PHOTOGRAPHY BY: GORD WYLIE

A MESSAGE FROM THE OSOYOOS INDIAN BAND, THE TOWN OF OLIVER, THE TOWN OF OSOYOOS AND RURAL AREA "A"

in 1993 and has been developed with an eco-friendly philosophy. More than one hundred bluebird boxes and two bat nurseries have been installed to encourage insect-eating guests to stay and dine in the vineyards. The Sonora Room restaurant, under French chef Dominique Couton, is one of the finest in the valley and an ideal place to taste Steve Wyse's wines by the glass. Burrowing Owl has built an enviable reputation for its reds, which are hard to get, especially now that their 2002 Meritage has won gold medals at both the Pacific Rim International Wine Competition and the Los Angeles County Fair in 2005. It's a cult winery if ever there was one.

Carriage House Wines

32764 BLACK SAGE ROAD, RR 1, SITE 46, COMP 19, OLIVER, BC V0H 1T0
(250) 498-8818 WWW.CARRIAGEHOUSEWINES.CA

YEAR FOUNDED: 1995 **FOUNDERS:** Dave and Karen Wagner
WINEMAKER: Dave Wagner **GRAPE VARIETIES:** (red) Pinot Noir, Merlot, Syrah, Cabernet Sauvignon; (white) Kerner **RECOMMENDED WINES:** Kerner Dry, Kerner Off-Dry, Merlot, Pinot Noir

Carriage House suggests something a little grander than this utilitarian wine facility. Dave Wagner, a local boy, had been looking for suitable land to grow grapes for a year before settling on this site on Black Sage Road. A few of the apricot trees remain from the orchard that the Wagners purchased in 1992, and you can picnic under the shade of one splendid old specimen that grows at the back of the winery. While this area is known for its muscular red wines made from Bordeaux varieties, Wagner has carved out a niche for his flagship white wine made from Kerner. As a testament to the abundance of black sage in the area, he named a blend of Chardonnay and Kerner "Ebonage White."

Desert Hills Estate Winery

30480—71 STREET (BLACK SAGE ROAD), OLIVER, BC V0H 1T0 (250) 498-1040
WWW.DESERTHILLS.CA

YEAR FOUNDED: 2002 **FOUNDERS:** Randy, Jessie, and Dave Toor
WINEMAKER: Elias Phiniotis **GRAPE VARIETIES:** (red) Syrah, Merlot, Cabernet Sauvignon, Gamay, Malbec; (white) Pinot Gris
RECOMMENDED WINE: Syrah

As a virtual winery, there isn't much to see here apart from the shack-like tasting room and a patch of grass for picnicking. The Toor brothers (Randy and Jessie are twins) were born in India. They grew up in Winnipeg and eventually moved to Oliver, where the family purchased a 25-acre apple orchard in 1988. Randy Toor converted part of the property to vineyards in 1995. The soil in this arid land resembles the sand on a beach—giving the red grapes a spicy, peppery note. At first the brothers sold their grapes to Domaine de Chaberton in the Fraser Valley. In 2002 they launched their own Desert Hills label and strengthened their association with the Domaine by contracting that winery's highly experienced oenologist, Elias Phiniotis, who also consults for Glenugie, to produce their wines.

A quick taste of the sample in the rudimentary tasting-room-cum-shop between Burrowing Owl and Black Hills wineries is all you need. If Randy Toor is there, you might want to linger and listen to his passionate discourse on wine.

Domaine Combret Estate Winery

32057 ROAD 13, OLIVER, BC, V0H 1T0 (250) 498-6966; 1-866-TERROIR
WWW.COMBRETWINE.COM

YEAR FOUNDED: 1992 **FOUNDER:** Robert Combret **WINEMAKER:** Olivier Combret **GRAPE VARIETIES:** (red) Cabernet Franc, Cabernet Sauvignon, Merlot, Gamay, Pinot Noir; (white) Chardonnay, Riesling
RECOMMENDED WINES: Chardonnay, Riesling, Chardonnay Icewine, Pinot Gris, Cabernet Sauvignon

Robert Combret, who immigrated to British Columbia from Provence in 1992, is a ninth-generation winemaker. He purchased the property long before the Golden Mile earned its soubriquet as the premier red-wine territory in the Okanagan.

Combret just wanted to find a region where he could grow grapes with minimal recourse to chemical sprays and pesticides. With his Montpellier-trained oenologist son Olivier, he designed the first gravity-feed winery in the province; it sits majestically on the Golden Mile Bench south of Oliver, and you can see it if you look up from the Black Horse Vineyard. Olivier, who now makes the wines, is, like all Frenchmen, a great believer in terroir (the effect of localized soils and microclimate on the flavours and structures of wines).

Combret makes highly individual wines in the French style—so much so that his Chablis-like St. Vincent Chardonnays are frequently awarded medals at the international Chardonnay du Monde competition judged at Château de Ravatys, the wine estate of the Pasteur Institute in Beaujolais. Olivier and his near neighbour Bill Eggert of Fairview Cellars have produced an impressive Bordeaux-style blend of Combret's Cabernet Franc with Eggert's Cabernet Sauvignon, which they call "Two Thumbs Up" and price at an eyebrow-raising $100 a bottle.

You'll have to visit either winery to purchase it and judge the digital accolade for yourself.

Welcome sign in Oliver.

Fairview Cellars

13147—334TH AVENUE, OLIVER, BC V0H 1T0 (250) 498-2211
BEGGERT@IMG.NET

YEAR FOUNDED: 1997 **FOUNDER:** Bill Eggert **WINEMAKER:** Bill Eggert
GRAPE VARIETIES: (red) Cabernet Sauvignon, Cabernet Franc, Merlot
RECOMMENDED WINES: The Bear's Meritage, Cabernet Sauvignon

Bill Eggert's motto is "From the heart…For the heart."
He is the embodiment of Canadian Gothic, a straight-
talking, no-nonsense farmer in a red flannel shirt and ball
cap. His tasting room, within an iron shot of the first hole
of the Fairview Mountain Golf Course, is a heritage log
cabin (located between the driving range and the first hole);
his cellar, where he barrel-ages his wines, is a bunker he
himself dug out of a hillside and then poured the concrete for. Bill learned how to make wine from Paul Bosc
in Ontario in the 1970s, while managing the vineyard of
the now defunct Charal Winery in Blenheim. He migrated
west and planted his own 6-acre vineyard in 1993 to the
three dominant red Bordeaux varieties "and one row of
Shiraz for abuse and punishment." As a result, he produces only red wines, as rugged and as extrovert as he is
himself. For his exceptional vintages, he reserves the title
"The Bear's Meritage." Bill explains how it came to be
named: "Bear is the nickname for my nephew Wesley
Bear. In 2000 he came to visit me. It was my first year
with my store open, I still had a full-time off-farm job, and
I was still building my underground cellar. As a result, I
had little time for the vineyard. Wesley Bear took over

that responsibility. The wines from 2000 showed the hard
work he did in the vineyard. I felt it only appropriate that
he get some recognition. I now use 'The Bear' in years I
feel are better than average."

It's worth a visit just to hear the story behind the name.
With Olivier Combret, Eggert has produced a blend of
Cabernet Franc and Cabernet Sauvignon called "Two
Thumbs Up," available only at either winery's shop. If
$100 is too steep for you, don't miss Eggert's other reds.

Gehringer Brothers Estate Winery

RR 1, SITE 23, COMP 4, OLIVER, BC V0H 1T0 (250) 498-3537; 1-800-784-6304

YEAR FOUNDED: 1981 **FOUNDERS:** Walter and Gordon Gehringer
WINEMAKER: Walter Gehringer **GRAPE VARIETIES:** (red) Pinot Noir,
Merlot, Cabernet Franc; (white) Pinot Gris, Pinot Blanc, Ehrenfelser,
Schönburger, Gewurztraminer, Sauvignon Blanc, Auxerrois, Chardonnay
RECOMMENDED WINES: Private Reserve Pinot Gris, Dry Rock
Chardonnay, Dry Rock Sauvignon Blanc, Auxerrois, Riesling,
Ehrenfelser, Cabernet Franc Icewine

The Gehringer family purchased their vineyard site, set
on a rocky bench on the west side of the Okanagan Valley,
in 1981. It was a fortuitous purchase because the area was
first called the Golden Mile half a century ago when its
frost-free microclimate made vegetable growing easy. Wine
journalist Dave Gamble told me the name was dusted off
in the mid-1990s and applied to the grape-growing area
along the bench above the flat land. Walter Gehringer
studied at the Geisenheim Institute (the first Canadian

OPPOSITE: Gehringer Brothers Esate Winery ABOVE: Bill Eggert of Fairview Cellars.

graduate of this illustrious wine school in the Rheingau), and his winemaking style reflects this training in the Germanic style of his wines and his deft touch with Riesling. He makes five different styles, from bone dry to Icewine, as they do in Germany. Walter worked initially with Andrés for five years as a winemaker before joining the family enterprise in 1984. His early wines were off-dry in style, but they have dried out in more recent vintages, especially since the introduction of the Dry Rock label of French varietals such as Chardonnay and Sauvignon Blanc (rather than traditional German grapes like Ehrenfelser and Schönburger). The winery, with its hexagonal, wood-trimmed tasting room, was built in 1985 and was one of the first in the Southern Okanagan.

Golden Beaver Winery
(formerly Gersighel Wineberg)

29690 HIGHWAY 97, RR 1, SITE 40, COMP 20, OLIVER, BC V0H 1T0 (250) 495-4991
WWW.GOLDENBEAVERWINERY.COM

YEAR FOUNDED: 1995 **FOUNDERS:** Dirk and Gerda De Gussem
WINEMAKERS: Dirk De Gussem, Gary Strachan (consulting) **GRAPE VARIETIES:** (red) Pinot Noir, Merlot; (white) Pinot Blanc, Chardonnay, Gewurztraminer, Riesling, Viognier **RECOMMENDED WINES:** not tasted

You find this rustic, small farm winery at the southern end of the Golden Mile. In 2006 Bruno Kelle, an electronics technician from Calgary, with his partner, Stella Schmidt, an accountant, purchased the property from

Dirk De Gussem. Kelle grew up on a tobacco farm in Tillsonburg, Ontario, which he eventually turned into a culinary herb operation before moving west in 1996. Schmidt, of Danish extraction, has close links to the land, too; her father bred field-trial dogs in Alberta and her sister farms pigs in Denmark. Dirk De Gussem will lend a hand in the winery under the watchful eye of consulting winemaker Gary Strachan. Kelle plans a new wine shop and an expansion to the current winery and will eventually build a residence on the property.

Golden Mile Cellars

13140–316A AVENUE, ROAD 13, OLIVER, BC V0H 1T0 (250) 498-8330
WWW.GOLDENMILECELLARS.COM

YEAR FOUNDED: 1998 **FOUNDERS:** Peter and Helga Serwo
WINEMAKER: Michael Bartier **GRAPE VARIETIES:** (red) Merlot, Pinot Noir, Syrah, Cabernet Franc, Cabernet Sauvignon; (white) Ehrenfelser, Chardonnay, Riesling, Chenin Blanc, Optima, Viognier **RECOMMENDED WINES:** Chardonnay, Merlot

Peter Serwo, a former builder, constructed a medieval castle for his winery and tasting room, complete with battlements and a conical copper dome. One of its towers is guarded by a suit of armour. The castle is positioned in the middle of the 20-acre vineyard he planted in 1982. The labels feature a crenellated crest, reflecting the winery's architecture. The view from the castle's facade across the Southern Okanagan Valley south of Oliver is spectacular. Golden Mile Cellars was purchased in 2003 by Mick and Pam Luckhurst—he in construction (no doubt impressed by Serwo's chutzpah in building a castle in the desert) and she a banker wooed into the industry by the romance of wine. Winemaker Michael Bartier is a Chardonnay specialist who has twice won the White Wine of the Year award at the Canadian Wine Awards. Altogether it's an intriguing place to visit—especially for the winery's masquerade ball, featuring medieval music, in October.

Hester Creek Estate Winery

13163–326 STREET, OLIVER, BC V0H 1T0 (250) 498-4435; 1-866-498-4435
WWW.HESTERCREEK.COM

YEAR FOUNDED: 1995 **OWNERS:** Curt Garland, David Livingstone
WINEMAKER: Eric von Krosigk **GRAPE VARIETIES:** (red) Cabernet Sauvignon, Cabernet Franc, Gamay Noir, Merlot; (white) Chardonnay, Pinot Blanc, Trebbiano, Semillon **RECOMMENDED WINES:** Pinot Blanc, Chardonnay/Semillon, Merlot, Cabernet/Merlot

Joe Busnardo planted the original 70-acre vineyard just south of Oliver on what is now the Golden Mile. Between 1968 and 1972 he put in an amazing range of European varietals for his Divino Estate, many from his native

TOP: Randy Picton of Nk'Mip Cellars. ABOVE: Bruce Nicholson of Jackson-Triggs Okanagan. RIGHT: Dark Horse Vineyard, where grapes are grown for Inniskillin Okanagan wines.

Veneto, including Trebbiano—the only winery in the Okanagan to make a wine from this workhorse Italian grape. In 1996 Busnardo sold the estate with its treasured old vines to a group of investors and relocated Divino on Vancouver Island. The new owners christened the winery Hester Creek (after the creek that runs in the gully between their property and the neighbouring Domaine Combret); one of the group, Frank Supernak, made the wines until his death in 2002. Another change of ownership occurred in 2004, when the company went into receivership. Curt Garland, who owns a trucking business, purchased it and immediately hired the peripatetic Eric von Krosigk to make the wines—a good move, considering the kudos Hester Creek products have received in national and international competitions.

The lovely vine-covered patio, where deli-style light lunches are served, looks out over the vineyard to Black Sage Bench and Mt. Baldy. The current winery building may be a parking lot by the time you visit because a major renovation is about to begin to build a spanking-new facility, which will be partly underground, as well as bed-and-breakfast accommodation.

Inniskillin Okanagan Vineyards

ROAD 11 WEST, RR 1, SITE 24, COMP 5, OLIVER, BC V0H 1T0
(250) 498-6663, (250) 498-6411; 1-800-498-6211 WWW.INNISKILLIN.COM

YEAR FOUNDED: 1994 **FOUNDERS:** Donald Ziraldo and Karl Kaiser
WINEMAKER: Sandor Mayer **GRAPE VARIETIES:** (red) Pinot Noir, Merlot, Cabernet Sauvignon, Cabernet Franc, Zinfandel; (white) Pinot Blanc, Pinot Grigio, Chardonnay, Gewurztraminer, Viognier, Riesling, Vidal
RECOMMENDED WINES: Meritage, Pinot Noir, Bear Cub Vineyard Zinfandel, Riesling Icewine

Karl Kaiser and Donald Ziraldo's first vintage in British Columbia was 1994, using grapes that had been grown on the Inkameep Vineyards in partnership with the Okanaquen Indian Band. The rocky 23-acre Dark Horse Vineyard that supplied the grapes is located on the western slope of the valley, north of Osoyoos Lake, and is the site of the winery. The labels, designed by a local artist, depict a horse and rider taken from an ancient rock carving on ancestral lands. The black label is reserved for non-oaked wines, the pearl label for wines that have spent time in oak, and the silver label for single-vineyard or site-specific

Winemaker Bruce Nicholson's trophy case must resemble Wayne Gretzky's. At the 2003 Canadian Wine Awards, Jackson-Triggs Okanagan was named Winery of the Year. That same year Nicholson was named Canadian Wine Producer of the Year for the third consecutive year at the International Wine & Spirits Competition in London. In 2004 he was named Best Canadian Producer at Vinitaly in Verona, and, in 2005, Winemaker of the Year at the San Francisco International Wine Competition. For specific wines from J-T's Okanagan portfolio, Nicholson has won numerous medals. Much of the reason for this success is the quality of the fruit produced in Vincor's extensive vineyard holdings in the Southern Okanagan and their meticulous management. The winery itself is far from glamorous—a vast industrial warehouse (with a separate cellar operation and barrel room for Vincor's Osoyoos Larose joint venture with Bordeaux's Groupe Taillan)—but the equipment inside is all state of the art. Unfortunately, you can't tour or taste here yet, but in 2007 Jackson-Triggs is planning to build a hospitality centre as part of a small estate winery on a newly purchased 30-acre site south of Tinhorn Creek.

Nk'Mip Cellars

400 RANCHER CREEK ROAD, OSOYOOS, BC V0H 1V0 (250) 495-2985
WWW.NKMIPCELLARS.COM, RESTAURANT: (250) 495-2986

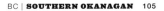

YEAR FOUNDED: 2002 **FOUNDERS:** Osoyoos Indian Band and Vincor International **WINEMAKER:** Randy Picton **GRAPE VARIETIES:** (red) Merlot, Pinot Noir, Cabernet Sauvignon, Cabernet Franc, Syrah; (white) Pinot Blanc, Chardonnay, Riesling **RECOMMENDED WINES:** Riesling, Pinot Blanc, Pinot Noir, Merlot Reserve

To the sound of drums, Chief Clarence Louis of the Osoyoos Indian Band cut a ceremonial rope of green sage to open North America's first aboriginal-owned and -operated winery on September 13, 2002. Green sage is a sacred plant used in cleansing ceremonies. The winery's name, Nk'Mip (pronounced In-ka-meep), comes from the local Salish dialect and means "place where the creek joins the lake." The Osoyoos Band has a history of viticulture dating back to 1968, when members first planted the Inkameep Vineyard. The 32,000-acre reservation that is home to the band contains 25 percent of all vineyard land planted in the Okanagan Valley.

Nk'Mip Cellars' attractive labels feature the company logo—a turtle (a symbol of wisdom and vision) painted as a pictograph on an arrowhead, a symbol of the power and heritage of the vineyard. This winery, with its 22-acre vineyard, is set dramatically in Canada's only pocket desert, where temperatures reach 41° Celsius. The Santa Fe–style building sits on an arid bench with rattlesnake-infested granite hills as a backdrop, overlooking Lake Osoyoos and close to the Washington State border. Across the lake you can see Vincor's Osoyoos Larose vineyards.

bottlings that bear the grower's name. In 2002 winemaker Sandor Mayer produced British Columbia's first Zinfandel with fruit from Vincor's Bear Cub Vineyard on the Osoyoos Lake bench. The wine won a gold medal at the annual Concours mondiale international wine competition in Brussels in 2005.

The winery itself is housed in a Spanish bodega-style building with a red tiled roof. The tasting room is small and neat with a long oak bar, ideal for tasting Sandor Mayer's award-winning wines.

Jackson-Triggs Okanagan Cellars

38691 HIGHWAY 97, OLIVER, BC V0H 1T0 (250) 498-4981; 1-800-665-2667
WWW.JACKSONTRIGGSWINERY.COM

YEAR FOUNDED: 1992 **FOUNDERS:** Don Triggs and Allan Jackson **WINEMAKER:** Bruce Nicholson **GRAPE VARIETIES:** (red) Cabernet Sauvignon, Merlot, Shiraz, Pinot Noir, Cabernet Franc, Malbec, Petit Verdot; (white) Chardonnay, Sauvignon Blanc, Riesling, Viognier, Gewurztraminer, Semillon **RECOMMENDED WINES:** Chardonnay, Cabernet-Shiraz, Shiraz, Meritage, Merlot, Riesling Icewine, Sparkling Icewine, Viognier, Gewurztraminer

Pascal Madevon of Osoyoos Larose Vineyard (OPPOSITE).

The band entered into a $7 million joint venture with Canada's largest wine company, Vincor International, to produce five varietal wines—Riesling, Pinot Blanc, Chardonnay, Pinot Noir, and Merlot. The wines are made by Randy Picton, who spent six years as associate winemaker at BC's CedarCreek Estate. The 18,000-square-foot gravity-feed winery is capable of producing 15,000 cases a year. For its first vintage in 2000, the facility made 3,300 cases.

Adjacent to the winery, the band has built a desert interpretive and heritage centre to help protect the remaining desert landscape and endangered species. A popular attraction for visitors is the snake pit, where the curious can get up close with metre-long rattlers that are captured, marked with electronic tracing chips, and returned to the wild. The boardwalk paths are festooned with signs telling visitors to be aware of rattlesnakes.

The winery is the second phase of a $25 million project that will include an all-season RV park, a nine-hole golf course, a hotel, and a conference hall on lakefront land adjoining the town of Osoyoos. This is a must-see operation. Once you've taken a look at the snakes in captivity at the nearby desert centre, you'll need a glass of wine. Seriously, Nk'Mip has cutting-edge technology and expert winemaking. The wines have improved beyond recognition from their opening vintage.

Osoyoos Larose Vineyard

BOX 1650, HIGHWAY, 97, OLIVER, BC V0H 1T0 (250) 498-4981

YEAR FOUNDED: 1998 **FOUNDERS:** Vincor International and Groupe Taillan **WINEMAKER:** Pascal Madevon **GRAPE VARIETIES:** (red) Merlot, Cabernet Sauvignon, Cabernet Franc, Malbec, Petit Verdot **RECOMMENDED WINE:** Osoyoos Larose

In 1999 Vincor entered into a joint venture with the giant Bordeaux shipper Groupe Taillan to create a wine of "global stature" in the Southern Okanagan Valley. Together they planted a 60-acre vineyard with all five Bordeaux red varieties. The first vintage was 2001. They called the wine Osoyoos Larose, a combination of the vineyard location in Osoyoos and Château Gruaud Larose, the flagship of six Bordeaux properties owned by Groupe Taillan.

The vines, a combination of different rootstock and clones, were prepared at the Mercier nursery in Bordeaux and shipped over to Canada to be planted by hand. The trellising system was selected to allow for superior canopy management and to promote good air movement and maximum sun exposure. The vines were planted much closer together than is usually found in Canada so as to produce a lower yield and more concentrated fruit quality. French oenology experts Michel Rolland and Alain Sutre

The view from Tinhorn Creek Vineyards (RIGHT).

consulted on the project, and the wine was made by Pascal Madevon, a former winemaker from Château La Tour Blanche in the Médoc. A blend of Merlot, Cabernet Sauvignon, and Cabernet Franc was aged in one- and two-year-old French barrels. Osoyoos Larose is the only winery in Canada to make a single wine. Currently the wine is made in the Jackson-Triggs facility in Oliver as a winery within a winery, but Vincor plans to construct a stand-alone winery for its flagship wine.

Paradise Ranch Wines Corp.

SUITE 901—525 SEYMOUR STREET, VANCOUVER, BC V6B 3H7 (604) 683-6040
WWW.ICEWINES.COM

YEAR FOUNDED: 1998 **FOUNDER:** James D. Stewart **WINEMAKER:** Alan Marks **GRAPE VARIETIES:** (red) Merlot; (white) Chardonnay, Riesling, Pinot Blanc **RECOMMENDED WINES:** Chardonnay Icewine, Merlot Icewine, Riesling Icewine

Paradise Ranch is the largest Icewine producer in British Columbia and one of the world's few wineries exclusively producing Icewines and Late Harvest wines. For their

first vintage in 1998, Paradise Ranch made eight different varietal Icewines—75 percent of the total Icewine production in British Columbia. Apart from the above-mentioned varietals, Paradise Ranch has also made Icewine from Gewurztraminer, Vidal, and Verdelet. In 2002 the vineyards, with their precipitous drop to the lake, were purchased by Mission Hill. James Stewart now buys grapes from independent growers in the Okanagan Valley and has plans to eventually open another winery in the Okanagan.

Silver Sage Winery

2032—87TH STREET, OLIVER, BC V0H 1T0 (250) 498-0319
WWW.SILVERSAGEWINERY.COM

YEAR FOUNDED: 1996 **FOUNDER:** Anna and Victor Manola **WINEMAKER:** Anna Manola **GRAPE VARIETIES:** (red) Merlot, Pinot Noir; (white) Pinot Blanc, Gewurztraminer **RECOMMENDED WINE:** Gewurztraminer

When Anna and Victor Manola, expatriate Romanians, purchased the property in 1996, the derelict vineyard on the bank of the Oxbow Creek was covered with silver

sage. They cleaned it out, planted 22 acres of vines, and built themselves an imposing house and winery on the property. It was a far cry from the Communist regime that Victor had escaped from in 1975 at the age of twenty. He managed to get his childhood sweetheart, Anna, to Canada when the regime collapsed. Anna Manola's father had been a winemaker in Romania overseeing an 1,100-acre vineyard, and Victor's father also had a winemaking and viticulture background. From the outset, the couple were determined to make totally natural wines without recourse to chemicals or sugar. They also took advantage of the ubiquitous sage to make a wine called Sage Grand Reserve, a semi-dry Gewurztraminer fermented with sage plants. In addition to the winery's production of organic Merlot, Pinot Noir, and the signature Silver Sage White, Anna also makes cherry, blueberry, and raspberry wine. Her latest off-beat product is called Flame, a white wine with a red chili pepper in the bottle that looks rather like a laboratory specimen. Tragically, Victor Manola was overcome by carbon dioxide fumes when he fell into a fermentation tank towards the end of the 2002 crush. In trying to rescue him, his consultant winemaker, Frank Supernak, also perished. As

a memorial to them, Anna closes the winery every year on November 10.

Although there is no restaurant here, the winery will cater for groups on the patio or in an on-site banquet hall that can seat ninety guests. There are also plans for accommodation, with six self-contained units.

Tinhorn Creek Vineyards

32830 TINHORN CREEK ROAD, OLIVER, BC V0H 1T0 (250) 498)-3743
WWW.TINHORN.COM

YEAR FOUNDED: 1993 **FOUNDERS:** Barb and Bob Shaunessy, Sandra and Kenn Oldfield **WINEMAKER:** Sandra Oldfield **GRAPE VARIETIES:** (red) Merlot, Cabernet Franc, Pinot Noir; (white) Chardonnay, Gewurztraminer, Pinot Gris, Kerner **RECOMMENDED WINES:** Merlot, Merlot Reserve, Merlot Oldfield's Collection, Cabernet Franc, Pinot Noir, Gewurztraminer, Kerner Icewine

Sandra Oldfield, an American, studied at California's celebrated wine school, UC Davis, where she met her husband, Kenn. The California connection inspired the type of winery the Oldfields created with the Shaunessys in 1993. Sandra Oldfield will tell you that they modelled Tinhorn Creek after Napa Valley's Newton Vineyard on Spring Mountain. Like Newton, this modernistic, mustard-yellow building is set majestically on a hillside—in this case, above Oliver's Golden Mile—its entrance embellished by a rock garden and a soothing water fountain. Inside, visitors can watch the winemaking process from interior galleries overlooking the stainless steel tanks, oak barrels, and cellar below.

The winery takes its name from the creek that runs through the property. In 1895 a gold-mining concern called the Tinhorn Quartz Mining Company was registered here. Now the only gold struck on the property is the medals Oldfield's wines win in national and international competitions. Ever since Tinhorn Creek's 1998 Merlot won Red Wine of Year at the Canadian Wine Awards, this variety has been Oldfield's signature wine, garnering medals in every competition in which it has been entered. The fruit comes from the 130-acre Black Sage Road vineyard, a property oil executive Bob Shaunessy bought in 1993. That same year he also purchased the 30-acre vineyard on the Golden Mile as the site for the winery.

In 2004, the Oldfields and their staff planted over 600 native shrubs, wildflowers, and bunchgrass in one part of the property to restore the area to an antelope-brush plant community to create a natural habitat for BC's endangered wildlife species.

This winery is one of the best-run operations in the valley (managed by Kenn Oldfield); you could eat off the cellar floor! And you won't find better red wines in the province. You may also be lucky to run into Zoe, Zippy, Jackal, and Sadie, the dogs on the property, or Kinko, the cat. And you'll enjoy the shopping experience there.

Similkameen Valley (see map on page 66)

Similkameen is not as well known in wine circles as the adjacent Okanagan Valley, nor has it been as highly developed as a vineyard sector. Currently, four wineries and one fruit winery are operating here, though that may well change as the cost of vineyard land rises for favoured Okanagan sites. Peller Estates has invested heavily in the region, creating the 65-acre Rocky Ridge Vineyard on a former alfalfa farm owned by local landowner Roger Hol. Actually, it's more a case of reinvesting, since the company—formerly known as Andrés Wines—was one of the first wineries as early as the 1960s to try to grow grapes in this hot, arid, windswept valley. You may recall a wine they made called Similkameen Superior.

Both the Okanagan and the Similkameen valleys start at the desert town of Osoyoos. The Okanagan Valley runs north for 250 kilometres; the Similkameen angles northwest for 100 kilometres. Similkameen, a former gold-mining area now given over to cattle ranching and horse farms, tends to attract rugged individualists, mavericks who find their own way. Take Orofino Vineyards, for instance, whose winery and shop are built out of straw bales, or Joe Ritlop of St. Laszlo Estate, who has been growing such retro North American hybrid grapes as Clinton and Interlaken since 1976. The frontier spirit is alive and well in the valley.

Similkameen is ideal for growing fruit, berries, and vegetables, so much so that Keremeos, the hub community of the valley, population 1,200, is known as the "Fruit Stand Capital of Canada." This is definitely red-wine country because the blistering heat of summer—hotter than the Okanagan—allows the grapes to ripen, and the cold nights guarantee good acidity. As in the Central and Southern Okanagan, growers have to irrigate the vineyards. The gravelly, sandy loam and silt-loam soils do not hold the water well, and the fierce winds that roar along the valley can dry the ground in minutes. Crowsnest Vineyards once lost its winery roof on a particularly blustery day; but the wind has its virtues because it keeps vineyard pests and frosts at bay, allowing growers to farm organically if they so desire.

The wineries, spread out along Highway 3 from Keremeos to Cawston, locate their vineyards on severely glaciated benchland terraces to take advantage of slopes that offer complex brown soils of sandy loam with varying amounts of gravel and stones. These stones can be eight or more inches in diameter.

Keremeos boasts one of the few remaining working flour mills in North America—a log house with its own water wheel built in 1877. You can also wander through the Heritage Gardens with their "living museum of wheat." And don't miss the turn-of-the-century covered bridge over the Similkameen River a few kilometres west of the village. If you visit in mid-September you can—as if it were not hot enough already—participate in the annual Pepper Festival.

TOURING WINERIES
in the Similkameen Valley

SINGLE DAY: Since it's only a few minutes' drive between Keremeos and Cawston, you can see all the wine activity in this hot, windy valley in a single day. For those with an interest in architecture, I would recommend stopping at Orofino to discover how you can build a winery out of straw bales. And, for some serious wine tasting, put Herder Winery on your itinerary.

WEEKEND: There are campsites and RV parks in Keremeos, but if you want something more luxurious, try the Cathedral Lakes Lodge. If you plan to spend the weekend in this area, having toured the five wineries here, you can spend the second day in Osoyoos in the Okanagan Valley. Or you can stay in the valley and divide your days between Crowsnest, St. Laszlo, and The Seven Stones on the first day and Herder and Orofino on the second. But if you do them all in one day, reserve the second for three Osoyoos wineries that will give you three very different experiences—Nk'Mip Cellars, run by the Osoyoos Indian Band; Burrowing Owl, with its commanding sweep of vineyard and fine-dining restaurant; and Tinhorn Creek.

St. Laszlo Vineyards. PREVIOUS PAGE AND RIGHT: Crowsnest Vineyards.

Crowsnest Vineyards

2036 SURPRISE DRIVE, CAWSTON, BC V0X 1C0 (250) 499-5129
WWW.CROWSNESTVINEYARDS.COM

YEAR FOUNDED: 1995 **FOUNDERS:** Hugh and Andrea McDonald
WINEMAKER: Ann Heinecke **GRAPE VARIETIES:** (red) Pinot Noir, Merlot,
Maréchal Foch, Samtrot; (white) Chardonnay, Riesling, Gewurztraminer
RECOMMENDED WINES: Pinot Noir, Riesling

Currently one of five wineries in the Similkameen Valley,
Crowsnest is named after Highway 3, the Crowsnest
Highway, and it's a true family affair—Olaf and Sabina
Heinecke, who bought the winery from the McDonalds in
1998; their daughter Ann, who makes the wine; and their
son Sascha, who manages the sales and oversees the dining
aspects. Set on the windy upper bench of the valley, the
winery commands a spectacular mountain view, especially
for sunsets. One of the oddities offered here is a wine made
from a red grape grown in Germany called Samtrot,
which Jancis Robinson describes in *Vines, Grapes and Wines*
as a "Meunier mutation…dogged by its very low yield."
The bistro serves a German menu, and the newly enlarged
covered patio offers a "Picnic on a Platter" as well as
such German specialities as rouladen, schnitzel, sauer-
kraut, and bratwurst. Plan to arrive at lunchtime.

Herder Winery & Vineyards

716 LOWE DRIVE, CAWSTON, BC V0X 1C0 (250) 499-5595 WWW.HERDER.CA

YEAR FOUNDED: 2004 **FOUNDERS:** Lawrence and Sharon Herder
WINEMAKER: Lawrence Herder **GRAPE VARIETIES:** (red) Cabernet
Sauvignon, Pinot Noir, Syrah, Merlot; (white) Pinot Gris **RECOMMENDED
WINES:** Pinot Noir, Pinot Gris, Chardonnay

Californian Lawrence Herder studied winemaking at
Fresno State University before embarking on an eight-
year winemaking career that took him to B.R. Cohn in
Sonoma, his own eponymous winery in Paso Robles,
Jackson-Triggs in the Okanagan, and Golden Mile Cellars
in Oliver. It was great training for the winery that he and
his Nanaimo-born wife, Sharon, a graphic designer, set
up in the Similkameen Valley to run themselves. While
they wait for their own 7.5-acre vineyard to come on
stream, they buy in grapes from local growers and produce vineyard-designated wines that exhibit bright
California style—including their bold, collectible labels.
It's a winery to watch.

Orofino Vineyards

2152 BARCELO ROAD, CAWSTON, BC V0X 1C0 (250) 499-0068
WWW.OROFINOVINEYARDS.COM

YEAR FOUNDED: 2003 **FOUNDERS:** John and Virginia Weber
WINEMAKERS: John Weber, Alan Marks (consultant) **GRAPE VARIETIES:**
(red) Merlot, Pinot Noir, Cabernet Franc; (white) Chardonnay,
Riesling, Muscat **RECOMMENDED WINES:** Merlot/Cabernet, Pinot Noir,
Pinot Gris, Chardonnay

Orofino is named for the mountain that overlooks the
property. It's a Spanish term harking back to earlier mining days meaning "fine gold," which could portend the
colour of the medals this small winery will consistently win
with its beautifully crafted wines. John Weber, a teacher
from Swift Current, Saskatchewan—about as far as you
can get from winegrowing in Canada—and his wife,
Virginia, a nurse with a diploma in horticulture, have hit
the ground running with their new winery. The 5.5-acre
vineyard was already sixteen years old when they acquired

it, and those well-seasoned vines provided them with mature fruit. Their 2,300-square-foot building, with its breezeway separating the winery from the tasting room, is unique because it's the only facility in the country constructed from straw bales. Orofino's earthen walls are 54 centimetres thick, maintaining a constant temperature inside; they provide sufficient insulation (RD-60) for the barrel cellar and tasting room against the heat of the Similkameen summers. "The bales allow our barrel building to remain at around 17° Celsius when it is 30° plus outside," says Weber.

The scenic picnic area is surrounded by the vineyard, trees (almond, oak, quince, maple, and walnut), and colourful magnolia and bougainvillea. Orofino has quickly become a cult winery; get there before the Webers run out of the little wine they produce. John Weber was honoured as the first recipient of the Frank Supernak Memorial Bursary sponsored by the Canadian Vintners Association.

St. Laszlo Vineyards Estate Winery

HIGHWAY 3, KEREMEOS, BC V0X 1N0 (250) 499-2856

YEAR FOUNDED: 1985 **FOUNDER:** Joe Ritlop **WINEMAKER:** Joe Ritlop Jr.
GRAPE VARIETIES: (red) Merlot, Pinot Noir, Cabernet Franc, Gamay Noir; (white) Gewurztraminer, Chardonnay, Siegerrebe, Perle of C'saba, Perle of Zala, Riesling, Interlaken, Verdelet **RECOMMENDED WINE:** Riesling

Joe Ritlop was born in the former Yugoslavian town of St. Laszlo, and his wines have an Eastern European feeling. He built the first winery in the Similkameen Valley (1984), although the 10 acres of vineyards—originally called Keremeos Vineyards—were planted as early as the 1970s. Ritlop is another industry maverick, having planted an eclectic variety of grapes, including such table grapes as Clinton and Interlaken. He believes in natural yeast fermentation and uses no chemicals. His son Joe Jr., who took over as winemaker, has introduced more classic varieties as well as fruit wines made from a range of berries, pears, peaches, and cherries. He has the largest collection of fruit and berry wines in the province, including a unique off-dry wine made from rose petals. I asked him how he made it and he replied, "It's a trade secret." Joe Sr. will tell you: "I will create my own wine in my own fashion. I cannot do anything else. We can make as good or better white wines here as in any European country."

The 4,000-square-foot winery, which Joe Jr. describes as "quaint" and I'd describe as unpretentious, is 1 kilometre east of Keremos, on Highway 3.

The Seven Stones Winery
(formerly Harmony-One Vineyards)

1143 HIGHWAY 3, CAWSTON, BC V0X 1C0 (250) 499-2144
SEVENSTONES@METHOP.NET

YEAR FOUNDED: 2000 **FOUNDER:** George and Vivianne Hanson
WINEMAKER: Alan Marks **GRAPE VARIETIES:** (red) Cabernet Sauvignon, Cabernet Franc, Syrah, Merlot, Pinot Noir; (white) Chardonnay
RECOMMENDED WINE: Meritage

George Hanson spent twenty-four years in the Yukon in the telecommunications industry before moving to the Similkameen Valley to fulfill a lifelong ambition to grow grapes and make wine—a dramatic change of climate and lifestyle. Initially, he named his gravity-flow winery Harmony-One because he saw himself as a conductor orchestrating all the different elements that go into winemaking. In 2005 Hanson changed the name to The Seven Stones, because there are seven rock formations in the valley, each with its own legend. "We thought this would be an interesting theme and we could provide valley information to our visitors to add to their experience," he says. The green-painted building that houses the winery and the tasting room is a 1,200-square-foot former workshop situated on sloping benchland overlooking the magnificent Similkameen River Valley and the mountains beyond. The summer heat in the valley has forced Hanson to install aerial sprinklers in his vineyard to irrigate the vines. The sprinklers are turned on at night, to avoid loss of precious water through evaporation. The talented winemaker Alan Marks, who produces Icewines for Paradise Ranch, makes the wine here.

Vancouver Island and the Wine Islands

The unofficial name the "Wine Islands" indicates that this wine-growing region is no longer just the preserve of Vancouver Island. In addition to the main island's sixteen wineries, there are now six vineyard and winery operations on four Gulf Islands scattered between Vancouver Island and the mainland. The Cowichan Valley around Duncan and the Saanich Peninsula northeast of Victoria account for almost 200 of the province's 5,500 acres, while the Gulf Islands' plantings total just under 100 acres.

Vancouver Island itself offers an exotic mix of seaside vistas, rich meadowland, lush rainforest, and forested mountains. The Gulf Islands make up an almost subtropical archipelago connected by a ferry system, which beguiles travellers with breathtaking scenery and seaside village destinations.

In average years the region enjoys warm, sunny summers, with most of the rainfall occurring in the winter months. In the growing season, warm days are followed by mild overnight temperatures that create a very shallow day-to-night temperature gradient, the exact opposite of the Okanagan. As in the Niagara region, which is tempered by the great reservoir of Lake Ontario, the islands are sometimes cosseted, at other times buffeted, by their proximity to the ocean. The more level temperatures favour a softer acid balance, which nudges the harsher tartaric acid into balance with the mellower malic acid. The wines reflect this quality, with a softer flavour profile that frames subtle but rich fruit character with clean, discrete acid.

A number of the wineries, such as Alderlea, Blue Grouse, Venturi-Schulze, and Vigneti Zanatta, pride themselves on growing and making wines exclusively from their estate-grown grapes. Others bring in selected varieties to augment their own production or to tide them over until their own young vineyards come on stream. Grape varieties that do well in the region include Siegerrebe, Gewurztraminer, Pinot Gris, Madeleine Sylvaner, Ortega, Pinot Noir, and Maréchal Foch, though more demanding varieties such as Merlot and Viognier are successful if plastic tents are erected over the rows in the spring to promote early growth and an earlier harvest. It's essential that all varieties have early ripening dates, because fungal activity associated with rains in later September often brings the growing season to an end. The payback, of course, is that Victorians enjoy pansies and other flowers in full bloom in February.

Try to stay for the sunsets; they are amazing and so, too, are the endless and relaxing views of fir-covered mountains and placid lakes. The artists who have settled on this and the smaller neighbouring islands have created a vibrant artisan community with their galleries, studios, potteries, and craft shows, as well as flourishing summer theatre and outdoor concerts. One sight not to miss is the 55-acre Butchart Gardens in Brentwood Bay, 20 kilometres north of Victoria.

TOURING WINERIES
on Vancouver Island and the Wine Islands

From Victoria, you can take either Highway 1 north, where the greatest concentration of wineries is to be found, or Highway 17 north, along the Saanich Peninsula towards Swartz Bay (the ferry point for Salt Spring and Saturna islands), where you'll find four wineries en route. It's best to call ahead and make appointments.

SINGLE DAY: Head north on Highway 1 to Alderlea Vineyards at Duncan, stopping on the way at Glenterra and Venturi-Schulze. Or, if you're pressed for time, concentrate on the wineries off Highway 17—Church & State for the architecture (and Butchart Gardens), Chalet Estate for lunch at Deep Cove Chalet across the road, and Marley Farm for the experience. If you want to avoid Victoria or the Malahat, you can take the Mill Bay ferry at Brentwood Bay by the airport, which takes you to Mill Bay, south of Duncan, and puts you in winery country—a trip of about twenty-five minutes.

WEEKEND: If you need pampering and great food, stay at Sooke Harbour House in Sooke on Whiffen Spit (a twenty-minute drive west of Victoria) or the Victoria Regent Hotel in Victoria. Visit Venturi-Schulze, Glenterra, and Alderlea. Stay the night in Duncan and take the Tsawwassen ferry from Swartz Bay (a thirty-five-minute car ride from Victoria) to the Gulf Islands or from Chemainus to Thetis Island. In the summer season the ferries are busy, and you may have to wait because of heavy traffic.

VANCOUVER ISLAND & THE WINE ISLANDS WINERIES

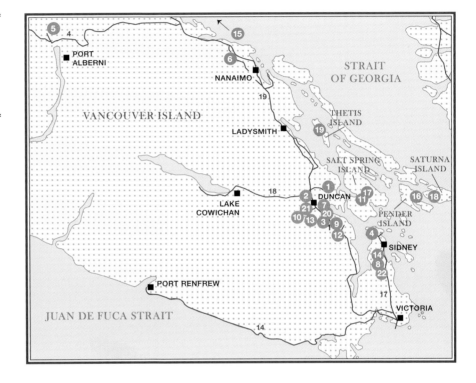

Alderlea Vineyards

1751 STAMPS ROAD, DUNCAN, BC V9L 5W2 (250) 746-7122

YEAR FOUNDED: 1998 **FOUNDERS:** Roger and Nancy Dosman
WINEMAKER: Roger Dosman **GRAPE VARIETIES:** (red) Maréchal Foch, Pinot Noir; (white) Bacchus, Pinot Gris, Auxerrois, Gewurztraminer
RECOMMENDED WINES: Auxerrois-Chardonnay, Pinot Gris, Pinot Noir, Merlot

Roger Dosman planted his vineyard in 1992 with some thirty different grape varieties. Through trial and error, he has winnowed these down to half a dozen but still feels he's producing too many labels (eight, including a port-style wine called Hearth). His two-storey white house is set in the middle of the vineyard, with a small tasting room attached. Dosman's meticulous care of the vineyard (he tents his Viognier, Merlot, and Pinot Noir with plastic sheets to protect them against spring frosts) and his careful winemaking have produced some of the best wines on

Nancy and Roger Dosman of Alderlea Vineyards.

the island. He produces a Maréchal Foch under the proprietary label Clarinet that sells out quickly. The Dosmans operate without email or website. "They find me," he says. Worth the effort, I'd say.

Entrance to Blue Grouse Estate. RIGHT: Blue Grouse founders
Hans and Evangeline Kiltz.

Averill Creek Vineyards

6552 NORTH ROAD, DUNCAN, BC V9L 6K9 (250) 715-7379
WWW.AVERILLCREEK.CA

YEAR FOUNDED: 2001 **FOUNDER:** Andy Johnston **WINEMAKER:** Andy
Johnston **GRAPE VARIETIES:** (red) Four clones of Pinot Noir, Merlot;
(white) Pinot Gris, Gewurztraminer **RECOMMENDED WINES:** not tasted

British-born Andy Johnson, a wine-loving doctor, spent
downtime from his Edmonton clinic by volunteering as a
cellar rat for vintages in Tuscany, Australia, France, and
New Zealand. The winemaking bug took hold and, after
over thirty years of medical practice, he searched Europe
and New Zealand for a suitable vineyard site. Eventually,
at the insistence of his family, he returned to his adopted
roots and settled on Vancouver Island, north of Duncan.
The steep southern slope of Mount Prevost, where he
purchased his property, is ideal for a gravity-feed winery—
the first on the island. The winery takes its name from a
small creek that flows through the property.

Blue Grouse Estate

4365 BLUE GROUSE ROAD, DUNCAN, BC V9L 6M3 (250) 743-3834
WWW.BLUEGROUSEVINEYARDS.COM

YEAR FOUNDED: 1989 **FOUNDERS:** Hans and Evangeline Kiltz
WINEMAKERS: Hans Kiltz, Richard Kiltz **GRAPE VARIETIES:** (red) Pinot
Noir, Gamay Noir, Black Muscat; (white) Pinot Gris, Ortega, Bacchus,
Siegerrebe **RECOMMENDED WINES:** Ortega, Pinot Gris, Black Muscat

Hans Kiltz's family has owned vineyards in Germany's
Rhine region for over three hundred years. When he and
his family immigrated to Canada, they bought a farm on
Vancouver Island in 1988. On the 31-acre property, carved
out of the forest, they found a neglected vineyard (the
first on Vancouver Island, planted by John Harper). A
trained veterinarian specializing in large animals, Kiltz
became a farmer; he revived the vineyard and began
making wine purely as a hobby. He loved it and, in 1993,
established a commercial operation, Blue Grouse, named
after the birds whose natural habitat it was. The wood-
panelled tasting room under the family home looks out
on to the vineyard and the evergreens beyond, making it
a relaxing spot to taste Kiltz's crisp German-style wines.
A special treat is his unique Black Muscat, the only one
grown in Canada.

Chalet Estate Winery

11195 CHALET ROAD, NORTH SAANICH, BC V8L 5M1 (250) 656-2552
WWW.CHALETESTATEVINEYARD.CA

YEAR FOUNDED: 2001 **FOUNDERS:** Michael Betts and Linda Plimley
WINEMAKER: Michael Betts **GRAPE VARIETIES:** (red) Cabernet
Sauvignon, Merlot and Syrah purchased from Osoyoos; (white) Ortega,
Bacchus, Pinot Gris **RECOMMENDED WINES:** Ortega, Cabernet Merlot

This winery is ideally situated across the road from one
of Vancouver Island's best restaurants, Deep Cove Chalet,
with its winkingly grumpy Swiss chef Pierre Koffel. If you

JOHN HARPER

THE UNSUNG HERO OF BC'S MODERN WINE INDUSTRY

Were it not for John Harper's pioneering efforts, the flourishing
vineyards of the Fraser Valley and Vancouver Island might not
be as advanced as they are today. When he died in 1991 at
the age of eighty-five, *B.C. Wine Trails* magazine wrote of the
legendary grape grower: "John Harper devoted his life to
grape growing and other horticultural pursuits. After working
as field man for major wineries, he undertook his own experiments with grape varieties at Cloverdale and later moved to
a larger site near Duncan, which is now Blue Grouse Vineyards.
John continued his varietal research on another location
which … became Glenterra Vineyards winery, and where his
neatly labelled rows of varietals can still be seen as part of
the present vineyards. The number of people who either knew
John or heard of his work is impressive, particularly on
Vancouver Island, where his experiments and trials of different
varietals laid the foundation for many of the present vineyards.
In fact, one of his dreams that was never realized was to
establish a winery of his own."

John Harper worked as a vineyardist for Andrés and Jordan
Ste. Michelle in the 1970s. In 1983 he retired to a farm on
Vancouver Island and began planting experimental vineyards
with material he had propagated at Cloverdale. The winery he
dreamed of would be realized by Hans Kiltz at Blue Grouse.
Harper advised Harry von Wolff at Château Wolff to plant Pinot
Noir and other premium varietals in his Nanaimo vineyard. He
also advised Claude Violet on what to plant in the Fraser Valley.
Marilyn Schulze at Venturi-Schulze recalls her husband,
Giordano Venturi, telling her he had purchased cool-climate
varieties from Harper in the 1970s: "It was after discovering
that John had moved to the Cowichan Valley to plant a vineyard
that Giordano seriously considered the area for his own vineyard. John propagated our Pinot Gris vines for us and he used
to pop by now and again to ask, 'So, how's my row doing?'
He passed away before the vines bore fruit, and we will sorely
miss being able to share a glass with him." Venturi-Schulze
now honours his memory with a wine they call Harper's Row,
a rich, fruity blend of Pinot Gris and Schönburger.

don't want to linger al fresco in the restaurant's garden, you sit on the winery's umbrella-shaded patio and enjoy winemaker Michael Betts's award-winning Pinot Gris. Betts, an Englishman, was taught his craft by the talented Frank Supernak. The winery boasts a large reception hall, which doubles as a barrel room when not in use for wedding receptions. In the small tasting room hangs a framed photo of the company president wearing half-moon glasses—an aging border collie named Cody whose recumbent body takes up much of the floor space.

Chase & Warren Estate Winery

6253 DRINKWATER ROAD, PORT ALBERNI, BC V9Y 8H9 (250) 724-4906
CHASEANDWARREN@SHAW.CA

YEAR FOUNDED: 2002 **FOUNDERS:** Vaughan Chase and Ron Crema
WINEMAKER: Vaughan Chase **GRAPE VARIETIES:** (red) Pinot Noir;
(white) Chardonnay, Bacchus, Muscat, Gewurztraminer
(and thirty other experimental varieties) **RECOMMENDED WINES:**
Gewurztraminer, Bacchus

Chase & Warren is off the beaten track and may not be on your route unless you are heading for the national parks of Port Alberni. This tiny facility (520 cases in all), with its 12-acre vineyard perched above the Alberni Valley on a southwest-facing glaciated slope, has the distinction of being the most westerly winery in Canada. Vaughan Chase planted "some decorative Gewurztraminer," which made a wine of sufficient quality that his brother-in-law, Ron Crema, encouraged him to plant other varieties. In 1966 the two of them did so with a vengeance. The wines they produce are Germanic in style.

Below the winery, a steam train takes visitors to and from the historic heritage site of McLean Mill. This is salmon-fishing country—Port Alberni styles itself the "Salmon Capital of the World"—so bring your rod if you have a mind. There is no Warren, incidentally—Vaughan Chase, a schoolteacher, thought that the pairing sounded more euphonious.

Château Wolff

2534 MAXEY ROAD, NANAIMO, BC V9S 5V6 (250) 753-9669
CHATEAUWOLFF@SHAW.CA

YEAR FOUNDED: 1987 **FOUNDER:** Harry von Wolff **WINEMAKER:** Mark
Hurworth **GRAPE VARIETIES:** (red) Pinot Noir, Dornfelder; (white)
Chardonnay, Bacchus, Viognier **RECOMMENDED WINES:** Pinot Noir,
Grand Rouge (dessert wine)

You can't get much smaller than Château Wolff's production (400–500 cases annually from 6 acres of organically farmed grapes), and you can't beat them for supreme optimism. Château Wolff is the most northerly winery on Vancouver Island, and the late Harry von Wolff chose to

plant Pinot Noir, Chardonnay, and Viognier—notoriously difficult varieties to ripen in a maritime climate. Yet they do, thanks to the naturally protected vineyard and the exposure to sunlight.

Von Wolff's European heritage is evident in the tasting room, with its large tapestry of the medieval city of Heidelberg. His years as a hotel food and beverage director, together with his love of Burgundy, led him to plant Pinot Noir and to make it for long aging. From the rocky cliff that towers above the vineyard, you get a great view of Mt. Benson and the valley below. The family intend to honour Harry von Wolff's dream by continuing to operate the winery.

Cherry Point Vineyards

840 CHERRY POINT ROAD, COBBLE HILL, BC V0R 1L0 (250) 743-1272
WWW.CHERRYPOINTVINEYARDS.COM

YEAR FOUNDED: 1994 **FOUNDERS:** Wayne and Helena Ulrich
WINEMAKERS: Simon Spencer, Todd Moore **GRAPE VARIETIES:** (red)
Pinot Noir, Agria, Castel; (white) Pinot Gris, Pinot Blanc, Auxerrois,
Ortega, Gewurztraminer, Müller-Thurgau, Siegerrebe, Ehrenfelser
RECOMMENDED WINES: Gewurztraminer, Valley Mist, Valley Sunset,
Blackberry Port

One of the glories of Cherry Point is the flower garden Helena Ulrich planted when she and her husband bought the property in 1990. The luxuriant profusion of blooms owes much to the sheep that graze on the property and the gravelly soil. Set among the flowers is a vast wine barrel that supports one end of the arbour and once doubled as a dog house for its erstwhile occupant—a welcoming Bouvier-wolfhound named T-Bone. Wayne Ulrich planted thirty-two varieties before narrowing

TOP: Cherry Point Vineyards plantings. ABOVE: The vineyard's entrance. RIGHT: Helena and Wayne Ulrich and Simon Spencer of Cherry Point.

down to eleven, and he was one of the first to plant the early ripening Hungarian variety Agria.

In addition to a portfolio of ten table wines, the winery produces a "port" made from blackberries. In the spring of 2004 the winery was purchased by the Cowichan Tribes, the largest First Nations community in British Columbia, making it the second band-owned-and-operated winery in North America (after Nk'Mip Vineyards) and the third in the world. This Native connection is reflected in Cherry Point's use of the sun symbol on its labels. The Cowichans plan to expand production, using fruit from other vineyards on their land. To capitalize on the success of the blackberry port, they have built a new Solera Room to age the wine. The wines on the lowest tier are partially drawn off for bottling and then topped up from barrels of a younger vintage.

Church & State Wines
(formerly Victoria Estate Winery)

1445 BENVENUTO AVENUE, BRENTWOOD BAY, BC V8M 1J5 (250) 652-2671
WWW.CHURCHANDSTATEWINES.COM, RESTAURANT: MADELEINE'S BISTRO,
(250) 652-2671

🍾 🍷$ 🍽 ⚙

YEAR FOUNDED: 1999 **FOUNDERS:** Eric von Krosigk and Fraser Smith
WINEMAKER: Bill Dyer (consultant) **GRAPE VARIETIES:** (red) Pinot Noir;
(white) Pinot Gris **RECOMMENDED WINES:** Pinot Noir Brut, Gamay, Merlot

Church & State, situated between Butterfly Gardens and Butchart Gardens on the Saanich Peninsula, is unashamedly geared to the tourist trade. Visitors enjoy tastings and cellar tours in the vast, barn-like building (21,000 square feet). The impressive redwood structure houses the winery, a shopping area, and a tapas bistro,

Madeleine's. Three-quarters of the grapes come from the Okanagan and Similkameen valleys, though the adjacent vineyard has thirty experimental varieties, which will be whittled down to a dozen. In the spring of 2005 Victoria businessman Kim Pullen took over the struggling winery, bought 14 acres of land along the Golden Mile to plant a vineyard, dumped $2 million worth of substandard wine, and hired Californian Bill Dyer as his consulting winemaker. Dyer, who made wine at Sterling Vineyards in Napa and currently consults to Marimar Torres in Sonoma, was the man who created the stylish wines for Burrowing Owl.

Divino Estate Winery

15100 FREEMAN ROAD, COBBLE HILL, BC V0R 1L0 (250) 743-2311
DIVINOWINERY@AOL.COM

YEAR FOUNDED: 1982 **FOUNDER:** Joseph Busnardo **WINEMAKER:** Joseph Busnardo **GRAPE VARIETIES:** (red) Cabernet Sauvignon, Merlot, Pinot Nero; (white) Tocai, Malvasia, Pinot Bianco, Pinot Grigio, Trebbiano, Chardonnay **RECOMMENDED WINES:** Pinot Grigio, Pinot Noir

Joe Busnardo marches to a different drum. A gruff, no-nonsense Italian immigrant, he bought his first farm in 1967 in Oliver. Against the advice of the wineries to which he would supply his crop, he imported twenty-six vinifera varieties from a friend's experimental vineyard in his native Treviso, plus fifty-six varieties from California's UC Davis. He was one of first to plant Pinot Bianco (Pinot Blanc) in BC, a grape that is now almost emblematic of the province's white wines. He sold the original winery, which opened its doors in 1982 in the Okanagan (now renamed Hester Creek Vineyards), and in 1996 bought his current property on Vancouver Island. Busnardo's passion for grape growing—particularly Italian varieties—and his aversion to oak barrels make for highly individual wines. You either love them or you don't.

Echo Valley Vineyards

4651 WATERS ROAD, DUNCAN, BC V9L 3Y2 (250) 748-1477
WWW.ECHOVALLEY-VINEYARDS.COM

YEAR FOUNDED: 2003 **FOUNDER:** Albert Brennink **WINEMAKER:** Eric von Krosigk **GRAPE VARIETIES:** (red) Gamay Noir, Pinot Noir, Agria, Dunkelfelder, Maréchal Foch; (white) Chardonnay, Chasselas, Gewurztraminer, Pinot Gris, Kerner **RECOMMENDED WINES:** Kerner, Pinot Gris

Albert Brennink, a Dutch-born architect, and his son Edward own a farm near Duncan which raised beef cattle. In 1999 they cleared 25 acres of land to plant an experimental vineyard at the foot of the Koksilah Ridge in the Cowichan Valley. They intended to farm organically and to irrigate the vines with their own well water

Ripe Gewurztraminer grapes at Glenterra Vineyards await harvest.

sourced from mountain streams. The Brennicks' European heritage is evident in the respect they have for the wine-making traditions of the specific regions where the grapes they grow originated. Their Chardonnay is made in Chablis style, their Pinot Gris in Alsace style, and their Kerner is resolutely Germanic. They also make a Gamay Nouveau as a winegrower in Beaujolais might.

Like other Vancouver Island vintners, they found that Ortega and Agria do best in their climate, and they have also had success with Alsace varieties such as Pinot Gris, Pinot Blanc, and Gewurztraminer.

Garry Oaks Winery

1880 FULFORD-GANGES ROAD, SALT SPRING ISLAND, BC V8K 2A5
(250) 653-4687 WWW.GARRYOAKSWINERY.COM

YEAR FOUNDED: 2000 **FOUNDERS:** Marcel Mercier and Elaine Kozak **WINEMAKER:** Elaine Kozak **GRAPE VARIETIES:** (red) Pinot Noir, Zweigelt, Léon Millot; (white) Pinot Gris, Gewurztraminer **RECOMMENDED WINES:** Pinot Gris, Pinot Noir, Fetish

Marcel Mercier, an environmental consultant, and Elaine Kozak, an economist, gave up the corporate world in 1999 to purchase a hundred-year-old fruit farm on Salt Spring Island. They created their terraced vineyard by carving out steep, south-facing, sandy-gravelly loam slopes at the foot of Mt. Maxwell that overlook the Burgoyne Valley. The 3,000-square-foot winery, with its gabled roof

Glenterra Vineyards

3897 COBBLE HILL ROAD, COBBLE HILL, BC V0R 1L0 (250) 743-2330
WWW.GLENTERRAVINEYARDS.COM

YEAR FOUNDED: 2000 **FOUNDERS:** John Kelly and Ruth Luxton
WINEMAKER: John Kelly **GRAPE VARIETIES:** (red) Pinot Noir; (white)
Pinot Gris, Pinot Blanc, Gewurztraminer **RECOMMENDED WINES:**
Vivace, Brio, Meritage

You can still discern John Kelly's Scottish burr even though he's been in British Columbia since 1969. His passion for wine eventually made him sell his business (making reflective products for road builders), take a course in oenology at Okanagan College, and look for property on Vancouver Island. The vineyard that Kelly and his partner, Ruth Luxton, puchased in 1998 was the second that John Harper had planted on Vancouver Island (Harper's first vineyard now belongs to Blue Grouse). As homage to Harper, John Kelly has maintained the original 1-acre plot with its forty different varieties, and he makes two wines from their grapes, Vivace (white) and Brio (red). The music-inspired Vivace is BC's most complicated wine—a blend of Müller-Thurgau, Bacchus, Pinot Gris, Siegerrebe, Schönburger, Ortega, Auxerrois, Chasselas, Ehrenfelser, Muscat, Wurzer, Huxelrebe, Regent, and Cantaro. Its red counterpart, Brio, is hardly less so, made from Dornfelder, Zweigelt, Dunkelfelder, Agria, Fruhburgunder, Lemberger, Haroldrebe, Maréchal Foch, Korento, and Merlot.

Glenterra's winery and tasting room are located in a garage-sized structure painted blue, and a patio-style restaurant is planned for 2006. As you sample the wines in the tiny tasting area, you can see into the winery proper with its tanks and barrels. Spend an hour here for historical reasons—and for the quality of Kelly's wines.

Godfrey-Brownell Vineyards

4911 MARSHALL ROAD, DUNCAN, BC V9L 6T3 (250) 715-0504
WWW.GBVINEYARDS.COM

YEAR FOUNDED: 1999 **FOUNDER:** David Godfrey **WINEMAKER:** David
Godfrey **GRAPE VARIETIES:** (red) Pinot Noir, Gamay, Cabernet
Sauvignon, Merlot, Maréchal Foch, Agria, Lemberger, Dunkelfelder;
(white) Pinot Gris, Chardonnay, Bacchus **RECOMMENDED WINES:** Pinot
Gris, Merlot

David Godfrey, a former English professor whose family grew grapes on their Cadboro Bay property, began looking for a site to plant his own 20-acre vineyard in 1993. It took him five years to find what he was looking for at the price he was willing to pay—in the Cowichan Valley. Godfrey didn't know then that the property he had chosen had once belonged to a second cousin of his grandmother whose name was Amos Brownell. Hence the name he gave his winery. Godfrey favours buxom red wines, as you

and cedar siding, consists of a compound with two buildings—the main processing facility and the barrel room, connected by a courtyard. Set on a slope, one wall of the barrel room, which doubles as a tasting room, is half underground, and that helps to maintain an even cellar temperature.

"I'm from pioneering stock," Elaine Kozak will tell you. "I grew up on a farm, and working the land never quite leaves your blood. Marcel was a science nerd with a sense of mischief who tended to poke around wherever curiosity led him (but where he shouldn't necessarily have been). In his teens, for example, he almost blew up his father's plumbing shop with the not-quite-kosher still he assembled in the attic."

Marcel Mercier may have been a self-taught distiller, but he learned his winemaking at his grandmother's knee, helping her make fruit wines in Alberta.

The name Garry Oaks comes from a species of oak tree, *Quercus garryana*, a.k.a Oregon white oak, which is unique to the Pacific Northwest region and grows on Salt Spring Island. The winery ages its Pinot Noir in barrels made from the Garry oak. The owners call their Bordeaux blend Fetish, rather than Meritage, and offer a unique Blaufrankisch called Labyrinth. They also have a small labyrinth marked out in stones between the old orchard and the pond.

Combine a visit here with the ferry ride and a day's outing on Salt Spring Island—especially on Saturday, the market day—and you'll have a memorable experience.

Saturna Island.

can tell from the varieties he has in his vineyard. Godfrey-Brownell, in partnership with the Oak Bay Beach Hotel, hosts a gourmet cycling tour through the Cowichan Valley. En route you get to visit a bakery and a *fromagerie* before arriving at the winery for a picnic with David Godfrey's wines.

Marley Farm Winery

1831D MOUNT NEWTON CROSS ROAD, SAANICHTON, BC V8M 1L1
(250) 652-8667 WWW.MARLEYFARM.CA

YEAR FOUNDED: 2000 **FOUNDERS:** Michael and Beverly Marley
WINEMAKER: Eric von Krosigk **GRAPE VARIETIES:** (red) Pinot Noir; (white) Pinot Grigio, Ortega **RECOMMENDED WINES:** Pinot Gris, Novine Red

Historically, Saanich has been a berry-growing area where the province's first wines were made, but the Marleys (Michael is a second cousin to reggae legend Bob Marley) always wanted their own grape winery. Set in the Mount Newton valley, the farm has sheep and geese that help with the weeding—and the fertilizing—now that the 5

acres of vines are planted. You'll find horses, chickens, turkeys, and pigeons—the whole farming experience—so it's a great place to bring the kids. The busy Eric von Krosigk produced the first wines from the 2001 vintage. The tasting room and wine boutique (painted in jazzy purple, yellow, and red, with a bleached wood ceiling) are housed in a stylishly contemporary building with an open-air restaurant at the back. In addition to the grape wines, Marley Farm also makes blackberry, kiwi, loganberry, and raspberry wine.

Marshwood Estate Winery

548 JADE ROAD, HERIOT BAY, QUADRA ISLAND, BC V0P 1H0 (250) 285-2068
MARSHWD@CONNECTED.BC.CA

YEAR FOUNDED: 2004 **FOUNDERS:** Kerry and Martina Kowalchuk
WINEMAKER: Kerry Kowalchuk **GRAPE VARIETIES:** (red) Pinot Noir; (white) Ortega, Agria, Pinot Gris, Dornfelder **RECOMMENDED WINE:** Ortega

Marshwood Estate, the first commercial winery to open on Quadra Island, is located on the east side of the island close to Rebecca Spit Provincial Park. The facility is nestled within 160 acres of woodland and marsh at the headwaters of Drew Creek, its vineyard planted on a long, wide slope of glacial moraine facing southwest. The Kowalchuks ran a successful commercial diving business, harvesting the ocean for octopus and sea cucumbers that they exported to the Far East. Now they harvest their land for grapes, raspberries, and strawberries. They learned to make wine by opening the island's first make-your-own-wine establishment, U-Vin, and, before they preached, they practised with the kits. "Ten years ago it was just an idea in our minds," says Martina, "and we began clearing the scrubby, over-logged land." They carved out roads with earth-movers and, in 1996, began planting a test plot of eighty Ortega vines. In 2004 Kerry and Martina Kowalchuk released their first grape and fruit wines.

Morning Bay Vineyard

6621 HARBOUR HILL ROAD, PENDER ISLAND, BC V0N 2M1 (250) 629-8351
WWW.MORNINGBAY.CA

YEAR FOUNDED: 2003 **FOUNDER:** Keith Watt **WINEMAKERS:** Keith Watt, Eric von Krosigk **GRAPE VARIETIES:** (red) Pinot Noir, Maréchal Foch; (white) Pinot Gris, Gewurztraminer, Riesling, Schönburger
RECOMMENDED WINES: not tasted

This new vineyard on Pender Island looks very dramatic from the air—a great bowl of terraces carved out of the forested hillside. Keith Watt, a former radio personality from Winnipeg, is convinced his top terraces will produce "some of the best Pinot Noir in Canada." The temperature profile, he claims, is closer to the coastal regions of California than anywhere else in Canada, and his 30-degree slope gives him great exposure and drainage. He got his winery experience working at Saturna Island Vineyards, and he began planting his own 6-acre vineyard in 2002. His first release of 2002 wines was made by Eric von Krosigk from Okanagan grapes. At the time of writing the winery is under construction, but the two-storey building will be large enough to host weddings and other events. The year 2005 will see the first vintage that uses Pender Island grapes.

Saltspring Island Vineyards

151 LEE ROAD, SALT SPRING ISLAND, BC V8K 2A5 (250) 653-9463
FAX: (250) 653-9464 WWW.SALTSPRINGVINEYARDS.COM

YEAR FOUNDED: 1997 **FOUNDERS:** Bill and Janice Harkley
WINEMAKERS: Paul Troop, Janice Harkley **GRAPE VARIETIES:** (red) Pinot Noir, Léon Millot; (white) Pinot Gris, Chardonnay **RECOMMENDED WINE:** Pinot Blanc

"We practice organic methods, which is a nice way of saying we have weeds," says Janice Harkley, an accountant by training, now a dedicated grape grower, winemaker, and blackberry picker. She and her husband, Bill, a retired Air Canada pilot, bought the property in 1998 and opened a B&B with two bedrooms (rated 4 kisses in the romantic travel guide *Best Places to Kiss in the Northwest*). Their 3-acre sandy vineyard adjacent to a gravel pit is set high on Lee Hill overlooking the Fulford Valley, so high in fact that a late spring frost does not concern the Harkleys, as their vineyard is unlikely to be touched by it. If you've cycled from Fulford Harbour to Ganges, here's where you would stop and admire your accomplishment of making the hill. You'll see a winery building that looks like a cross between a barn and a chapel, although it was built in 2001.

In 2002 the Harkleys received the first winery licence granted on Salt Spring Island. "We enjoyed that distinction for exactly one half-hour," recalls Janice, as Garry Oaks, their neighbour down the hill, received theirs thirty minutes later. Saltspring's colourful label features "Eartha," a voluptuous earth goddess floating above the island like a Chagall cartoon. Since 2003 they have bottled their whites under screwcap (good for them!). They also make a delicious port-style wine from wild blackberries. Visitors can sample locally made cheeses paired with Saltspring Vineyards wines.

Saturna Island Vineyards

8 QUARRY TRAIL, PO BOX 54, SATURNA ISLAND, BC V0N 2Y0
(250) 539-5139; 1-877-918-3388 WWW.SATURNAVINEYARDS.COM
RESTAURANT: SATURNA ISLAND VINEYARDS BISTRO, (250) 539-3521

YEAR FOUNDED: 1995 **FOUNDERS:** Lawrence and Robyn Page
WINEMAKER: Daniel Lagnaz **GRAPE VARIETIES:** (red) Pinot Noir, Merlot, Pinot Meunier; (white) Chardonnay, Pinot Gris, Gewurztraminer, Muscat
RECOMMENDED WINES: Semillon Chardonnay, Chardonnay

From the air, Saturna Island Vineyards' Falconridge vineyard, sited on the second largest of the Gulf Islands at the southern end of the chain, presents a dramatic picture: a carpet of green running from a bench above the rocky shoreline to a sheer granite and sandstone cliff face stippled with pine and arbutus trees. The winery's 60 acres of vines, planted between 1995 and 2000, are divided into four vineyards—Rebecca's Vineyard (named for lawyer Larry Page's daughter), Robyn Vineyard (named for his wife), Longfield Vineyard, and the largest vineyard, Falconridge, adjacent to the winery. The vineyards have to be fenced off from the hungry attentions of feral goats. The winemaking facility is housed in a 10,000-square-foot steeply roofed barn, not far from the post-and-dowel wine shop, with a bistro that serves light lunches in the summer season. Ultimately, a cooking school and Vineyard Inn are planned. On Canada Day the islanders hold a lamb barbecue in Winter Cove Marine Park at the other end of the island.

Baskets of Pinot Noir grapes after harvest at Vigneti Zanatta Winery. OPPOSITE: Marilyn Schulze and Giordano Venturi of Venturi-Schulze Vineyards.

Thetis Island Vineyards

90 PILKEY POINT ROAD, THETIS ISLAND, BC V0R 2Y0 (250) 246-2258
WWW.CEDAR-BEACH.COM, ACCOMMODATION: CEDAR BEACH OCEAN LODGE,
(250) 246-2258

YEAR FOUNDED: 2004 **FOUNDER:** Colin Sparkes **WINEMAKER:** Colin Sparkes **GRAPE VARIETIES:** (red) Pinot Noir, Merlot, Dornfelder, Agria, Shiraz, Pinotage, Cabernet Sauvignon; (white) Pinot Gris, Gewurztraminer, Chardonnay, Sauvignon Blanc **RECOMMENDED WINES:** not tasted

Colin Sparkes, an Englishman given to mountain climbing and sea kayaking, and his partner, Carola Daffner, a German who shares his taste for adventure, run an oceanfront B&B (formerly "an English gentleman's country retreat") on Thetis Island. To prove to would-be vacationers that the climate is Mediterranean, they planted 1,800 vines, including such warm-weather varieties as Shiraz and Pinotage. They are also playing it safe with cool-climate early ripeners such as Dornfelder and Agria. The winery, a small lean-to that processes the fruit from the south-facing hillside vineyard at the centre of the island (a ten-minute walk from the beach), is protected on three sides by stands of arbutus. Sheep graze in the 10-acre vineyard and control the grass, which grows between the rows of vines and holds moisture in the sandy, gravelly soil. The couple's border collie sheepdog, Katinka, has proven more effective than electric fences in deterring birds, deer, and raccoons from eating the grapes. In addition to touring the vineyard and tasting, the B&B offers kayaking, cycling, Finnish sauna, swimming, snorkelling, and wildlife spotting. A romantic getaway for the wine lover or sports enthusiast, Thetis Island attracts an international clientele.

Venturi-Schulze

4235 TRANS-CANADA HIGHWAY, COBBLE HILL, BC V0R 1L0 (250) 743-5630
WWW.VENTURISCHULZE.COM

YEAR FOUNDED: 1993 **FOUNDERS:** Giordano Venturi, Marilyn Schulze **WINEMAKERS:** Giordano Venturi, Michelle Schulze, Marilyn Schulze **GRAPE VARIETIES:** (red) Pinot Noir; (white) Pinot Gris, Kerner, Siegerrebe, Schönburger, Ortega, Chasselas, Auxerrois **RECOMMENDED WINES:** Brut Rosé, Pinot Noir, Indigo

Giordano Venturi, from Italy, and Marilyn Schulze, who is originally from Australia, purchased a hundred-year-old farm in 1988. Through hard work, they have created a small, garage-style operation that has become something of a hidden treasure, given how difficult it is to acquire these wines. The couple's perfectionism can be seen in the pristine condition of the vineyard, which sees no chemicals and is farmed without irrigation. "This is the island. We've got to roll with the punches," says Venturi. To combat the twin threats of inclement weather and birds, he has to tent the vines with plastic in early spring to protect against late frost and to ensure ripeness, and he nets the entire vineyard in the late summer against the birds.

Venturi-Schulze wines are highly individual and intense; the lesser-known varieties are given proprietary brand names—Indigo for Schönburger, Sole for Kerner, and Brandenberg 3 for Madeleine Sylvaner. The couple raised a lot of eyebrows in 1996 when they bottled their entire portfolio of wines, including sparkling, under crown caps to avoid cork taint. Today the industry is catching up to them with the use of screwcaps. In addition to the wines, Venturi, a native of Modena, makes a popular balsamic vinegar.

The couple live in a much-renovated and expanded 1893 farmhouse adjacent to the winery and the isolated vinegar house (you don't want vinegar near wine because it will turn the wine). This winery is a must-taste situation, but watch out for the sign; Venturi-Schulze is on the Trans-Canada Highway, but it's hard to find. An appointment is imperative, as the proprietors "value their privacy and spend as much time as possible in the vineyard and winery."

Vigneti Zanatta Winery

5039 MARSHALL ROAD, DUNCAN, BC V9L 6S3 (250) 748-2338
WWW.ZANATTA.CA, RESTAURANT: VINOTECA, (250) 709-2279

YEAR FOUNDED: 1989 **FOUNDERS:** Zanatta family **WINEMAKERS:** Jim Moody, Loretta Zanatta **GRAPE VARIETIES:** (red) Pinot Noir; Castel, Léon Millot, Cabernet Sauvignon, Merlot; (white) Auxerrois, Cayuga, Madeleine Sylvaner, Ortega, Pinot Gris, Siegerrebe **RECOMMENDED WINES:** Ortega, Pinot Grigio, Fatima Brut

Dennis Zanatta, true to his Italian heritage, planted vines to make his own wine on the 120-acre farm he purchased

in 1958. Those initial plantings in a 5-acre plot, along with more than one hundred varieties, became part of the Duncan Project in the 1980s, a forward-thinking government-sponsored experiment to discover the best wine grapes to grow in this cool region. Zanatta sent his daughter Loretta to the Veneto region in Italy, where they make Prosecco, to study winemaking (she specialized in sparkling wines) and, on her return, the family opened the first winery on Vancouver Island. The winery uses only island-grown fruit, one of the few that do. In 1996 the Zanatta family restored their charming 1903 farmhouse, with its wrap-around porch, and created a wine bar–restaurant that serves delicious country-style food grown on the farm or by their neighbours. Loretta and her husband, Jim Moody, now run the winery; Dennis Zanatta is retired and tends his own vineyards. There's a lot of island wine history here as one of the first vineyards on the island.

Winchester Cellars

6170 OLD WEST SAANICH ROAD, VICTORIA, BC V9E 2G8 (250) 920-7042
WWW.WINCHESTERCELLARS.COM

YEAR FOUNDED: 2004 **FOUNDER:** Ken Winchester **WINEMAKER:** Ken Winchester **GRAPE VARIETIES:** (red) Pinot Noir, Maréchal Foch; (white) Ortega, Bacchus, Pinot Gris, Chardonnay **RECOMMENDED WINES:** Pinot Noir, Pinot Gris

Ken Winchester spent fourteen years in California, though he confesses to being a Burgundian at heart ("I'm all about French oak"). His specialty is Pinot Noir, and his first efforts, tasted from the barrel, are very encouraging. He is also a trained distiller and will be making grappa and brandy in addition to his wines. Winchester began making wine in Montreal in 1983 as a home winemaker. While working as the editorial director for a publishing house in San Francisco, he took a course in oenology and viticulture at California's UC Davis. Following a stint in Paso Robles growing grapes and making wine, he returned to Canada to become winemaker at Victoria Estate (now renamed Church & State). He has the only certified organic vineyard on Vancouver Island, one of three in the province. Drive down a tree-shaded farm lane, and you reach the two-storey converted red barn ("It was single storey," says Winchester. "We literally raised the roof"). On the lower floor, two sets of double doors open up to the barrel room. A wide wooden staircase leads to the second-floor tasting room—as comfortable as your own living room, with a sofa and a fireplace. If Ken Winchester is in the cellar, he can usually be persuaded to pull a barrel sample or two to illustrate the mystery of Pinot Noir, the Holy Grail of wine grapes, the most difficult to grow and vinify. In 2005 Winchester was the only Canadian invited with his Pinot Noir to the prestigious International Pinot Noir Conference in Oregon, where producers of this legendary "heartbreak" grape gather every year.

CHAPTER THREE

ONTARIO

Ontario is the largest wine region in Canada and the best known internationally. As of 2005, there were 130 operating wineries in the province (including fruit wineries), eighty-five of which make VQA wines. So successful has the industry become that it has attracted the attention of the Burgundy shippers Boisset, Michel Picard, and Michel Laroche, as well as local entrepreneurs who are willing to invest millions of dollars to make Ontario wine. You have only to tour the wineries in Niagara to see the extent of such investment in vineyard development, infrastructure, and winemaking hardware.

The architecture of the facilities ranges from the traditional French château style (Château des Charmes, Peller) to Ontario Gothic (Peninsula Ridge, Angels Gate) to contemporary (Jackson-Triggs, Stratus, Tawse, Flat Rock, Fielding, and Huff). Every wine region needs a magnet and, when it is built, Vincor's Le Clos Jordanne will attract visitors from all over the world. This joint-venture project between Vincor and Boisset will be housed in a unique building designed by the pre-eminent Canadian architect Frank Gehry. The critical mass of wineries in the Niagara Peninsula has created a "Napa North"

PREVIOUS SPREAD: Harvesting grapes at Cave Spring Cellars.
BELOW: Alfresco wine tasting at Château des Charmes.

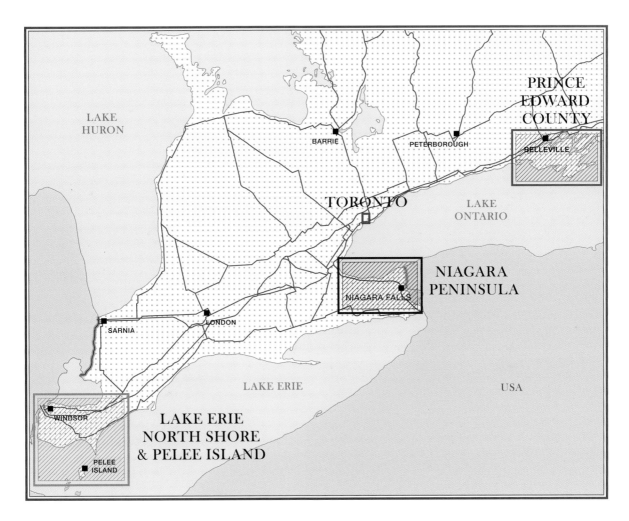

THE WINE REGIONS OF ONTARIO

phenomenon. Fine restaurants, cooking classes, bike tours, concerts, theatre, jazz festivals, and winery events have generated a tourism boom that sees bus-loads of local and foreign visitors flocking through winery tasting rooms.

After seeing Niagara Falls, everyone, it seems, wants to discover Ontario wines. Lake Erie North Shore has suddenly blossomed with a host of new wineries, and this growing number will attract tourists to the southwest corner of the province. Ontario's newest region, Prince Edward County, already has the infrastructure in place—the restaurants, B&Bs, festivals, and activities—to entice the wine traveller. It all adds up to a one compelling idea: Ontario wine is glamorous, and the world has begun to take notice.

The cradle of the Canadian wine industry was not the Niagara Peninsula, where the greatest vineyard

acreage is to be found, but a good 70 kilometres north in a town named Cooksville. Today it is part of Mississauga, a city of 680,000 people just west of Toronto. It was here, on the banks of the Credit River, that a retired German soldier, Corporal Johann Schiller, settled on 20 acres of land granted to him by the Crown for his military service in Canada in the early years of the nineteenth century. Schiller, the acknowledged father of Canadian wine, had winemaking experience in the Rhine Valley of his native land. By 1811 he had domesticated the wild labrusca vines that grew along the banks of the Credit River and supplemented them with American hybrids from Pennsylvania. Schiller made enough wine to satisfy his own needs and to sell to his neighbours.

There is no documentary evidence about Schiller's winery enterprise over the years, but an

Harvesting Gewurztraminer grapes at Strewn Winery.
OPPOSITE: Freshly picked grapes at Cave Springs Cellar.

enterprising French aristocrat, Count Justin M. de Courtenay, resurrected it in 1864 as the Vine Growers Association. De Courtenay doubled the size of the vineyard by planting Clinton and Isabella grapes. His label, Clair House, became the largest brand in Ontario, and his wine was exhibited in Paris to celebrate Canada's nationhood in 1867. In the same year, a farmer in Queenston named Porter Adams was shipping grapes to the Toronto market for home winemakers, and John Kilborn, a farmer who owned 17 acres on Ontario Street in Beamsville, was selling his wine locally for $1.75 a gallon. With typical vintners' braggadocio, he wrote in the *Canadian Agriculturalist* that his wine "probably would bring in more if we asked for it. At all events it is worth four times as much as the miserable stuff sold by our merchants under the name of wine."

Winemaking in the late nineteenth century was more of a basement hobby than a business. When it was not sold through the kitchen door, it would have been available at the local drugstore. The problem for those early winemakers, whether they made it for their own consumption or for profit, was the alcohol level. Native hybrids such as Isabella and Catawba are low in sugar but high in acidity, so sugar had to be added during fermentation to bring up the alcohol level.

The first growers along the Niagara Peninsula mostly planted their vines to service the fresh fruit trade. One of the best table varieties, as well as a much-favoured taste in jams and jellies, was the Concord grape, whose flavour is familiar to us today in grape juice and virtually all grape-flavoured products. This hardy, unkillable grape was propagated by a Massachusetts grower who rejoiced in the name of Ephraim Wales Bull. He named it after the town he lived in.

The only problem with the Concord grape is that it makes awful wine, and, ever since 1988, it and its labrusca kin have been banned from Ontario table wines. As grape juice it can be enjoyable, but when fermented it concentrates a natural chemical compound called methyl anthranilate that gives the wine the unfortunate odour of an agitated fox. Yet Concord, because it was easy to grow and gave high yields, was to become the workhorse grape of the Ontario wine industry up until the 1940s. And, as the major component in the "Duck" range of pop wines, the Concord grape provided 90 percent of company profits until the late 1970s. (In order to mask the foxy bouquet and flavour, Canadian wineries indulged in the questionable practice of "stretch"—the addition of sugar, colouring agents, and water. An imperial ton of grapes can yield about 160 gallons of wine. Through stretching, the large commercial wineries were able to get up to 2,400 litres, or 620 gallons, per tonne.)

The Americans sent not only their grapes north but their entrepreneurs, too. In the 1860s most of the winemaking operations in Ontario were small-volume enterprises, a sideline for farmers who had crops other than grapes to harvest. In 1866 "a

company of gentlemen from Kentucky," according to a letter in the *Canadian Farmer*, "who have been in the grape business for 14 years, have purchased a farm on Pelee Island and planted 30 acres this spring, and intend to plant 20 acres next spring." They named their winery Vin Villa, the stone ruins of which can still be seen on the island. Vin Villa sold grapes and finished wine to an enterprising grocer in Brantford, Major J.S. Hamilton, whose store was granted a royal charter to sell wine and liquor in 1871. Eventually Hamilton took over Vin Villa, and the company that bore his name was sold in 1949 to London Winery (which was acquired by Vincor in 1996).

By 1890 there were thirty-five commercial wineries in Ontario, two-thirds of which were located in Essex County in the southwest of the province. The pre-eminence of Essex as Canada's grape-growing centre lasted for thirty years. By 1921 the grape vines—close to 2,000 acres—had been torn out and replaced by more profitable cash crops such as tobacco and soft fruit. A mere 50 acres of vines remained, but this concentration was still greater than anywhere else in Canada.

In 1873 George Barnes started a winery in St. Catharines on the banks of the old Welland Canal. There was no mistaking the company's purpose in the name on the wine label: Ontario Grape Growing and Wine Manufacturing Company, Limited. What this moniker lacked in imagination, it compensated for in longevity. The company operated as Barnes Wines until 1988, when Château-Gai purchased it.

George Barnes's vines had been in the ground for one year when Thomas Bright and his partner, F.A. Shirriff, opened a winery in Toronto. In naming it the Niagara Falls Wine Company, the pair must have instinctively realized they would have to move nearer their grape supply—and move they did in 1890, to the outskirts of that border town. In 1911 the company changed its name to T.G. Bright and Company. Over eighty years later, Cartier and Inniskillin would merge with T.G. Bright to form Vincor, Canada's largest winery.

The closing years of the nineteenth century showed remarkable growth for Ontario's wine

TOP: Pinot Noir under netting at Cave Springs Cellars.
ABOVE: Tying off vines in early spring in Jordan.
RIGHT: Century-old wine barrel at Pelee Island Winery.

industry. By the advent of the twentieth century, the Niagara Peninsula boasted 5,000 acres under vine. But two events set the burgeoning wine industry off on a path of incipient self-destruction: the First World War and Prohibition. When the war broke out, the government's need for industrial alcohol to make explosives synchronized with the popular sentiment for Prohibition, and, within two years, the distilleries were converted to the production of industrial alcohol for the war effort. The *Ontario Temperance Act* was passed on September 15, 1916, by the government of Sir William F. Hearst, himself an active Methodist layman and dedicated temperance advocate. All bars, clubs, and liquor stores would be closed for the duration of the war. Amazingly, a strong grape growers' lobby managed to have native wines exempted from the provisions, and wine became the only alcoholic beverage that could be sold legally in the province.

When Prohibition was introduced, there were ten operating wineries in Ontario. When it finally ended on October 31, 1927, the Board of Liquor Commissioners had granted no fewer than forty-seven licences. Prohibition, more than any other factor, had turned Canadians into a nation of wine drinkers. In 1920, some 21 million Canadians consumed 221,985 gallons of domestic wine. A decade later the figure was 2,208,807 gallons—for Ontario alone. The favourite by far (80 percent) was a red port-style wine of maximum alcoholic strength made from Concord grapes. (These products were known affectionately as "block & tackle wines"—after consuming a bottle, you could walk a block and tackle anyone.)

In an effort to regulate both the production of wine and the growing public consumption, the government created the Liquor Control Board of Ontario—with the emphasis on control. Big companies such as Brights and Jordan began buying up the licences of less viable operations—not for their equipment or stock but for the retail store that each winery was allowed to operate. Through these amalgamations, the number of wineries in Ontario was reduced from sixty-one to eight, and no new licences would be granted until 1975, when two

VINCOR INTERNATIONAL

441 COURTNEY PARK DRIVE EAST
MISSISSAUGA, ON L5T 2V3 (416) 504-3647

Vincor International is Canada's largest wine producer. From its origins as Château-Gai and Brights Wines, it is now better known through its individual winery labels: Inniskillin, Sawmill Creek, Braeburn Cellars, Ancient Coast, L'Ambiance, Jackson-Triggs, and Le Clos Jordanne in Ontario; and Sumac Ridge, Hawthorne Mountain Vineyards, Inniskillin Okanagan, Jackson-Triggs, and Osoyoos Larose in British Columbia. Vincor also owns wineries in Quebec, New Brunswick, California (R.H. Phillips), Washington State (Hogue Cellars), Western Australia (Goundrey, Amberley), New Zealand (Kim Crawford), and the United Kingdom (Western Wines). And it operates a chain of wine retail stores called the Wine Rack.

In the first decade after it was founded in 1993, Vincor became a wine company of international stature. Thanks to an aggressive acquisition strategy, it is currently the fourth-largest wine conglomerate in North America after E. & J. Gallo, Constellation, and the Wine Group.

Chronology

1874 Niagara Falls Wine Company established
1889 Cartier Wines founded
1911 Niagara Falls Wine Company renamed T.G. Bright & Company
1975 Inniskillin founded
1986 Brights acquires Jordan & St. Michelle Cellars
1989 Management buyout of Cartier Wines
1992 Cartier Wines acquires Inniskillin
1993 Cartier-Inniskillin merges with Brights to become Vincor; Jackson-Triggs label launched
1996 Vincor buys Dumont Vins et Spiritueux in Quebec; Vincor acquires Okanagan Vineyards; Vincor acquires London Winery
1997 Vincor acquires RJ Grape Inc.
1998 Vincor acquires R.J. Spagnols Wine & Beer Making Supplies Ltd.; Vincor acquires Groupe Paul Masson winery in Quebec; Le Groupe Taillan and Vincor plant the Osoyoos Larose vineyard in BC
1999 Le Clos Jordanne Winery and Vineyards established with Boisset of Burgundy
2000 Vincor buys Sumac Ridge and Hawthorne Mountain Vineyards in BC
2001 Vincor buys Hogue Cellars, Washington State; Jackson-Triggs opens Niagara winery
2002 Vincor buys Goundrey Wines in Western Australia
2003 Vincor buys Kim Crawford Wines of Auckland, New Zealand
2004 Vincor buys Amberley Estate of Margaret River, Australia; Vincor buys Western Wines in the UK

small boutique operations were started—Inniskillin and a sparkling-wine facility named Podamer. These two fledgling wineries joined the six big boys: Barnes, Brights, Château-Gai, Jordan, London, and Andrés.

Ontario wines were still being made from labrusca varieties and hybrids such as Maréchal Foch, Baco Noir, Seyval Blanc, and Vidal. Although Brights had been experimenting with Chardonnay as early as 1955, the Horticultural Research Institute in Vineland warned growers against planting vinifera varietals, which, it said, could not survive Canadian winters. The major thrust of the commercial wineries was to blend off-shore wines with their locally grown product, a practice legitimized by the *Wine Content Act* of 1972. Two years before, Andrés had sold off the Ontario vineyards it had purchased in 1962, and Brights soon followed Andrés' lead.

A few dedicated growers, including Bill Lenko and John Marynissen, defied the conventional wisdom and planted Chardonnay and Cabernet Sauvignon in their Niagara Peninsula vineyards; and a youthful nurseryman named Donald Ziraldo supplied interested growers with vinifera plants from his Niagara-on-the-Lake farm. Hermann Weis, who owns St. Urbans-Hof winery in the Mosel, provided his Weis clone Riesling to interested growers and eventually set up his own winery, Vineland Estates, in Ontario.

The seminal event in Ontario's wine story occurred in 1974, when Donald Ziraldo and his Austrian partner, Karl Kaiser, made the first batch of Maréchal Foch from their own grapes in a converted barn on the Niagara Parkway. The following year they got their licence as Inniskillin and moved to their current location just west of the Ziraldo nursery. The co-founders of Ontario's first new retail winery since Prohibition had one clear standard: 100 percent locally grown wines, preferably vinifera. Inniskillin became the model for an exciting new breed of estate or farm wineries that made wines from their own vineyards: Château des Charmes (1978), Newark (1979, now Hillebrand), Reif Estate (1982), Vineland Estates (1983), Konzelmann Estates (1984), Stoney Ridge (1985), Cave Spring Cellars (1986), and Henry of Pelham (1988).

Barrel-aging cellar at Jackson-Triggs Niagara Estate Winery.

The philosophies and practices of these new vintners were enshrined in the regulations of the Vintners Quality Alliance (VQA), the single most important piece of legislation to save the industry from extinction. The small players had become the engine that propelled Ontario wines, dragging the large commercial players reluctantly along in their combined wake.

The small estate wineries captured consumers' palates, and the Big Six (Andrés, Barnes, Brights, Château-Gai, Jordan, and London) found their market share eaten into by these new upstarts. To increase revenues, the Big Six expanded into other provinces and began to consolidate. Brights bought Jordan; Château-Gai snapped up Barnes. In 1989 a buyout of Château-Gai from Labatts by a team of its managers, led by Allan Jackson and Don Triggs, created Cartier Wines, a company destined to swallow up Inniskillin, Brights, and London before turning its gaze on British Columbia, Quebec, and then the world.

Once Ontario's VQA wines began to win medals in international competitions—and, more important, the hearts and taste buds of Ontario consumers—new entrepreneurs emerged to start their own wineries. Between 1990 and 2003 the total rose to thirty-six. This second wave of small wineries included farmers who saw bigger profits from making wine than from selling their grapes to the major wineries. It also included second careerists who had been successful in other enterprises and looked at wineries as both an investment and a lifestyle choice.

While the old guard were influenced by their winemaking experience in France and Germany or by their taste for European wines, the new winemakers were more New World in their vision. They had been trained in oenology in Australia (Joe Will at Strewn, Sue-Ann Staff at Pillitteri), had winemaking experience in South Africa, New Zealand, and the United States, or were the first graduates from the Cool Climate Oenology and Viticulture Institute (CCOVI) and Niagara College.

The industry is currently redefining itself with subappellations in the Niagara Peninsula, an exercise in differentiating soil types and microclimates that will add another layer of sophistication and complexity to consumer choice. The emergence of a fourth viticultural area in Ontario, Prince Edward County, to join Niagara Peninsula, Lake Erie North Shore, and Pelee Island, is only the beginning of this quest for new and less costly land on which to plant vineyards. Already intrepid growers are moving as far north as Thunder Bay, Owen Sound, Roseneath, and Collingwood and as far east as Chesterville. With global warming, who knows how far north vineyards will be planted in the future?

NIAGARA PENINSULA SUBAPPELLATIONS

In November 2004 the Vintners Quality Alliance announced the establishment of eleven subappellations of the Niagara Peninsula. The region, located on the northern shore of Lake Ontario and reaching inland to the Niagara Escarpment, was first designated as the Niagara Peninsula appellation in 1988. The concept is to differentiate the varying soils and microclimates that affect the flavour and style of the wine grown in that particular zone.

The boundaries of these newly created subappellations were determined by the physical characteristics of the zones—climate (the most important factor), topography, soil, and geology, as well as practical considerations such as keeping contiguous vineyards within a given subregion.

The use of a subappellation name on a wine label will be optional and will not necessarily denote a

Mechanical harvesting of Riesling grapes in Jordan, Ontario.

superior product. Quality and content standards will remain the same as for Niagara Peninsula–designated wines. Subappellation wines must contain at least 85 percent of wines from the stated subregion, with up to 15 percent from within the boundaries of the Niagara Peninsula appellation. In the near future, labels will carry such designations as Niagara Lakeshore, Niagara River, Four Mile Creek, Beamsville Bench, St. Davids Bench, Short Hills Bench, Lincoln Lakeshore, Twenty Mile Bench, Creek Shores, and Vinemount.

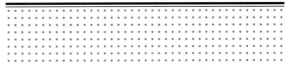

UNITY WINES

UNITY WINE
CABERNET SAUVIGNON-MERLOT
2002

Canada's major wine regions are separated by vast distances, and winemakers usually restrict their grape purchases to a small geographic area within their own appellation. In 2003, however, Vincor released a Chardonnay and Cabernet Sauvignon Merlot from the 2001 vintage under the Unity Wine label, which they repeated in 2002.

Following the Australian model, in which wines from different regions can be blended, Vincor's chief winemaker, Rob Scapin, blended wines made from grapes grown in the Niagara Peninsula with wines produced in BC's Okanagan Valley. The grapes came from Jackson-Triggs properties in both regions, and the final blend was bottled in Ontario. "It's all about learning how wines made in different climatic regions, with different geographical characteristics and different soils, can work to bring the very best out of each other," says the Australian-born Scapin. "Several New World countries, and Australia in particular, move wine between appellations to craft sensational wines that both capture and enhance the best of their diverse terroirs."

Because unity wines are a blend of two appellations, they do not as yet qualify for the Vintners Quality Alliance designation. Even without the blessing of a VQA label, these wines show what can be done when the best barrels of each appellation are blended. Bring it on, I say.

Lake Erie North Shore could also be divided into three subappellations, while Pelee Island is a homogenous appellation of its own. Prince Edward County is waiting to be designated the province's fourth viticultural area.

This further refinement in the appellation process may well be confusing for the consumer. But it will subtly differentiate wine styles and give the winemaker the opportunity to express the flavours that relate directly to the unique soil structure, microclimates, and exposures of a given district.

Niagara Peninsula (See map on page 140)

The Niagara Peninsula is Ontario's fruit and salad bowl, a place where you could plant a walking stick and it would take root and blossom. It is easier to catalogue what does not grow in this fertile crescent than what does.

This region may not be as scenically stunning as other wine regions of the world (South Africa, for example, Germany's Mosel Valley, or BC's Okanagan Valley), but where else can boast such attractions as Niagara Falls and the *Maid of the Mist* boat, the historic town of Niagara-on-the-Lake, the Shaw Festival, and the British stockade Fort George? Add in the restaurants, the hiking and biking trails, and all the events staged by the wineries throughout the year, and you have an irresistible destination for both the wine connoisseur and those who are only mildly wine curious. The proximity to the New York State border makes the Niagara Peninsula an easy destination for American tourists.

We owe the incredibly rich soils of the vineyards here to our southern neighbours. The slow, inexorable square dance of glaciers during the Late Pleistocene and Early Holocene periods deposited their sediments in beds stripped bare by even earlier glacier drifts. From sandy loam to silty clay over shale bedrock, these soils came to us courtesy of Wisconsin—soils rich in minerals and trace elements that add complexity to Ontario's Chardonnays, Pinot Noirs, and Cabernet.

The Niagara Peninsula is situated just north of the 43rd parallel, placing it squarely between latitudes 30° and 50°, the global band where wine grapes flourish. If you trace the latitude as it runs through Europe, you'll find that it passes through such respected wine regions as the Côtes du Rhône, Chianti Classico, and Rioja. Then again, these European appellations are not blessed with Canadian winters, which can start late in the fall and last into April, making for a comparatively short growing season. Niagara summers, when they come, are usually very hot, but their heat in wine country is moderated by the lake effect. Lakes Ontario and Erie create offshore winds that cool the vines in summer and, in favoured sites on the Niagara Escarpment, carry away the frost in winter. The lakes also act as hot-water bottles, storing the heat of summer and giving it off in winter.

The Escarpment that runs from Hamilton, Ontario, to Watertown, New York, is the major reason why the Niagara Peninsula is able to support viticulture. Constantly eroding, it used to be the coastline of a primordial sea. Now it runs parallel to Lake Ontario and rises over 200 metres above sea level at its highest point. This massive rock formation, 430 million years old—nearly twice as old as the Appalachian Mountains—existed well before the first Ice Age and gave birth to Niagara Falls.

A combination of wind, water, and rock makes grape growing possible in a landscape that can be covered with snow for as much as six months of the year. The warm air blown ashore from the lakes runs up the face of the Escarpment and, as it cools, it falls back down the slope in a circular motion. This constant, tumbling airflow carries away frost and dries the vines, protecting them from rot.

TOP: Horseshoe Falls, Niagara Falls. ABOVE: April magnolia blossoms, Niagara-on-the-Lake.

TOURING WINERIES
in the Niagara Peninsula

There are more than sixty wineries in the Niagara Peninsula alone, so it would take you a few weeks to visit them all. If all you can spare is a day or two, plan a trip that does not involve a lot of driving. The concentration of wineries breaks down into three well-defined areas: Winona–Grimsby–Beamsville, Vineland–Jordan–St. Catharines, and Niagara-on-the-Lake. Most tourists want to head directly for Niagara-on-the-Lake because it is one of the prettiest towns in Canada and replete with history. In the summer months, however, its streets, shops, and restaurants are busy with tourists. From the maps provided here, select an area you would like to visit and zero in on a route that will take you to no more than four or five wineries a day (unless you're a wine writer or have a competent designated driver with navigational abilities).

Winona-Grimsby-Beamsville area

SINGLE DAY: If you're coming from Toronto, your first destination should be farthest from home. Don't miss Peninsula Ridge (for lunch or dinner), Angels Gate, Fielding Estate, and Crown Bench.

WEEKEND: If you want to stay in the area, head on the second day for Thomas & Vaughan, Mountain Road, and Crown Bench and then go to Legends on the lake side of the Queen Elizabeth Way (QEW).

Vineland-Jordan–St. Catharines area

SINGLE DAY: Wineries not to be missed here are Tawse, Vineland Estates (lunch on the terrace), Flat Rock, and Cave Spring Cellars (dine at On The Twenty).

WEEKEND: Add Malivoire, Willow Heights, Stoney Ridge, and Creekside.

Niagara-on-the-Lake area

SINGLE DAY: Don't miss Jackson-Triggs and Stratus, which are next door to each other, and Inniskillin. For a change of pace, drop in on Marynissen.

WEEKEND: On day two, try the wineries along the lakeshore, Strewn and Konzelmann, then Peller Estates, Lailey, and Château des Charmes.

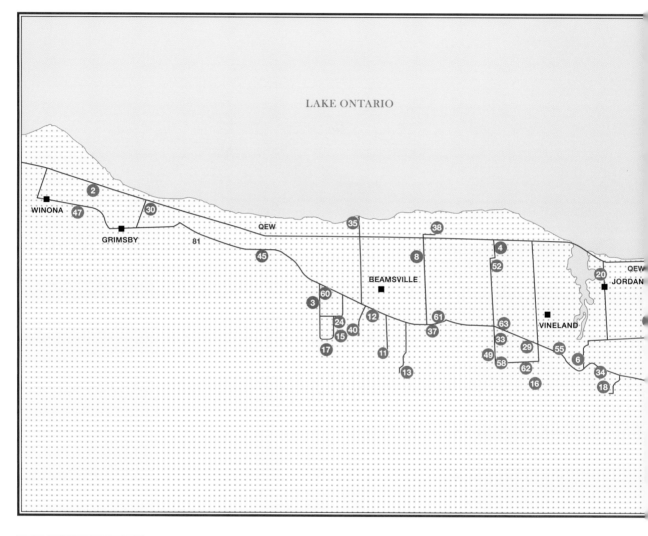

LAKE ONTARIO

NIAGARA
PENINSULA
WINERIES

1 ANCIENT COAST WINES
2 ANDRÉS WINES
3 ANGELS GATE WINERY
4 BIRCHWOOD ESTATE WINES
5 CAROLINE CELLARS WINERY
6 CAVE SPRING CELLARS
7 CHÂTEAU DES CHARMES
8 CORNERSTONE WINERY
9 COYOTE'S RUN ESTATE WINERY
10 CREEKSIDE ESTATE WINERY
11 CROWN BENCH ESTATES
   WINERY
12 DANIEL LENKO ESTATE WINERY
13 DE SOUSA WINE CELLARS
14 DOMAINE VAGNERS
15 EASTDELL ESTATES WINERY
16 FEATHERSTONE ESTATE
   WINERY & VINEYARD

17 FIELDING ESTATE WINERY
18 FLAT ROCK CELLARS
19 FROGPOND FARM
20 HARBOUR ESTATES WINERY
21 HARVEST ESTATE WINES
22 HENRY OF PELHAM FAMILY
   ESTATE WINERY
23 HERNDER ESTATE WINES
24 HIDDEN BENCH VINEYARDS
   AND WINERY
25 HILLEBRAND ESTATES WINERY
26 INNISKILLIN WINES
27 JACKSON-TRIGGS NIAGARA
   ESTATE WINERY
28 JOSEPH'S ESTATE WINES
29 KACABA VINEYARDS
30 KITTLING RIDGE ESTATE
   WINES & SPIRITS

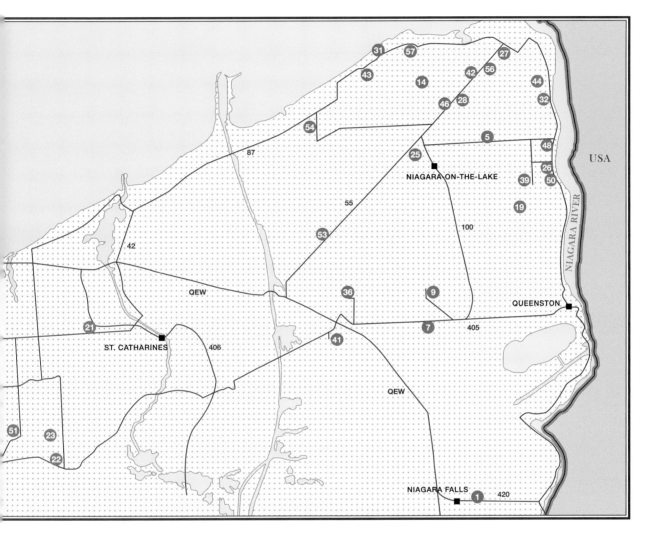

Angels Gate Winery. OPPOSITE: Entrance to Andrés Wines.

Alvento Winery

3048 SECOND AVENUE, VINELAND, ON L0R 2E0 (905) 562-1212
BMOOS@TOTAL.NET

YEAR FOUNDED: 2001 **FOUNDERS:** Morrie Neiss, Elyane Grenier,
and Bruno Moos **WINEMAKER:** Bruno Moos **GRAPE VARIETIES:** (red)
Merlot, Cabernet Franc, Nebbiolo; (white) Viognier **RECOMMENDED
WINES:** not tasted

From 1983 through 1999, Elyane and Bruno Moos ran a
winery in Soiana, Tuscany, where they made Sangiovese
(a Chianti-style wine) and Vermentino (a white wine)
from 7.5 acres of land situated on top of a typical Colline
Pisane hill. The wines were good enough to be com-
mended in Italy's leading wine guide, *Gambero Rosso*.
Frustrated by Italian bureaucracy, they sold the winery
and moved to Niagara. In 2001 they purchased land on
the west side of Jordan Harbour, across from Harbour
Estate. The winery, adjacent to the red-brick house where
the couple live, is in an old barn that has been renovated
and augmented. "It's not a big monument," says Moos,
"but it looks neat. It has character and is very efficient."
Unfortunately, the initial planting of vines was destroyed
by the freezing winter of 2002, but the couple persevered.
Bruno Moos's intention is to follow the Chianti model
and to age his red wines for two years in French oak and
then for one year in the bottle. The first release in 2006
will be a 2004 vintage of a Bordeaux-style blend. The
winery plans to open in 2006.

Ancient Coast Wines

4887 DORCHESTER ROAD, NIAGARA FALLS, ON L2E 6N8
WWW.ANCIENTCOAST.COM

YEAR FOUNDED: 2000 **FOUNDER:** Vincor International **WINEMAKER:**
Mira Ananicz **GRAPE VARIETIES:** (red) Baco Noir, Cabernet Franc,
Cabernet Sauvignon, Merlot; (white) Vidal, Chardonnay, Riesling,
Auxerrois **RECOMMENDED WINE:** Vidal Icewine

Ancient Coast is a label for a series of inexpensive varietal
wines created by Vincor in 2000. The attractive label
design with fossils embedded in rock represents the Niagara
Escarpment, "a vast limestone spine that snakes through
the Great Lakes region. The escarpment was in prehistoric
times the shore of an immense lake that receded and left
fossils in the rocks." These everyday wines exhibit a light
fruit character. Tastings are available at the store
attached to the winery.

Andrés Wines

697 SOUTH SERVICE ROAD, GRIMSBY, ON L3M 4E8 (905) 643-4131

YEAR FOUNDED: 1970 **FOUNDER:** Andrew Peller **WINEMAKER:** Heidi
Montgomery **GRAPE VARIETIES:** supplied by growers **RECOMMENDED
WINE:** Domaine d'Or

Andrés is a name synonymous with Baby Duck, probably
the first wine that most Canadians growing up in the

WIND MACHINES

1970s and 1980s ever tasted. The company was founded by Andrew Peller, a Hungarian immigrant. He opened the British Columbia plant in Port Moody in 1961 and the Ontario plant in 1969. The company also has bottling facilities in Nova Scotia and Alberta, where such popularly priced wines as Hochtaler and Domaine d'Or (blended with offshore wines) still bear the Andrés label. The company has over 100 stores under the Vineyard Estates Wines banner and owns Hillebrand and Thirty Bench in Ontario and Casabello, Sandhill, and Red Rooster in BC. To distance themselves from the Baby Duck image, the company created the Peller Estates label in 1997 and built a monumental château-style winery, also called Peller Estates, in Niagara-on-the-Lake.

Angels Gate Winery

4260 MOUNTAINVIEW ROAD, BEAMSVILLE, ON L0R 1B2 (905) 563-3942;
1-877-ANG-GATE WWW.ANGELSGATEWINERY.COM

YEAR FOUNDED: 2000 **FOUNDERS:** A group of Toronto investors
WINEMAKER: Natalie Spytkowsky **GRAPE VARIETIES:** (red) Cabernet Franc, Cabernet Sauvignon, Gamay, Pinot Noir, Syrah, Merlot; (white) Chardonnay, Gewurztraminer, Riesling **RECOMMENDED WINES:** Chardonnay Old Vines, Cabernet Franc, Merlot

In 1995 a group of thirteen Bay Street investors with a passion for wine planted a 10-acre vineyard on land once owned by the Congregation of Missionary Sisters of Christian Charity—hence the angelic connection. In the

In spite of global warming, vineyards can be destroyed when early fall frosts or Canadian winters that last into spring freeze the vines. On January 27, 2005, the mercury dipped to –28° Celsius. Such polar temperatures are not unusual between December and March—making Ontario a consistent producer of Icewine. With such temperatures, labrusca and hybrid varieties are less at risk, but the tender *Vitis vinifera*, the favoured wine grapes, can be wiped out in a single night. A vinifera vine can tolerate temperatures down to approximately –23° Celsius for a short time as long as the sap has not risen—when the vine is dormant. Below that temperature there will be extensive bud damage, resulting in crop loss or, even worse, damage to the canes and the graft.

Altering the ambient temperature around the vines can save a vineyard from destruction. Growers can protect their vines by installing wind machines mounted on 10 metre steel towers. The blades, 5.5 metres in diameter, similar to those of a helicopter, are driven by gas or liquid propane. Their intermittent action—rotating once every four or five minutes—draws the warmer air above the vines down to canopy level, mixing it with the colder air at vine level. This action can raise the temperature around the grape clusters as much as five degrees. The wind machines cost between $25,000 and $45,000 each, and the cost of running them in a 50-acre vineyard for a night can be $1,500 in fuel alone. Expensive, but not as expensive as having to replant a vineyard and wait three years for the first commercial crop. Since 2003, many wineries have been incorporating this technology into their vineyards, and there are now more than 200 wind machines in the region.

1950s the property was used as a mink farm and then abandoned when fur went out of favour. A new winery was built in 2001 and opened for visitors a year later. Lunch is served on the patio. The winery, across the road from Thirty Bench, also owns a 25-acre vineyard 5 kilometres away. Natalie Spytkowsky is a talented young winemaker whose Chardonnay 2003 was chosen as the official white wine of the Legislative Assembly of Ontario in 2004.

Birchwood Estate Wines

4679 CHERRY AVENUE, BEAMSVILLE, ON L0R 1B1 (905) 562-VINE (8463);
1-866-644-2524 WWW.BIRCHWOODWINES.CA

YEAR FOUNDED: 2000 **FOUNDER:** Andrew Green **WINEMAKERS:**
Thomas Green, Jason Roller (assistant) **GRAPE VARIETIES:** (red)
Cabernet Sauvignon, Cabernet Franc, Baco Noir, Gamay Noir, Pinot
Noir, Merlot; (white) Riesling, Seyval, Gewurztraminer, Chardonnay,
Auxerrois, Pinot Gris, Vidal **RECOMMENDED WINES:**Gewurztraminer/
Riesling, Auxerrois, Pinot Noir, Cabernet Franc Icewine

You can easily miss this small winery as you flash by on the QEW in the direction of St. Catharines. But if you take the South Service Road exit, you arrive at a small driveway marked at the entrance by two wine barrels. The winery is a simple shed in weathered grey barn wood, standing on the plain leading up to the Beamsville Bench in its own vineyard—a tranquil retreat from the traffic of the motorway nearby. For such a small property, it's had a colourful history: it was owned formerly by Willow Heights and, before that, named Vine Court. Andrew Green of Diamond Estate Wines founded the current winery.

Thomas Green and Jason Roller share the winemaking duties here with those at Diamond Estates' other properties: Lakeview Cellars, Thomas & Vaughan, and EastDell. The Salmon River label is reserved for large-volume blended VQA wines, and, generally, you'll find solid, unpretentious, wallet-friendly wines here. The Icewine samples are free, unlike those at most other wineries, where there is a small charge.

Caroline Cellars Winery

1028 LINE 2, VIRGIL, ON L0S 1T0 (905) 468-8814 WWW.LAKEITFARMS.COM

YEAR FOUNDED: 2002 **FOUNDERS:** Rick and Elfriede Lakeit and family
(Justine, Stephanie, Rick Jr., and Jaclyn) **WINEMAKERS:** Rick Lakeit,
Mike Komar **GRAPE VARIETIES:** (red) Cabernet Franc, Cabernet
Sauvignon, Pinot Noir, Baco Noir, Maréchal Foch, Merlot; (white) Vidal,
Riesling, Chardonnay, Sauvignon Blanc, Pinot Gris **RECOMMENDED
WINES:** Late Harvest Riesling, Cabernet Franc

Four generations of Lakeits have farmed and grown grapes in the Niagara Peninsula. In 1978 Caroline Lakeit helped her son Rick, one of her nine children, to realize his dream of owning his own farm. Today the Lakeit family, who are related to the Hernder family, still live and work that same piece of property on the outskirts of Niagara-on-the-Lake. In memory of his mother, Rick Lakeit named the winery after her. The gabled winery building, with its timbered tasting bar and wine boutique, has rustic charm.

Upstairs, the loft, with its pine-planked walls, high peaked ceiling, and maple hardwood floor, can accommodate 120 people for private events. Jens Gemmrich of Frogpond consults on the winemaking, which is carried out by Rick Lakeit and Mike Komar. Komar is a student winemaker from the Cool Climate Oenology and Viticulture Institute. Caroline Cellars also produces a range of fruit wines.

CLOCKWISE FROM TOP LEFT: The vineyard at Caroline Cellars Winery; On the Twenty Restaurant at Cave Spring Cellars; Len Pennachetti of Cave Spring; wine shop at Cave Spring.

Cave Spring Cellars

3836 MAIN STREET, JORDAN, ON L0R 1S0 (905) 562-3581
WWW.CAVESPRING.CA, RESTAURANT: ON THE TWENTY, (905) 562-5336;
1-800-701-8074

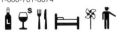

YEAR FOUNDED: 1986 **FOUNDERS:** Pennachetti family and Angelo Pavan **WINEMAKER:** Angelo Pavan **GRAPE VARIETIES:** (red) Pinot Noir, Cabernet Franc, Merlot, Gamay, Cabernet Sauvignon; (white) Riesling, Chardonnay, Sauvignon Blanc, Chenin Blanc, Gewurztraminer **RECOMMENDED WINES:** Riesling CSV, Chardonnay CSV, Chardonnay Musqué, Indian Summer Riesling, Riesling Icewine, Gamay, Cabernet-Merlot

Imagine having a winery in the main street of your village—and one of wine country's best restaurants to boot. Cave Spring, in Jordan Village (a much-visited tourist destination), is housed in a gracious long greystone building, originally an apple warehouse, that dates back to 1870. The entire enterprise—winery, restaurant, and luxury inn on the other side of the street—has its foundation on benchland vineyards planted in 1978 by Len Pennachetti and his father. Vineyard holdings have subsequently grown to 175 acres. They discovered the original site they wanted by scouting the area in a small plane. In 1986, with mature vinifera vines at their disposal, they teamed up with winemaker Angelo Pavan and Tom Muckle (also a founding partner of Thirty Bench) to open a winery, which bears the name of the farm, on the slope above the village. The first estate-grown Riesling and Chardonnay they produced heralded the quality that has been consistent ever since. Pavan is a much-awarded winemaker who produces some of the best Chardonnay and dry and sweet Riesling in the country. His Gamay is pretty good, too. Spend some time here and spoil yourself with lunch at the bright and airy On the Twenty restaurant.

Château des Charmes

1025 YORK ROAD, NIAGARA-ON-THE-LAKE, ON L0S 1P0 (905) 262-4219
WWW.CHATEAUDESCHARMES.COM

YEAR FOUNDED: 1978 **FOUNDER:** Paul Michel Bosc **WINEMAKERS:** Pierre-Jean Bosc, Paul M. Bosc **GRAPE VARIETIES:** (red) Cabernet Sauvignon, Cabernet Franc, Merlot, Pinot Noir, Gamay Noir "Droit," Gamay Noir; (white) Chardonnay, Riesling, Sauvignon Blanc, Aligoté, Auxerrois, Gewurztraminer, Viognier, Vidal **RECOMMENDED WINES:** St. Davids Bench Chardonnay, Gewurztraminer, Viognier, Late Harvest Riesling, Riesling Icewine, Brut Sparkling, Cabernet Merlot, Cabernet Sauvignon, Equuleus

Paul Michel Bosc, a fifth-generation winemaker from Algeria by way of France, is a major figure in the pioneering efforts of the modern Canadian wine industry. After studying oenology at the University of Dijon in Burgundy and subsequently managing a large wine cooperative in Algeria, he immigrated to Canada in 1963. Bosc began his illustrious winemaking career in Canada with Château-Gai Wines (eventually Vincor) before creating his own winery with his lawyer-partner Rodger Gordon in 1978. The original winery was an unprepossessing cement-block bunker set in the vineyard, but with the success of his wines came the finances to buy vineyard land in St. Davids and, ultimately, to build a landmark Loire-style château to house the new winery facility. There is a sense of grandeur here as you enter the main door and see the curved staircase and the well-appointed tasting room on the ground floor. With his wife, Andrée, and two sons, Paul-André and Pierre-Jean, Bosc has created an impressive portfolio of wines in the French style based on four separate vineyards totalling 279 acres. Along the

OPPOSITE: Musicians park their instruments in the vineyard of Château des Charmes (ABOVE) during the winery's 25th anniversary celebration.

way he has introduced several new varieties to the province, such as Aligoté, Viognier, and Savagnin, and, from his original vineyard, developed a new clone of Gamay (Gamay Droit).

He has long affiliated himself and his company with such organizations as the National Research Council to undertake research projects covering many subjects—carbonic maceration, clonal selection, reverse osmosis, vine performance relative to tile drainage, new canopy management techniques, and climate control through the use of wind-machine technology. For his services to the Ontario wine industry, Paul Michel Bosc was awarded the Order of Canada in 2005.

Bosc is a dedicated equestrian with his own horse-breeding stable, and he has named his flagship Bordeaux blend Equuleus. This winery excels in sparkling wines, Chardonnay, Late Harvest Riesling, Riesling Icewine, and Bordeaux-style reds. Enjoy the outdoor patio, where you can eat lunch and try a glass of wine.

Cornerstone Winery

4390 TUFFORD ROAD, BEAMSVILLE, ON L0R 1B0 (905) 563-6758
WWW.CONERSTONEWINERY.COM

YEAR FOUNDED: 2005 **FOUNDERS:** Jerry and Wanda Kopanscy
WINEMAKER: Frank Zeritsch **GRAPE VARIETIES:** (red) Cabernet Franc, Cabernet Sauvignon, Gamay; (white) Chardonnay, Sauvignon Blanc, Vidal **RECOMMENDED WINES:** Cabernet Franc, Vidal Icewine

Jerry and Wanda Kopanscy's winery, a wooden frame building with metal siding and covered porches on both sides, is located at the junction of John Street and Tufford Road; the corner is marked by a large stone—hence the name they chose for their label. The couple purchased the 19-acre property in 1998 and planted an initial 6 acres of vines, adding an acre or so each year. An industrial mechanic by trade, Jerry Kopanscy had no experience of winemaking, although he studied agriculture at university. To do Cornerstone's cellar work, he hired Frank Zeritsch, who made wines at Thirty Bench. Their first commercial crop in 2002 was Cabernet Franc, from which Zeritsch produced a wine that won a bronze medal at Toronto's Wine & Cheese Show in 2005. Just in case you get carried away by the romance of owning a winery, a note of caution. "This is a sixteen-to-eighteen-hour-a-day operation," says Kopanscy. In addition to the wine, a range of fruit wines is made here.

Coyote's Run Estate Winery

485 CONCESSION 5 ROAD, ST. DAVIDS, ON L0S 1P0 (905) 682-8310; 1-877-COYOTE3 WWW.COYOTESRUNWINERY.COM

YEAR FOUNDED: 2003 **FOUNDERS:** Jeff Aubry, Gerald Aubry, and Steven Murdza **WINEMAKER:** David Sheppard **GRAPE VARIETIES:** (red) Pinot Noir, Cabernet Franc, Merlot, Cabernet Sauvignon, Shiraz; (white) Chardonnay, Pinot Gris, Vidal **RECOMMENDED WINES:** Chardonnay, Cabernet Franc

Winemaker David Sheppard's twenty-one-year stint with Inniskillin has paid off for this small winery. His first four wines created quite a sensation when they were released in 2004 and won medals at the Canadian Wine Awards. The next year his Chardonnay Reserve took the gold medal at the Ontario Wine Awards. Sheppard's wines, especially the Chardonnay and Pinot Noir, remind me of Karl Kaiser's, his erstwhile boss at Inniskillin, who had a special affinity for these varieties.

The property was once the lakebed of glacial Lake Iroquois, giving it a rich complexity of soils. "What really excites us," says Patti Aubry, "is the unique dividing line that runs across our property, splitting it into two sections. On one side, we have the dark brown clay soil that is common to the area, while the other side has a lighter red clay soil that is rather rare." These soil types give a definite sense of terroir to their wines, particularly their Pinot Noir. Coyote's Run is a winery to watch.

Creekside Estate Winery

2170 FOURTH AVENUE, JORDAN STATION, ON L0R 1S0 (905) 562-0035; 1-877-262-9463 WWW.CREEKSIDEESTATEWINERY.COM, RESTAURANT: CREEKSIDE WINE DECK AND GRILL, (905) 562-0035 EXT. 235

YEAR FOUNDED: 1998 **FOUNDERS:** Laura McCain Jensen and Peter Jensen **WINEMAKERS:** Rob Power, Craig McDonald **GRAPE VARIETIES:** (red) Bordeaux reds, Pinot Noir, Shiraz; (white) Sauvignon Blanc, Pinot Gris, Chardonnay **RECOMMENDED WINES:** Sauvignon Blanc, Signature Merlot, Signature Shiraz, Laura's Blend

Peter Jensen and his wife, Laura McCain, got inspired to make their own wine while honeymooning in the Napa

Valley. Before their marriage, Jensen had operated several wine stores in Toronto, producing budget wines from concentrates. On their return from California, the couple decided to get into the business of growing grapes and making wine. Their first step in 1997 was to purchase the Habitant Vineyards in Nova Scotia, which they renamed Blomidon Ridge Estate. Two years later they bought two 30-acre farms and a small winery in Jordan Station called VP Cellars. Under their first winemaker, Australian Marcus Ansems, they grew rapidly from a 5,000-case winery to close to 30,000 cases before Ansems left to work in British Columbia for Blasted Church and then Therapy Vineyards.

Creekside made an early mark with its Sauvignon Blanc and its flagship Laura's Blend, a Bordeaux-style red that could well be mistaken for a claret. But don't miss the Shiraz, Australia's icon grape. Ansems convinced the Jensens to plant this variety before it became a favourite among winemakers. Ansems' assistant, Rob Power, took over winemaking duties in 2002 and is perpetuating his extrovert style. The Jensens' other project is a 50-acre vineyard in St. Davids planted to Shiraz, Pinot Noir, Cabernet Sauvignon, and Merlot as well as Chardonnay and Viognier, and, in time, it will become a second winery. The two wines bearing the label for golfer Mike Weir Estate Winery are made here at Creekside.

Crown Bench Estates Winery

3850 ABERDEEN ROAD, BEAMSVILLE, ON L0R 1B7 (905) 563-3959; 1-888-537-6192 WWW.CROWNBENCHESTATES.COM

YEAR FOUNDED: 1999 **FOUNDERS:** Peter Kocsis and Livia Sipos
WINEMAKER: Peter Kocsis **GRAPE VARIETIES:** (red) Pinot Noir, Cabernet Franc, Cabernet Sauvignon, Merlot; (white) Chardonnay, Vidal
RECOMMENDED WINES: Reserve Chardonnay, Vidal Icewine, Livia's Gold, Reserve Cabernet Franc

The extended Kocsis family has a meritorious history as grape growers in the Niagara Peninsula—growers who eventually turned into commercial winery operators (see also Mountain Road and Thomas & Vaughan). Peter Kocsis, whose father had been a deputy minister of agriculture in his native Hungary before immigrating to Canada, purchased a 15-acre vineyard in the mid-1970s with the idea of planting Chardonnay. The Kocsis vineyard fruit was much sought after by other winemakers, who turned it into award-winning wines. Peter Kocsis decided that he should get into the game, too.

Crown Bench Estates, set high on the Beamsville Bench, is as much a nature reserve as a winery, as it borders on the Bruce Trail. From the well-tended vineyard you can see Lake Ontario and, on a clear day, the Toronto skyline. Streams, waterfalls, ponds (with nesting Canada

OPPOSITE: Creekside Estate Winery. ABOVE: Empty bottles await filling at Crown Bench Estates Winery (LEFT).

geese and ducks), and bordering forests filled with wildlife make it a destination for nature lovers.

Apart from the more conventional wines from the mature vineyards, Crown Estate also markets a series of Icewines flavoured with such surprising ingredients as roasted jalapeno peppers, ginger, maple syrup, and a variety of berries. One of their best wines is a dessert-style Chardonnay called Livia's Gold.

Daniel Lenko Estate Winery

5246 KING STREET WEST, BEAMSVILLE, ON L0R 1B3 (905) 563-7756
WWW.DANIELLENKO.COM

YEAR FOUNDED: 1999 **FOUNDER:** Daniel Lenko **WINEMAKERS:** Daniel Lenko, Ilya Senchuk **GRAPE VARIETIES:** (red) Cabernet Franc, Cabernet Sauvignon, Pinot Noir, Merlot, Syrah; (white) Chardonnay, Viognier, Riesling, Gewurztraminer, Vidal **RECOMMENDED WINES:** Old Vines Chardonnay, Viognier, Late Harvest Vidal, Dry Riesling, Cabernet Franc

If ever there was a disconnect between the appearance of the physical plant and the quality of the wine produced there, it's here at Lenko Estate. You would think you'd come to a suburban home with a barn in the backyard. Well, you have, but you've also arrived at one of the best wineries in the province.

Danny Lenko is usually sold out of his wines, and he doesn't give winery tours, but it's worth dropping by because you might find him under a vintage car with a wrench in his hand. Better still, you might get invited into the family home for a wine tasting and homemade apple pie in Helen Lenko's simple kitchen. The success of this small estate winery is based on Jim Warren's consultancy, Danny Lenko's uncompromising winemaking, and the ongoing care and attention Daniel's father, Bill Lenko, lavished on the 35-acre vineyard for over forty years. The Old Vines Chardonnay is made from some of the most venerable planted in the region, going on thirty years. The wines Lenko coaxes from them are rich, concentrated, and delicious. Go early in the spring when Daniel Lenko still has wines to sell.

De Sousa Wine Cellars

3753 QUARRY ROAD, BEAMSVILLE, ON L0R 1B0 (905) 563-7269
WWW.DESOUSAWINES.COM

YEAR FOUNDED: 1990 **FOUNDERS:** John De Sousa Sr. and John De Sousa Jr. **WINEMAKERS:** John De Sousa Jr., Andrzej (Andre) Lipinski **GRAPE VARIETIES:** (red) Maréchal Foch, Baco Noir, Cabernet Sauvignon, Merlot, Cabernet Franc, Touriga Nacional; (white) Riesling, Vidal, Chardonnay, Sauvignon Blanc **RECOMMENDED WINES:** Cabernet Franc Reserve, Sauvignon Blanc

The De Sousa family has the distinction of owning the only winery in downtown Toronto (802 Dundas Street West). It was opened in 1998 as a fermenting facility and

ABOVE: De Sousa Wine Cellars. ABOVE RIGHT: EastDell Estates Winery. LEFT: Daniel Lenko of Daniel Lenko Estate Winery.

Domaine Vagners

1973 FOUR MILE CREEK ROAD, NIAGARA-ON-THE-LAKE, ON L0S 1J0
(905) 468-7296 MVAGNERS@SCOTTLABSLTD.COM

YEAR FOUNDED: 1993 **FOUNDER:** Martin Vagners **WINEMAKER:** Martin Vagners **GRAPE VARIETIES:** (red) Cabernet Sauvignon, Merlot, Pinot Noir; (white) Riesling **RECOMMENDED WINES:** Creek Road Red, Pinot Noir, Riesling

Martin Vagners claims, with some justification, to be Canada's smallest producer and is determined to remain so. His 5-acre vineyard, planted in 1990, is as small as you can go and still be called a commercial winery. Vagners works for Scott Laboratories, a company that supplies yeast, fining agents, and other supplies to the wine industry. His Domaine is more of a garage with a rustic interior where he keeps his reshaved French oak barrels. Because he uses only his own grapes, quantities vary according to the abundance of the harvest. Tasting and sales are somewhat restricted, so call ahead for availability. As a Bordeaux fan, Vagners' interest lies in red wines based on Cabernet and Merlot, although his Pinot Noir is an exciting wine.

EastDell Estates Winery

4041 LOCUST LANE, BEAMSVILLE, ON L0R 1B2 (905) 563-9463
WWW.EASTDELL.COM, RESTAURANT: THE VIEW RESTAURANT, (905) 563-9463,
ACCOMMODATION: HERON'S NEST CABIN, (905) 563-9463

YEAR FOUNDED: 1999 **FOUNDERS:** Susan M. O'Dell and Michael East
WINEMAKERS: Jim Warren, Scott McGregor **GRAPE VARIETIES:** (red) Cabernet Sauvignon, Cabernet Franc, Merlot, Pinot Noir; (white) Chardonnay, Riesling, Gewurztraminer **RECOMMENDED WINES:** Summer Rosé, Bistro Blanc, Riesling

Michael East and his partner, Susan O'Dell (hence EastDell), purchased this 62-acre Beamsville property in 1996. Before getting into winemaking three years later, they sold grapes to other wineries (East had been a home winemaker before buying the vineyard).

Coming from a business background, the couple decided to cater to the corporate world by promoting their winery as ideal for business meetings, events, and executive retreats. Certainly, the sense of wooded seclusion here will get the creative juices flowing, as will the

hospitality centre a year after the death of John De Sousa Sr., who taught his son how to make wine in the rugged, barrel-aged Portuguese style. You can't tour this Toronto facility, but you can dine in the restaurant, Lisbon by Night (416-603-6522), two storeys above the cellar, or you can shop for De Sousa wines in the boutique and gift shop on the first floor.

The primary winemaking site for De Sousa is high on the Beamsville Bench. The family purchased the original farm of 22 acres in 1979, and they have augmented it over the years as adjacent land came up for sale. Here the modern two-storey winery building has a distinctive Portuguese ambiance, with its traditional kitchen. Visitors, if they so desire, can sample De Sousa's red wines from a tannin-softening clay cup—a Portuguese tradition that really works.

John De Sousa is ably backed up by winemaker Andre Lipinski, who was assistant winemaker at Vineland Estates and created the original wines of Legends Estate before moving on to Fielding Estates Winery. He is responsible for all De Sousa's Reserve wines.

restaurant menu based on local produce and the accompanying wines. The blue heron, the logo on the company's labels, speaks to the estate's location on the migration path for a wide variety of birds.

The View Restaurant, with its large picture windows, was built entirely of wood and stone that was found on the property itself and offers a great view of the Escarpment and Lake Ontario. The Loft, a private space for tastings and functions above the winery, overlooking the Bench Boutique, features a soaring cathedral ceiling and skylights. Below the winery, beside a small lake, is a rentable cabin called the Heron's Nest.

The company acquired Thomas & Vaughan in 2004, and Birchwood and Lakeview Cellars in 2005, and is now merged with Diamond Estates.

Featherstone Estate Winery & Vineyard

3678 VICTORIA AVENUE, VINELAND, ON L0R 2C0 (905) 562-1949
WWW.FEATHERSTONEWINERY.CA

YEAR FOUNDED: 1999 **FOUNDERS:** David Johnson and Louise Engel
WINEMAKER: David Johnson **GRAPE VARIETIES:** (red) Cabernet Franc, Pinot Noir, Gamay, Merlot; (white) Chardonnay, Sauvignon Blanc, Riesling, Gewurztraminer **RECOMMENDED WINES:** Vidal Blanc, Gewurztraminer, Estate Riesling, Gemstone Red

Like many Canadian winery owners, David Johnson began as a home winemaker—a passion that deflected him from his day job to the vineyards of Niagara. With his wife,

Louise Engel, Johnson operated the Guelph Poultry Gourmet Market, which they started together in 1986. Since its founding, Featherstone has established itself as an insecticide-free estate winery, releasing ladybugs and lacewings to control aphids and using pheromone traps to control the more serious hazard of grape berry moth. Johnson is also experimenting with the use of woodchips under the vines to control weeds and conserve moisture—an especially valuable function during the months of July and August.

Featherstone was one of the first wineries to use Canadian oak barrels for its 2002 Chardonnay. If the weather is fine, you can order lunch on the verandah. You might even get a glimpse at the hawk that Louise Engel keeps on the property to scare off scavenging birds.

CLOCKWISE FROM TOP LEFT: Featherstone Estate Winery & Vineyard; Ed and Nadja Madronich of Flat Rock Cellars; Fielding Estate Pinot Noir; sculpted rock at Featherstone Estate.

Fielding Estate Winery

4020 LOCUST LANE, BEAMSVILLE, ON L0R 1B2 (905) 563-0668; 1-888-778-7758
WWW.FIELDINGWINES.COM

YEAR FOUNDED: 2005 **FOUNDERS:** Ken and Marg Fielding **WINEMAKER:** Andrzej (Andre) Lipinski **GRAPE VARIETIES:** (red) Merlot, Cabernet Sauvignon, Syrah, Cabernet Franc, Pinot Noir; (white) Riesling, Chardonnay, Pinot Gris, Viognier, Gewurztraminer, Sauvignon Blanc
RECOMMENDED WINES: Riesling Semi-Dry, Vidal Fireside White, Chardonnay Musqué

Ken and Marg Fielding hit the ground running. Within a year of opening their winery, they were already producing 8,000 cases under the watchful eye of winemaker Andre Lipinski, whose special talent with Chardonnay became evident at Vineland Estates and at Legends (he also consults to De Sousa).

Fielding's modern, clean-lined winery, located within a beautifully maintained 30-acre vineyard, is designed in a contemporary Canadiana design, with the warmth and feel of cottage country. From the tasting bar, large glass panels afford a unique view of the winery operations and a breathtaking view across Lake Ontario.

Fielding's wines have won medals in provincial and national competitions since their first release. Be sure to try them, specially the Chardonnay.

Flat Rock Cellars

2727–7TH AVENUE, JORDAN, ON L0R 1S0 (905) 562-8994
WWW.FLATROCKCELLARS.COM

YEAR FOUNDED: 2000 **FOUNDER:** Ed Madronich **WINEMAKERS:** Ann Sperling (consulting winemaker), Marlize Beyers (assistant winemaker)
GRAPE VARIETIES: (red) Pinot Noir; (white) Chardonnay, Riesling
RECOMMENDED WINES: Riesling, Chardonnay, Pinot Noir

Set high on the Escarpment into the side of a hill, lawyer Ed Madronich's striking contemporary winery (two six-sided spaces linked by a bridge over a five-storey, gravity-flow facility in concrete, steel, wood, and glass) has a commanding view of the 75-acre vineyard. The wine shop, on two levels erected on enormous steel legs, has a 360° windowed panoramic view. The winery gets its name from the huge flat rocks that were excavated from the site to put drainage tiles under each row of vines. The geothermal heating and cooling system involving 15,000 feet of piping is just one of the innovative technologies in this space-age facility. Australian Darryl Brooker made an immediate impression with his maiden vintage here, especially with Riesling and Pinot Noir. When he was hired away by Hillebrand, high-profile consultant Ann Sperling was retained to oversee the vineyards and winemaking with South African–trained Marlize Beyers.

Flat Rock was the first winery in Ontario to commit its entire portfolio of wines to screwcap closures, including

its Icewine (a world first). Ed Madronich Jr., who runs the winery with his father, describes the experience for the visitor as "fun, welcoming, approachable, and unpretentious." I couldn't have said it better. Whether you're a fan of contemporary architecture or you just love wine, don't miss Flat Rock.

Frogpond Farm

1385 LARKIN ROAD, RR 6, NIAGARA-ON-THE-LAKE, ON L0S 1J0
(905) 468-1079 WWW.FROGPONDFARM.CA

YEAR FOUNDED: 2001 **FOUNDERS:** Jens Gemmrich and Heike Koch
WINEMAKER: Jens Gemmrich **GRAPE VARIETIES:** (red) Cabernet Franc, Merlot; (white) Riesling **RECOMMENDED WINES:** Cabernet-Merlot, Riesling

Jens Gemmrich learned his winemaking in Heilbronn, Württemberg, Germany, where his family owned a winery.

He spent ten years as the winemaker at Stonechurch before he and Heike Koch bought a small family farm and decided to make it an all-organic operation. Frogpond was the first Ontario winery to be certified by the Organic Crop Producers & Processors as fully organic.

The couple tore out 10 acres of apple trees to create their vineyard. Their organic philosophy for their grape growing extends to other natural features on the property. Rainwater caught in the pond they made provides a habitat for a large number of wildlife species, all of which add to the biodiversity of the farm.

Gemmrich's winemaking philosophy is to be as non-interventionist as possible. "To get the best out of grapes," he says, "let Nature do the work."

You won't find Frogpond wines anywhere but here and, to taste them, you enter the family home; the tasting room is in the garage. Frogpond is unique among Canadian wineries in bottling its products in 500 millilitre bottles rather than the standard 750 millilitre.

OPPOSITE: Flat Rock Cellars' winery. TOP: Henry of Pelham Family Estate Winery. ABOVE: Brothers Paul, Matthew, and Daniel Speck of Henry of Pelham.

Harbour Estates Winery

4362 JORDAN ROAD, JORDAN STATION, ON L0R 1S0 (905) 562-6279; 1-877-439-9463 (HEW-WINE) WWW.HEWWINE.COM

YEAR FOUNDED: 1999 **FOUNDERS:** Darlene and Fraser Mowat **WINEMAKER:** Ken Mowat **GRAPE VARIETIES:** (red) Baco Noir, Merlot, Cabernet Sauvignon, Cabernet Franc; (white) Chardonnay, Riesling, Sauvignon Blanc, Vidal **RECOMMENDED WINES:** Riesling, Chardonnay, Baco Noir

"Come for the wine and stay for the view" is the invitation from Fraser and Darlene Mowat that few visitors can resist. Harbour Estates, with its 550 metre waterfront, is located at the most prominent point in Jordan Harbour as seen from the QEW. It bills itself as "Niagara's winery on the water," a theme that is carried through the design that offers an outdoor experience in all seasons, complete with trail systems through surrounding woods. A boardwalk on the harbour is planned, as is a new winery to replace the building behind the tasting room. Fraser's son Ken (born 1982) is one of the youngest winemakers in Canada and is a dab hand at making Icewine. In 2001, at the tender age of nineteen, Ken took over the winemaking duties from Jeff Innes, who now makes wine at Rockway Glen and the Grange of Prince Edward.

Harvest Estate Wines

1179 FOURTH AVENUE, ST. CATHARINES, ON L2R 6P9 (905) 682-0080 WWW.HARVESTWINES.COM

YEAR FOUNDED: 2001 **FOUNDER:** Fred Hernder **WINEMAKER:** Ray Cornell **GRAPE VARIETIES:** (red) Cabernet Franc, Cabernet Sauvignon, Merlot, Baco Noir, Zweigelt, Maréchal Foch; (white) Riesling, Gewurztraminer, Chardonnay, Vidal **RECOMMENDED WINES:** Dry Riesling, Riesling Icewine

Fred Hernder of Hernder Estates bought this property for his children, Chris and Angela. The winery is essentially a second label for Hernder Estates and also produces a range of fruit wines. The winery, restaurant, and fruit and bakery market are all housed in the chalet-like Harvest Barn, with its vaulted ceiling and imposing stone fireplace. The great expanses of wall display the works of local artists and artisans. Here Ray Cornell, Hernder's winemaker, produces wines that are pleasingly forward and table ready at wallet-friendly prices.

Henry of Pelham Family Estate Winery

1469 PELHAM ROAD STREET, RR 1, ST. CATHARINES, ON L2R 6P7 (905) 684 8423; 1-877-735-4267 WWW.HENRYOFPELHAM.COM, RESTAURANT: COACH HOUSE CAFÉ, (905) 684-8423

YEAR FOUNDED: 1988 **FOUNDERS:** Speck family **WINEMAKERS:** Ron Giesbrecht, Sandrine Epp (assistant) **GRAPE VARIETIES:** (red) Baco Noir, Pinot Noir, Cabernet Sauvignon, Cabernet Franc, Merlot; (white) Chardonnay, Riesling, Sauvignon Blanc **RECOMMENDED WINES:** Cuvée Catharine Rosé Brut, Cabernet-Merlot, Reserve Baco Noir, Barrel-Fermented Chardonnay, Riesling Icewine

The Speck brothers, Paul, Matthew, and Daniel, have run this winery with its 150 acres of vineyards since the premature death of their father in 1993. In 1982 Paul Speck Sr. bought the property that had belonged to his ancestors as far back as 1794. The original owner was Nicholas Smith, whose son Henry (after whom the winery is named) built a coaching inn in 1842. This historic building now serves as the tasting room, wine store, and restaurant, and Henry's visage graces the wine labels.

The Specks were in the vanguard of planting vinifera grapes back in the early 1980s and showed themselves to be venturesome enough to be the first Ontario winery to introduce screwcaps for their premium Barrel-Fermented

Chardonnay in 2003. Their winemaker, Ron Giesbrecht, has produced some of the best wines in the province, including an intense, flavourful Baco Noir. Giesbrecht's top wines are the Speck Family Reserve Chardonnay, Pinot Noir, and Cabernet Merlot blend. These wines are a selection of the best barrels produced from low-yielding vines over twenty years old. There is also a Riesling under this label that is not aged in oak.

Don't miss the Canadian art gallery in the coaching inn, where tastings with Canadian cheeses, tours, and sales are now conducted. This winery should not be missed.

Hernder Estate Wines

1607–8TH AVENUE, ST. CATHARINES, ON L2R 6P7 (905) 684-3300
WWW.HERNDER.COM

YEAR FOUNDED: 1993 **FOUNDER:** Fred Hernder **WINEMAKER:** Ray Cornell **GRAPE VARIETIES:** (red) Cabernet Franc, Cabernet Sauvignon, Merlot, Zweigelt, Baco Noir, Maréchal Foch; (white) Riesling, Gewurztraminer, Chenin Blanc, Chardonnay, Pinot Gris, Chardonnay Musqué, Morio Muscat, Vidal **RECOMMENDED WINES:** Riesling Reserve, Proprietors Reserve Gewurztraminer, Chambourcin

The Hernder family has been making wine in Canada since 1939, when Gottfried Hernder emigrated from Germany. His son Fred acquired a historic 1867 cattle barn on the Niagara Bench, believing it to be the perfect location for processing juice. Fred Hernder moved on to wine, with his first vintage of Vidal in 1991, and opened to the public two years later. With 500 acres on seven different farms, Hernder is one of the largest vineyard operators in Ontario. The expansive barn, with its adjacent ornamental pond, covered bridge, and landscaped gardens, is a much-sought-after venue for weddings.

Ray Cornell, Hernder's soft-spoken, down-to-earth winemaker, has been winning medals for his off-dry Riesling for several years. He makes a broad range of varietals, as well as fruit wines, and believes in long aging for his reds. Don't miss his Unfiltered Cabernet Franc.

The Hernders own a second winery near to this location, Harvest Estate.

Hidden Bench Vineyards and Winery

4152 LOCUST LANE, BEAMSVILLE, ON L0R 1B0 (905) 563-8700
WWW.HIDDENBENCH.COM

YEAR FOUNDED: 2004 **FOUNDER:** Harald Thiel **WINEMAKER:** Jean Martin Bouchard **GRAPE VARIETIES:** (red) Pinot Noir, Merlot, Cabernet Sauvignon, Cabernet Franc, Malbec, Petit Verdot; (white) Chardonnay, Riesling, Sauvignon Blanc, Gewurztraminer **RECOMMENDED WINES:** not tasted

"I have always had an interest in wine from a very young age," writes Harald Thiel, the Montreal-born lawyer who sold his flourishing audio-visual services company to become a vintner. "My interest gelled in 1980–81 when I studied for a year in France and had the opportunity to sample some memorable wines and to tour the winemaking regions." As a successful businessman, Thiel's passion for wine led him to found the Gourmet Food and Wine Show in Montreal, but he wanted to get even closer to the wine business by starting up his own winery. He spent eighteen months looking for suitable properties in Niagara

TOP AND LEFT: Vineyard tour and facade at Hillebrand Estates Winery. ABOVE: Hernder Estate Wines.

before purchasing the 28.5-acre Locust Lane Vineyard (planted in 1998) and the mature 26-acre Rosomel Vineyard (planted in 1975). Both are located on the Beamsville Bench.

For his winemaker, Thiel engaged a fellow Quebecer, Jean Martin Bouchard. He studied oenology at Charles Sturt University in Australia and has garnered a wealth of experience internationally, working the crush in Australia, Alsace, Rhône, and Germany, as well as at Sumac Ridge in British Columbia.

The temporary facility is a basic barn converted to a gravity-flow winery. The selection of winemaking equipment and the uncompromising attention to detail show that this operation aims at the highest quality. It's definitely a winery to watch.

Hillebrand Estates Winery

1249 NIAGARA STONE ROAD (REGIONAL ROAD 55), NIAGARA-ON-THE-LAKE, ON L0S 1J0 (905) 468-7123; 1-800-582-8412 WWW.HILLEBRAND.COM
RESTAURANT: (905) 468-7123

YEAR FOUNDED: 1979 **FOUNDER:** Joseph Pohorly **WINEMAKER:** Darryl Brooker **GRAPE VARIETIES:** (red) Cabernet Sauvignon, Cabernet Franc, Merlot; (white) Chardonnay, Riesling, Sauvignon Blanc, Gewurztraminer, Muscat, Vidal **RECOMMENDED WINES:** Trius Grand Red, Trius Brut, Trius Icewine, Trius Riesling, Showcase Cabernet Sauvignon

Hillebrand has undergone a number of reincarnations since Joe Pohorly created a small farm winery called Newark in 1979. Pohorly sold Newark to the Swiss bitters company Underberg, which renamed the property Hillebrand Estates and capitalized it lavishly by the standards of the day. In 1994 Underberg sold the company to Andrés, which continued the expansion.

You'll find the winery on the highway leading into Niagara-on-the-Lake. It looks like a colonial settlement of gleaming white buildings, with the vineyards stretching out far behind. In fact, the company owns only 2 acres here. It has 75 acres off site, and thirty-five contracted growers who supply it with grapes.

During his fifteen years as winemaker, J-L Groulx did much to give the wines a stylish French profile, especially with the Trius label, before being wooed away to the new Stratus winery in 2004. His successor in 2005 was the talented Australian Darryl Brooker, who was the first winemaker at Flat Rock. Brooker's style is more New World, so I expect to see more fruit-driven wines from Hillebrand in future.

Hillebrand, with its fine-dining restaurant and popular series of outdoor jazz, blues, and classical concerts, has led the way in promoting agri-tourism to the Niagara area. These events are extremely popular in the summer months. Visitors bring their lawn furniture and umbrellas and picnic on the grass while listening to great Canadian performers. Hillebrand also offers one of the very best winery tours in Niagara.

Inniskillin Wines

1499 LINE 3, NIAGARA-ON-THE-LAKE, ON L0S 1J0 (905) 468-2187;
1-888-466-4754 WWW.INNISKILLIN.COM

YEAR FOUNDED: 1975 **FOUNDERS:** Donald Ziraldo and Karl Kaiser
WINEMAKER: James Manners **GRAPE VARIETIES:** (red) Pinot Noir,
Gamay, Merlot, Cabernet Franc, Cabernet Sauvignon; (white)
Chardonnay, Riesling, Pinot Grigio, Pinot Blanc, Viognier, Chenin Blanc
RECOMMENDED WINES: Founders' Chardonnay, Vidal Icewine, Riesling
Icewine, Pinot Noir Reserve, Chardonnay Reserve, Sparkling Vidal
Icewine, Cabernet Franc, Klose Vineyard Cabernet Sauvignon.

On July 31, 1975, Karl Kaiser and Donald Ziraldo were
granted the first winery licence in Ontario since 1929.
The story of how it happened is worth retelling here. The
flamboyant extreme skier Donald Ziraldo received his
degree in agriculture from the University of Guelph in
1971 and began running the family nursery that specialized in fruit trees and grapevines. The stolid, academic
Karl Kaiser, a native of Austria, once studied for the
priesthood, but the church's loss was the Ontario wine
lover's gain. Abandoning ecclesiastical pursuits, Kaiser
moved to Canada in 1968 after meeting and marrying his
Canadian wife, Silvia. A dedicated home winemaker with
a degree in chemistry, Kaiser met Ziraldo when he came
to the nursery to buy some French hybrid vines. The two
men, so different in temperament, struck up a friendship
and talked for hours about Ontario wine over a bottle of
Kaiser's homemade product. After a lot of dreaming and
talking, they decided to apply for a winery licence. "The
late General George Kitching, chairman of the Liquor
Control Board of Ontario, shared our vision of creating
a premium estate winery producing varietal wines from
grapes grown in the Niagara Peninsula," recalls Ziraldo.
Their first red wine was a Maréchal Foch 1974 that they
called Vin Nouveau. Ten years later, this initial effort was
still very much alive and tasted like an old Burgundy.

The original Inniskillin winery was housed in an old
packing shed at the Ziraldo family nursery, 2 kilometres
east of its current location. The first owner of the property
had been a Colonel Cooper, who served in an Irish reg-
iment, the Inniskillin Fusiliers, during the War of 1812. On
completing his military service, he was granted Crown
land, which he named Inniskillin Farm.

In 1978 Ziraldo and Kaiser relocated to their present
site, the Brae Burn Estate. The contemporary Inniskillin
winery combines the partners' experience, with architectural features of both Old World and New World wine
regions blending in with the surrounding vineyards. The
historic barn, thought to have been influenced by Frank
Lloyd Wright, contains the shop and tasting room on the
ground floor, with a huge loft above for private receptions.
A smaller adjacent barn, part of the self-guided tour, is
now a museum.

To Inniskillin goes the credit of creating the international market for Canadian Icewine, when the Vidal 1989
won a major prize at Vinexpo in Bordeaux. In addition,
Karl Kaiser was the first Ontario winemaker to make a
vineyard-designated Chardonnay in the Burgundian style
(at one time Inniskillin had five single-vineyard
Chardonnays) and to champion Pinot Noir as a great
grape for Ontario's climate. In 1993 Inniskillin was the first
Canadian winery to enter into a joint production venture
with a French company, when it invited Jaffelin's Burgundy
specialist, Bernard Repolt, to help select the best barrels

CLOCKWISE FROM TOP: The winery; entrance; and moose sculpture by Charles Pachter at Inniskillin Wines.

of its Chardonnay and Pinot Noir for a label called Alliance. Kaiser now concentrates on Inniskillin's Icewine production in both Ontario and BC, leaving the day-to-day winemaking decisions for the rest of the portfolio to others, first to Australian Philip Dowell, and then to his Aussie colleague James Manners.

Inniskillin was purchased by Cartier in 1992, forming the nucleus of the company that would soon become Vincor International.

DONALD ZIRALDO
CANADA'S WINE AMBASSADOR

The March 1998 issue of *Wine Tidings* magazine featured a smiling Donald Ziraldo on its cover. Wearing a black baseball cap with the Inniskillin logo picked out in gold letters, Ziraldo was seated on the Great Wall of China with a bottle of Inniskillin Vidal Icewine and a glass by his side. The headline read: "Inniskillin Icewine Cracks China."

That was typical Ziraldo—showman, salesman, promoter, merchant-traveller, ambassador—bringing the message of Ontario wines to the world at a time when his peers were at home worrying if they could compete with California. On that trip Ziraldo visited Beijing, Shanghai, Singapore, and Hong Kong, opening up those Asian markets to his Icewine and paving the way for his competitors.

Ask any foreigner if they know the name of a Canadian winery. In a heartbeat they will answer "Inniskillin." No one has done a better job in beating the drum for Canadian wines while furthering the interests of the winery that Donald Ziraldo and Karl Kaiser founded in 1974.

Ziraldo, the son of Italian immigrants, was born in St. Catharines in 1948, a few miles from the farm where he began his career as a nurseryman. While his winemaker-partner Karl laboured in the cellar and the laboratory, Donald travelled the world carrying with him wines for all to taste. An avid skier, he does a lot of his business on the slopes of Europe, New Zealand, and Vale, Colorado. Always with a beautiful woman on his arm and dressed in the latest Italian designer clothes, Donald Ziraldo also has a serious side. He collects Art Deco *objets d'art* and is a vocal defender of Niagara Region's agricultural land. He was the founding chairman of the VQA and was instrumental in creating the Cool Climate Oenology and Viticulture Institute at Brock University, whose building is named Inniskillin Hall. For his contributions to the Canadian wine industry, he was awarded the Order of Canada in 1993.

Jackson-Triggs Niagara Estate Winery

2145 NIAGARA STONE ROAD (HIGHWAY 55), RR 3, NIAGARA-ON-THE-LAKE, ON
L0S 1J0 (905) 468-4637; 1-866-589-4637 WWW.JACKSONTRIGGSWINERY.COM

YEAR FOUNDED: 2001 **FOUNDERS:** Don Triggs and Allan Jackson
WINEMAKERS: Kristine Casey, Lydia Tomek (assistant) **GRAPE VARI-
ETIES:** (red) Pinot Noir, Cabernet Sauvignon, Cabernet Franc, Merlot;
(white) Chardonnay, Riesling, Gewurztraminer, Sauvignon Blanc, Vidal
RECOMMENDED WINES: Delaine Vineyard Riesling, Delaine Vineyard
Pinot Noir, Proprietor's Grand Reserve Meritage, Grand Reserve
Chardonnay, Vidal Icewine, Cabernet Franc Icewine

The Jackson-Triggs label (named for Vincor founding partners Don Triggs and Allan Jackson) first appeared in 1993,
but it wasn't until 2001 that the large portfolio of wines
got its own dedicated winery.

In that year Jackson-Triggs opened its spectacular,
ultra-contemporary winery on the highway into Niagara-
on-the-Lake. The three-tiered, partial gravity-flow facility
covers 47,000 square feet and is set back from the road in
its own 26-acre vineyard. The design was inspired by traditional farm buildings, with their post-and-beam frames
and wide barn doors. Its materials are a combination of
natural stone at its base, native fir roof trusses, high-tech
aluminum framing, and vast windows that showcase the
vineyard at every turn. The vaulted underground cellar,
with its tiers of French and American oak barrels, is
impressive. Visitors can also enjoy food and wine pairings
in the tasting gallery. The quarter-acre of Pinot Noir vines
that was planted at the entrance to the winery in 2001 was
dedicated to Adrienne Clarkson, the former governor
general. Proceeds from the sale of this small block of Pinot
Noir are donated in perpetuity to a charity of the present
incumbent's choice.

In 2000 Jackson-Triggs entered into a joint venture with
the giant Burgundy shipper Boisset to build a winery called
Le Clos Jordanne to produce Burgundy-style Chardonnay
and Pinot Noir from a 35-acre vineyard. Jackson-Triggs's
flagship wines come from the Delaine Vineyard, a 95-acre
property on the Niagara Parkway not far from the winery
and owned by Don and Elaine Triggs (hence the name),
which was planted in 1999. Riesling, Chardonnay, and
Pinot Noir under this label are some of the best wines I've
tried from this winery.

Jackson-Triggs produces a large portfolio of wines under
four price categories—Proprietors' Selection, Proprietors'
Reserve, Proprietors' Grand Reserve, and the Delaine
Vineyard labels—and many people find these distinctions
quite confusing. The Proprietors' Reserve Meritage is one
of the best-value Ontario wines on the market.

Joseph's Estate Wines

1811 NIAGARA STONE ROAD (HIGHWAY 55), RR 3, NIAGARA-ON-THE-LAKE,
ON L0S 1J0 (905) 468-1259; 1-866-168-1259 WWW.JOSEPHSESTATEWINES.COM

YEAR FOUNDED: 1992 **FOUNDER:** Joseph Pohorly **WINEMAKERS:**
Joseph Pohorly, Katherine Reid **GRAPE VARIETIES:** (red) Merlot,
Cabernet Franc, Cabernet Sauvignon, Pinot Noir, Zweigelt, Baco Noir,
Chancellor, Petite Sirah; (white) Chardonnay, Riesling, Gewurztraminer,
Muscat Ottonel, Vidal, Pinot Gris **RECOMMENDED WINES:** Merlot
Reserve, Pinot Gris, Vidal Icewine

Joseph Pohorly was one of the first winery owners in
Niagara and one of the first to produce Icewine (1983).
He converted the family farm on Niagara Stone Road to
Newark Wines (the original name of Niagara-on-the-
Lake) in 1979 and became the third cottage winery in
the peninsula. Before his stint as a winemaker, Pohorly
earned his living as a secondary school teacher for twenty years and then pursued yet another profession—as a
civil engineer and architectural engineer. In 1982 the
Swiss company Underberg invested in the winery and
renamed it Hillebrand Estates. Pohorly eventually sold
his shares to the Swiss company and left to pursue other
interests. He designed and built the Colonel Butler Inn,
a hotel in Niagara-on-the-Lake that he ran for a number
of years with his wife, Betty. But he found the call of

winemaking too strong to resist. In 1992 he purchased a
20-acre fruit farm just down the road from Hillebrand
and converted the orchard to vineyards. Four years later
he opened his attractive stone-faced winery, fronted by its
beautifully maintained formal flower garden. In 2003
Pohorly augmented the tiny, cramped winery building to
a 10,000-sqare-foot facility. In addition to wines, fortified
wines, and fruit wines, he also pioneered a process to
extract cold-pressed grapeseed oil, a powerful antioxidant,
which he launched on the market in 2003.

Kacaba Vineyards

3550 KING STREET, VINELAND, ON L0R 2C0 (905) 562-5625
WWW.KACABA.COM

YEAR FOUNDED: 1997 **FOUNDERS:** Michael and Joanna Kacaba
WINEMAKER: John Tummon **GRAPE VARIETIES:** (red) Cabernet
Sauvignon, Cabernet Franc, Syrah, Merlot; (white) Pinot Gris, Chardonnay
RECOMMENDED WINES: Meritage, Merlot, Pinot Noir, Gamay

Mike Kacaba, a Toronto lawyer, purchased this beautiful
property—a former horse farm—in 1997 before it could
be parcelled up for a housing development. The entrance
to the estate is flanked by Niagara ledge rock, and the
curving driveway is lined with sugar maples. A silver bridge
spans a ravine terraced and planted with one of Ontario's
first major plantings of Syrah. On the other side of the
ravine are rows of mainly Bordeaux reds, with roses
planted at the end of each row. Once you are there, the
skyline of Toronto is visible across Lake Ontario.

The red-roofed winery is a model of compact efficiency. John Tummon, who took over winemaking duties in
2005, is a very talented amateur-turned-professional whose
winemaking career began while he was in university in
1972. He is the only amateur winemaker to win the title of
Winemaker of the Year as well as Champion Cider Maker
for three consecutive years at the provincial level.

When you visit, you can enjoy a picnic on the patio.

Kittling Ridge Estate Wines & Spirits

297 SOUTH SERVICE ROAD, GRIMSBY, ON L3M 1Y6 (905) 945-9225
WWW.KITTLINGRIDGE.COM

YEAR FOUNDED: 1992 **FOUNDER:** John Hall **WINEMAKER:** John Hall
GRAPE VARIETIES: (red) Merlot, Cabernet Franc, Cabernet Sauvignon,
Baco Noir, Maréchal Foch, Shiraz; (white) Chardonnay, Riesling,
Gewurztraminer, Vidal, Seyval **RECOMMENDED PRODUCTS:** Maréchal
Foch, Icewine & Brandy, Inferno Pepper Pot Vodka, Oh Canada Maple
Whisky Liqueur

Kittling Ridge was originally a distillery founded in 1971
by Otto Rieder, a Swiss stillmaster who made a range of
eaux-de-vie, brandy, vodka, and whisky. John Hall joined

OPPOSITE: Jackson-Triggs Niagara Estate Winery. ABOVE: John Hall
and daughter Beth of Kittling Ridge Estate Wines & Spirits.

the company as CEO in 1992 and applied for a winery licence, which was granted in 1993. Hall assumed control of the winery-cum-distillery in 1998. In that year he began construction of a seventy-nine-room hotel just north of the winery, across the QEW at Casablanca Boulevard. While Kittling Ridge produces a large portfolio of wines in its industrial facility, its main business is the production of spirits (vodka, whisky, brandy, and rum), liqueurs, coolers, and cocktails. The wines produced here are very commercial and bargain priced. Hall is a creative marketer: some of his off-beat products include Icewine and Brandy (launched in 1993), Inferno Pepper Pot Vodka (featuring a red pepper in the jug-like bottle), and Oh Canada Maple Whisky Liqueur.

John Hall states his philosophy on his website: "If you don't like our wine, return it—we will drink it."

Konzelmann Estate Winery

1096 LAKESHORE ROAD (BETWEEN FIRELANES 5 AND 6), RR 3
NIAGARA-ON-THE-LAKE, ON L0S 1J0 (905) 935-2866
WWW.KONZELMANNWINES.COM

YEAR FOUNDED: 1988 **FOUNDER:** Herbert Konzelmann **WINEMAKERS:**
Herbert Konzelmann (winemaster), Matthias Boss (winemaker) **GRAPE**
VARIETIES: (red) Merlot, Pinot Noir, Cabernet Sauvignon, Zweigelt,
Baco Noir; (white) Riesling, Chardonnay, Gewurztraminer, Pinot Blanc,
Vidal **RECOMMENDED WINES:** Vidal Icewine, Chardonnay Grand
Reserve, Riesling Grand Reserve, Special Select Late Harvest Vidal

Herbert Konzelmann's great-grandfather Friedrich Konzelmann was a restaurateur and a winemaker in his native Württemberg. In 1958 Herbert joined the winery Friedrich had created in Stuttgart in 1893 and, under his management, the capacity grew to 380,000 litres. (Konzelmann keeps the memory of that family enterprise alive by featuring the doors of the old winery on his labels.) In 1980 Herbert Konzelmann decided to emigrate to Canada when developers began encroaching on vineyard land. On a visit to Niagara, he was so impressed with the potential for grape growing that he took soil samples back to Germany in margarine containers for analysis. Four years later he relocated his family to Niagara-on-the-Lake and purchased a farm on the shore of Lake Ontario, three minutes' drive from the town. For his red varieties, he bought another farm inland from the lake, bringing his total vineyard up to 83 acres.

A tireless experimenter, Konzelmann introduced vertical vine training to the region—a process that allowed wind and sun to draw moisture from the fruit, increasing sugar content and intensity of flavour while still maintaining the delicate acid balance. He was also the first winemaker in Ontario to use rotary fermenters to extract more colour for his red wines. Herbert Konzelmann's Old World charm pervades both the wines and the ambiance of this winery on the lake.

TOP: Donna Lailey of Lailey Winery. ABOVE: Lakeview Cellars Estate Winery. LEFT: Mural at Kittling Ridge Estate.

Lailey Vineyard

15940 NIAGARA PARKWAY, NIAGARA-ON-THE-LAKE, ON L0S 1J0 (905) 468-0503
WWW.LAILEYVINEYARD.COM

YEAR FOUNDED: 2000 **FOUNDERS:** Donna and David Lailey, Derek and Judith Barnett, Yves Starreveld and Tonya Lailey **WINEMAKER:** Derek Barnett **GRAPE VARIETIES:** (red) Cabernet Sauvignon, Cabernet Franc, Merlot, Zweigelt, Pinot Noir; (white) Chardonnay, Gewurztraminer, Muscat Ottonel, Riesling, Sauvignon Blanc **RECOMMENDED WINES:** Cabernet Sauvignon, Merlot, Cabernet Franc, Zweigelt, Chardonnay Reserve

In 1970 Donna Lailey and her husband, David, bought 20 acres of farmland along the Niagara Parkway from David's father. They replaced the hybrids with vinifera varieties and, over the years, turned the property into one of Ontario's finest vineyards. After growing grapes here for 25 years, Donna decided to open a contemporary-style winery because the winemakers—commercial and amateur—she had been selling her fruit to consistently won medals in local and international competitions. Her founding partners include daughter Tonya and her husband, Yves Starreveld, and winemaker Derek Barnett and his wife, Judith. Derek Barnett, an Englishman, was familiar with Lailey fruit because he had worked with it for ten years at Southbrook, initially as farm manager and then as winemaker.

A former Ontario Wine Awards Winemaker of the Year, Barnett was the first to release a Chardonnay and a Pinot Noir aged in Canadian oak barrels. He makes top-flight Chardonnays and richly extracted Cabernet Franc and Cabernet Sauvignon.

Drop in to try the spicy, sappy effect of Canadian oak on Lailey wines.

Lakeview Cellars Estate Winery

4037 CHERRY AVENUE, VINELAND, ON L0R 2C0 (905) 562-5685; 1-866-644-2524
WWW.LAKEVIEWCELLARS.ON.CA

YEAR FOUNDED: 1991 **FOUNDERS:** Eddy and Loraine Gurinskas **WINEMAKERS:** Thomas Green, Jason Roller (assistant) **GRAPE VARIETIES:** (red) Cabernet Sauvignon, Merlot, Vidal, Syrah; (white) Pinot Gris, Chardonnay, Riesling **RECOMMENDED WINES:** Cabernet Sauvignon, Cabernet Merlot, Baco Noir, Gewurztraminer, Chardonnay

Eddy Gurinskas, a successful, medal-winning amateur winemaker, took early retirement from Canadian National Railways in 1990 and bought a 13-acre fruit farm on the Beamsville Bench. He converted the farm into a vineyard and began to pursue his hobby as a professional. His small, rustic winery produced robust, richly extracted red wines from Bordeaux varietals. The prime focus of Lakeview Cellars has been Cabernet Sauvignon. "It is my favourite grape variety," he says. "I enjoy wine with body and tannins that need to age for four or five years." His winemakers, Thomas Green and Jason Roller, now make the wines in Gurinskas's style, continuing a tradition of bold, expressive reds while expanding the portfolio with four Icewines and a port-style fortified wine called Starboard. In 2003 the winery was purchased by Diamond Estates, a holding company that merged with EastDell in 2005. At the end of that year the actor Dan Ackroyd invested $1 million in Diamond Estates, which now controls four Niagara wineries.

If you're interested in how the vineyard affects the flavour of the finished wine, take Lakeview's vineyard tour and you'll become an instant expert. You can even take an eight-week course in belly dancing at the winery if you have a mind to.

Driveway into Legends Estates winery.
OPPOSITE: Thomas Bachelder of Le Clos Jordanne.

Le Clos Jordanne

2540 SOUTH SERVICE ROAD, JORDAN STATION, ON L0R 1S0 (905) 562-9404
THOMAS.BACHELDER@LECLOSJORDANNE.CA

YEAR FOUNDED: 2000 (first vines planted) **FOUNDERS:** Boisset and
Vincor International **WINEMAKERS:** Thomas Bachelder (viniculteur/vine-
yard manager & winemaker), Isabelle Roy-Meunier (assistant in both
roles) **GRAPE VARIETIES:** (red) Pinot Noir; (white) Chardonnay, Pinot
Gris, Riesling **RECOMMENDED WINES:** Chardonnay, Pinot Noir

This winery's name should, of course, be Le Clos Jordan,
but there is a Jordan winery in Sonoma that prevents the
owners from spelling it that way. The title, irrespective of
spelling, speaks to the French influence of the Burgundy
shipper Boisset—co-partner with Vincor in this enterprise.
The model is resolutely Burgundian in terms of grape
selection, planting (tight spacings with some 2,200 vines per

acre), and oak barrels from Burgundian coopers. Thomas
Bachelder, a Montrealer who has made top-flight Pinot
Noir and Chardonnay in Burgundy and in Oregon, wants
to stress the terroir of the four vineyards he has to work
with (to restrict vegetative growth and ensure that the vines'
roots go deep to pick up trace elements from the soil).
These first wines, tasted from the barrel, are some of the
best I have tried from Ontario. Bachelder and his assistant, Isabelle Roy-Meunier, another Montrealer, will be
producing three quality levels of wine from the estate's
vineyards—Bench Reserve, Single Vineyard, and a
Grand Vin. Currently, they are making the wines in the
old Lakeshore Nurseries building, a low olive-green structure along the QEW outside St. Catharines. The winery,
designed by Frank Gehry, will not be visible from the road
but, when it is completed in 2010, will draw the attention
of the world to the Ontario wine scene.

Legends Estates

4888 ONTARIO STREET NORTH, BEAMSVILLE, ON L0R 1B3 (905) 563-6500
WWW.LEGENDSESTATES.COM

YEAR FOUNDED: 2000 **FOUNDER:** Paul Lizak **WINEMAKER:** Paul Lizak
GRAPE VARIETIES: (red) Pinot Noir, Cabernet Sauvignon, Cabernet
Franc, Merlot; (white) Chardonnay, Gewurztraminer, Chenin Blanc,
Muscat Ottonel, Riesling, Pinot Gris, Chardonnay Musqué
RECOMMENDED WINES: Chardonnay, Gewurztraminer, Pinot Noir

Nestled on the shores of Lake Ontario in Beamsville, just
one minute off QEW Exit 64, is a winery that made an
immediate impression with its first release. In the few
years since it was founded as a fruit winery in 1996,
Legends has been making excellent Chardonnays and
Gewurztraminers that have won gold medals in the
Ontario Wine Awards competitions. The Lizak family
farms 155 acres of fruit trees and 45 acres of vines.

The utilitarian winery is not architecturally distinguished, but the wines produced by winemaker Paul Lizak
make you forget your surroundings. Lizak learned his winemaking on the job, first from consultant Jim Warren and
then from Andre Lipinski.

Lizak plans to build a modern winery with a restaurant
overlooking Lake Ontario, but no date has been fixed.

Maleta Vineyards & Estate Winery

450 QUEENSTON ROAD, RR 4, NIAGARA-ON-THE-LAKE, ON L0S 1J0
(905) 685-8486 WWW.MALETAWINERY.COM

YEAR FOUNDED: 1998 **FOUNDERS:** Stan and Marilyn Maleta
WINEMAKERS: Daniel Pambianchi, Arthur Harder **GRAPE VARIETIES:**
(red) Cabernet Franc, Cabernet Sauvignon, Merlot, Gamay Noir, Syrah;
(white) Riesling, Chardonnay **RECOMMENDED WINES:** Meritage,
Gamay Noir, Riesling

Stan Maleta, a former car dealer, and his wife, Marilyn,
launched Maleta Vineyards & Estate Winery in 1998 on

FRANK GEHRY'S FUTURISTIC WINERY

In the millennium year, Vincor teamed up with the large
Burgundy shipper Boisset for a joint venture—one designed
to mirror their operation in British Columbia with the Bordeaux
shipper Groupe Taillan. While the BC enterprise was dedicated to making a Bordeaux-style red wine, the goal in Ontario
is to replicate the quality of fine red and white Burgundy. The
vines for Le Clos Jordanne were shipped from a nursery in
Burgundy and planted in 2000. Much of the interest in this
endeavour to produce ultra-premium Chardonnay and Pinot
Noir in Ontario centres on the world-renowned architect commissioned to design the winemaking facility—Frank Gehry.
His dramatic concept has curved white stucco walls and a roof
of furled metal that he likens to "a silver cloud floating over
the vineyard, with the winery spreading out beneath it."

The multi-level, gravity-flow building, set back 450 metres
from the road, stands at the centre of the sloping vineyard,
enclosed by woodland. The design incorporates huge glass
columns and suspended catwalks above the vats. Visitors on
guided tours will be able to see the entire winemaking operation from the large central hall. Expected to open in 2010, this
first complete building designed by Gehry in Canada should
be a magnet for wine lovers and architecture buffs alike.

ABOVE: Shiraz Mottiar and Martin Malivoire of Malivoire Wine Company. RIGHT: The winery's sorting table. OPPOSITE: Row-end rose bushes in Malivoire's vineyard.

Queenston Road in Niagara-on-the-Lake. The property is adjacent to what was once the historic Sunnieholme Winery, founded in 1918, and on land reputed to be the site of Niagara's first commercial vineyard, developed in the mid-1800s. The winemaking takes place in a bright pink Quonset hut with a burgundy-coloured façade that puts you in mind of a western movie set. The tasting room here has to be one of the smallest in the province.

In 2004 Daniel Pambianchi's company, Cadenza Wines, purchased Maleta. Like Maleta, Pambianchi was a dedicated home winemaker whose experiences found expression in a 294-page book, *Techniques in Home Winemaking: A Practical Guide to Making Château-Style Wines*. His passion for his hobby lured him from the telecommunications business into professional winemaking. He plans to double production to 3,000 cases and to add Pinot Noir to the portfolio.

Malivoire Wine Company

4260 KING STREET EAST, BEAMSVILLE, ON L0R 1B0 (905) 563-9253;
1-866-644-2244 WWW.MALIVOIRE.COM

YEAR FOUNDED: 1999 **FOUNDERS:** Martin Malivoire and Moira Saganski
WINEMAKERS: Shiraz Mottiar, Ann Sperling (consultant) **GRAPE VARIETIES:**
(red) Pinot Noir, Maréchal Foch, Gamay; (white) Chardonnay, Pinot
Gris, Gewurztraminer, Chardonnay Musqué, Melon **RECOMMENDED**
WINES: Moira Chardonnay, Gewurztraminer, Pinot Gris, Pinot Noir,
Old Vines Foch

Martin Malivoire's company makes special effects for the movie industry, but his passion for wine led him to open a winery. His state-of-the-art facility is unique—three attached Quonset huts set on a hillside with a 10 metre drop to allow a totally gravity-flow operation (the wine is moved along at each stage from crush to tank to barrel without the use of pumps). The entranceway, with its local stone pillars and rock gardens, softens the utilitarian lines of the compactly designed facility. Recently added is a 46 metre barrel cellar that maintains the architectural integrity of the site; it, too, is an elongated Quonset hut, set half underground, which has been insulated to maintain a constant cool temperature of 12° Celsius. Malivoire's distinctive labels feature the company's controversial logo—a ladybug (which is also the name of their rosé). The insect is used in the Moira Vineyard instead of insecticides and is unrelated to the Asian ladybug, which compromised a portion of Niagara's 2001 vintage.

From the outset, Malivoire wanted to produce the best rosé in Canada and, with the help of winemaker Ann Sperling, he has achieved that goal. Sperling also makes some of the best Chardonnay in the country. Her wines made from Moira Vineyard fruit (Chardonnay and Gewurztraminer) are stunning in their rich fruit flavours, and so too is her chunky, smoky Old Vines Foch. In August 2005 her assistant Shiraz Mottiar took over as winemaker, with Sperling staying on in a consulting capacity. Mottiar was one of the first graduates from Brock University's Cool Climate Oenology and Viticulture

Institute in 2000. In 2002 he flew to Australia's Yarra Valley to participate in the crush at Coldstream Hills. The winery's founder, wine judge and author James Halliday, described Mottiar in his book *Wine Odyssey: A Year of Wine, Food and Travel* as "one of the stars of the vintage." With such praise, I expect the Malivoire wines to maintain their high standard.

Maple Grove Estate Winery

4063 NORTH SERVICE ROAD, BEAMSVILLE, ON L0R 1B0 (905) 562-7415

YEAR FOUNDED: 1993 **FOUNDER:** Giovanni Follegot **WINEMAKER:** Giovanni Follegot **GRAPE VARIETIES:** (red) Cabernet Sauvignon, Cabernet Franc, Merlot, Pinot Noir; (white) Chardonnay, Pinot Gris **RECOMMENDED WINES:** Pinot Gris, Cabernet Sauvignon

This tiny, rustic, barn-like facility is the second winery owned by Giovanni ("Johnny") and Rosanna Follegot. In 1992 the Follegots began acquiring vineyard property between Beamsville and Vineland to supply the grapes for the couple's major operation, Vinoteca, north of Toronto in Woodbridge. Maple Grove is situated on the shore of Lake Ontario, within site of the QEW, on an 18-acre vineyard. The range of Maple Grove wines is available only at the winery and the hours can be eccentric, so call ahead.

Marynissen Estates Winery

1208 CONCESSION 1, NIAGARA-ON-THE-LAKE, ON L0S 1J0 (905) 468-7270
WWW.MARYNISSEN.COM

YEAR FOUNDED: 1991 **FOUNDER:** John Marynissen **WINEMAKER:** Sandra Marynissen **GRAPE VARIETIES:** (red) Cabernet Sauvignon, Cabernet Franc, Merlot, Gamay Noir, Syrah, Malbec, Petite Sirah; (white) Chardonnay, Riesling, Gewurztraminer, Sauvignon Blanc, Vidal **RECOMMENDED WINES:** Chardonnay, Cabernet Merlot, Vidal Icewine

John Marynissen, an immigrant from Holland in 1952, was the first grape grower to plant Cabernet Sauvignon in Canada (1978) and one of the earliest champions of vinifera grapes in Ontario. An award-winning amateur winemaker with several international trophies for his Chardonnays and Rieslings, Marynissen turned professional in 1991. Since then, Marynissen Estates has gained an admirable reputation for its concentrated, fruit-driven red wines. The winery is a rural barn-style building of 10,000 square feet, packed to the rafters with French and American oak barrels (the winery ages its Chardonnay and Cabernet Sauvignon in both types and bottles them separately). Sandra Marynissen and her husband, Glen Muir, took over the winemaking duties from her father in 2001, though he still oversees and advises.

This winery, just outside Niagara-on-the-Lake, is a favourite stopping point for cycle tours.

Mountain Road Wine Company

4016 MOUNTAIN STREET, BEAMSVILLE, ON L0R 1B7 (905) 563-0745
WWW.MOUNTAINROADWINE.COM

YEAR FOUNDED: 1999 **FOUNDER:** Steve Kocsis **WINEMAKERS:** Steve Kocsis, Jon Witkowski **GRAPE VARIETIES:** (red) Gamay, Cabernet Franc, Cabernet Sauvignon, Baco Noir, Maréchal Foch; (white) Chardonnay, Riesling, Vidal **RECOMMENDED WINES:** Cabernet Sauvignon, Maréchal Foch, Mountain Road Red, Chardonnay Reserve

The simple hand-drawn label of Steve Kocsis's wines gives a graphic description of his vineyard's location on the Beamsville Bench and its relationship to Lake Ontario. The escarpment is drawn in a thick black line and, just as it flattens out to a bench, the line turns green, before turning black again and sloping down to the blue of the lake. A sun shines perennially in the sky above the slope. The Kocsis family is well known in this region; his cousin Thomas started Thomas & Vaughan, and his cousin Peter, Crown Bench.

Steve Kocsis purchased his property in 1981 and, two years later, planted a vineyard with Vidal, Chardonnay, and Gamay. In subsequent years he bought two more farms—Hillside Drive and Fly Road—to give him a total of 80 acres. He made his first wine, a Maréchal Foch, in 1982 and his first Vidal Icewine in 1999. He and his family live on the property and his tasting room is in his basement. Mountain Road produces long-lived Burgundian-style Chardonnay of great distinction, and his barrel-aged blended reds are cellar contenders that age well.

LEFT: Marynissen Estates Winery. ABOVE: Niagara College Teaching Winery.

Niagara College Teaching Winery

135 TAYLOR ROAD, NIAGARA-ON-THE-LAKE, ON L0S 1J0
(905) 641-2252, EXT. 4070 WWW.NIAGARAC.ON.CA; WWW.NETWINERY.CA
RESTAURANT: NIAGARA CULINARY INSTITUTE (NCI) DINING ROOM,
(905) 641-2252 EXT. 4619, ACCOMMODATION: NIAGARA COLLEGE RESIDENCE
AND CONFERENCE CENTRE, (905) 641-4435, SUMMER MONTHS
(DORMITORY ROOMS)

YEAR FOUNDED: 2000 **FOUNDERS:** Jon Ogryzlo and Dan Patterson
WINEMAKERS: Jim Warren, Jordan Harris (assistant) **GRAPE VARIETIES:**
(red) Cabernet Sauvignon, Cabernet Franc, Pinot Noir, Shiraz, Gamay
Noir, Baco Noir; (white) Chardonnay, Riesling, Sauvignon Blanc, Vidal
RECOMMENDED WINES: Barrel-Fermented Chardonnay, Sauvignon
Blanc, Pinot Noir, Riesling, Vidal Icewine

Niagara College boasts the only teaching winery in
Canada. The three-year course gives students a working
knowledge of all aspects of grape growing, vineyard management, and winemaking. Jim Warren, the peripatetic
Ontario winemaker who founded Stoney Ridge and has
consulted to myriad Ontario wineries, teaches the next
generation of winemakers how to coax the best flavours
out of Ontario grapes. As well as being a teaching facility,
the college is a commercial operation: its wines are for
sale in the campus store (the only academic premises in
Canada with its own wine cellar), and, because they're
priced to sell and they've done very well in competitions
such as the Canadian and the Ontario Wine Awards, the
2,500 cases move quickly. Proceeds from their sale help
to finance the programs of the School of Horticulture
and Agribusiness.

The facility itself resembles a small estate winery that
makes hand-crafted wines. The grapes the students process
come mainly from the Jack Forrer Vineyard, a 6-acre
teaching and research plot at the Glendale Campus in
Niagara-on-the-Lake. The "vine library" here features the
top twelve *Vitis vinifera* varieties grown in Canada and
demonstrates vine spacing, rootstocks, and trellising systems. Chardonnay, oaked and unoaked, and Riesling are
the wines to try.

Niagara Vintners Incorporated

548 LINE NO. ONE, NIAGARA-ON-THE-LAKE, ON L0S 1T0 (905) 468-4119
HKLASSEN@NIAGARAVINTNERS.COM

YEAR FOUNDED: 2004 **FOUNDER:** Helmut Klassen **WINEMAKER:** Robert
Summers **GRAPE VARIETIES:** (red) Cabernet Franc, Cabernet
Sauvignon, Merlot, Gamay, Baco Noir; (white) Chardonnay,
Gewurztraminer, Riesling, Pinot Grigio **RECOMMENDED WINE:**
Chardonnay

No one thought of creating a cooperative winemaking
venture among Niagara's grape growers until now. It was
the brainchild of Helmut Klassen, a former plant manager who spent twenty years in the auto industry. As a
teenager, Klassen worked at Brights, where he got a good
grounding in vineyard management. When he left his
posts in Detroit and the Far East, he returned to Niagara
and his first love—wine. Klassen, who was a director of
the Grape Growers Marketing Board, convinced a group
of twenty Niagara Peninsula farmers, whose combined
vineyards total 4,300 acres, to come together to open their
own winery. The simple barn-like, green-roofed facility,
currently under construction on 30 acres at Highway 55
just west of Virgil, has geothermal heating and a zero-
discharge system for sewage.

The company's philosophy is to produce bargain-
priced wines (between $10 and $15) in an environmentally
friendly way. Robert Summers, formerly with Andrés, is
the man who will coordinate receiving and fermenting the
grapes from members of this exciting new project.

Palatine Hills Estate Winery

911 LAKESHORE ROAD, RR 3, NIAGARA-ON-THE-LAKE, ON L0S 1J0
(905) 646-9617 WWW.PALATINEHILLSESTATEWINERY.COM

YEAR FOUNDED: 1998 **FOUNDERS:** John and Barbara Neufeld
WINEMAKER: David Hojnoski **GRAPE VARIETIES:** (red) Baco Noir,
Merlot, Cabernet Franc, Cabernet Sauvignon, Zweigeltrebe; (white)
Seyval Blanc, Geisenheim 318, Vidal, Chardonnay, Riesling,
Gewurztraminer, Sauvignon Blanc **RECOMMENDED WINES:** Vidal
Icewine, Chardonnay, Gewurztraminer

You might say that John Neufeld backed into winemaking.
He has been a grape farmer since 1972 and was a former

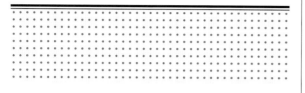

CCOVI

BROCK UNIVERSITY'S COOL CLIMATE OENOLOGY
AND VITICULTURE INSTITUTE

The Cool Climate Oenology and Viticulture Institute at Brock University in St. Catharines, Ontario, is Canada's leading wine school—the only institution in the country that grants degrees in winemaking and grape growing. Established in 1996, CCOVI accepted its first eight students the following year, all of whom graduated from the three-year course in 2000. Four are now winemakers in California, two are working in the wine industry, Rob Power is winemaker at Creekside, and Shiraz Mottiar is winemaker at Malivoire.

The institute is housed in Inniskillin Hall, a $6.1 million building on Brock's campus that features a biotechnology laboratory with all the latest equipment, a viticulture laboratory, a student winery, and a wine cellar. A major focus of CCOVI's academic activities is research into all aspects affecting the health of the Canadian wine industry. Currently, researchers are investigating problems associated with the Asian ladybug. The beetle was first noted as a pest in 2001, and the university has since collaborated with local and international scientists to develop and host several information and training sessions on the subject for winemakers and growers. It is also conducting research into ways to detect fraudulent Icewine. In China, Taiwan, and Hong Kong, the incidence of counterfeit Icewine is damaging the image of Canada's icon wine and losing hundreds of thousands of dollars in sales to the exporting wineries.

The current director of the institute is a research specialist, Dr. Isabelle Lesschaeve, from the Champagne region, who has her own consulting firm and has worked for the National Institute of Agronomical Research in Dijon. Dr. Lesschaeve received her PhD from the University of Burgundy in France, having studied food science with a specialty in sensory evaluation.

In addition to CCOVI's research programs, a range of courses right up to the doctoral level is available in winemaking and viticulture. The institute also offers a certification program for sommeliers.

The restaurant (left) and winery (right) at Peninsula Ridge Estates Winery.

chair of the Ontario Grape Marketing Board (now Grape Growers of Ontario). In the late 1990s he collaborated with winemaker David Hojnoski to produce a small batch of Icewine from grapes left over after he had fulfilled his contracts to other wineries. In 2001 Neufeld and Hojnoski began making other table wines and juices for export to New York and Pennsylvania. The following year Neufeld entered his intensely honeyed, tropical-fruit-flavoured Palatine Hills Vidal Icewine 1998 in the Ontario Wine Awards and walked off with the Wine of the Year trophy. John and Barbara Neufeld originally had no plans to open a winery retail outlet, but the public clamour for the award-winning Icewine was so great that they decided to apply for a retail licence for their farm-gate operation.

The result—their small, neatly understated winery retail store located in the 168-acre vineyard. Since the average production is only 8,000 cases, Neufeld still sells grapes and juice to other wineries in Ontario and to wineries south of the border. He intends to increase production to 25,000 cases over the next few years. The winery name, Palatine Hills, appears on old maps of the Niagara district dating back to the 1780s, when United Empire

were miffed by his flagrant beer advertising on radio. (Under the guise of advertising the products of his ice factory, Peller Ice, they accused him of subliminally promoting Peller Beer and refused to grant him a winery licence.) Eight years later his son Dr. Joe Peller purchased the winery in Grimsby, from which the phenomenon of Baby Duck was launched in the mid-1970s. The success of this carbonated, labrusca-based pop wine was initially a financial blessing and then a curse, as the rest of the industry turned to vinifera products, leaving Andrés saddled with the pop wine image. In 1991 the company changed the name on its labels to Peller Estates and concentrated on producing varietal wines of increasing quality, culminating in its Signature series. These rich, oak-aged wines show how far the company has come from the Quack-pack days of Baby Duck.

To underline this commitment to quality, Peller Estates built an impressive new winery, with cellars worthy of a Hollywood movie set, in a 25-acre Niagara-on-the-Lake vineyard (it owns another 120 acres off site and also buys from twenty-two contracted growers). Housed here in this French château-style building surrounded by vines is one of the best restaurants in the peninsula. Chef Jason Parsons presides over a magnificent chandeliered dining room that looks out onto the vineyard. You can also eat on the outdoor terrace to be closer to the vines. If you dine here, start with a glass of Cristalle sparkling wine (spiked with Icewine) and order a bottle of the Signature Cabernet Franc to complement the local produce.

Peller Estates also owns Hillebrand Estates, Thirty Bench, and around one hundred retail wine stores called Vineyard Estates Wines.

Loyalists who were originally from Germany brought the name with them.

David Hojnoski is particularly adept at producing full-bodied Chardonnay and spicy Gewurztraminer that is true to its varietal character. These are the wines to try and, of course, his Icewines.

Peller Estates Winery

290 JOHN STREET EAST, RR 1, NIAGARA-ON-THE-LAKE, ON L0S 1J0
(905) 468-4678; 1-888-673-5537 WWW.PELLER.COM
RESTAURANT: (905) 468-4678

YEAR FOUNDED: 2001 **FOUNDER:** Andrew Peller **WINEMAKER:** Lawrence Buhler **GRAPE VARIETIES:** (red) Cabernet Franc, Cabernet Sauvignon, Merlot; (white) Riesling, Chardonnay, Pinot Gris, Gewurztraminer, Muscat, Vidal **RECOMMENDED WINES:** Cristalle (sparkling), Signature Series Riesling Icewine, Signature Series Vidal Icewine, Signature Series Cabernet Franc, Signature Series Merlot

Andrew Peller was fifty-eight when he founded Andrés Wines in Port Moody, BC, in 1961. He would have started his business in Ontario, but provincial bureaucrats

Peninsula Ridge Estates Winery

5600 KING STREET WEST, PO BOX 500, BEAMSVILLE, ON L0R 1B0
(905) 563-0900 WWW.PENINSULARIDGE.COM, RESTAURANT: (905) 563-0900

YEAR FOUNDED: 2000 **FOUNDER:** Norman D. Beal **WINEMAKER:** Jean-Pierre Colas **GRAPE VARIETIES:** (red) Cabernet Sauvignon, Cabernet Franc, Merlot, Syrah; (white) Chardonnay, Sauvignon Blanc **RECOMMENDED WINES:** Sauvignon Blanc, INOX Chardonnay, Equinox (Sauvignon Blanc/Chardonnay blend), Arcanum (Meritage blend with Syrah)

Norman Beal had not intended to open a winery in Ontario when he left a highly successful career in the petroleum industry. He was searching for properties in California and New York State. At the urging of family members, he abandoned the idea of investing in California and came home from Connecticut to create Peninsula Ridge at a cost of $4.5 million. He bought the Beamsville property in March 1999, with its beautifully sited Victorian farmhouse that resembles a non-threatening version of Norman Bates's family home in *Psycho*. Beale planted 25 acres of vineyard on the property (a former apple orchard)

TOP: Pillitteri Estates Winery. ABOVE: Its winemaker, Sue-Ann Staff. RIGHT: October pumpkin harvest at Puddicombe Estate Farms & Winery.

the best I have tasted in Ontario. Equally surprising is Colas' choice of Syrah to blend in his Meritage-style red, an exciting wine that gets better with every vintage as the vines mature.

The farmhouse is now a sophisticated restaurant, and the retail store and tasting bar are housed in a tastefully restored 1855 post-and-beam barn. The coach house that stands behind the farmhouse is used for private and corporate events and for weddings catered by the Peninsula Ridge restaurant chefs.

Pillitteri Estates Winery

1696 NIAGARA STONE ROAD (REGIONAL ROAD 55), RR 2,
NIAGARA-ON-THE-LAKE, ON LOS 1JO (905) 468-3147 WWW.PILLITTERI.COM

YEAR FOUNDED: 1993 **FOUNDER:** Gary Pillitteri **WINEMAKER:** Sue-Ann
Staff **GRAPE VARIETIES:** (red) Merlot, Cabernet Franc, Cabernet
Sauvignon, Gamay Noir; (white) Chardonnay, Gewurztraminer, Pinot
Grigio, Riesling, Sauvignon Blanc, Vidal Blanc; (Icewines) Vidal,
Riesling, Gewurztraminer, Cabernet Franc, Cabernet Sauvignon,
Chambourcin, Chardonnay, Merlot **RECOMMENDED WINES:** Riesling
Icewine, Vidal Icewine, Gewurztraminer Icewine, Family Reserve
Merlot, Family Reserve Cabernet Franc

The antique Sicilian donkey cart that has pride of place in the winery's reception area speaks to founder Gary Pillitteri's heritage. A grape grower since his arrival from Italy in 1948, Pillitteri was an enthusiastic amateur

and a further 25 acres on Quarry Road on the Beamsville Bench, and he built a magnificent 3,800-square-foot L-shaped, underground cellar.

Beale also had the good sense to hire a top-notch winemaker—the Burgundian Jean-Pierre Colas, who had earned an international reputation for his white wines while working at Domaine Laroche in Chablis. You would expect Colas to excel with Chardonnay, both unoaked and oaked, but the real surprise is his Sauvignon Blanc,

Puddicombe Estate Farms & Winery

1468 HIGHWAY 8, WINONA, ON L8E 5K9 (905) 643-6882
WWW.PUDDICOMBEFARMS.COM

YEAR FOUNDED: Puddicombe label established 1998 **FOUNDERS:**
Murray and Carolyn Puddicombe **Winemaker:** Lindsay Puddicombe
GRAPE VARIETIES: (red) Cabernet Franc, Pinot Noir, Maréchal Foch,
Gamay Noir, De Chaunac, Baco Noir, Concord; (white) Seyval,
New York Muscat Riesling, Vidal, Chardonnay, Sauvignon Blanc,
French Colombard, Viognier, Niagara, SV 23512 **RECOMMENDED**
WINES: Muscat, Colombard, Viognier, Sauvignon Blanc, Vidal Icewine,
Gamay; Iced Apple

The Puddicombe family have owned this family farm
since 1797 and have been growing grapes here since 1940.
The 300-acre farm's location within the city limits of
Hamilton makes it the first winery on the Niagara wine
route and an easy drop-in place, especially if you're travelling with kids. Today the winery offers a total family
experience, with train rides, a petting zoo, and a children's
play area, as well as pick-your-own grapes, fruits, and
vegetables in season.

Murray Puddicombe teamed up with Jim Warren in
the early days of Stoney Ridge to use his fruit farm as the
site for the winery. This partnership dissolved in 1997 over
philosophical differences, and the Ottawa-based Cuesta
Corporation bought Stoney Ridge, relocating it to
Vineland. But the Puddicombe family remained in the
business and introduced its own portfolio of grape wines
to add to the fruit wines it produced (there are now 160
acres of vines). Puddicombe's daughter Lindsay is the
winemaker, and she is particularly strong in aromatic
varieties such as Muscat, Colombard, and Riesling. But
don't miss Puddicombe's Iced Apple (think Icewine made
from apples, as they do in Quebec).

Reif Estate Winery

15608 NIAGARA PARKWAY, RR 1, NIAGARA-ON-THE-LAKE, ON L0S 1J0
(905) 468-7738 WWW.REIFWINERY.COM

YEAR FOUNDED: 1982 **FOUNDER:** Ewald Reif **WINEMAKERS:** Klaus W.
Reif, Roberto DiDomenico **GRAPE VARIETIES:** (red) Cabernet Franc,
Cabernet Sauvignon, Merlot, Pinot Noir, Baco Noir, Zinfandel, Gamay;
(white) Chardonnay, Gewurztraminer, Riesling, Pinot Gris, Sauvignon
Blanc, Chenin Blanc, Kerner, Vidal, Seyval Blanc, Geisenheim
RECOMMENDED WINES: Vidal, Select Late Harvest Vidal, Vidal Icewine,
Cabernet Sauvignon, Meritage, Cabernet Merlot

When Klaus Reif's uncle Ewald opened his winery in
1983, it was only the fourth in Niagara-on-the-Lake. Ewald,
a thirteenth-generation winemaker from Germany, began
as a grape grower in Ontario in 1977, selling grapes to
Inniskillin, a short tractor ride down the scenic Niagara
Parkway. Eventually, he began making his own wine. In

winemaker whose success with Icewine in a local competition encouraged him to start his own commercial operation
in 1993. Now Pillitteri is an all-family enterprise, with
siblings, cousins, and friends contributing grapes and
expertise. The winery complex, with its farmer's market,
wrap-around balcony, trophy area, and five tasting bars,
has been designed to accommodate large numbers of visitors. Its architectural look, according to Gary's son
Charlie, is "Old World conversing with New World"—
the idea of traditional winery design with contemporary
styling. A feature worthy of the *Guinness Book of Records* is
the 12.7 metre concrete tasting table in the Roman-vaulted
barrel cellar, set with twenty-three chairs (Gary's lucky
number). The wine library, to be completed in 2007, will
accommodate past vintages of Pillitteri wines, other
Ontario wines, and Charlie Pillitteri's personal collection.
The flagship wine here is Icewine—eight different varieties—which accounts for one-third of Pillitteri's production
and is sold to nineteen countries around the world.

The young winemaker, Sue-Ann Staff, a former
Ontario Wine Awards Winemaker of the Year, comes from
five generations of Ontario grape growers and studied
oenology at Australia's Roseworthy College. Her style of
winemaking reflects the Australian penchant for bold,
fruit-driven flavours with soft tannins and whispers of
vanilla oak. The Family Reserve range may be costly, but
they define the quality that can come out of Ontario
vineyards, helped along by careful winemaking.

1987 his nephew Klaus, who got his training at Germany's renowned Geisenheim Institute, immigrated to Canada to take over the winemaking. Klaus Reif's first Vidal Icewine captured the attention of the influential American wine critic Robert Parker Jr., who included it in his list of the ten best wines of the year in 1989. The retail store and tour centre are located in a historic stagecoach house on the property.

In 1990 Reif was joined by Roberto DiDomenico, a graduate from the University of Guelph with a specialized honours degree in microbiology, and they now share the winemaking duties. Since DiDomenico's arrival, the production emphasis has shifted from aromatic, German-style white wines to elegant yet powerful French-style reds, particularly Cabernet Sauvignon–based blends. Building on the reputation of Tesoro 1995, a red Meritage blend that excited industry and critics alike when it was released in 1998, Reif introduced a premium line of Cabernet, Merlot, and Pinot Noir under the First Growth label in 2001. These strapping, age-worthy wines, made from low-yielding vines with a minimum age of twelve years, are oak aged for at least two years.

Ridgepoint Wines

3900 CHERRY AVENUE, VINELAND, ON L0R 2C0 (905) 562-8853
WWW.RIDGEPOINTWINES.COM, RESTAURANT: LA CANTINA (LUNCH ONLY),
(905) 562-8853

YEAR FOUNDED: 2002 **FOUNDERS:** Mauro and Anna Scarsellone
WINEMAKER: Arthur Harder **GRAPE VARIETIES:** (red) Merlot, Cabernet Sauvignon, Cabernet Franc, Pinot Noir, Nebbiolo, Sangiovese; (white) Chardonnay, Riesling **RECOMMENDED WINES:** Nebbiolo, Riesling Dry

Mauro Scarsellone is a chartered accountant pursuing his hobby with gusto. He began planting his 18-acre vineyard in 1995. He and his wife, Anna, built a wooden, 4,000-square-foot, European-style winery over a cellar to replace the shed where they made their first wines in 2001.

Scarsellone is convinced you can successfully make good big red wines in Ontario, and so he has planted more than half his vineyard to Cabernet Sauvignon, Merlot, and Pinot Noir. He also chose to plant two Italian grape varieties that are notoriously difficult to grow in Ontario's climate—Nebbiolo and Sangiovese—the latter in honour of his Italian family heritage and a first for Ontario. "Maybe it's my Italian blood," he says. "When someone tells me good red wine can't be done in Ontario, it makes me all the more determined to try." And he may be right—certainly the Nebbiolo 2001, its first vintage, augurs well for the future. It didn't taste of Piedmontese soil, but it was a delicious, fruity wine.

The ubiquitous Jim Warren consulted on the first vintage in 2001, and now Arthur Harder, who made wine at Hillebrand, presides over the cellar. The welcome here is effusive, especially if you like Italian wines.

Riverview Cellars Estate Winery

15376 NIAGARA PARKWAY, RR 1, NIAGARA-ON-THE-LAKE, ON L0S 1J0
(905) 262-0636 WWW.RIVERVIEWCELLARS.COM

YEAR FOUNDED: 2000 **FOUNDERS:** Sam Pillitteri and Mike Pillitteri
WINEMAKER: Fred Di Profio **GRAPE VARIETIES:** (red) Merlot, Cabernet Franc, Cabernet Sauvignon, Baco Noir; (white) Chardonnay, Riesling, Gewurztraminer, Vidal **RECOMMENDED WINES:** Cabernet Franc Reserve, Riesling Icewine

The Pillitteri family is something of a wine dynasty in the Niagara Peninsula. This small winery, with its 25-acre vineyard owned by Sam and Lina Pillitteri, is located on the Niagara Parkway—with a view of the Niagara River—close to Niagara Falls.

Riverview originally supplied grapes for seven years to the winery run by Gary Pillitteri, before Gary convinced his brother to start up an operation of his own. Winemaker Fred Di Profio learned his craft working for five years with Sue-Ann Staff at Pillitteri Estate, and he learned well.

The most popular wine here is Fontana Dolce, sold in half-bottles, a kind of red version of White Zinfandel—a sweet blend of Cabernet Sauvignon, Merlot, and Baco

Joseph DeMaria of Royal DeMaria Wines.
OPPOSITE: Ridgepoint Wines.

Noir. It's ideal for making Sangria (a recipe for which appears on Riverview's website). It's worth stopping for the Fontana Dolce, if you like sweet wines.

Rockway Glen Golf Course & Estate Winery

3290 NINTH STREET, ST. CATHARINES, ON L2R 6P7 (905) 641-5771;
1-877-ROCKWAY (762-5929) WWW.ROCKWAYGLEN.COM
RESTAURANT: (905) 641-1030 EXT. 228

YEAR FOUNDED: 2001 **FOUNDERS:** Catharine and Bruce Strongman and BSH Developments **WINEMAKER:** Jeff Innes **GRAPE VARIETIES:** (red) Merlot, Cabernet Sauvignon, Shiraz, Cabernet Franc, Gamay; (white) Chardonnay, Vidal **RECOMMENDED WINES:** Vidal, Cabernet-Merlot

Rockway Glen's spacious clubhouse is home to a winery, restaurant (Continental cuisine), and glassed-in banquet room that looks out onto the golf course. One unique feature is Le musèe du vin, a well-displayed collection of eighteenth- and nineteenth-century wine artifacts and implements from France; it's worth visiting for the graceful antique staircase alone. The wine shop sells locally made wine jellies as well as "classic and risqué stemware."

Winemaker Jeff Innes has worked in cellars in Georgia and Uruguay as well as in Ontario's Harbour Estates and the Grange of Prince Edward.

You don't have to be a member to dine at the club, so you can enjoy Jeff Innes's wines while deconstructing the golfers' swings from the comfort of the table.

Royal DeMaria Wines

4551 CHERRY AVENUE, BEAMSVILLE, ON L0R 1B1 (905) 562-6767;
1-888-793-8883 WWW.ROYALDEMARIA.COM

YEAR FOUNDED: 1998 **FOUNDER:** Joseph DeMaria **WINEMAKER:** Joseph DeMaria **GRAPE VARIETIES:** (red) Merlot, Cabernet Sauvignon, Cabernet Franc, Pinot Noir; (white) Chenin Blanc, Pinot Gris, Gewurztraminer, Vidal, Riesling, Muscat, Pinot Blanc, Sauvignon Blanc, Chardonnay **RECOMMENDED WINES:** Vidal Icewine, Chardonnay Icewine, Gewurztraminer Icewine, Pinot Gris Icewine

When Joseph DeMaria, a hairdresser and self-taught winemaker, gave his winery the title "Royal," it attracted the attention of Buckingham Palace. In October 2002 the winery received notice that Queen Elizabeth II had requested to see his product. DeMaria promptly assembled

a gift package: it included his much-medalled Riesling Icewine 1999, which had been awarded the Vinexpo 2001 Grand prix d'honneur in Bordeaux—the same prize Inniskillin won for its Vidal 1989 ten years earlier.

Royal DeMaria bills itself as "Canada's Icewine Specialists." DeMaria's fascination with Icewine began in 1991, when he first tasted it while touring Niagara wineries. He began making it as a basement vintner before he purchased 25 acres in Vineland in 1996 to produce it commercially. While most Ontario wineries are content to make Icewine from Riesling and Vidal, and sometimes Gewurztraminer or Cabernet Franc, DeMaria makes this winter wine from twelve different varieties plus a Meritage blend. He began making Icewine in 1998 and has won a trunkful of medals in competitions around the world: at the time of writing, Royal DeMaria Wines has won fifty gold medals in forty-eight competitions, and a total of 169 medals in five vintages. You would never guess this success from the simple two-storey white winery building with little decoration.

DeMaria wines are seductively sweet, but a great Icewine must have perfect balance to create the tension between the residual sugar and the acidity. The winery produced the world's first Meritage Icewine. Uniqueness, it seems, comes at a price: this wine, marketed in 375 millilitre bottles, was priced on release at $395. As stocks dwindled, the price rose to a staggering $5,000 a bottle. The average price for Ontario Icewines in this half-bottle format is about $50.

Southbrook Winery

581 STONE ROAD WEST, NIAGARA-ON-THE-LAKE, ON L0S 1J0 (905) 832-2548
WWW.SOUTHBROOK.COM

YEAR FOUNDED: 1991 **FOUNDER:** William Redelmeier **WINEMAKERS:** Ann Sperling, Steve Byfield (assistant) **GRAPE VARIETIES:** (red) Cabernet Sauvignon, Cabernet Franc, Merlot; (white) Chardonnay, Sauvignon Blanc, Vidal **RECOMMENDED WINES:** Triomphe Cabernet Merlot, Triomphe Chardonnay, Sauvignon Blanc, Cabernet Franc; Framboise (fruit wine)

For many years, Bill Redelmeier and his wife, Marilyn, ran a highly successful market garden on their farm—over 285 acres of lush, rolling countryside between Richmond Hill and Maple, only 24 kilometres north of Toronto. An avid wine collector, he then decided to open a winery in his century-old milking barn. The adjacent barn where cows were milked is now the barrel-aging room, its massive stone walls thick enough to provide an even, cool temperature all year round. Redelmeier took French wines as his model and sourced the best fruit he could from Niagara growers, including grapes from Donna Lailey for his vineyard-designated wines. Southbrook's first vintage was 1992, under the stewardship of Derek Barnett, who created a style of richly textured wines that his successor, Colin Campbell, emulated since taking over in 2002. The Triomphe range of Sauvignon Blanc, Chardonnay, and Cabernet Sauvignon are great wines. So too is Triomphus Vidal Icewine. In addition to table wines, Southbrook produces some of the best fruit wines in Canada and has the distinction of being the first Canadian fruit wine (Framboise) to be sold at Harrod's in London.

Southbrook is an enjoyable place to visit not only to sample wine but also to see the farm products grown here. You can shop in the farmer's market, pick your own raspberries, or select a pumpkin or a Christmas tree.

Bill Redelmeir has purchased property in Niagara-on-the-Lake and intends to move the winemaking operation there by the spring of 2007. He also had the foresight to add Ann Sperling to his winemaking team.

Stonechurch Vineyards

1242 IRVINE ROAD, RR 5, NIAGARA-ON-THE-LAKE, ON L0S 1J0
(905) 935-3535; 1-800-935-3500 WWW.STONECHURCH.COM

YEAR FOUNDED: 1990 **FOUNDERS:** Lambert and Grace Hunse **WINEMAKER:** Terence van Rooyen **GRAPE VARIETIES:** (red) Baco Noir, Cabernet Sauvignon, Cabernet Franc; (white) Chardonnay, Riesling, Vidal, Morio Muscat, Gewurztraminer **RECOMMENDED WINES:** Morio Muscat, Reserve Cabernet Sauvignon, Vidal Icewine

A previous owner of the Hunse family farm mortgaged the property to raise funds to build a church of stone when

LEFT: Southbrook Winery and its owner, Bill Redelmeier (TOP).
ABOVE: Fermenters at Stoney Ridge Estate Winery.

dissolved in 1997, Warren found new investors in Ottawa, who moved the operation to Vineland. Barry Katzman and Glen Hunt's company, Wines of Woods End, merged with Stoney Ridge to give it marketing muscle, and, eventually, Warren sold his shares to them so he could concentrate on his burgeoning winemaking responsibilities. He officially retired from the company in 1999, but he still keeps his hand in, producing the wines for the Founder's Signature Collection with his former assistant winemaker Liubomir Popovici, a Romanian, who now controls the cellar and is making first-rate wines. Don't miss his Cabernet Franc Reserve. In 2002 Barry Katzman, now president of Creekside, inaugurated the Stoney Ridge Wine Library, a collection of limited-edition wines and back vintages that had not previously been released to the public. With the departure of Katzman, the winery was acquired by Mark Bonham, a Toronto financier.

Jim Warren was notorious for the number of wines he would make in a given vintage (one year he had sixty-two labels). Stoney Ridge has cropped that down to a more manageable thirty or so products in its portfolio, including a cranberry wine. Like Topsy, this is a winery that grew—and it grew piecemeal, a bit at a time, with extra buildings added on as needed. Check out the old wines in the library and take home a bottle of Charlotte's Chardonnay, a non-oaked wine with a rich pineapple and peach flavour, which Warren makes as a tribute to his wife.

the congregation could not finish the construction. Lambert and Grace Hunse planted their vineyard in 1972, and their late son, Rick, and his wife, Fran, opened the winery in 1990. The self-guided vineyard trail is an education in grape growing. Winemaker Jens Gemmrich, from Germany, was in charge of the cellar until South African Terence van Rooyen left Cilento to take over winemaking duties for the 2004 harvest.

Stoney Ridge Estate Winery

3201 KING STREET. VINELAND, ON L0R 2C0 (905) 562-1324
WWW.STONEYRIDGE.COM

YEAR FOUNDED: 1985 **FOUNDER:** Jim Warren **WINEMAKERS:** Liubomir Popovici (chief), Jim Warren (founding) **GRAPE VARIETIES:** (red) Baco Noir, Pinot Noir, Cabernet Franc, Cabernet Sauvignon, Merlot; (white) Sauvignon Blanc, Pinot Grigio, Chardonnay, Chenin Blanc, Gewurztraminer, Vidal **RECOMMENDED WINES:** Unoaked Chardonnay, Bench Series Barrel-Fermented Gewurztraminer Icewine, Pinot Grigio, Pinot Noir, Reserve Cabernet Sauvignon

Stoney Ridge, like its founder, has moved around a lot. When Jim Warren created the winery in 1985, its home was in a small barn and garage on the Weylie farm in Stoney Creek. In 1989 Warren partnered with fruit farmer Murray Puddicombe and moved the facility to the Puddicombe property in Winona. When that partnership

Stratus Vineyards

2059 NIAGARA STONE ROAD (REGIONAL ROAD 55), NIAGARA-ON-THE-LAKE, ON L0S 1J0 (905) 468-1806 WWW.STRATUSWINES.COM

YEAR FOUNDED: 2000 **FOUNDER:** private owner **WINEMAKER:** J-L Groulx **GRAPE VARIETIES:** (red) Cabernet Sauvignon, Cabernet Franc, Malbec, Syrah, Petit Verdot, Merlot, Gamay; (white) Sauvignon Blanc, Semillon, Viognier, Gewurztraminer, Chardonnay **RECOMMENDED WINES:** Stratus White, Stratus Red, Merlot

Stratus, the neighbouring winery to Jackson-Triggs in Niagara-on-the-Lake, looks like an enormous industrial box store with windows, but it houses the most sophisticated winemaking operation in the province, governed by a rigorous Old World winemaking philosophy: the finished wine is a blend of the best barrels, sometimes of different varietals as in Bordeaux, or different clones of the same grape as in Burgundy. J-L Groulx, a Loire Valley native who trained in Burgundy and Bordeaux, was the winemaker at Hillebrand Estates for many years before teaming up with winery consultant Peter Gamble to design this ultra-modern facility. Groulx and Gamble believe in long hang time for their grapes, dramatically low yields (maximum 2.5 tonnes per acre), and the blending of varietals. The winery is 100 percent gravity flow for the grapes and the wines, to ensure the gentlest handling at all phases of production. Once the wine has finished its journey down

PETER GAMBLE
THE CONSCIENCE OF THE ONTARIO WINE INDUSTRY

Sorting tables at Stratus Vineyards.

"It's been a wonderful decade and a half for Ontario wine lovers. And although we've just suffered an unprecedented three damaging winters in a row—and there's been some backsliding on quality goals and bulk wine importation—the next decade should prove to be Ontario's finest yet. With all that has been learned about our vineyards and viniculture, there's a growing recognition, with some new and vibrant players leading the way, that Ontario's winemakers must reach for the stars. Let the world's warmer, easier growing regions do the *vin ordinaire* while we narrow our focus to the top."

Winemaker, consultant, wine judge, winery executive, and wine writer Peter Gamble has worn many hats in the Ontario wine industry, none more crucial than his role as the founding executive director of the VQA in its seminal first decade. Gamble came to the job with experience as a winemaker in the early 1980s with Newark Wines, now Hillebrand Estates. To get a foot in the door, he offered his services unpaid in exchange for access to the vineyards, the cellars, the laboratory, and the winemakers. During his seven-year tenure as the VQA's public face, he became a tireless ambassador for Ontario and Canadian wines and a passionate advocate of high-quality appellation products. A founding director of Cuvée, the annual celebration of Ontario wines in March, and a driving force behind the creation of the Canadian Wine Library at Brock University's Cool Climate Oenology and Viticulture Institute, he now concentrates on his consulting business of winery start-ups, an enterprise that has taken him as far afield as the United Kingdom, France, Italy, Mexico, Argentina, New Zealand, and South Africa. In Canada he helped create Stratus and Benjamin Bridge. His latest projects include consulting to Ravine Vineyard Estate Winery, to be built on a 25-acre site on the St. Davids Bench in Niagara, and, with his partner, Ann Sperling, helping to start up the family winery in British Columbia to be called Sperling Vineyards.

to the barrel cellar for aging, it is transported up, for bottling, in steel tanks by means of a central elevator, rather than being pumped up under pressure. Stratus is one of the few Canadian wineries that use large French oak vats, rather than stainless steel tanks, to ferment the wines. It also believes in long barrel aging. As a result, the wines are some of the best made in Canada. The flagship wines are simply labelled Stratus Red and Stratus White, and wines not selected for the Stratus series go into a second label called Wildass.

The winery, owned by a group of investors, is certified LEED—Leadership in Energy and Environmental Design—a North American standard for rating the sustainability of commercial and industrial buildings. A ground-loop geothermal system of twenty-five wells dug 82 metres into the ground uses the earth's energy for all of its heating and cooling needs. Stratus is a winery not to be missed—for its contemporary architecture, its state-of-the-art technology, and, above all, its wines and its weekly wine and food seminars.

Strewn Winery

1339 LAKESHORE ROAD, RR 3, NIAGARA-ON-THE-LAKE, ON L0S 1J0
(905) 468-1229 WWW.STREWNWINERY.COM, RESTAURANT: TERROIR LA CACHETTE, (905) 468-1222

YEAR FOUNDED: 1997 **FOUNDERS:** Joe Will and Jane Langdon
WINEMAKER: Joe Will **GRAPE VARIETIES:** (red) Merlot, Cabernet Franc, Cabernet Sauvignon; (white) Riesling, Chardonnay, Gewurztraminer, Sauvignon Blanc, Pinot Blanc, Vidal (for Icewine and Select Late Harvest) **RECOMMENDED WINES:** Strewn Three, Merlot Terroir, Riesling Terroir, Riesling Icewine, Vidal Icewine

Joe Will began his winemaking career in the Okanagan, before sharpening his skills at Roseworthy College in

facility with the most modern equipment on the Bench. The dramatic sloped roof of the contemporary winery, reflected in an ornamental pond, suggests the height within that allows for a gravity-feed operation on six levels, together with three barrel-aging cellars.

Winemaker Deborah Paskus convinced Tawse to create a winery in Niagara rather than purchasing a property in his beloved Burgundy. A bottle of the legendary Temkin-Paskus Chardonnay (a collaboration between wine writer Steven Temkin and Paskus in the 1990s to produce a few pampered barrels of Burgundy-style white wine) so impressed Moray Tawse that he purchased 25 acres of Beamsville Bench and proceeded to build a winery. This acreage included the Vinc Vineyard, containing twenty-five-year-old Chardonnay vines and thirty-year-old Riesling. Paskus, who also makes wine at Closson Chase, produces some of the most concentrated Chardonnays in Canada. The wine she will make from these old vines, I predict, will set the benchmark for this variety in Ontario. Tawse has named the 3.5-acre Chardonnay portion of this vineyard Robyn's Block, after one of his daughters. The 1.5-acre Riesling portion is named for his other daughter: Carly's Block.

While the primary focus here is Chardonnay, Tawse also produces small amounts of Cabernet Franc, Pinot Noir, and Riesling. Make an appointment to see this property; even the most jaded palate will be impressed.

Australia. On his return to Canada, he joined Pillitteri as its founding winemaker. His first crush under his Strewn label (the 1994 vintage) was done at Pillitteri. Three years later he purchased his own facility with partner Newman Smith. Joe and his wife, Jane Langdon, took over an abandoned 35,000-square-foot fruit cannery built in the 1930s and transformed it with great flair and taste into a winery, a restaurant with a cooking school attached (see www.winecountrycooking.com), and their own home. Will's winemaking style relies heavily on his sense of the soils in his 26-acre vineyard. He calls his top wines Strewn Terroir, and he makes them only if he feels the vintage has delivered the quality he's looking for. The same sense of the land is reflected in the name of the restaurant, Terroir la Cachette, which is decorated in a variety of earth-tone colours. With a rustic, countrified interior and an extensive outdoor patio, the restaurant-cum-wine-bar serves a Provençal menu and is a favourite stopping place for winery visitors—especially cyclists, who enjoy the pastoral ride along Lakeshore Road out of Niagara-on-the-Lake.

Tawse Winery

3955 CHERRY AVENUE, RR 1, VINELAND, ON L0R 2C0 (905) 562-9500
WWW.TAWSEWINERY.CA

YEAR FOUNDED: 2001 **FOUNDERS:** Moray Tawse and family
WINEMAKERS: Deborah Paskus; Brian Hamilton, Paul Pender (assistants)
GRAPE VARIETIES: (red) Pinot Noir, Cabernet Franc, Merlot; (white) Chardonnay, Riesling **RECOMMENDED WINES:** Chardonnay, Riesling, Cabernet Franc, Pinot Noir

Investment banker Moray Tawse is a serious Burgundy collector and, when he decided to get into the wine business, he spared no expense creating an elegant, small-capacity

The Thirteenth Street Wine Corp.

3983–13TH STREET, JORDAN STATION, ON L0R 1S0 (905) 562-9463
WWW.13THSTREETWINES.COM

YEAR FOUNDED: 1998 **FOUNDERS:** Gunther Funk, Ken Douglas, Herb Jacobson, and Erv Willms **WINEMAKERS:** Gunther Funk, Ken Douglas, Herb Jacobson, Erv Willms **GRAPE VARIETIES:** (red) Pinot Noir, Gamay, Merlot, Cabernet Franc, Cabernet Sauvignon, Syrah; (white) Chardonnay, Riesling **RECOMMENDED WINES:** Premier Cuvée (sparkling), Riesling, Chardonnay Reserve, Gamay, Gamay Reserve, Cabernet Merlot

Thirteenth Street is owned by four families who operate out of tiny premises on Gunther Funk's farm on the Jordan plain. Lawyer Ken Douglas and mechanical engineer Herb Jacobson share the winemaking duties with Funk and Erwin Willms. All four founders started off as highly accomplished home winemakers. They source their fruit from vineyards owned by Funk and Willms and other small growers who believe in low yields. Their common philosophy of low-yield, small-batch production has paid off handsomely in terms of medals won for their small but quality-driven portfolio of wines. They make the best Gamay in Canada (like a mouthful of black cherries), a concentrated Chardonnay with toasty pear and pineapple flavours, and a zesty sparkling Riesling. If you like wines that make a statement, don't miss Thirteenth Street.

Thirty Bench Vineyard & Winery

4281 MOUNTAINVIEW ROAD, BEAMSVILLE, ON L0R 1B2 (905) 563-1698
WWW.THIRTYBENCH.COM

YEAR FOUNDED: 1994 **FOUNDERS:** Tom Muckle, Yorgos Papageorgiou, Franz Zeritsch, Livio DiNello, James Forrest, and Fred Oliphant **WINEMAKERS:** Tom Muckle, Yorgos Papageorgiou, Franz Zeritsch **GRAPE VARIETIES:** (red) Pinot Meunier, Cabernet Franc, Cabernet Sauvignon, Merlot, Pinot Noir; (white) Riesling, Chardonnay, Pinot Gris, Gewurztraminer **RECOMMENDED WINES:** Semi-Dry Riesling, Chardonnay, Red Blend

Thirty Bench takes its name from the nearby Thirty Mile Creek on the Beamsville Bench. The winery is housed in a long wood barn set in the vineyard directly across the road from Angels Gate. The enterprise began as a partnership in the late 1970s—a Riesling-growing operation that, by 1980, had expanded to 39 acres with a whole range of vinifera varietals. Today the winemaking is a team effort, each member with his own area of specialization. Dr. Tom Muckle, a pathologist from Hamilton, is the Riesling man; Yorgos Papageorgiou, professor emeritus of geography and economics at McMaster University, makes the vaunted Benchmark red wines and the Chardonnay; and Austrian-born Frank Zeritsch, who owned a winemaking shop in Hamilton, produces the company's Icewines. The hallmark of Thirty Bench wines is their concentration of fruit flavours from long hang time on the vine. This super-maturity results in high-alcohol and intensely flavoured wines that sometimes go over the top but can age for several years. The winery and its 70 acres were acquired by Peller Estates in May 2005, but the Thirty Bench team will continue making the wines.

Thomas & Vaughan Estate Winery

4245 KING STREET, BEAMSVILLE, ON L0R 1B0 (905) 563-7737
WWW.THOMASANDVAUGHAN.COM

YEAR FOUNDED: 1998 **FOUNDERS:** Thomas Kocsis and Barbara Vaughan **WINEMAKER:** Thomas Green **GRAPE VARIETIES:** (red) Maréchal Foch, Baco Noir, Cabernet Franc, Merlot, Cabernet Sauvignon; (white) Chardonnay, Pinot Gris, Vidal Blanc **RECOMMENDED WINES:** Cabernet Franc, Meritage, Cabernet Sauvignon, Riesling Botrytis Affected

Thomas Kocsis, of the ubiquitous Kocsis clan of grape growers and winemakers, took his wife's birth name (Vaughan) to christen the winery they founded in 1998. The small wood-frame facility, with its 38-acre vineyard, is right on Highway 8—the main Wine Route through the area—located at the base of the Escarpment. Thomas, a second-generation winegrower with over two decades of vineyard experience, decided to concentrate on red varieties for his winery. His winemaker, Thomas Green, produces beefy, well-structured Cabernets and a Meritage blend that are much admired—and rightly so. The winery

TOP AND ABOVE: Vineland Estates Winery. OPPOSITE: Courtyard at Willow Heights Estate Winery.

offers a series of tours, a complimentary self-guided tour, and three tours with tasting at a nominal charge.

In 2004, Thomas & Vaughan was purchased by EastDell Estates.

Vincor International Headquarters

441 COURTNEY PARK DRIVE EAST, MISSISSAUGA, ON L5T 2V3 (905) 564-6900
WWW.VINCORINTERNATIONAL.COM

YEAR FOUNDED: 1874 (Falls Wine Company) **FOUNDERS:** Thomas G. Bright and Francis Shirriff **GRAPE VARIETIES:** See individual Vincor wineries for details

Vineland Estates Winery

3620 MOYER ROAD, VINELAND, ON L0R 2C0 (905) 562-7088;
1-888-VINELAND (846-3526) WWW.VINELAND.COM

🍾 🍷 🍴 🛏 👤ˢ

YEAR FOUNDED: 1983 **FOUNDER:** Hermann Weis **WINEMAKER:** Brian
Schmidt **GRAPE VARIETIES:** (red) Merlot, Cabernet Franc, Sangiovese,
Seurat, Pinot Noir, Cabernet Sauvignon; (white) Riesling, Chardonnay,
Chardonnay Musqué, Pinot Gris, Pinot Blanc, Pinot Menunier,
Sauvignon Blanc **RECOMMENDED WINES:** Cabernet Franc, Vidal
Icewine, Riesling Dry, Riesling Semi-Dry, Riesling Icewine, Chardonnay
Unoaked, Gewurztraminer, Sauvignon Blanc

Vineland Estates is one of the handsomest and best-sited
wineries in Ontario, with extensive vineyard holdings
stretching over 275 acres. From its large cedar deck,
diners can see across the undulating St. Urban Vineyard
to Lake Ontario and the Toronto skyline in the distance.
In 1979 the Mosel winegrower Hermann Weis planted two
50-acre vineyards to Riesling in Vineland. Using this fruit,
Dieter Guttler opened the original Vineland Estates winery
in 1983. Ownership passed to the Weis family five years
later and, in 1992, they sold the property to John Howard.
He expanded the original winery, preserving the 1845
farmhouse as a tasting room and restaurant, and restored
the historic stone carriage house for functions. He also
built a new winery with a distinctive stone tower. In 2003
Howard sold his interest to construction magnate Freddy
DeGasperis. Vineland Estates has the distinction, or
perhaps challenge, of selling Canada's most expensive red
wine, a Meritage priced at $125 a bottle. Winemaker Brian
Schmidt and his brother Allan before him have made
Riesling the signature variety here, whether in dry, off-
dry, sparkling, or Late Harvest and Icewine styles. The
restaurant, which specializes in local food products beautifully prepared, is a destination on its own. The wine
boutique, with its magnificent wooden bar and upstairs
loft, houses the best wine store in Niagara. The whole site
is definitely worth a visit.

Willow Heights Estate Winery

3751 KING STREET, VINELAND, ON L0R 2C0 (905) 562-4945
WWW.WILLOWHEIGHTSWINERY.COM

YEAR FOUNDED: 1994 **FOUNDER:** Ron Speranzini **WINEMAKER:** Ron
Speranzini **GRAPE VARIETIES:** (red) Gamay Noir, Merlot, Cabernet
Franc, Cabernet Sauvignon; (white) Chardonnay, Riesling,
Gewurztraminer **RECOMMENDED WINES:** Riesling, Chardonnay
Reserve, Vidal Icewine, Tresette

Ron Speranzini's winery would not be out of place in the
Mediterranean. The garden courtyard is enclosed by an
airy arbour that partially conceals the complex of villa-style
buildings behind. Built in 1998, it replaced a more modest
structure and represents the confidence the owner had in
his wines and the future of his label. Like so many Ontario
winemakers, Speranzini, whose former life was in the steel
industry, began as an amateur who won a sufficient
number of national competition trophies to encourage
him to enter the commercial world. His first offering, a
Chardonnay Reserve 1992, won the top honour in its category at Cuvée, Ontario's annual celebration of VQA
wines. Chardonnay is Willow Heights' calling card, but
Speranzini also makes a top-notch Meritage red called
Tresette—a blend of Cabernet Sauvignon, Cabernet Franc,
and Merlot—as well as a delicious Riesling.

Lake Erie North Shore

The Erie shore, according to Parks Canada, "encompasses the greatest biodiversity" of any region in Canada, standing as it does at the northern limit of the Carolinian forest zone that covers most of the eastern United States. It is home to hundreds of species found nowhere else in the country—including Canada's only lizard, the five-lined skink that graces the label of Pelee Island Winery's Cabernet Franc.

Lake Erie North Shore is really Canada's south coast, a region that is more southerly than one-third of the continental United States. Driving it is like crossing the Prairies, only here corn and soybeans take the place of wheat fields, punctuated by orchards and berry fields. You can see just how rich and fertile this pancake-flat land is by the number of greenhouses around Leamington, the "Tomato Capital of Canada," that light up the night sky. The easy terrain here makes it a paradise for neophyte cyclists. The marinas of Leamington and Kingsville are a magnet for boaters, and scuba divers congregate along the 35 kilometre arc of the Pelee Passage to explore the two hundred shipwrecks along this most treacherous, reef-ridden strip in Lake Erie. More sedate pleasures are also available, such as the Jack Miner Bird Sanctuary, Point Pelee National Park, and the 35-acre Colasanti's Tropical Gardens. Bird lovers will want to visit the area during the month of May, which is designated as the Festival of Birds, or just roam the broad beaches and lie on the dunes watching the mass migrations.

Lake Erie's grape-growing zone hugs the shore and arcs in a bow shape from Amherstburg, at the mouth of the Detroit River, to Ridgetown, northeast of Blenheim, with 300 acres of vineyard dotted in clusters throughout the rich farmland of Essex, Kent, and Elgin counties. Although this region is home to a number of wineries, it is significantly smaller in vineyard surface than Pelee Island. The main concentration of vines is found around Harrow, where Colio Estate is located, and Kingsville, where Pelee Island Winery has its winemaking facility and has planted supplementary vineyards on the mainland. A lesser concentration of vines is found to the northeast of Amherstburg. The third area of grape growing is east, between Blenheim and Cedar Springs.

The terrain here is relatively flat, based on limestone bedrock. In Essex County, in the south towards Harrow, Kingsville, and Leamington, the predominant soil type is Brookston clay and clay loam. As you approach the shore, the soil changes to sandy loam that allows for better drainage. The area around Blenheim is slightly higher in elevation, with soils ranging from well-drained gravelly and sandy loams to the less porous clays.

Like Pelee Island, Lake Erie North Shore enjoys a longer, warmer growing season than the Niagara Peninsula, being farther south and exposed to great bodies of water. With Lake St. Clair to the north, the Detroit River to the west, and Lake Erie to the south, this area of southwest Ontario is virtually surrounded by water. The presence of so much water has a cooling effect in the heat of summer and, in the late fall, when the growing season is over, it gives off its stored warmth.

TOURING WINERIES in the Lake Erie North Shore region

The drive from Toronto to Kingsville/Harrow, the heart of the region, takes about four hours, so a single-day trip does not leave you much time to visit the wineries here.
SINGLE DAY: Head straight for Colio, an old established winery, which will give you a good feel for the style of wines made here.
WEEKEND: The extra day will allow you to explore the many new wineries that are opening up in the region. Don't miss Viewpointe, Sanson, Sprucewood, and Mastronardi.

LAKE ERIE NORTH SHORE & PELEE ISLAND WINERIES

1 ALEKSANDER ESTATE WINERY
2 COLCHESTER RIDGE ESTATE WINERY
3 COLIO ESTATE WINES
4 D'ANGELO ESTATE WINERY
5 ERIE SHORE VINEYARD
6 MASTRONARDI ESTATE WINERY
7 MEADOW LANE WINERY
8 MUSCEDERE VINEYARDS
9 PELEE ISLAND WINERY
10 QUAI DU VIN ESTATE WINERY
11 SANSON ESTATE WINERY
12 SMITH & WILSON ESTATE WINES
13 SPRUCEWOOD SHORES ESTATE WINERY
14 VIEWPOINTE ESTATE WINERY

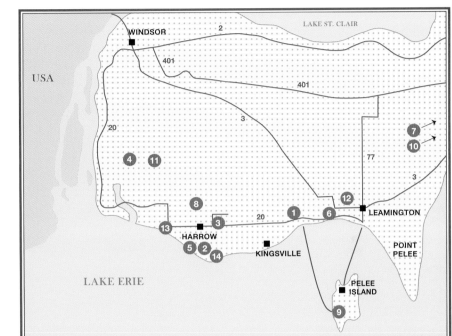

Aleksander Estate Winery

1542 COUNTY ROAD 34, RUTHVEN, ON N0P 2G0 (519) 326-2024
MAIL@ALEKSANDERESTATE.COM

YEAR FOUNDED: 2004 **FOUNDER:** Aleksander Bemben **WINEMAKER:** Aleksander Bemben **GRAPE VARIETIES:** (red) Cabernet Sauvignon, Cabernet Franc, Chambourcin; (white) Riesling **RECOMMENDED WINE:** Riesling

Aleksander Bemben worked at Pelee Island Winery in Kingsville from its creation in 1983 and, for many years, was the assistant winemaker there. In 1998 he purchased farmland in Ruthven, halfway between Leamington and Kingsville, about a kilometre inland from the shore, and planted the 5-acre vineyard in 2000. According to Izabela Bemben, who works with her father and is a graduate of the Cool Climate Oenology and Viticulture Institute program at Brock University, "The winery is not very fancy. It's a converted farm building where we have a small retail store."

In addition to grape wines, this small family-operated concern also makes fruit wines.

Colchester Ridge Estate Winery

108 COUNTY ROAD 50 EAST, HARROW, ON N0R 1G0 (519) 738-9800
WWW.COLCHESTERRIDGE.COM

YEAR FOUNDED: 2001 **FOUNDER:** Bernard Gorski **WINEMAKER:** Bernard Gorski **GRAPE VARIETIES:** (red) Cabernet Sauvignon, Merlot; (white) Chardonnay, Gewurztraminer **RECOMMENDED WINE:** Cabernet Sauvignon

Bernard Gorski, a dedicated home winemaker, has been around grapes and farming all his life. "I've been actively farming," he says, "since I was eight years old in 1962, so I know the horticultural part of the program." Gorski owns a 300-acre farm in Harrow and, with his brother Ted, runs a tanker trucking company that hauls wine for blending in bulk from California to Ontario wineries. "In my sales calls I was exposed to all the winemakers," he recalls. "Looking at the process, the machines, and what has to be done for many years, I finally jumped in with both feet." In 2001 Gorski planted 12 acres of vines on his farm, with the intention of starting his own winery, and installed a single wind machine to combat the frost.

Currently, he makes the wine in a farm building but is converting another barn 200 metres from the lake into the winery building. "It will not look like a barn when I'm done," promises Gorski.

Colio Estate Wines

1 COLIO DRIVE, PO BOX 372, HARROW, ON N0R 1G0 (519) 738-2241;
1-800-265-1322 WWW.COLIOWINES.COM

YEAR FOUNDED: 1980 **FOUNDER:** Enzo de Luca **WINEMAKER:** Carlo Negri **GRAPE VARIETIES:** (red) Gamay, Merlot, Cabernet Franc, Dornfelder, GM 318, Pollux, Villard Noir, Zweigeltrebe; (white) Chardonnay, Vidal 256, Sauvignon Blanc, Seyval Blanc, Riesling **RECOMMENDED WINES:** CEV Merlot, CEV Cabernet Franc, CEV Signature Cabernet-Merlot, CEV Vidal Icewine, CEV Lily Sparkling Wine, Pinot Grigio

In the late 1970s the city of Windsor was twinned with Udine in Friuli. Some local expatriate Friulani businessmen, headed by Enzo de Luca, who grew up with the wines from the Collio region of northeastern Italy, decided they could establish a winery in Harrow and replicate the experience. They hired a Friulano winemaker, Carlo Negri, and called their winery Colio (hoping that the name spelled differently would not invoke the ire of their compatriots at home). The company is now owned by de Luca and Joe Berardo, the proprietor of the Portuguese wine conglomerate Bacalhôa (formerly J.P. Vinhos).

When Colio opened in Harrow, it gave new life to Canada's oldest and most historic wine region. At the end of the nineteenth century, Lake Erie North Shore was the epicentre of the nascent Canadian wine industry. Far removed from its major market (a four-hour drive from Toronto), Colio has had to build its consumer base more efficiently than wineries closer to the Golden Horseshoe. It is a commercial winery in the best sense of the word: the owners believe in volume but have maintained creditable quality in their bargain-priced wines. Their flagship wines, labelled with Carlo Negri's signature, are powerful with bright fruit, and their long barrel aging makes them good candidates for laying down. Negri, who has produced wine here for more than twenty-five years, also makes the sparkling Icewine for Pillitteri here.

Colio sources its grapes from some 200 acres of vines in the Kingsville-Colchester area. It sold the original 100-acre vineyard in Harrow to Tony Mastronardi, who started up his own winery in Kingsville. With its imposing stone facade, the winery houses over 1.2 million litres of cooperage in both stainless steel and oak. The vast barrel cellar, kept cool and humid by timed sprays of mist, is decorated with two 10-metre-long murals of grape pickers.

In 2005 Enzo de Luca and Joe Berardo purchased nearly 21 acres of vineyard land on the Niagara Parkway, a shrewd business decision to get a presence in the lucrative Niagara market. They plan to build a winery there in the future.

D'Angelo Estate Winery

5141 CONCESSION 5, RR 4, AMHERSTBURG, ON N9V 2Y9 (519) 736-7959;
1-888-598-8317 DANGELOWINES@ON.AIBN.COM

YEAR FOUNDED: 1989 (vineyard planted 1983) **FOUNDER:** Sal D'Angelo **WINEMAKER:** Sal D'Angelo **GRAPE VARIETIES:** (red) Cabernet Franc, Maréchal Foch, Baco Noir, Chambourcin, "a new variety—a cross between Cabernet Sauvignon and Maréchal Foch"; (white) Vidal, Chardonnay **RECOMMENDED WINES:** Cabernet Franc, Maréchal Foch, Select Late Harvest Vidal, Vidal Icewine

Winemakers will tell you that wines are made in the vineyard: you need great grapes to make great wine. As a vineyardist, there is none better than Sal D'Angelo, the 1999 Ontario Grape King. He clocks up the air miles these days between the Okanagan in British Columbia, where he lives, and Lake Erie North Shore, to preside over the winemaking in both his properties.

The D'Angelo family brought the winemaking tradition over with them from Italy in 1955 and, from his boyhood days, the young Salvatore helped his father with the crush at home. He learned his viticulture from his grandfather when he returned to Italy as a young man. He was back in Canada in 1979, looking for vineyard land in southwestern Ontario. An accomplished amateur winemaker, D'Angelo wanted to start his own winery. In 1983 he purchased 50 acres in Amherstburg, just south of Windsor, planted his first vineyard, and, six years later, opened his winery. His voracious reading about wine culture over the years drew D'Angelo to the Okanagan Valley, where, after several visits, he finally purchased a property in Naramata in 2001, financing it by selling a second 12-acre vineyard he owned in Colchester. This

LEFT: Carlo Negri of Colio Estate Wines. ABOVE: Cabernet vineyards at Colio Estate.

vineyard became Viewpointe Estate, where he still plays a role as a consulting winemaker.

Sal D'Angelo makes one of the best Maréchal Foch wines in Ontario. Although it has won him many medals, he has high hopes for a new grape he has planted—a crossing of Cabernet Sauvignon and Maréchal Foch. "It looks like Foch," he says, "but it tastes like Cabernet and ripens later than Foch. At the present time we don't know what to call it. Fobernet?"

Erie Shore Vineyard

410 COUNTY ROAD 50 WEST, RR 3, HARROW, ON N0R 1G0 (519) 738-9858 WWW.ERIESHORE.CA

YEAR FOUNDED: 2002 **FOUNDERS:** Harvey and Alma Hollingshead **WINEMAKER:** Harvey Hollingshead **GRAPE VARIETIES:** (red) Cabernet Franc, Chambourcin, Baco Noir, Zweigelt; (white) Chardonnay, Riesling, Vidal **RECOMMENDED WINES:** Autumn Harvest Vidal, Summer Sun Cabernet Rosé, Duet

Harvey and Alma Hollingshead, both graduates in agriculture with careers in banking, planted their 15-acre vineyard in 1997, making Erie Shore Canada's most southerly winery (there is no actual winery on Pelee Island). The Hollingsheads began selling juice to home winemakers before opening their winery facility in December 2002. What they don't use themselves they sell to other winemakers, such is the demand for grapes in the region. The winery's label features a large stylized E that contains blue water, emblematic of their position 600 metres from Lake Erie's shoreline. They are one of the few facilities that recycle their own bottles, buying them back at 25 cents each.

Mastronardi Estate Winery

1193 CONCESSION 3 EAST, KINGSVILLE, ON N9Y 2E5 (519) 322-2987; (519) 326-1417 (TEMPORARY) WWW.MASTRONARDIWINES.COM

YEAR FOUNDED: 2003 **FOUNDERS:** Tony, Eadie, and Rino Mastronardi **WINEMAKER:** Lyse Leblanc **GRAPE VARIETIES:** (red) Cabernet Franc, Cabernet Sauvignon, Baco Noir, Zinfandel, Zweigelt; (white) Chardonnay, Geisenheim, Gewurztraminer, Pinot Gris, Riesling, Riesling-Traminer, Seyval, Vidal **RECOMMENDED WINES:** Cabernet Franc, Vidal Icewine

The Mastronardi brothers, Tony and Rino, bought the 100-acre vineyard as a going concern from Colio Estate in 2002. That year they had 100 percent winterkill. The brothers decided to uproot the vines and build greenhouses to grow tomatoes and peppers (their core business), because the low-lying vineyard was subject to both frost damage and winterkill.

Tony was heartened, though, by the fact that Colio saved 35 percent of its crop that same year by introducing wind machines into the company's Kingsville vineyard, so he decided to leave the old Harrow Estate vineyard in place and put in his own wind machines. He purchased six from a California company and, in 2003, Mastronardi Estate had a full crop. Tony Mastronardi is now a distributor for the wind machine company. "I'm having more fun in growing the vineyards and making wine than in greenhouses," he says

Currently the wine is made in an old barn on the property. The brothers hired a winemaker long familiar with Essex County fruit, Lyse Leblanc, who used to run her own 3,500-case winery in Harrow.

Meadow Lane Winery

44892 TALBOT LINE, RR 3, ST. THOMAS, ON N5P 3S7 (519) 633-1933 WWW.MEADOWLANEWINERY.COM

YEAR FOUNDED: 1998 **FOUNDERS:** Walter and Debbie Myszko **WINEMAKER:** Walter Myszko **GRAPE VARIETIES:** (red) Merlot, Cabernet Franc; (white) Zweigelt, Hiberand **RECOMMENDED WINES:** Gooseberry Wine, Framboise

The Myszko family's winery is situated east of St. Thomas, across from the airport, on a 45-acre farm in a meadow surrounded by thick woodlands. The farm produces a variety of berries and stone fruits from which Walter Myszko makes thirteen different fruit wines, including raspberry, elderberry, blackcurrant, plum, gooseberry, and nectarine—a skill he learned in his native Poland.

Myszko immigrated to Canada at the age of fifteen to live with his aunt and uncle on their tobacco farm. In his college years, he cultivated his interest in winemaking, perfecting his technique on the fruits grown on the family farm before turning to wine grapes. The warmth of the welcome alone is worth the visit.

Muscedere Vineyards

7457 COUNTY ROAD 18, HARROW, ON N0R 1G0 (519) 252-7966
WWW.MUSCEDEREVINEYARDS.COM

YEAR FOUNDED: 2006 **FOUNDERS:** Fabio and Roberto Muscedere
WINEMAKERS: Fabio Muscedere, Roberto Muscedere **GRAPE VARI-
ETIES:** (red) Cabernet Franc, Pinot Noir, Cabernet Sauvignon, Malbec,
Merlot, Syrah; (white) Vidal, Riesling, Sauvignon Blanc, Pinot Gris,
Chardonnay **RECOMMENDED WINE:** Chardonnay

Since 2004, the brothers Fabio and Rob Muscedere (pronounced Moo-shed-eray) have operated Canada South
Wine Tours, a company that shuttles visitors for day-long
tours of wineries around Essex County. They hit on a
creative symbiosis here, because the highlight of the bus
tour is a lunchtime stop at the brothers' new winery. The
wine gene seems to have skipped a generation in the
Muscedere family, since the grandfather owned a winery
in Italy, but Fabio and Rob's father, a machine operator,
was content just to buy a 150-acre retirement farm and
let a local farmer grow soybeans. "We didn't know what
we had in our backyard," says Roberto Muscedere, an
engineer turned vintner, "until, five or six years ago, we
realized we had a piece of land that was ideal for growing
grapes. We researched it, we did trial plantings of different clones, different rootstocks, until we found the right
ones for our soil."

The brothers make their wine in the basement of a
brick farmhouse on the property with the help of veteran
grower Sal D'Angelo, preferring to invest in the best
equipment rather than in bricks and mortar for a new
winery. For their first crush in 2004, they made seventy-five
cases each of a buttery, unoaked Chardonnay and a fresh,
light, and fruity Cabernet Franc from their own 5-acre
vineyard, and 130 cases of Riesling from purchased grapes.

Quai du Vin Estate Winery

45841 FRUITRIDGE LINE, RR 5, ST. THOMAS, ON N5P 3S9 (519) 775-2216
WWW.QUAIDUVIN.COM

YEAR FOUNDED: 1988 **FOUNDER:** Roberto Quai **WINEMAKERS:** Roberto
Quai, Jamie Quai (assistant) **GRAPE VARIETIES:** (red) Concord, Pinot
Noir, Merlot; (white) Riesling, Vidal, Chardonnay, Seyve-Villard, Niagara,
Aurore **RECOMMENDED WINE:** Vidal

Roberto Quai's father, Redi, planted the vineyard in 1970.
Roberto and his wife, Lisa, started making wine in 1988
and officially opened the winery two years later. Set on a
plateau a half-hour drive south from London, the winery,
with its product-stuffed store, offers a superb view of Lake
Erie. Here you'll find a surprisingly wide range of native
North American (labrusca) varieties as well as hybrids and
viniferas. Quai offers some of the most eccentric wines
available in the province, cross blending fruit and grape to
get such combinations as watermelon and Vidal, peach

and Chardonnay, cranberry and Elvira, and a sweet wine
made from partially evaporated maple sap—and vintage-
dated to boot. Quai pioneered the concept of a 25-cent
deposit charge on bottles in Ontario. In addition to being
environmentally conscious, he is something of a showman.
To draw visitors to his winery he puts on poker tourna-
ments, music trivia competitions, and amateur astronomer
nights, as well as rock 'n' roll and blues performers.

Sanson Estate Winery

9238 WALKER ROAD, RR 1, MCGREGOR, ON N0R 1J0 (519) 726-9609
WWW.SANSONESTATEWINERY.COM

YEAR FOUNDED: 1997 **FOUNDER:** Dennis Sanson **WINEMAKER:** Dennis
Sanson **GRAPE VARIETIES:** (red) Estate Baco Noir, Cabernet Franc,
Cabernet Sauvignon, Merlot, Syrah, Zweigelt; (white) Vidal Blanc, Pinot
Gris, Chardonnay, Sauvignon Blanc **RECOMMENDED WINES:** Baco Noir
Reserve, Sauvignon Blanc, Vidal Icewine

Dennis Sanson, a former hospitality school teacher and
professional chef, began making wine in his garage. True
to his down-to-earth style, his retail wine store on the 90-
acre property is housed in a former chicken barn. Sanson
initially bought the property to grow vegetables, in
particular heirloom tomatoes, and to raise cattle, pigs, and
poultry. He grows some of his own grapes (Baco Noir
and Vidal), but the rest he buys from contract growers. His
4,000-square-foot winery, with its ample patio garden,
was designed to blend in with the existing farm structures
that date from around 1840. It also houses an event hall
that can accommodate 120 people.

Smith & Wilson Estate Wines

8368 WATER STREET, RR 1, BLENHEIM, ON N0P 1A0 (519) 676-5867
SMITH.WILSON@SOUTHKENT.NET

YEAR FOUNDED: 2004 **FOUNDERS:** George and Mary Smith
WINEMAKERS: George Smith, Mary Smith **GRAPE VARIETIES:** (red) Baco
Noir, Cabernet Franc, Cabernet Sauvignon, Chambourcin, Gamay, Petit
Verdot, Merlot, Pinot Noir, Zwiegelt; (white) Chardonnay,
Gewurztraminer, Pinot Gris, Riesling, Sauvignon Blanc, Vidal, Viognier
RECOMMENDED WINES: Gewurztraminer, Rondeau

Smith & Wilson sounds suspiciously like a firearms
manufacturer, but it's much less threatening as a combination of George Smith and Mary Wilson. The couple are
long-time grape growers who turned professional in 2004,
making five grape wines and a fruit wine (raspberry-
apple). "Through the years of selling our grapes to Pelee
Island and Sanson," says Mary, "we've met the winemakers. They were all very encouraging." The property
stretches to the lake and ends abruptly, with an 18 metre
drop straight into the water. The Smith & Wilson label
features a line drawing of the couple's house, which
contains the tasting room.

A southwest Ontario vineyard before bud break.

Sprucewood Shores Estate Winery

7258 COUNTY ROAD 50 WEST, HARROW, ON N0R 1G0 (519) 738-9253
GORD@SPRUCEWOODSHORES.COM, RESTAURANT: (519) 738-9253

YEAR FOUNDED: 2006 **FOUNDER:** Gordon Mitchell **WINEMAKER:** Tanya
Mitchell **GRAPE VARIETIES:** (red) Cabernet Franc, Cabernet Sauvignon,
Gamay Noir, Merlot, Pinot Noir; (white) Chardonnay, Pinot Gris, Vidal
RECOMMENDED WINE: Pinot Noir

Like many operations starting up in Essex County,
Sprucewood Shores is a true family business. Gordon
Mitchell, a former plant manager at the Daimler-Chrysler
factory in Ajax, planted his vineyard in 1990. "I still had
dirt between my toes," he confesses. "I grew up on a mixed
farm, dairy and grain producing, down in the Windsor
area. So we're kind of moving back to where we started."

The winery, constructed above two barrel cellars, is a
combination of Tuscan and Canadian lakeshore architecture: limestone quarried in Amherstburg along with
board-and-batten finish around the wainscoted stones on
the sides and back. It stands in the 35-acre vineyard 150
metres from the lake. The family plans to open two or
three bedrooms in their home as a B&B.

Tanya Mitchell, Gordon's daughter, is a chemical engi-
neer who took over the winemaking. The other children—
Stephan, Marlaina, and Jacob—are also involved in the
operation. For the inaugural vintage in 2004, Tanya
Mitchell produced four red wines: Pinot Noir, Cabernet
Franc, Cabernet Sauvignon, and Merlot.

Viewpointe Estate Winery

151 COUNTY ROAD 50 EAST, HARROW, ON N0R 1G0
WWW.VIEWPOINTEWINERY.COM

YEAR FOUNDED: 2000 **FOUNDERS:** John, Steve, and Jean Fancsy
WINEMAKERS: John Fancsy, Joceyln Clark (assistant) **GRAPE VARIETIES:**
(red) Cabernet Franc, Cabernet Sauvignon, Merlot, Pinot Noir, St. Laurent,
Sangiovese, Syrah, Tempranillo; (white) Auxerrois, Chardonnay,
Chardonnay Musqué, Gewurztraminer, Pinot Gris, Riesling, Sauvignon
Blanc, Semillon, Viognier **RECOMMENDED WINES:** Cabernet Franc,
Cabernet Merlot, Pinot Noir

John Fancsy and his brother Stephen think big. They
bought into a California vine nursery to supply themselves
with their plant needs and, currently, have seventeen
different varieties in their three Lake Erie vineyards. They
both gave up lucrative jobs as automobile engineers to start
Viewpointe, which will become something of a showplace
for Essex County. The gravity-flow facility is located right
on the bluff of Lake Erie in Harrow.

Viewpointe Estate Winery is made up of three vineyard
parcels: Walnut Grove (planted in 2000), Northviewpointe
(planted in 2001), and Viewpointe (planted in 1999 and
acquired from Sal D'Angelo in 2001). After two or three
years, when these vines are mature, they should produce
about 14,000 cases. At full capacity, the production will
be in the 25,000-case range. The emphasis here is on red
wines made from Cabernet Franc, Cabernet Sauvignon,
and Merlot.

Pelee Island (See map on page 183)

Lying about 25 kilometres off the mainland of southern Ontario in Lake Erie is Canada's best-kept secret. A ninety-minute ferry ride from either Kingsville or Leamington, this 10,000-acre island, shaped like the face of a fox, is Canada's most southerly inhabited point and its smallest viticultural area. (The most southerly point in Canada is actually Middle Island, a tiny uninhabited island, now a national park and said to be the place where Al Capone once had a house.)

Historically, Pelee Island is where Vin Villa, the first commercial winery in Canada, was built in 1866 (its haunting remains can still be seen). The winery was built by a Kentucky gentleman farmer named Thaddeus Smith, who bought 40 acres on Sheridan Point at the northern part of the island. Out of the solid rock he excavated a cellar measuring 4 metres deep, 13 metres wide, and 20 metres long and covered it with two enormous stone arches. Above the cellar Smith built the basement of his house and, for the winery, an entranceway large enough for a horse and wagon filled with grapes to enter. Over the basement, Smith constructed a Southern-style mansion from the stones carved out of the wine cellar, and he filled the house with antiques. Vin Villa was destroyed by fire in 1963 and, today, only the ivy-covered stone walls remain—like those of a ruined monastery. You can see a model of what Vin Villa looked like in its prime near Pheasant Farm, where 20,000 game birds are raised for the annual May hunt. (The contemporary Pelee Island Winery, founded in 1984, is on the mainland at Kingsville.)

There are no cows on Pelee Island, no deer, and no skunks, but this land is teeming with wildlife, including red foxes, rabbits, and wild turkeys. But its greatest glory is its bird life, especially the diversity of waterfowl. The island is on the migration path for birds and the monarch butterfly flying south for the winter. Many of the creatures that inhabit the island or use it as an airport can be found on the labels of Pelee Island Winery.

Pelee Island shares the same geological structure as Essex County—light brown stony loam over a bed of clay that covers limestone bedrock, the latter dating back to the Devonian age, some 400 million years ago. Shaped like an inverted saucer in profile, at its highest point the island is a mere 12 metres above the level of the lake. Drainage is a problem, so the vineyards have been planted in the southwestern corner and the centre of the island, where there is a concentration of dark Brookston clay. This type of clay drains better than the heavy black Toledo clay that characterizes the soil on the rest of the island.

Pelee Island, with its safe beaches, fishing, Red Cedar Savannah Nature Reserve, and historic lighthouse and Vin Villa site, is a place to explore by car, by bike, or on foot. The ferry ride is long enough to calm city tensions and prepare you for the hyper-relaxed pace of the island.

**TOURING THE WINERY
on Pelee Island**

SINGLE DAY: Because Pelee Island Winery is located on the mainland at Kingsville, you can spend an hour there tasting, but the real experience is on the island itself, where you'll find the wine pavilion. So plan to spend the day there. Once you find it, you'll wish you had booked into a B&B or brought your camping gear so you could spend more time exploring the island. Check the ferry schedule, because the boat leaves from either Leamington or Kingsville, depending on the month. If you arrive on foot, you can rent bikes or simply take the winery's shuttle bus to the pavilion. WEEKEND: Book a B&B and drive to see the ruins of Vin Villa, then visit the Pelee Island Winery pavilion. You can buy frozen hamburgers there and grill them yourself on the communal barbecues. The next day explore the island, but don't miss Pheasant Farm or the ancient lighthouse. Just be aware that if you visit during harvest time, you'll be sharing the ferry with grapes, corn, and soybeans.

Historic map of Pelee Island, 1866.

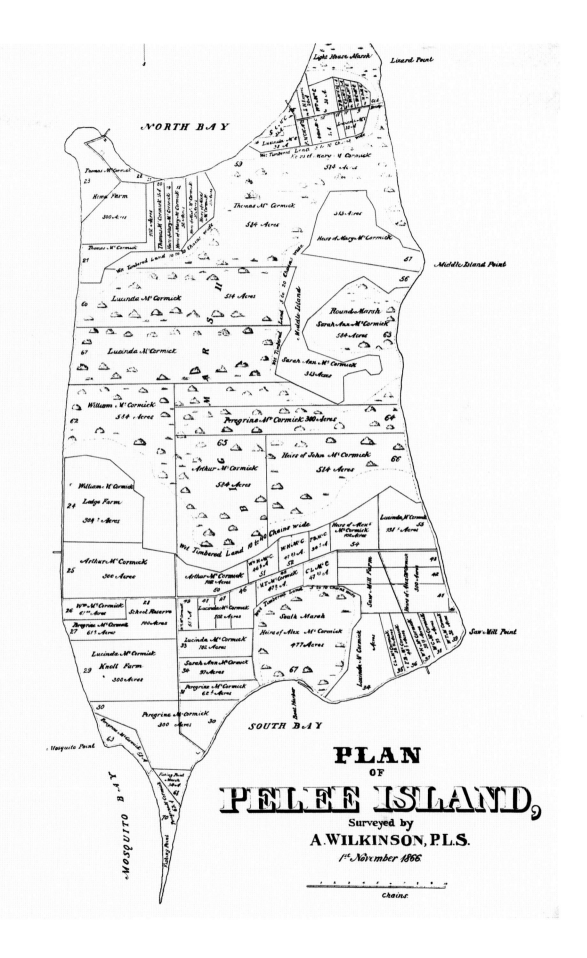

PLAN
OF
PELEE ISLAND,
Surveyed by
A. WILKINSON, P.L.S.
1st November 1866.

chains.

THE ISLAND APPELLATION

At the turn of the twentieth century, Pelee Island was three distinct islands. Dykes were built and the inland marshes filled in to create a single island 14.5 kilometres north to south and 5.6 kilometres at its widest point—the largest island in the Lake Erie basin. The roads you drive today were built on the dykes, and pumping stations are still used to safeguard against flooding. There are fewer than 300 permanent residents, but numbers swell fourfold during the summer season, with cottagers and other vacationers (there are eighteen B&Bs here). Eighty percent of the island's surface is planted to wheat, corn, grapes, and soybeans. Henry Ford planted the first soybeans on Pelee Island because his automobile company made steering wheels out of them. The 500 acres of vineyards planted at the centre of the island are the property of Pelee Island Winery, the only winery in Canada to have an appellation all to itself.

What makes Pelee Island most viable as a wine-growing area is Lake Erie, the shallowest of all the Great Lakes and, as a result, the one with the warmest surface temperature. The lake has a moderating effect on the cold air masses blowing in from the Arctic in winter. The warmer climate during spring, summer, and fall allows for a longer growing season than in the Niagara Peninsula, though in January and February you might not believe that the island is on the same latitude as Rome and California's Mendocino County. The snow that is created by the interaction of wind, air, and open water acts as a protective insulation for the vines. Because of the high water table, the wines of this region can be somewhat lighter than those grown on the mainland. Winemakers who seek richer, more concentrated taste profiles often cut down the number of bunches on the vine.

LEFT: Aerial view of Pelee Island. ABOVE: Pelee Island Winery.
BOTTOM LEFT: Antique poster of Pelee Island Winery.
BOTTOM RIGHT: Historic Pelee Island barrel overgrown with vines.

Pelee Island Winery

455 SEACLIFF DRIVE (COUNTY ROAD 20), KINGSVILLE, ON N9Y 2K5
(519) 733-6551; 1-800-597-3533 WWW.PELEEISLAND.COM

YEAR FOUNDED: 1984 **FOUNDERS:** Wolf von Teichman and the Strehn
family **WINEMAKERS:** Walter Schmoranz, Martin Janz **GRAPE VARI-
ETIES:** (red) Cabernet Franc, Gamay Noir, Zweigelt, Cabernet
Sauvignon, Merlot; (white) Chardonnay, Riesling, Gewurztraminer, Pinot
Gris, Vidal **RECOMMENDED WINES:** Vinedressers Cabernet Franc
Reserve, Zweigelt/Gamay, Pinot Gris Vendage Tardive

Pelee Island Winery enjoys four distinctions: it's unique in
its appellation; it was the site of Canada's first commercial
winery, Vin Villa, in 1866; it's the only winery that has to
ferry its fruit from the vineyard to the winery; and it was
the first Ontario winery to produce a commercial quan-
tity of Icewine (Vidal 1983) and the first red Icewine
(Lemberger and Blaufränkisch 1989).

In 1980 Austrian winemaker Walter Strehn planted
Riesling, Chardonnay, and other German varieties on
Pelee Island. Three years later he shipped the grapes back
to Kingsville on the mainland for processing. When Strehn
returned to his homeland, another Austrian, Walter
Schmoranz, took over the winemaking.

The winery, built in 1984 and subsequently remodelled,
resembles a prosperous church, with white walls and
windows defined in local stone. But the real experience
is on the island itself, where you will find the Pelee Island
Wine Pavilion. From the ferry dock, buses shuttle visitors
to the impressive contemporary barn building, approached
by a pathway marked by rose bushes. Dominating the
interior is a huge wooden wine press from Germany
dated 1723; around it is a museum of winemaking equipment, antique bottles, and a photo essay on how corks
are made. You can sip the wines on the covered balcony
or sit under picnic umbrellas on the expansive grass patio.

The wealth of flora and fauna in the area—over 10,000
indigenous species of plants and animal life—is celebrated
in the variety of the winery's bird and animal labels.
Pelee Island makes over twenty-five different wines.

Prince Edward County

Think of Prince Edward County as Sonoma to Niagara's Napa, slightly less developed and sophisticated but more rural and bucolic than its established neighbour to the west. The region was settled by United Empire Loyalists fleeing the American Revolution, who cleared the land they settled and planted barley and hops. A testament to the wealth of those industrious nineteenth-century farmers, who supplied American breweries with their hops and malted barley, are the fieldstone farm houses and solid brick homes of Picton, Wellington, and Bloomfield.

With the introduction of tariffs against these products in 1880, the local farmers turned to green peas and other vegetables suitable for canning. A thriving cheese industry developed because the region could sustain animal feed crops as well as fruit orchards. Even grapes were grown. As early as the 1870s, there was a winery in Hillier whose wines were good enough to take a gold medal at the Centennial Exposition in Philadelphia.

Prince Edward County might seem an unlikely wine region—an island, formerly a peninsula, that jutted out into Lake Ontario midway between Toronto and Kingston. The dredging of the 8 kilometre Murray Canal between 1882 and 1889 effectively cut off the county from the mainland, creating an island of 250,000 acres with an estimated 800 kilometres of shoreline. The land here is essentially a large limestone plateau, rising to its highest point at 150 metres above sea level. The presence of upper-bedrock limestone soil has attracted winegrowers who seek to produce the Holy Grail—Pinot Noir. Much of the county has a shallow soil depth before you reach bedrock, but relatively low rainfall, coupled with the ameliorating effects of the Bay of Quinte and Lake Ontario, makes it ideal land for growing orchard fruits, tomatoes, corn, peas—and wine grapes.

Still, it's what's above the ground that will intrigue the wine traveller. This is a landscape of undulating pasture land and lovely villages with old farmhouses, pioneer barns, and handsome Victorian mansions. The shoreline culminates in one of the greatest natural beach areas in Canada, Sandbanks Provincial Park, beloved of campers and daytrippers. The major cluster of wineries is in Hillier Township, where the surface gravelly clay–loam soil, reddish brown in colour, is high in limestone fragments and well drained as a result. The climate here, and in Athol, North Marysburg, and Hallowel, is moderated by the large bodies of water that surround the county, but the temperature is, on average, lower than that of the Niagara Peninsula. The last spring frost can be as late as mid-May, and the first frost in mid-October, giving Prince Edward a slightly shorter growing season than Ontario's other viticultural regions. Winter is the enemy here and the growers have to bury their vines.

Prince Edward County created an agri-tourism infrastructure before it had a critical mass of wineries. It has a winery route, a taste trail, and events such as the Taste of the County that include restaurants, cheese producers, organic growers, and lamb, beef, and pork producers.

**TOURING WINERIES
in Prince Edward County**

The county is compact enough for you to visit four or five wineries in a day with ease. The main concentration is between Hillier and Picton. An excellent website (www.tastetrail.ca) gives you information on some of the wineries, but it is a better resource for restaurants, accommodation, and local retailers of interest.

SINGLE DAY: For a good cross-section of styles and sizes of wineries, don't miss Huff Estates, the Grange, Long Dog, and Closson Chase.

WEEKEND: B&Bs proliferate in the county, as well as excellent restaurants, including the Milford Bistro (Milford), Merrill Inn (Picton), and Angeline's (Bloomfield). In addition to the wineries mentioned above, spend your second day visiting By Chadsey's Cairns (for history buffs), Norman Hardie Winery (for top-flight wines), Sandbanks Estate (for sheer charm), and the Black Prince (for its wide selection of wines).

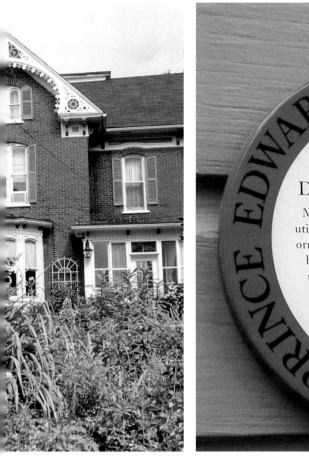

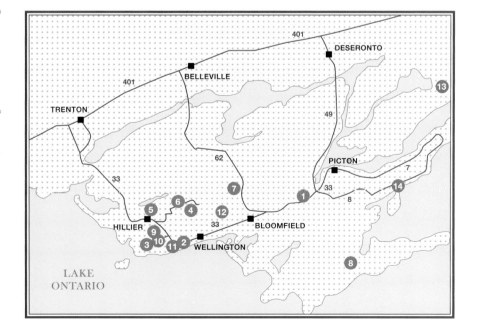

LEFT: Bed-and-breakfast house in Wellington. ABOVE: Prince Edward County heritage marker at Long Dog Vineyard & Winery.

PRINCE EDWARD COUNTY WINERIES

1 BLACK PRINCE WINERY
2 BY CHADSEY'S CAIRNS WINERY & VINEYARD
3 CARMELA ESTATES WINERY
4 CLOSSON CHASE WINERY
5 DOMAINE LA REINE
6 THE GRANGE OF PRINCE EDWARD
7 HUFF ESTATES WINERY
8 LONG DOG VINEYARD & WINERY
9 NORMAN HARDIE WINERY
10 ROSEHALL RUN VINEYARDS
11 SANDBANKS ESTATE WINERY
12 SUGARBUSH VINEYARDS
13 THIRTY THREE VINES
14 WAUPOOS ESTATES WINERY

OPPOSITE: Historic graveyard at By Chadsey's Cairns Winery & Vineyard. ABOVE: Richard Johnston and Vida Zalnieriunas of By Chadsey's Cairns.

Black Prince Winery

13370 LOYALIST PARKWAY, RR 1, PICTON, ON K0K 2T0 (613) 476-4888;
1-866-470-9463 WWW.BLACKPRINCEWINERY.COM

YEAR FOUNDED: 2001 **FOUNDERS:** John Sambrook, Geoff Webb, and Val O'Donovan **WINEMAKER:** Geoff Webb **GRAPE VARIETIES:** (red) Chambourcin, Pinot Noir, Maréchal Foch, Cabernet Franc; (white) Auxerrois, Chardonnay, Riesling **RECOMMENDED WINES:** Auxerrois, Baco Noir

John Sambrook, general manager of the Opimian Society, a wine-buying cooperative, for over thirty years, dreamed up the idea of a winery in Prince Edward County in 2000. Sambrook, an Englishman, named the winery after the warrior son of Edward III who led the English at the Battle of Crécy at the age of sixteen and won the Battle of Poitiers. The suit of armour that stands at the entrance to the tasting room is a favourite photo op for visitors. Behind the suburban-looking house on this 50-acre property is an old horse barn where the winery is located and, behind that, a 9-acre vineyard planted in sandy loam soil.

Marshland is currently being reclaimed to plant more vineyards. The winery also buys in grapes from Ontario as well as juice from California for Opimian Society wines. In its first year, Black Prince crushed 8 tonnes of locally grown grapes and imported 36 tonnes. Plan to visit in June for the medieval joust.

By Chadsey's Cairns Winery & Vineyard

17432 LOYALIST PARKWAY, RR 1, WELLINGTON, ON K0K 3L0 (613) 399-2992
WWW.BYCHADSEYSCAIRNS.COM

YEAR FOUNDED: 2003 **FOUNDERS:** Richard Johnston and Vida Zalnieriunas **WINEMAKER:** Vida Zalnieriunas **GRAPE VARIETIES:** (red) Gamay, Pinot Noir, St. Laurent; (white) Riesling, Chardonnay, Gewurztraminer, Muscat, Chenin Blanc **RECOMMENDED WINES:** Riesling, Gewurztraminer, Pinot Noir

Ira Chadsey (1828–1905) was an eccentric Loyalist and professed atheist who settled this 200-year-old farm and fenced in its boundaries with a series of fourteen cairns built from fieldstone and interspersed with Victorian metal posts. In 1995 Richard Johnston, a former New Democrat MPP and past president of Centennial College, Scarborough, bought this historic property overlooking Wellington Bay, near Picton, and planted his vineyard four years later. All four historic barns on the property are part of the winery operation—the former horse barn is now the winery, and a beautifully proportioned old red-brick Quaker meeting hall has been transformed into the wine shop. In addition to 20 acres of vines, Johnston and his wife, Vida, keep a flock of Cotswold sheep and other farm animals. The pioneer cemetery on the property, with gravestones dating back to 1805, is a treat for amateur genealogists.

Carmela Estates Winery

1186 GREER ROAD, RR 1, WELLINGTON, ON K0K 3L0 (613) 399-3939;
1-866-578-3445 WWW.CARMELAESTATES.CA

YEAR FOUNDED: 2002 **FOUNDERS:** Bob and Sherry Tompkins **WINEMAKER:** Norman Hardie **GRAPE VARIETIES:** (red) Cabernet Franc, Pinot Noir; (white) Riesling, Chardonnay, Pinot Gris **RECOMMENDED WINES:** Chardonnay, Riesling, Cabernet Franc

Mike Peddlesden, who now manages the vineyards at the Grange of Prince Edward, was the guiding force behind this winery when it was opened in 2002 as Peddlesden Wines. He sold his interest to his partners, Bob and Sherry Tompkins, two years later, and they renamed it Carmela after Sherry's mother. They brought in a new winemaker: Norman Hardie had extensive experience making wine in his native South Africa as well as in

Burgundy, New Zealand, California, and Oregon before he settled in Canada's newest wine region. The Burgundy varieties—Chardonnay and Pinot Noir—are Hardie's strong suit, and they, in turn, should ultimately prove to be the signature wines of the county.

Carmela's state-of-the-art processing facility is housed in a soaring cathedral-like building—a large custom-built, contemporary-styled Ontario bank barn with huge picture windows looking over the 22-acre vineyard and an ash forest beyond. The stone steps of the entranceway are marked on both sides by goldfish ponds, fed with running water from twin wine barrels. To the right is an outdoor chess set. Inside you'll find a bright, contemporary tasting room and wine shop as well as an adjacent hall offering banqueting and convention opportunities. Enjoy a picnic in the grounds or rent the villa for the night.

Closson Chase Winery

629 CLOSSON ROAD, HILLIER, ON K0K 2J0 (613) 399-1418; 1-888-201-2300
WWW.CLOSSONCHASE.COM

YEAR FOUNDED: 2001 **FOUNDERS:** Seaton McLean, Andy Thomson, Michael MacMillan, Sonja Smits, Eugene McBurney, William Fanjoy, and Deborah Paskus **WINEMAKER:** Deborah Paskus **GRAPE VARIETIES:** (red) Pinot Noir; (white) Chardonnay **RECOMMENDED WINES:** Pinot Noir, Chardonnay

The partners couldn't decide on what to call their winery, so they looked at the nearest cross streets—Closson and Chase. The self-contained winery—a building within a building—is housed in a magnificent 130-year-old double milk barn that has been cleverly renovated. Sheets of Plexiglas sheathe the walls and maintain the integrity of

Domaine la Reine

PO BOX 66, CONSECON, ON K0K 1T0 (613) 394-0236
WWW.DOMAINELAREINE.CA

YEAR FOUNDED: 2003 **FOUNDERS:** Geoff Heinricks and Lauren Grice
WINEMAKER: Geoff Heinricks **GRAPE VARIETIES:** (red) Pinot Noir
RECOMMENDED WINE: Pinot Noir

Domaine la Reine, as bricks and mortar, does not exist as yet. It is what Geoff Heinricks, a former contributor to *Frank* magazine, refers to as "a winery within a winery, operating within Closson Chase Vineyards." The wines are made and sold there, but the fruit is sourced from Heinricks's own vineyard, which he planted in 1995 with some thirty different clones of Pinot Noir. This "virtual winery" arrangement will continue until Domaine la Reine has its own facility (either in 2006 or 2007, or when Closson Chase needs the full space).

"I fervently believe in Hillier as one of the most tantalizing and rewarding areas to grow and make Pinot Noir in Canada, if not the New World," confides Heinricks, a committed pioneer grower in the county who has chronicled his struggle to create a Pinot Noir vineyard in *A Fool and Forty Acres*. He's also written the viticultural primer for the Prince Edward County Economic Development Office. When he builds his own cellars on his property, they will be integrated into the limestone farmhouse buildings.

The first releases of his Domaine la Reine wines are under the Grand Hiver label, which will become the Domaine's second label when the high-density (3,630 vines per acre) vineyards at the Domaine and those at his supplier, Little Creek Vineyard, mature further. Grapes and vineyards are maintained organically, though they are not certified.

Heinricks will make a maximum of 1,000 cases of wine, and he plans to expand his vineyard to include the red Austrian variety St. Laurent, "a white mutation from our vineyard now called Pinot Lauren (named after his wife)," and the Melon de Bourgogne (Muscadet).

The Grange of Prince Edward

990 CLOSSON ROAD, HILLIER, ON K0K 2J0 (613) 399-1048; 1-866-792-7712
WWW.THEGRANGEWINES.COM, RESTAURANT: (613) 399-1048;
1-866-792-7712

YEAR FOUNDED: 2004 **FOUNDERS:** Robert N. Granger and Caroline
Granger **WINEMAKER:** Jeff Innes **GRAPE VARIETIES:** (red) Pinot
Noir, Gamay, Cabernet Franc; (white) Chardonnay, Pinot Gris,
Riesling **RECOMMENDED WINES:** Trumpour's Mill Gamay Noir,
Chardonnay Reserve

In 1974, Bay Street lawyer Robert Granger and his wife, Diana, purchased a Loyalist farm near Hillier. They lovingly restored the 1875 farmhouse, the barn, and Trumpour's sawmill and landscaped the grounds around

OPPOSITE: Cabernet Franc vines await planting in Wellington.
TOP: Andy Thompson, his wife, Pat Phillips, winemaker Deborah Paskus, and Sonja Smits of Closson Chase Winery.
ABOVE: The Grange of Prince Edward.

the old structure, with all its gaps between the boards, while ensuring comfort inside. The vermilion-painted tasting room, with its tin-sided bar, is an ideal spot to enjoy the only two wines Deborah Paskus makes here— Pinot Noir and Chardonnay (she is also the winemaker at Tawse). But what wines! Paskus is known for her intense, Burgundian-style Chardonnays and Pinot Noirs, produced without compromise from low-tonnage grapes fermented in the best French oak barrels. Though Paskus may profess that Closson Chase is "unsophisticated in terms of technology," the décor and glassware suggest an upmarket wine-bar experience. The winery's evocative labels, based on shipping flags, were designed by the renowned Newfoundland artist David Blackwood. The colours are recreated in the stained glass at the main entrance to the winery.

the creek that runs through the property, creating two pond sites. In 2001 they planted the first of five vineyards. The imposing barn that dates back to 1826 now houses the winery. The open-plan tasting room, with its handsome bird's-eye maple bar and magnificent fieldstone fireplace, is located in the former hayloft and is furnished with local Canadiana pieces. The barrel cellar is below in the old milking stalls. The Grangers' daughter, Caroline, a former Dior model and actor, came home from Paris to run the vineyards, having taken a two-year course in vineyard management at Loyalist College in Belleville.

Winemaker Jeff Innes makes wines under the Trumpour's Mill label from Niagara grapes. He also collaborates with a Burgundian consultant from Puligny-Montrachet on the production of Pinot Noir and Chardonnay, grown here in the 50-acre vineyard. "Our goal is to learn from Burgundy," says Caroline Granger. "I love the elegance and understatement of those wines." Be sure to include this winery on your tour.

Huff Estates Winery

2274 COUNTY ROAD 1, BLOOMFIELD, ON K0K 1G0 (613) 393-5802
WWW.HUFFESTATES.COM, ACCOMMODATION: THE INN AT HUFF ESTATES,
(613) 393-5802

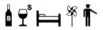

YEAR FOUNDED: 2000 **FOUNDER:** Frank (Lanny) Huff **WINEMAKER:**
Frédéric Picard **GRAPE VARIETIES:** (red) Merlot, Cabernet Franc,
Cabernet Sauvignon; (white) Pinot Gris, Chardonnay **RECOMMENDED**
WINES: Chardonnay, Merlot, Rosé

What Mission Hill is to the Okanagan and Le Clos Jordanne will be to Niagara, Huff Estate is to Prince Edward County—a go-to winery that, since its opening in 2004, is already a magnet for tourists. The modern industrial building is set back from the road at Huff's Corners (named for Lanny Huff's family, who settled here as United Empire Loyalists in 1825). An 8-acre vineyard (one of the three owned by Huff, totalling 43 acres) leads up to the winery, which sits on top of Mount Pleasant, one of the highest points in the county. Its position allows for a gravity-feed operation to the barrel cellar below.

Huff is the proverbial local boy made good. A chemical engineer, he made a tidy fortune in the plastics business over forty years and spent a reputed $6 million to build a state-of-the-art winery with a sunken cellar, high technology, and even a helicopter pad that will facilitate corporate getaways to the twenty-suite country inn that opened in 2006.

Huff was the first winery in the region to grow Merlot (at the South Bay vineyard, close to Lake Ontario). To make his wines, Lanny Huff hired the young Burgundy-trained winemaker Frédéric Picard, who has worked vintages in South Africa, Chile, California, and Tuscany, and most recently with fellow Frenchman Jean-Pierre Colas at Peninsula Ridge. Picard plans to make a sparkling wine, an intelligent choice because the grapes for sparkling wine

The historic 1875 Dulmage driveshed at Long Dog Vineyard & Winery. RIGHT: The winery's mailbox.

don't have to be as ripe as those for table wine. You can purchase a light lunch here on the patio. Enjoy!

Long Dog Vineyard & Winery

104 BREWERS ROAD, MILFORD, ON K0K 2P0 (613) 476-4140
WWW.LONGDOG.CA

YEAR FOUNDED: 1999 **FOUNDERS:** James Lahti, Steven Rapkin, and
Victoria Rose **WINEMAKERS:** James Lahti, Dan Sullivan **GRAPE VARI-**
ETIES: (red) Pinot Noir, Gamay; (white) Chardonnay, Pinot Gris
RECOMMENDED WINES: Chardonnay, Pinot Gris, Pinot Noir

James Lahti, an IMAX film producer and accomplished home winemaker, bought the farm as a retreat in 1997 and planted the first 1,300 vines himself in 1999. Buried behind the first Pinot Noir vine he planted is "Otto the Wonder Dog," a wire-haired Dachshund that gives the winery its name. Lahti operates Long Dog out of two barns dating back to 1860 and 1870. Both have been

marvellously restored. The larger of the two—a former horse stable with a silver-painted roof—houses a series of old milk tanks purchased for fermenting his Pinot Noir. The smaller building used to be a pig barn ("I call it the Swinery," he says). It is now mercifully odourless and is where Lahti ferments and barrel ages his white wines in French and Hungarian oak.

Long Dog is a complete estate winery, using only its own grapes, one of the few that does not resort to bringing in fruit from Niagara. In the tasting room across the road from the barns, you can sample some of the best wines made in Prince Edward County. Lahti credits the quality of his Pinot Noir to the concentration of limestone in his soil, a constituent that Prince Edward County shares with Burgundy.

Long Dog wines are not inexpensive, but then, neither is Burgundy. Lahti, ably assisted by his winemaker friend Dan Sullivan, has set the pace for the county with his richly textured Chardonnay, peachy Pinot Gris, and authentic Pinot Noir.

Norman Hardie Winery

1152 GREER ROAD, WELLINGTON, ON K0K 3L0 (613) 961-9836
NJH@ROGERS.COM

YEAR FOUNDED: 2004 **FOUNDERS:** Norman J. Hardie and Oliver Lennox-King **WINEMAKER:** Norman J. Hardie **GRAPE VARIETIES:** (red) Pinot Noir; (white) Chardonnay, Riesling, Pinot Gris **RECOMMENDED WINES:** Chardonnay, Pinot Noir

Norman Hardie makes the wine for Carmela, but has always wanted his own winery, designed to his specifications of functionality (a gravity-flow operation with an underground barrel chamber). Now he has achieved his dream, virtually across the street from Carmela. The winery, incorporating Hardie's house, is a contemporary New Age barn with a metal roof and redwood-stained pine siding that melds into the farmscape around him. Hardie's two-storey home is connected to the winery by a breezeway. The building is judiciously situated on a steep slope, allowing for a gravity-flow operation and a barrel chamber to be carved out of the hillside. Remnants of the exposed rock in the cellar show the metre-deep band of solid limestone that runs through the property—ideal base soil for Pinot Noir. Like James Lahti at Long Dog, Hardie ferments his wines in horizontal milk tanks to ensure that his whites get maximum lees contact for flavour (he stirs the lees of the juice two or three times a day for five days before fermentation to extract maximum flavour), and he gives his reds long skin contact for colour. A unique feature for visitors is the outdoor wood-burning BBQ and pizza oven for summertime Saturday luncheons, accompanied by a wine tasting with Hardie in the barrel chamber or overlooking the cellar in the loft. Hardie's winemaking experience in South Africa and Burgundy shows in the finely structured, richly flavoured wines he's making here. All Hardie wines are bottled under screwcap. This winery is definitely one to watch.

Dan and Lynn Sullivan and their children, Megan and Dylan, of Rosehall Run Vineyards. OPPOSITE: On the winery's 150-acre farm.

Rosehall Run Vineyards

1243 GREER ROAD, HILLIER, ON K0K 3L0 (613) 399-1183

YEAR FOUNDED: 2001 **FOUNDERS:** Dan Sullivan, Cam Reston, Lynn Sullivan, and Cindy Zwicker-Reston **WINEMAKER:** Dan Sullivan **GRAPE VARIETIES:** (red) Pinot Noir; (white) Chardonnay, Chardonnay Musqué, Ehrenfelser **RECOMMENDED WINES:** Pinot Noir, Chardonnay

Dan Sullivan has received high praise and many awards for his wines at the amateur level. These include Best Wine in Canada 2001 for his 1999 Chardonnay; gold medal in Intervin's amateur division competition for his 1999 Baco Noir; and Best Chardonnay 2003. He also received silver medals at the Amateur Winemakers of Ontario competition for his Icewine. Sullivan bought the 150-acre picturesque farm property in 2000 and planted 15 acres of vinifera vines, including 7 acres to four different clones of Pinot Noir. Currently he is making his wines in a small barn on the property next to Carmela on Greer Road, but he plans to build a new winery and is "toying with doing a sparkling wine." Since the 2002 crush, Sullivan has also provided technical and oenological assistance to Long Dog Winery.

Sandbanks Estate Winery

17598 LOYALIST PARKWAY, WELLINGTON, ON K0K 3L3 (613) 399-1839
WWW.SANDBANKSWINERY.COM

YEAR FOUNDED: 2000 **FOUNDER:** Catherine Langlois **WINEMAKER:** Catherine Langlois **GRAPE VARIETIES:** (red) Cabernet Franc, Pinot Noir, Baco Noir; (white) Vidal, Riesling **RECOMMENDED WINES:** Cabernet Franc, Baco Noir, Dunes Vidal, Riesling

Sandbanks Estate is a small family operation owned by Catherine Langlois and her husband, Rene Lorenzo (marketing director for Pelee Island Wines). The winery facility is in the basement of the couple's A-frame house, behind the 5.5-acre vineyard right on Highway 33, the Loyalist Parkway, with a view of the lake. Langlois makes her red wines here and her whites (which require cooling apparatus) at Black Prince. Langlois studied hotel management in Montreal and, in 1994, won a bursary to work the harvest in Burgundy. On her return to Ontario, she was offered a job by Pelee Island Winery, not in the cellar but, because she is bilingual, selling their wines in Ottawa. The sales experience, coupled with her training as a sommelier and a winemaker, gave Langlois the expertise and the confidence to open her own winery. She intends to use only Sandbanks Estate fruit and to buy any varieties she does not grow herself, such as Chardonnay, from within the county. Sandbanks wines show what training in Burgundy can do: Catherine Langlois' wines have pure, clean lines and taste profiles true to their varieties. Don't miss the opportunity to taste them.

Sugarbush Vineyards

1286 WILSON ROAD, RR 1, HILLIER, ON K0K 2J0 (613) 399-9000
WWW.SUGARBUSHVINEYARDS.CA

YEAR FOUNDED: 2002 **FOUNDERS:** Robert and Sally Peck **WINEMAKERS:** Robert Peck, Sally Peck **GRAPE VARIETIES:** (red) Pinot Noir, Cabernet Franc, Gamay; (white) Chardonnay, Riesling, Gewurztraminer **RECOMMENDED WINES:** not tasted

Robert Peck, who "would rather be in the vineyard than sitting behind a desk," is a former computer engineer who

Waupoos Estates Winery and its founder Ed Neuser with his grandson Eric (RIGHT).

followed his dream of becoming a vintner in the county where he was born. The Pecks purchased a farm in Hillier in 2002 and began planting a vineyard with the help of Robert's parents. At the back of the vines there is a 6-acre stand of sugar maples, hence the name of their winery (and another revenue stream from the maple syrup they intend to produce).

At the time of writing, the winemaking operation resides in the basement of their newly built home on the property. In the future they plan to build a customized facility in stone and stucco, mirroring the look of their house. The couple's ten-year sojourn in Calgary led them into the wine world, and their nostalgia for the city leads them to celebrate with an annual breakfast on the first weekend of the Calgary Stampede. The Pecks found their inspiration in the small wineries of the Okanagan while on a visit during their honeymoon in 1997. They were especially influenced by their visit to Fairview Cellars, where Bill Eggert taught them how to prune vines.

Thirty Three Vines

9261 HIGHWAY 33 (LOYALIST PARKWAY), CONWAY, ON K0K 2T0 (613) 373-1133
WWW.PEC.ON.CA/33VINES, RESTAURANT: (613) 373-1133

YEAR FOUNDED: 2004 **FOUNDERS:** Paul and Marilyn Minaker
WINEMAKER: n/a **GRAPE VARIETIES:** (red) Cabernet Franc, Merlot, Pinot Noir; (white) Chardonnay, Riesling **RECOMMENDED WINES:** not tasted

Paul Minaker, a telecommunications consultant, had an epiphany in the Napa Valley during a year-long work contract in 1997 that turned him from a beer drinker into a wine lover. The urge to make wine brought him back to his roots in Prince Edward County, particularly to Cherry Valley, where he had spent his summers as a child. Minaker searched for property here until he found a 7-acre site right on the Loyalist Parkway (Highway 33, hence the winery's name), overlooking the Adolphus Reach inlet on Lake Ontario. "It was a farm," Minaker recalls, "with a wonderful old 6,600-square-foot barn and a big red CN

caboose that I'm sure intrigues everyone in the 50,000 cars that pass by each summer." In 2004 he began planting his vineyard and, in addition, acquired a further 22 acres near a hundred-year-old limestone schoolhouse that his grandfather attended and, later, where his grandmother taught.

The caboose is being outfitted to become the winery's initial tasting room. A large patio is planned that overlooks the vineyard and the water. The winery opens in 2006.

Waupoos Estates Winery

3016 COUNTY ROAD 8, PICTON, ON K0K 2T0 (613) 476-8338
WWW.WAUPOOSWINERY.COM, RESTAURANT: GAZEBO RESTAURANT,
(613) 476-8338

YEAR FOUNDED: 2001 **FOUNDERS:** Ed Neuser and Rita Kaimins
WINEMAKER: Amy Mumby **GRAPE VARIETIES:** (red) Baco Noir, St.
Laurent, De Chaunac, Pinot Noir; (white) Vidal, Seyval Blanc,
Geisenheim, Chardonnay, Riesling, Auxerrois, Gewurztraminer, Pinot
Blanc **RECOMMENDED WINES:** Riesling, Chardonnay

Ed Neuser and Rita Kaimins have the distinction of founding the pioneer winery in Prince Edward County. The couple came to Canada from Germany in 1983 and purchased a farm in Waupoos (an Indian name for rabbit) with a spectacular slope running down to Prince Edward Bay. Ten years later they tore out an apple orchard and planted their first vineyard of Vidal grapes. Neuser buys his red grapes from Klaus Reif in Niagara, a long-time association that resulted in Reif convincing him to grow grapes. Reif also trained his former winemaker, Jason MacDonald, who was born in the county. Amy Mumby, his assistant, is now making the wines.

The Neusers' home, the meticulously kept vineyard, the pavilion-like winery and boutique built of local limestone, and the restaurant below make a picture-perfect setting for a winery tour—especially if you arrive by boat at Waupoos's own marina, a half-hour walk away (or, if you reserve, Neuser will pick you up and deliver you back). Waupoos Estates is somewhat removed from the main concentration of wineries in Prince Edward County but worth the scenic drive, though many visitors arrive by boat. "We get twenty-five dinghies a day arriving in our sheltered bay in the summer," says Ed Neuser.

ASSOCIATION DES VITICULTEURS DE L'EST ONTARIEN

East of Prince Edward County, in the Ottawa area, the Association of Grape Growers of Eastern Ontario encourages the planting of vineyards (visit http://site.voila.fr/aveo2/). A growing number of vineyards between Brockville and Ottawa could soon become active commercial wineries. Among the first, potentially, is Domaine du Cervin and Le Verger des Pins.

DOMAINE DU CERVIN
13845 ROUTE GIBEAULT, CHESTERVILLE, ON K0C 1H0
(613) 448-2245; (613) 448-3461

YEAR FOUNDED: 2004 **FOUNDER:** Sammuel Gutknecht **WINEMAKER:**
Sammuel Gutknecht **GRAPE VARIETIES:** (red) Baco Noir, St. Laurent,
De Chaunac, Pinot Noir; (white) Vidal, Seyval Blanc, Geisenheim,
Chardonnay, Riesling, Auxerrois, Gewurztraminer, Pinot Blanc
RECOMMENDED WINE: Icewine

Samuel Gutknecht, who came to Canada in 1995, named his winery after a mountain in his native Switzerland. In that year he planted 500 vines on the rocky clay soil of an old dairy farm he purchased. His labels depict a red deer, emblematic of the herd of 300 that shares the property and whose meat products are sold at the winery.

LE VERGER DES PINS
1818 SAINT-FÉLIX, BOURGET, ON K0A 1E0 TEL: 613-487-2064
PCDORAN@HMNET.NET

Since 1995 Paul Doran has been growing apples, cherries, pears, and apricots as well as table grapes and grapes for wine on land that is south of Bourget. His vineyard is planted on a sandy knoll, in the lee of the Larose Forest. Doran produces two wines under the colourful Château Bourget label, L'Ancêtre and L'Espiègle, both a blend of grapes and apple wine.

Toronto and North of Toronto

Wineries in a suburban setting or in an industrial mall just outside the Greater Toronto Area may not be as interesting to see as those in the Niagara Peninsula, Lake Erie North Shore, Pelee Island, or Prince Edward County, but they have the advantage of being close at hand and you won't get stuck in traffic on the Queen Elizabeth Way (QEW). You'll also find wineries in rural settings north of the GTA within an hour's drive. Even without the pastoral settings, you will still have the opportunity to taste the wines and to talk to the people who make them.

While many of the wineries in the GTA and farther north have to truck the grapes or fermenting wine up from the Niagara Peninsula, there are those that have their own vineyard sites.

TOURING WINERIES
in Toronto and North of Toronto

You won't find vineyards at Cilento, Magnotta, or Vinoteca, but you will find a range of wines not available at the LCBO; and at Magnotta you can see a collection of original paintings commissioned for their labels. **SINGLE DAY:** Visit all three wineries in Woodbridge and Vaughan. You could also take in Ocala in the afternoon. **WEEKEND:** Once you have toured the wine shops of Cilento, Magnotta, and Vinoteca, spend the night in a local inn. Next day, for the vineyard experience, visit Willow Springs in Stouffville and Chesslawn in Caledon.

Chesslawn Vineyard & Winery

8859 CASTLEDERG SIDEROAD, CALEDON, ON L7E 0S7 (905) 857-2989
WWW.CHESSLAWNWINERY.COM

YEAR FOUNDED: 2005 **FOUNDERS:** David and Lisa Matson
WINEMAKER: David Matson **GRAPE VARIETIES:** (red) Baco Noir, Maréchal Foch, Pinot Noir, Cabernet Sauvignon; (white) Seyval Blanc, Vidal, Chardonanay, Riesling **RECOMMENDED WINES:** Chesslawn Gold (Chardonnay), Cabernet Sauvignon

David Matson, a tenth-generation Irish Canadian, got the wine bug while studying applied science at Pennsylvania State University. In addition to his studies, he spent two consecutive harvests volunteering at Pennsylvania's Mount Nittany Winery. After graduating, Matson returned to the family's 175-acre dairy farm in Caledon intent on starting his own winery operation in the gently rolling Albion Hills. In 2001 he and his wife, Lisa (they met at Penn State), planted an initial 1.3-acre experimental plot in a former alfalfa field that they subsequently expanded to 7 acres of vines.

The colonial-style winery that the Matsons built themselves is a fifty-minute drive from Toronto. Given its name, you would expect to find a giant chess set on the lawn, but Matson's father called the farm after the abundance of chestnut trees on the property, and "Chestlawn" just didn't sound right. David Matson is a hands-on winemaker who bottled his inaugural vintage in 2005. He believes in long oak-aging for his Chardonnay (two years) and intends to produce an Icewine in the future.

Cilento Wines

672 CHRISLEA ROAD, WOODBRIDGE, ON L4L 8K9 (905) 264-9463;
1-888-245-WINE HTTP://CILENTO.SITES.TORONTO.COM

YEAR FOUNDED: 1995 **FOUNDERS:** Angelo and Grace Locilento
WINEMAKERS: Adrian Ariel Carabajal **GRAPE VARIETIES:** (red) Merlot, Baco Noir, Gamay, Cabernet Sauvignon; (white) Riesling, Chardonnay, Vidal **RECOMMENDED WINES:** Riesling Brut, Sauvignon Blanc Reserve, Riesling Reserve, Chardonnay Reserve

Grace Locilento's grandmother used to own a vineyard in Italy, so it was natural for the young girl to dream of

Cilento Wines.

TORONTO & NORTH OF TORONTO WINERIES

1 CHESSLAWN VINEYARD
  & WINERY
2 CILENTO WINES
3 MAGNOTTA WINERY
  CORPORATION
4 OCALA ORCHARDS
  FARM WINERY
5 SILVER PEAK WINE CELLARS
6 VINOTECA WINERY
7 WILLOW SPRINGS WINERY

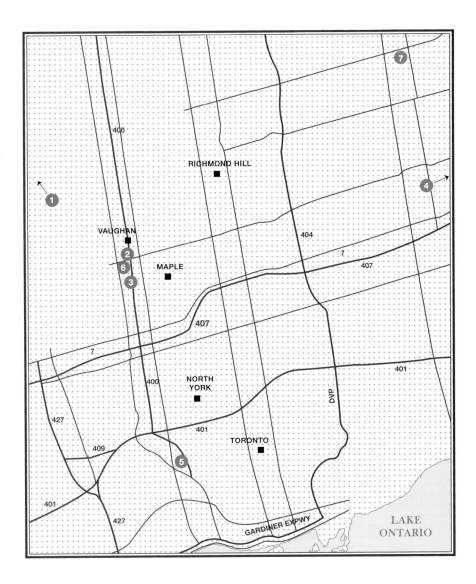

opening a winery when she emigrated with her family in 1952. The Locilentos initially bought a juice company and began by supplying juice and wine accessories to home winemakers, but their ultimate goal was to make wine themselves. In 1995 they realized their ambition. Two years later they built a California mission–style winery facility in Woodbridge, north of Toronto. Cilento trucks its grapes up from the Niagara Peninsula to this two-storey building, measuring 36,000 square feet, whose walls are decorated with life-sized murals of traditional European winemaking activities. In 2004, when their long-time winemaker, South African Terence van Rooyen, left to join Stonechurch (whose vineyards were the source for Cilento's grapes), the winery went into decline. Now it is back on track with its newly hired winemaker from Argentina, Adrian Ariel Carabajal. It's too soon to say whether he will be carrying on with the bold, full-flavoured style that characterized van Rooyen's wines, but since he comes from the Penaflor group of wineries, the odds are that his wines will be big.

Magnotta Winery Corporation

271 CHRISLEA ROAD, VAUGHAN, ON L4L 8N6 (905) 738-9463; 1-800-461-9463
WWW.MAGNOTTA.COM

YEAR FOUNDED: 1990 **FOUNDERS:** Gabe and Rossana Magnotta
WINEMAKERS: Peter Rotar, Marco Zamuner **GRAPE VARIETIES:** (red)
Cabernet Sauvignon, Cabernet Franc, Merlot; (white) Riesling,
Sauvignon Blanc **RECOMMENDED WINES:** Sparkling Ice, Riesling
Icewine, Pinot Gris, Cabernet Franc, Cabernet Franc Icewine

Gabe and Rossana Magnotta started in the wine business
by importing juice for sale to home winemakers. They
now head a public company with the third-largest sales
volume in Ontario after Vincor and Andrés, and they did
it through their own sales outlets by producing offshore
blends and VQA wines at bargain prices. Their claim to
be the most awarded winery in Ontario is born out by the
1,800 trophies on display in the awards room at their flagship facility in Vaughan, north of Toronto. This room
opens onto a much-photographed fountain garden. The
60,000-square-foot building, with its cathedral ceiling,
houses the winery, a distillery, and a brewery. The walls are
hung with paintings that have graced their wine labels,
including works by Group of Seven artists A.Y. Jackson
and Arthur Lismer and those the Magnottas have specially commissioned.

The company has a winery facility in Beamsville (where
it distills its grappa) and four vineyards totalling 180 acres
in Niagara. It also owns a 351-acre vineyard in Chile's
Maipo Valley that supplies it with juice and wine.
Magnotta makes over 150 different products, including
an Amarone-inspired VQA red wine and the world's first
sparkling Icewine, the first Icewine grappa, and the first
eau-de-vie distilled from Icewine.

Bringing wine to the people is the watchword here. The
bargain-priced Icewines, particularly Cabernet Franc and
Riesling, are worth tasting, as is their Cabernet Sauvignon.
Visit the Vaughan headquarters and you're sure to find
something that tickles your palate.

Ocala Orchards Farm Winery

971 HIGH POINT ROAD, RR 2, PORT PERRY, ON L9L 1B3
(905) 985-9924; 1-866-985-9924 WWW.OCALAWINERY.COM

YEAR FOUNDED: 1995 **FOUNDER:** Irwin L. Smith **WINEMAKER:** Irwin L.
Smith **GRAPE VARIETIES:** (red) Maréchal Foch, Baco Noir, Cabernet
Sauvignon; (white) Vidal, Pinot Gris, Gewurztraminer, Riesling, Seyval
Blanc **RECOMMENDED WINES:** Riesling, Cabernet Sauvignon

A winery as far north as Port Perry may sound improba-
ble, but the ameliorating effect of nearby Lake Scugog
makes grape growing possible on the Oak Ridges
Moraine. The original farm that Irwin and Alissa Smith
inherited raised Holstein cattle in Irwin's grandfather's

day, and apples in his father's. In 1995 Irwin returned to
the family farm after seventeen years of selling musical
instruments in the area, to help his father turn the farming
enterprise into a fruit and grape winery. The winemaking
operation is housed in an early-twentieth-century dairy
barn complete with timber beams, board floors, and oak
doors. Ocala boasts 20 acres of vines and 15 acres of
orchards. From these fruit sources the winery produces
over thirty different wines from orchard fruits, berries, and
grapes, including a product they call Vin de Glace because
VQA regulations restrict the name Icewine to the three
recognized viticultural areas of Niagara Peninsula, Lake
Erie North Shore, and Pelee Island. The white wines here
are better than the reds, but the pricing is remarkably low
compared with their competition to the southwest. Fruit-
wine fanciers will appreciate the sweet black-currant wine.

Silver Peak Wine Cellars

130 INDUSTRY STREET, UNIT 42, TORONTO, ON M6M 5G3 (416) 763-7236
INFO@SILVERPEAKWINES.COM

YEAR FOUNDED: 1988 **FOUNDER:** Angelo Rigitano **WINEMAKER:** Angelo
Rigitano **GRAPE VARIETIES:** (red) Merlot, Baco Noir, Cabernet Franc;
(white) Riesling, Chardonnay, Muscat Ottonel, Seyval Blanc
RECOMMENDED WINES: Cabernet Franc, Chardonnay

From 1992 to 1998 Angelo Rigitano made four or five
wines a year for the Toronto restaurant C'est What? to
augment its innovative all-Ontario list. A self-taught
winemaker, he sourced his grapes from various growers
in Niagara. In 1998 he decided to start his own commercial operation, working out of an industrial unit in
Toronto. You can't taste his wines here, but you can
order them with dinner in several Toronto restaurants.
In 2004 Rigitano made 50 cases of champagne-method
sparkling wine.

Vinoteca Winery

527 JEVLAN DRIVE, WOODBRIDGE, ON L4L 8W1 (905) 856-5700; 1-866-313-5700
WWW.VINOTECA.SITES.TORONTO.COM

YEAR FOUNDED: 1989 **FOUNDERS:** Giovanni and Rosanna Follegot
WINEMAKER: Giovanni Follegot **GRAPE VARIETIES:** (red) Merlot,
Cabernet Sauvignon, Cabernet Franc, Pinot Noir, Sangiovese,
Syrah; (white) Pinot Gris, Chardonnay, Gewurztraminer, Riesling, Vidal
RECOMMENDED WINES: Cabernet Sauvignon, Chardonnay,
Sauvignon Blanc

Giovanni ("Johnny") and Rosanna Follegot opened their
first winery in the Greater Toronto Area in a Woodbridge
industrial park in 1989, far removed from their grape
supply in Niagara and imported grapes from Giovanni's
own vineyard in Italy. In 1991 the couple acquired a farm
at the foot of the Niagara Escarpment near Beamsville and
planted a vineyard to make VQA wines. Two years later

TOP: Ocala Orchards Farm Winery. ABOVE: Magnotta Winery Corporation.

they converted a 2,500-square-foot barn on the property to a winery and called it Maple Grove. The retail store for the Maple Grove label is at the side of the barn and is staffed only on weekends. The main operation continues to be at the Woodbridge site—a modern, custom-built structure that looks more like an office building than a winery. Shopping for wine here is like shopping in an Italian supermarket. Whatever you need is available, from wine by the barrel (18 litres) to everyday house wines, older vintages of Follegot's succulent Cabernet Sauvignons, custom-labelled bottles, and wine accessories.

Willow Springs Winery

5572 BETHESDA ROAD, STOUFFVILLE, ON L4A 7X3 (905) 642-WINE (9463)
WWW.WILLOWSPRINGSWINERY.CA

YEAR FOUNDED: 2001 **FOUNDERS:** Mario and Julie Testa **WINEMAKER:** Michael Traynor **GRAPE VARIETIES:** (red) Baco Noir, Sabrevois, Frontenac; (white) Chardonnay, Seyval Blanc, Lucy Kuhlmann, Geisenheim **RECOMMENDED WINES:** Baco Noir, Geisenheim; Empire Apple

Mario Testa's grandfather, a home winemaker, planted a row of willows on the family farm that gave Mario the inspiration for naming the 2,200-square-foot winery he created in 2001. The custom-built barn, with its deep verandah, steeply raked roof, and gabled windows, has great charm as well as functionality. If the idea of a winery off Markham Road, 50 kilometres north of Toronto, sounds strange—you don't get much farther north than this in Ontario if you want to grow wine grapes for a living— keep in mind that the varieties planted in this vineyard are found in Quebec, where temperatures are even colder. Winemaker Michael Traynor, a graduate of the Wine Technology program at Loyalist College in Belleville and vineyard manager for Huff Estates in Prince Edward County, produces his Merlot, Cabernet Sauvignon, Cabernet Franc, Gamay, and Sauvignon Blanc from grapes purchased in Niagara. In addition to wine and fruit wines, the Testas sell jams, chutneys, and other wine-related products.

QUEBEC

CANADA'S UNDISCOVERED WINE REGION

The impulse for Quebecers to make wine must have some ancestral root in their French heritage. Why do they even try? Shut your eyes and think of a vineyard scene: What do you see? Rows of plump clusters of purple grapes nestling in green leaves? The sun beating down from a cloudless sky? Napa Valley? The gentle slopes of Burgundy? Chianti's terra-cotta-tiled hilltop towns?

Now think Quebec City, where the mercury can drop to −40°C in winter—too cold even for Icewine because, at those polar temperatures, the grape bunches simply disintegrate. Yet there are over forty wineries in the province of Quebec, stretching in a large arc from west of Montreal to the Eastern Townships (Cantons-de-l'Est) to northeast of Quebec

City. And more are poised to open. While Prince Edward County in Ontario loses vines during the winter, that region's climate is positively balmy compared to Quebec's. On June 3, 1986, a surprise frost killed 90 percent of the fruiting buds in the Dunham vineyard of Vignoble l'Orpailleur. In the mid-1990s, when Roland Harnois planted his first vines at

PREVIOUS SPREAD: The vineyard at Domaine de l'Île Ronde.
BELOW: Winemaker Marcel Mitan.

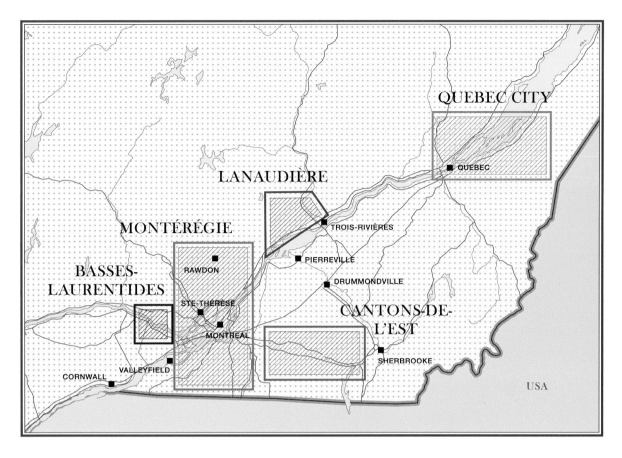

THE WINE REGIONS OF QUEBEC

Domaine Royarnois in Saint-Joachim, near Ste. Anne-de-Beaupré, he lost two-thirds of the plants because the roots froze. Yet, like the owners of L'Orpailleur, he persevered and replanted his vineyard with hardier varieties that would survive the cold. Now he has a flourishing vineyard.

These Quebec vintners grow varieties you may never have heard of—Frontenac, Sabrevois, Elmer Swenson 517, Vandal-Cliche, and Ste-Croix—grapes that can withstand winter temperatures down to −35°C. And the flavour profiles are not what you may be used to. A wine drinker will probably find these wines lean and tart compared to those of British Columbia and Ontario, but they work well if you carefully select your accompanying dishes.

In the 1860s, when Ontario's wine industry became a commercial enterprise with the founding of Vin Villa on Pelee Island, southern Quebec already had thirty vineyards spread over 100 acres of land planted to old American hybrids. But these vineyards didn't last long. By the end of the nineteenth

century the vines had been slowly wiped out by the cold. When Canada started importing inexpensive European wines before and after Prohibition, the effort and expense to keep the vineyards alive were too great. By 1935, only 5 acres remained in "la belle province."

During the 1980s, national pride dictated that Quebec needed a wine industry, and today more than 500 acres are cultivated in the province's five major growing regions. While the language may be French and the winemakers look to France for their inspiration, there is nothing conservative and traditional about the way Quebec vignerons go about their business. They grow several varieties in their vineyards to determine which will do best in their particular soil and microclimate. And, since the grape harvests are very small (most are boutique enterprises making a few hundred to a couple of thousand cases a year), they have to blend these different grapes. That means you will find wines labelled with proprietary names—Vignoble la

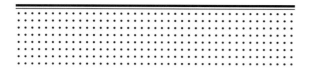

ALAIN BREAULT
VINEYARDIST EXTRAORDINAIRE

"Every mountain between Montreal and Orford has a vineyard now." So claims Alain Breault, and he must know because he has sold the winter-hardy vines he propagates in his green-houses in Abbotsford to over 700 growers in Quebec, Central and Eastern Ontario, and the Maritimes. Ponytailed Breault is the thirteenth generation of his family in Canada. Of Acadian descent, his great-great-grandfather, a farmer, established his family in Dunham in the early part of the twentieth century. Breault's interest in wine was sparked by a visit to the Napa Valley in 1982 with his brother Jacques. On his return he associated himself with Hervé Durand, who had asked the world's leading ampelographer, Pierre Galet of Montpellier, what grape varieties could be grown in Quebec. Galet advised Durand to try Aurore, Seyval Blanc, and Rayon d'Or—all French hybrids—and to bury them for the winter. Breault, with the L'Orpailleur team, propagated these vines in a greenhouse and planted them in 1982. Only the Seyval Blanc was successful.

In 1986 the Breault brothers left L'Orpailleur to start their own winery, Les Arpents de Neige, an ironic homage to Voltaire's famous derogatory quip. Alain left the struggling, debt-ridden winery in 1991 to start up his own grape propagation business, Viticulture A & M, with his wife, Mariette. He travels constantly, developing new varieties that will withstand Quebec's long, hard winters. A dedicated evangelist in the cause of Quebec wines, Breault is spearheading the drive to get growers to plant the new winter-hardy varieties that have been developed at the University of Minnesota. He believes that the best varieties to plant in Quebec are Sabrevois and Frontenac for red wines and Louise Swenson for whites. Breault predicts that Frontenac Gris, the white version of Frontenac, will become the grape for Quebec Icewine. It can withstand temperatures of –36°C. Winter-hardy himself, Breault's only personal concession to winter is to wear socks with his open-toed sandals.

Bauge's La Patriarche, Vignoble Isle de Bacchus' Le 1535, or Les Blancs Coteaux's La Vieille Grange—but rarely will you find the grape variety on the label unless it's a Seyval Blanc. Many of these wineries also grow apples for cider as well as grapes for wine; and one product, Iced Apple Wine (Ice Cider), rivals English Canada's Icewine not only in quality but in price as well.

Naturally, politics in Quebec is never far from the surface in any enterprise. Quebec's winemakers are a highly individual lot, willing to express an opinion about their endeavours when asked—or even when not asked. Two main lines of thought became evident to me during my travels through the province: one school thinks that Quebec should grow authentic, original wine grapes unique to the province (Sabrevois and Frontenac); the other school believes that growers should plant grapes that are also grown in Ontario, such as Baco Noir and Vidal, the rationale being that, if the crop is destroyed during a calamitous winter, winemakers can always buy in these varieties so they will have some wine to sell. (But then, this attitude is similar to the dual mindset in Ontario's Prince Edward County, whose winters are almost as severe.)

The major problem with Quebec wines, according to Gilles Benoît, proprietor of Vignoble des Pins and the most progressive of Quebec's winemakers, is that his fellow Quebecers are not drinking them. "It's the tourists who buy the wines," he says. If that sounds like Ontario ten years ago, Quebec's future is rosy, because sales will happen thanks to the critical mass of wineries, which stimulates growth in agri-tourism.

Quebec's wineries are concentrated in five main regions—a configuration that makes touring easy in the sense that you can concentrate on one area at a time and follow its wine route. A day trip out of Montreal will allow you to visit the three wineries in Basses-Laurentides, a lovely mountainous region with forests and lakes. Montérégie, a rich agricultural area divided by the Richelieu River, close to whose banks you'll find many of the wineries and cideries, is probably the most promising region in Quebec because it enjoys the most temperate climate—if any part of Quebec could claim to be temperate. The wineries in Montérégie are spread out, off the main roads, and therefore require the attention of a good navigator. The major concentration of Quebec wineries is in the Eastern Townships (Cantons-de-l'Est), divided between those clustered around the picturesque town of Dunham and those in Magog-Sherbrooke, an area of gently rolling hills, cornfields, and orchards. The most recently developed wine region is Lanaudière, situated along the north shore of the St. Lawrence as you drive from Montreal

towards Quebec City. Finally there is Quebec City itself, the most unlikely of wine regions and, in my opinion, the most interesting from a tourism point of view. Here you have at your disposal the history and heritage of French North America, which calls to you from every church spire and cobblestone.

QUEBEC'S WINE-MAKING TRADITION
On September 7, 1535, Jacques Cartier dropped anchor off what he described as "a great island" in the St. Lawrence. There he found masses of wild

Detail of winery barn at Vignoble des Pins.

Farmhouse (left) and hundred-year-old barn (right) at Vignoble les Blancs Coteaux.

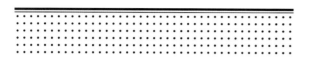

HILLING UP
A VINEYARD'S WINTER COAT

The major threat to Quebec's vineyards is winter. When the temperature dips below –25°C, most buds on French hybrid vines will freeze. Growers in what are euphemistically called cool climates, such as Quebec and Prince Edward County in Ontario, have devised strategies to protect their vineyards during the bitterest days of winter. Some growers use straw as a cover, or plastic sheets tented over the wires. But it is more efficient to protect the buds for next year's shoots by hilling up—lowering the canes on their trellis wires and back-plowing through the rows to throw earth up onto the vines, covering their trunks and lower canes. In the spring the vines have to be uncovered.

The French oenologist Hervé Durand, one of the founding partners of L'Orpailleur, first used the concept of hilling in Quebec in 1982. He had visited vineyards in Russia and China, where he saw farmers bury their vines to protect them against the harsh winters. The vines have to be buried in early November, before the ground freezes, and then be uncovered in the spring to expose the buds to sunlight. But hilling and unhilling are expensive operations. According to Robert Le Royer of Le Royer St. Pierre, "burying 16 acres of vines cost us $8,200 for labour and machinery." It is estimated that hilling adds 7 to 10 percent to the cost of a bottle.

riparia grapes growing up the trees. He called the island Isle de Bacchus, but, on reflection—thinking that might be too frivolous a title for his masters in Paris—he renamed it Isle d'Orléans as a tribute to Charles, duc d'Orléans, the third son of his monarch, François I.

The Jesuit missionaries who followed in Cartier's footsteps brought with them barrels of sacramental wine and, when they ran out, they tried to make wine by using the native wild grapes. The wine they produced was tolerable enough to be sipped at mass, but not to be quaffed by the early settlers in quantities capable of warming their hearts during the long winters in New France.

Voltaire, the French satirist and the embodiment of the eighteenth-century Enlightenment, referred famously to New France as "*quelques arpents de neige*" (a few acres of snow), not the most hospitable environment in which to plant vineyards. At that time the French upper classes imported their red wine from France or Spain, while the underclass was reduced to brewing a drink from fir branches that they called "spruce beer."

Quebec City is almost on the same latitude as Burgundy's Côte d'Or, so the new arrivals dreamed of recreating the wine scene they remembered from France in their adopted homeland. During the eighteenth and nineteenth centuries, they made various attempts to establish a wine industry in

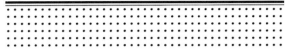

SEYVAL BLANC
THE GRAPE THAT SAVED QUEBEC

In 1980, when Christian Barthomeuf created the first vineyard in modern times in Quebec, he chose to plant Maréchal Foch and Pinot Noir for red wine and Seyval Blanc for white. Only the Maréchal Foch and Seyval survived the winter. Seyval Blanc, a French–American hybrid grape, was also the first choice of Charles-Henri de Coussergues when he planted the vineyard at L'Orpailleur in 1982. Ever since, this hardy white grape has become the most widely planted variety in the province—the mainstay of its white wines. You'll find Seyval Blanc in every cool growing region in the world, including such unlikely wine-growing areas as Minnesota, Wisconsin, and southern England, where the climate demands winter-hardiness and early ripening.

Seyval ripens two weeks before that ubiquitous red variety Concord. When fermented, Seyval Blanc makes crisp white wine with citrus flavours that lends itself to barrel aging. Think of it as a cameo Chablis. It goes well with fish and seafood, especially the sparkling version of the wine.

But the days of Seyval Blanc as the white grape of choice for Quebec's vignerons may be numbered. According to Alain Breault, the main supplier of vines to Quebec's wine growers, "Consumers and winemakers want more aromatic whites," varieties such as Geisenheim 322, Cayuga White, and Frontenac Gris.

Lower Canada, but most were abandoned because of the severity of the climate, which could not support the vinifera vines they attempted to grow. However, winemakers are a persistent lot and, by the 1860s, some thirty vineyards south of Montreal covered around 100 acres. Most of the religious orders had their own plots, thanks to the pioneering efforts of a French nobleman, Count Justin de Courtenay, who was convinced that Lower Canada could produce wines that would outperform their Burgundian model.

In 1864, de Courtenay pulled up stakes and moved to Ontario, where he purchased Clair House, the vineyard originally planted by Johann Schiller. But de Courtenay's legacy lived on as other growers struggled to keep their vineyards alive with winter-hardy labrusca varieties imported from the United States. The most notable was the Beaconsfield Vineyard at Pointe Claire, planted in 1877 by a

Mr. Menzies, who joined forces with one George Gallagher two years later. But the growing temperance movement had a stifling effect on would-be vintners. Unlike Ontario, where winemaking thrived after the introduction of Prohibition, the vineyards of Quebec languished. By 1935, only about 5 acres of vines remained.

The soldiers who returned from Europe in 1945 brought with them a taste for European wine. The waves of European immigrants who followed had the knowledge and the experience to grow grapes and vinify them, if only on a hobby basis. But still the problem of climate bedevilled postwar efforts in Quebec to kickstart a commercial wine industry using home-grown grapes.

Ice can split the trunk of a vine stock, and even the hardiest labrusca varieties are susceptible to winterkill. Most vines can survive temperatures down to –25°C, but in Quebec the mercury can drop to as low as –41°C. The vine shuts down to protect itself and will become active only when the temperature finally reaches a consistent 10°C. A certain number of heat units (known as growing degree-days, calculated on the daily mean temperature above 10°C) is required during the growing season for grapes to ripen. The total average heat units during this season in Quebec are less than 1,000, although certain favoured sites enjoy higher readings because of their microclimates. Iberville, Quebec, gets 1,410 heat units, compared to 1,566 units in Vineland in the Niagara Peninsula and 1,629 units in Oliver, BC. (By contrast, the Médoc region of Bordeaux, France, has 1,472 heat units; Hawkes Bay, New Zealand, has 1,583 units; and Napa Valley, California, has 2,118 units.)

Quebec has highly localized microclimates, especially around Dunham and Magog, that allow the hardier vine stocks to thrive. Topographical features such as large bodies of water or well-protected south-facing slopes offer the grower an opportunity to plant carefully selected varietals. But always there is the problem of winterkill. The most radical measure to safeguard the plants is burial, to protect the buds for the following year's growth. The early settlers in the mid-eighteenth century covered their small

Statuary at Vignoble de la Chapelle Ste. Agnès. OPPOSITE: The historic church at Saint-Jean-Port-Joli by Vignoble du Faubourg.

acreage of vines with horse manure to protect the plants during the winter, a solution as ineffective as it is impractical today. The process used now is called "hilling"—banking earth over the fruiting spurs and the canes by back-plowing between the rows of vines. However, the newly propagated vines from Minnesota, such as Frontenac, Sabrevois, and Louise Swenson, don't require burial.

The growth and future health of the Quebec wine industry will depend on the ability of the wineries to attract tourists. If visitors come, they will buy the wines, enchanted by the historic buildings, the pastoral landscape, the traditional cuisine, the cheese makers, *cidreries*, chocolatiers, bakeries, and, above all, the warmth of the welcome. The vintners' pride in their products is infectious, as you will discover when you visit these wineries, each as individual and fascinating as the men and women who work with the grapes in this most difficult of climates. Wherever there is passion and dedication to grape growing, the potential is there to make fine wines. Quebec is a generation behind Ontario and British Columbia in terms of the selection of varieties that are best for its terroir. But as the winemakers discover the best clones to plant and the most effective trellising and pruning methods, and allow time for their vines to mature, Quebec will produce wines that will astonish you.

Montérégie

This region is Quebec's Garden of Eden; you can grow virtually any fruit, vegetable, cereal, or winter-hardy vine you want in this gorgeous valley along the Richelieu River. The region is a welcoming mix of fruit growers, market gardeners, chocolate sellers, stockbreeders, and winegrowers. And if it looks more like cider country than wine land, it's because the town of Rougemont is the apple capital of the province. In late spring the hills are white with apple blossom. The southern part of the region sits on an ancient beach of Lake Champlain, whose waters receded 12,000 years ago, leaving behind a rich geological mix of sand, loam, clay, and pebbles. The predominant soil in the vineyards is clay–loam mixed with light sand—ideal for wine growing because it is not too rich and it drains well.

A short detour off the wine route will take you to Chambly, to tour its historic fort, built in 1709, or to watch the yachts rise and fall in Chambly's manually operated lock system, dating back to 1843. A local restaurant, Fourquet-Fourchette (known for matching its dishes with beers from the nearby Unibroue brewery), features the historic cuisine of New France. At Mont-St-Hilaire you can visit an art museum featuring the paintings of some of Quebec's most eminent artists, Paul-Émile Borduas, Jordi Bonet, and Ozias Leduc, all of whom lived in the area. Mont-St-Hilaire's nature reserve, recognized as a biosphere by UNESCO, is the refuge of 185 species of birds and several mammals. And if it's animals you're looking for, give yourself time to explore the Safari Park near Havelock and the Jardins de Versailles at Mont-St-Grégoire. For sports enthusiasts, there are 800 kilometres of bike, hiking, and cross-country ski trails. What better way to arrive at a winery?

**WINE TOURING
in Montérégie**

SINGLE DAY: Make the town of Iberville your base and visit Vignobles des Pins, Vignoble Clos de la Montagne, and Vignoble de Lavoie or, if you have the time, drive farther north to Vignoble St-Denis.
WEEKEND: Start at Vignoble Marathonien and follow the wine route to Lacolle and north, driving the Chemin des Patriots along the Richelieu River to St-Denis-sur-Richelieu, a route that takes you past seven wineries. Book a B&B around Iberville.

Vignoble Angell

134, RANG ST-GEORGES, ST-BERNARD-DE-LACOLLE, QC J0J 1V0
(450) 246-4219

YEAR FOUNDED: 1985 **FOUNDER:** Jean-Guy Angell
WINEMAKER: Guy Angell **GRAPE VARIETIES:** (red) De Chaunac, Merlot, Pinot Noir; (white) Seyval Blanc, Vidal, Chardonnay
RECOMMENDED WINES: not tasted

Jean-Guy Angell, the owner of a string of karate schools across the country, is one of the pioneers of the Quebec wine industry. Angell planted his first 200 vines in 1978 along Highway 202, near the American border at St.-Bernard-de-Lacolle. Now his son Guy makes the wine from 18 acres of vines. The growing season here is longer than virtually anywhere else in the province by about two weeks, time that allows the Angells to nurture such tender vinifera as Chardonnay, Merlot, and Pinot Noir. The winery is located in the basement of a charming 1813

stone house (the cellar was carved out of rock), a favourite wedding venue (the catering staff in the banquet hall will spit-roast a lamb or a pig) and a tour-bus stop for visitors from the United States.

Vignoble Cappabianca

586, BOULEVARD ST-JEAN-BAPTISTE, MERCIER, QC J6R 2A7
(450) 691-1515 PAULA@SYMPATICO.CA

FOUNDED: 1997 **FOUNDER:** Francesco Lapenna **WINEMAKER:** Francesco Lapenna **GRAPE VARIETIES:** (red) Lucie Kuhlmann, Maréchal Foch, Seyval Noir, Pinot Noir; (white) Seyval Blanc, Vidal **RECOMMENDED WINES:** Lucia Rosso, Late Harvest Seyval

Francesco Lapenna comes from a long line of Italian winemakers who hail from Campobasso in Molise province. "I remember my grandfather first and then my father making grape juice into wine," Lapenna will tell

Vignoble Angell.

you. "It always evoked praise from the friends who were invited to dine."

Unfortunately, Lapenna's grandfather lost the family vineyard in Italy during the Second World War. The 8-acre vineyard Lapenna and his father planted in Mercier in 1990 is a sacred trust to that memory. The winery looks rather industrial, situated as it is on the main road into Montreal, but appearances can be deceiving, because the winemaking is very precise and careful. The taste of Lucia, the light red, is delightful. I didn't taste his Icewine, but his mother assures me it's terrific.

Vignoble Clos de la Montagne

330, RANG DE LA MONTAGNE, MONT-ST-GRÉGOIRE, QC J0J 1K0
(450) 358-4868 WWW.CLOSDELAMONTAGNE.COM

YEAR FOUNDED: 1988 **FOUNDERS:** Aristide Pigeon and Denise-Andrée Marien **WINEMAKER:** Jean-Paul Martin **GRAPE VARIETIES:** (red) De Chaunac, Maréchal Foch, Chancellor, Seyval Noir; (white) Vidal, Geisenheim 318 **RECOMMENDED WINES:** Cuvée Versailles, Cuvée Joffrey, Cuvée Frère André

This attractive green-roofed winery is set back from the highway behind a stand of weeping willows at the foot of the impressive Mont-St-Grégoire. Montrealers Aristide Pigeon and his partner, Denise-Andrée Marien, bought the derelict property in 1988 ostensibly to create a stained-glass studio, evidence of which is visible in the lattice windows of the winery tasting room. They restored the apple and pear orchards and planted a 5-acre vineyard. Then, in 1992, the couple began producing wine seriously with a very compact operation. In addition to producing wines

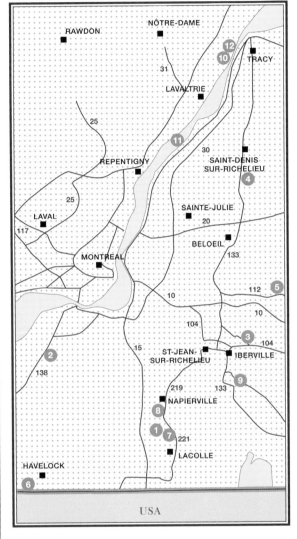

MONTÉRÉGIE & LANAUDIÈRE WINERIES

MONTÉRÉGIE

1 VIGNOBLE ANGELL
2 VIGNOBLE CAPPABIANCA
3 VIGNOBLE CLOS DE LA MONTAGNE

4 CIDRERIE-VIGNOBLE CLOS SAINT-DENIS
5 VIGNOBLE DE LAVOIE
6 VIGNOBLE DU MARATHONIEN
7 VIGNOBLE MOROU
8 VIGNOBLE DES PINS
9 VIGNOBLE LE ROYER ST PIERRE

LANAUDIÈRE

10 VIGNOBLE CARONE
11 VIGNOBLE DE L'ILE RONDE
12 VIGNOBLE AUX PIEDS DES NOYERS

and aperitifs, they also make cider. Other non-vinous points of interest are the exotic birds and llamas penned on the property. Pigeon used to raise horses and wanted "something to play with." The winery holds an annual cider festival in May.

Cidrerie-Vignoble Clos Saint-Denis

1149, CHEMIN DES PATRIOTES, ST-DENIS-SUR-RICHELIEU, QC J0H 1K0
(450) 787-3766 WWW.CLOS-SAINT-DENIS.QC.CA

YEAR FOUNDED: 1990 **FOUNDERS:** Guy Tardif, François Tardif, and Ghislaine Meunier **WINEMAKER:** Jean-Yves Plamandon **GRAPE VARIETIES:** (red) Ste-Croix; (white) Eona **RECOMMENDED WINES:** Pomme de Glace; Cuvée St. Denis Blanc

Set back from the Richelieu River in an unending stretch of cornfields, this oasis of vineyards and orchards is dominated by a stately hundred-year-old barn weathered to a silvery grey. Nearby, the old chicken coop has been converted into rooms for invited guests. On this 38-acre property, 20 acres have been planted to vines on clay–loam soil. The enterprise is divided between apples and grapes, although the late Guy Tardif told me, "Apple wine is our bread and butter."

The venture started as a retirement project after Tardif left politics (he was a minister in René Lévesque's government in the 1970s), but it is now a full-time occupation for his agronomist son François.

Visitors with a technical bent should ask Tardif to show them the special machine he and his father developed that can press the juice from either apples or grapes. Tardif's Cuvée St. Denis, made from Ste-Croix, with five months in oak, is the best of this variety I have tasted. Pomme de Glace (Iced Apple), the mainstay of the business (8,000 cases as opposed to 2,000 of wine), is widely available through Quebec's liquor distribution system (SAQ). This awarded product prompted Guy Tardif to quip, "It has won just about as many medals as the Canadian Olympic team."

The wine shop in the magnificent old barn is a delightful space for tasting wine.

The entrance sign at Vignoble du Marathonien.

Vignoble de Lavoie

100, RANG DE LA MONTAGNE, ROUGEMONT, QC J0L 1M0
(450) 469-3894 WWW.DE-LAVOIE.COM

YEAR FOUNDED: 2000 **FOUNDERS:** Francis Lavoie and Robert Poitevin
WINEMAKER: Francis Lavoie **GRAPE VARIETIES:** (red) Maréchal Foch,
Baco Noir, De Chaunac, Lucie Kuhlmann; (white) Seyval Blanc,
Cayuga, Geisenheim **RECOMMENDED WINES:** Onir (Seyval, Cayuga,
Geisenheim), La Tourelle (Maréchal Foch, Baco Noir); Ace (Ice Cider)

This custom-built winery, nestled at the foot of Mount
Rougemont and set in its own vineyard (planted in 1998),
commands a magnificent view of the mountain. The
modern facility speaks to the architectural talents of
Robert Poitevin, who was one of the owners. The Lavoie
family grew apples for eighteen years before they decided
to get into the wine business. Lavoie and Poitevin opened
the winery in 2000 and it produces two blended red
wines and two blended whites from 12 acres of vines,
and three different styles of cider. It's very relaxing to
sit on the patio here and sip a glass of the Ice Cider.

Vignoble du Marathonien

318, ROUTE 202, HAVELOCK, QC J0S 2C0 (450) 826-0522
WWW.MARATHONIEN.QC.CA

YEAR FOUNDED: 1990 **FOUNDERS:** Jean and Line Joly **WINEMAKER:**
Jean Joly **GRAPE VARIETIES:** (red) Maréchal Foch, De Chaunac, small
experimental lots of Merlot and Cabernet Franc; (white) Seyval Blanc,
Cayuga, Vidal, Geisenheim 318 **RECOMMENDED WINES:** Vidal Icewine,
Boisé d'Havelock

A leisurely drive up a gravel lane past apple trees and
neatly manicured lawns will lead you to this 4-acre vineyard in front of an attractive white house with a large
covered balcony. You've arrived at Vignoble du
Marathonien, very near the American border at Havelock.
This is one of the southernmost wineries in Quebec and
the property of Jean Joly, engineer and marathon runner.
Joly and his father-in-law purchased this apple farm in
1989 and planted a vineyard the following year. A sign
at the entrance reads: "Planting vines in Quebec is like
running a marathon. It takes as much perseverance,
determination and work to reach the finish line that is
the harvest, and to receive the medal that is the tasting
of the wine."

The labels of three of Joly's wines carry a cartoon-like
illustration of a long-distance runner in full stride—in
fact, more of a balletic hurdler than a marathoner. Try a
glass of Boisé d'Havelock, a crisp, grapefruit-flavoured
Seyval Blanc aged six months in wood, as you gaze out
across the vines and dream that this could be your summer
place in Quebec.

Vignoble Morou

238, ROUTE 221, NAPIER, QC J0J 1L0 (450) 245-7569
WWW3.SYMPATICO.CA/MOROU/

YEAR FOUNDED: 1991 **FOUNDER:** Étienne Héroux **WINEMAKER:** Yvon J.
Roy **GRAPE VARIETIES:** (red) De Chaunac, Maréchal Foch, Chancellor,
Gamay; (white) Geisenheim, Cayuga, Seyval Blanc, Vidal
RECOMMENDED WINES: La Closerie, Clos Napierois White

Étienne Héroux, a retired chemical engineer, planted a
vineyard in 1987 with eighteen different varieties in light
sand-and-clay soil. He opened the winery four years later,
having carefully whittled the number down to four red
varieties and six whites. In 2003 Héroux sold the enterprise
to Yvon Roy, an accountant and dedicated home winemaker, and Suzanne Labrèque. Despite having sold the
property, he still keeps a loving paternal eye on both the
vineyard and the winemaking at Vignoble Morou. Set in
open farmland near Napier, the charming, well-preserved
stone house, shaded by a huge weeping willow, dates
back to the mid-eighteenth century. A small store for
purchasing wine is housed in a two-car garage detached
from the house.

Vignoble des Pins

136, GRAND SABREVOIS, STE-ANNE-DE-SABREVOIS, QC J0J 2G0
(450) 347-1073 VIGDESPINS@AOL.COM

YEAR FOUNDED: 1986 **FOUNDERS:** Gilles Benoît and Laurie Clarke
WINEMAKER: Gilles Benoît **GRAPE VARIETIES:** (red) Maréchal Foch,
Frontenac, Sabrevois, Zweigelt; (white) Cayuga, Geisenheim 322
RECOMMENDED WINES: Late Harvest Geisenheim, Pin Blanc (Cayuga),
Frontenac

Gilles Benoît is one of the most accomplished and innovative winemakers in Quebec. His winery, situated on the
plain in Ste-Anne-de-Sabrevois, south of Iberville, is named
after the stands of red and white pines he planted around
the property to protect his vines from the wind. In 2002
Benoît made the first wine from Frontenac grapes in the
province. Alain Breault sold him Sabrevois vines in 1995
and, as a tribute to Benoît's success with them, Breault
convinced Elmer Swenson, the Wisconsin grape breeder,
to allow him to rename the Swenson 219 clone Sabrevois,
after the town where Benoît has his vineyard operation.
Certainly, it's the best wine made from this variety I have
tasted, with complex flavours of blackberry, tobacco leaf,
coffee bean, and bitter chocolate.

If you've ever dreamed of making wine, Gilles Benoît
is the man you should visit. He has realized his dream: to
plant a manageable 5-acre vineyard, stay small, and make
wines the way he wants. As a small operation, Benoît can
take the time to experiment, including laying straw on top
of his hilled-up tender vinifera vines during winter months
and making a sparkling wine by hand. His tiny tasting-
room-cum-wine-shop has become a mecca for Quebec
wine enthusiasts.

Vignoble Le Royer St-Pierre

182, ROUTE 221, ST-CYPRIEN-DE-NAPIERVILLE, QC J0J 1L0
(450) 245-0208 WWW.VIGNOBLEROYER.COM

YEAR FOUNDED: 1989 **FOUNDERS:** Robert Le Royer and Lucie St-Pierre
WINEMAKER: Robert Le Royer **GRAPE VARIETIES:** (red) Maréchal Foch,
Cabernet Franc, Ste-Croix, Frontenac, Chancellor; (white) Cayuga,
Geisenheim 318, Kay Gray, St. Pepin **RECOMMENDED WINES:** La
Lambertois Carte Noire, Givre Noir

Robert Le Royer planted his first vines in 1983 on his
brother-in-law's farm near Mirabel Airport. There he
experimented with over fifty grape varieties on 6 acres,
hoping to find the most suitable grapes for the Quebec
climate, before searching for a farm of his own. Le Royer

RÉJEAN GUERTIN

ON HIS HARVESTING WAGON

Réjean Guertin, the proprietor of Artisans de Terroir, invented
a vehicle to save his pickers the strain of backache during
harvest. In Quebec, the canes of the vines are kept near to
the ground to protect them from the cold, so pickers have to
bend low to gather the grape clusters. Basically, Guertin's
invention is a three-wheeled go-kart. Pickers sit in the seat
and propel themselves along the row by foot, with their
backs supported. The plastic pail for the grapes is mounted
next to the picker. Several other wineries have copied
Guertin's idea.

eventually purchased 52 acres in Napierville, and he and
his wife, Lucie, decided to grow wine instead. Le Royer
converted the old barn into the winery, and the majestic
wooden silo attached to the farmhouse became the tasting
room—a favourite with visitors. Le Royer pressed an old
carriage house into service, too, as a private tasting room.
Royer holds an annual Fête des Vendanges in September,
but reservations are essential.

Le Royer's wines reflect his personality: positive, well-
balanced, and firm. Although there is no restaurant here,
the winery does offer catered meals.

Wine tour and tasting at Vignoble des Pins.

Lanaudière (See map on page 219)

Lanaudière, one of the first areas of New France to be settled, is relatively new as a winegrowing region. Currently, three wineries are located in this linear stretch running north of Montreal along the north shore of the St. Lawrence, before you reach Quebec City.

If you hug the shoreline, you'll be treated to impressive vistas of the river and pass through some historic villages, but you'll miss the full beauty of the Laurentian Mountains, with their lakes and forests, their waterfalls and rushing streams tumbling to the north, beyond a wide agricultural plain. By the nineteenth century, Lanaudière was one of the richest agricultural areas of Quebec. Tobacco was an important crop, and the old houses where the leaves were dried can still be seen. Montrealers come here in the spring to taste the new maple syrup and to dine in the quaint inns and restaurants. If you're an outdoors type who likes hiking, backpacking, canoeing, and cross-country and backcountry skiing, bring your gear. For the music lover, there's the annual Lanaudière Music Festival in July–August that attracts international artists. For the birdwatcher, the place to go is south of Berthierville, on the Îles de Sorel. And, somewhat surprisingly perhaps, you'll find wine here, too, because the ameliorating influence of the St. Lawrence makes grape growing possible.

Although there are few wineries here as yet, Anthony Carone of Vignoble Carone predicts that there will be more to come. "The Lanaudière region," he contends, "ranks among Quebec's very best grape growing regions." It offers several advantages: the sandy and silt–loam soils allow grape varieties to thrive and acquire more intense flavours, aromas, and textures, and the proximity to two major markets, Montreal and Quebec City, makes it easy for customers to visit the wineries. The grandiose Domaine de l'Île Ronde is a particularly big draw, but be prepared to take to the water.

> **TOURING WINERIES
> in Lanaudière**
>
> **SINGLE DAY:** Plan to spend a day at Domaine de l'Île Ronde. This island winery is a boat ride away from the historic village of St-Sulpice. On the way back, explore the village.
>
> **WEEKEND:** Take in all three wineries of the region at a leisurely pace, with a stop at Îles-des-Moulins in Terrebonne, five beautifully restored nineteenth-century industrial buildings: the flour mill (1846), sawmill (1804), seigneurial office (1850), bakery (1803), and new mill (1850).

Vignoble Carone

75, ROY STREET, LANORAIE, QC J0K 1E0 (514) 887-2728
WWW.VIGNOBLECARONE.COM

YEAR FOUNDED: 2002 **FOUNDER:** Carone family **WINEMAKER:** Anthony Carone **GRAPE VARIETIES:** (red) Cabernet Severnyi, Frontenac, Landot, Léon Millot, Regent, GR-7, Rondo; (white) Geisenheim 331, Vandal-Cliche **RECOMMENDED WINES:** Lanoraie, Frontenac

Cloistered in a suburban cul-de-sac, forty-five minutes' drive northeast of Montreal, you'll find a 22-acre field planted with a variety of vegetables (the Carone family business) and then, surprisingly, a 5-acre plot of vines—Anthony Carone's preoccupation and passion. In 2002

Carone and his Italian family renovated the existing farmhouse to build in a climate-controlled cellar and a fermentation room, intending to produce 1,000 cases of mainly red wine made in the Italian tradition of field blending (grape varieties grown together). Carone's signature wine, Lanoraie, named after the town, is made from Cabernet Severnyi, a Cabernet Sauvignon–Severnyi cross (Carone is the only commercial grower in Quebec to cultivate this grape). The smoky, red-berry–flavoured wine is aged in new American oak for six months before bottling and is rather like a barrel-aged Beaujolais. Vignoble Carone offers four wines: Novello, a Quebecois take on Italy's *vino novello*, Frontenac, Lanoraie, and the white Vandal-Cliche.

The winery at Domaine de l'Île Ronde.

Domaine de l'Île Ronde

POST OFFICE BOX 322, ST-SULPICE, QC J5W 4L9 (514) 771-7161
WWW.DOMAINEDELILERONDE.COM

YEAR FOUNDED: 2000 **FOUNDERS:** Joceyln Lafortune and the
Vandanaigue family **WINEMAKER:** Yves Trépanier **GRAPE VARIETIES:**
(red) Sabrevois, Frontenac, Maréchal Foch; (white) Vandal-Cliche, St.
Pepin **RECOMMENDED WINES:** Saint-Sulpice (Ste-Croix, Maréchal
Foch), La Fortune Rosé, La Fortune Blanc (white port-style)

The island is dominated by a magnificent newly built
château, a blend of traditional French and contemporary
California styles covering 10,000 square feet. It's a little at
odds with the small stone cottages dotted about the island,
but it has a certain intrinsic grandeur in spite of its
modernity. The 20-acre vineyard is the most densely
planted in the province and the most immaculately manicured, reflecting the care and attention lavished on it by its
owner, Jocelyn Lafortune. An insurance appraiser born in
Saint-Sulpice, Lafortune made fruit wines as a young man.

Unless you have your own boat or you're part of a
group tour, you may not get to visit Domaine de l'Île
Ronde. The winery specializes in fortified wines that
Lafortune would like to hold for five years before release.
However, economics dictate that he sell them after three
years. He buys the alcohol he needs from the SAQ but
wants to get an alembic still to make his own.

Vignoble aux Pieds des Noyers

71, GRANDE CÔTE EST, LANORAIE, QC J0K 1E0 (450) 887-1050
VIGNOBLEAUXPIEDSDESNOYERS@MSN.COM

YEAR FOUNDED: 2004 **FOUNDER:** Alain Bussières **WINEMAKERS:**
Fabrice Lafon, Alain Bussières, Hugo Bussières **GRAPE VARIETIES:** (red)
Seyval Noir, Zweigelt, Maréchal Foch, Chelois, De Chaunac; (white)
Chardonnay, Chardonnay Musqué, Cayuga, Vandal-Cliche, Seyval
Blanc, Gewurztraminer **RECOMMENDED WINES:** L'Incrédule (red blend),
Le Délinquant (fortified)

You can flash right by this tiny winery as you speed
through the town of Lanoraie, but it's worth a stop as
long as Alain Bussières is home. He's a fireman with a
passion for wine, and it shows in his large portfolio. The
6-acre vineyard behind his house, planted in 1998, is
named after the butternut tree. The wines surprised me
with their high standard of quality, given that Bussières
is always on call and winemaking is more of a hobby for
him. These wines are available only at the winery.

Cantons-de-l'Est

The first settlers in the eighteenth century called this scenic part of Quebec "Eastern Townships," a name that was later translated into French as Cantons-de-l'Est. It's a region of covered bridges and affluent towns and villages with solid Victorian brick houses, elegant Normandy-style châteaux, and fieldstone barns. The antique stores along the route may distract you from your dedicated pursuit of the wineries, as will the shops that sell locally made pâtés, cheeses, sausages, and chocolates.

Cantons-de-l'Est is the cradle of Quebec viticulture. It was here that the modern industry began in 1980, when Christian Barthomeuf planted the first vineyard at Domaine des Côtes d'Ardoise in the picturesque town of Dunham. The region is actually two defined areas: the western part centred on Dunham is known as Haut-Yamaska, after the river than runs through it, and the eastern sector centred on Magog is known as Estrie.

Dunham, at the crossing of the Richelieu and St. Lawrence valleys, was the first township to be developed in the 1790s. This charming town is the unofficial wine capital of Quebec, where the gravel slopes of the surrounding hills offer a longer frost-free growing season. Around the Magog area, the proximity of lakes Memphrémagog and Massawippi and the hills and heights of Mont Orford Provincial Park create a benevolent microclimate for grape growing. The vines are protected against May frosts by the movement of cold air falling down the slopes into the vast sink of the St. Lawrence Valley.

The soils in Haut-Yamaska range from pebbly gravel and sand (reflected in the name of Vignoble de la Sablière—"the sandbox"—at St-Armand near the Vermont border) to gravel and slate as you get near to Dunham (the name of its seminal winery, Côtes d'Ardoise—"slopes of slate"—tells that story). This mix of gravel and slate extends to every slope of the Montérégienne mountains. The soil around Magog is less porous, made up of glacial deposits of clay silt and pebbles.

If you visit this region in September during harvest time, you can participate in the annual Fête des Vendanges in Magog, which attracts over 50,000 wine lovers. For the adventurous, there's also hang-gliding and parachute jumping in the Farnham area, but that's not recommended if you've visited a few wineries.

**TOURING WINERIES
in Cantons-de-l'Est**

SINGLE DAY: Head for Dunham, but be careful not to collect a speeding ticket. From this base, you can easily see five wineries in a day if you like. But don't miss L'Orpailleur (have lunch here and spend the afternoon in the grounds of Domaine des Côtes d'Ardoise). If you prefer to stay away from crowds, drop by Les Blancs Coteaux (next door to L'Orpailleur). For a visit that will entertain the whole family, stop in at La Bauge's winery-cum-zoo. The Yamaska wineries are, on the whole, more interesting than Estrie's, and they are easier to find. Still, although this region is closer to Montreal, the scenery of lakes and mountains around Magog is beautiful. For art lovers with a sweet tooth, see Chapelle Ste. Agnès (go in fall for the trees). For wine nuts, don't miss Les Pervenches—for the best wines in the province.
WEEKEND: Take in Dunham (see above) and Les Chants de Vignes in Magog.

Vignoble Domaine de l'Ardennais

158, CHEMIN RIDGE, STANBRIDGE EST (EAST), QC J0J 2H0
(450) 248-0597 WWW.VIGNOBLEDELARDENNAIS.COM

YEAR FOUNDED: 1994 **FOUNDER:** François Samray **WINEMAKER:** Gary Skinner **GRAPE VARIETIES:** (red) Seyval Noir, Maréchal Foch, De Chaunac; (white) Seyval Blanc, Vidal, Riesling, Cayuga, Muscat
RECOMMENDED WINES: Domaine de L'Ardennais Chancellor, Le Mûrier, La Flamboyante, Le Partois

L'Ardennais speaks to the native soil of its French founder, who was born in the Ardennes. Gary and Lucie Skinner bought the property from François Samray in 2002 and have maintained its original look—a cluster of ancient barns set amid the sugar maples. Their sheltered 10-acre vineyard, with its small lake and woodlot—one of the warmest spots in Quebec—lies in a dip behind the winery. The Skinners live on the property with their daughter and are prepared to welcome visitors at reasonable hours. They grow a small amount of Muscat in a large greenhouse. In

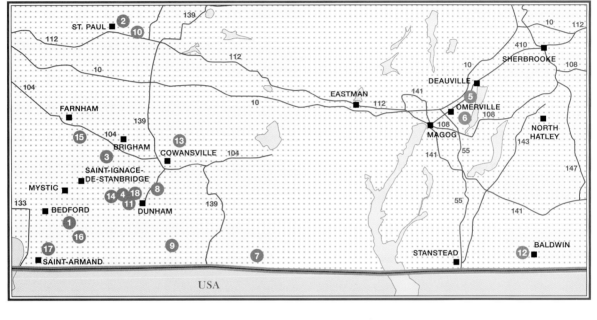

1 VIGNOBLE DOMAINE DE
   L'ARDENNAIS
2 VIGNOBLE LES ARTISANS
   DU TERROIR
3 VIGNOBLE LA BAUGE
4 VIGNOBLE LES BLANCS
   COTEAUX
5 VIGNOBLE LE CEP D'ARGENT

6 VIGNOBLE LES CHANTS
   DE VIGNE
7 VIGNOBLE DE LA CHAPELLE
   STE. AGNÈS
8 VIGNOBLE CLOS STE-CROIX
9 VIGNOBLE CLOS SARAGNAT
10 VIGNOBLE COTEAU ST-PAUL
11 VIGNOBLE DES CÔTES
   D'ARDOISE

12 DOMAINE FÉLIBRE
13 VIGNOBLE LA MISSION
14 VIGNOBLE L'ORPAILLEUR
15 VIGNOBLE LES PERVENCHES
16 VIGNOBLE DOMAINE DU RIDGE
17 VIGNOBLE DE LA SABLIÈRE
18 VIGNOBLE LES TROIS
   CLOCHERS

CANTONS-DE-L'EST WINERIES

addition to their wines, they also make a series of fruit wines, including a blend of blackberry juice, Gamay, Muscat, and grape juice mixed with raspberry concentrate and alcohol. The wine shop sells an interesting range of items, including emu oil.

Vignoble les Artisans du Terroir

1150, DE LA MONTAGNE, SAINT-PAUL-D'ABBOTSFORD, QC J0E 1A0
(450) 379-5353

FOUNDED: 1997 **FOUNDER:** Réjean Guertin **WINEMAKER:** Réjean Guertin **GRAPE VARIETIES:** (red) Chancellor, Lucie Kuhlmann, Ste-Croix, Sabrevois, Frontenac; (white) Vidal, Geisenheim, Seyval, Cayuga, St. Pepin **RECOMMENDED WINES:** Premises d'Automne White, Premises d'Automne Red

When Réjean Guertin purchased the property in 1977, it was flush with apple trees. Since Guertin had always grown vines in his garden, he planted the 10-acre vineyard behind the orchard in 1997 and, two years later, he bottled his first wines.

Apples are still a large part of the operation at Artisans du Terroir. You can buy them by the bushel, along with his wines, in the wood barn by the highway.

All of Guertin's wines are currently blends, but he intends to plant up to 80 percent Frontenac in the future and to make more red wine. Try to schedule a visit during harvest time in order to see the unique harvesting wagons that Réjean has invented, as well as the colourful sails of the paragliders that take off from nearby Mount Yamaska in the summer months. Guertin also raises llamas and exotic birds.

Vignoble la Bauge

115, DES ERABLES, BRIGHAM, QC J2K 4E1 (450) 266-2149
WWW.LABAUGE.COM

YEAR FOUNDED: 1987 **FOUNDER:** Alcide Naud **WINEMAKER:** Simon
Naud **GRAPE VARIETIES:** (red) Frontenac, Chancellor, Sabrevois; (white)
Seyval Blanc, Geisenheim, Vidal, plus an experimental 1-acre plot of
different varieties **RECOMMENDED WINES:** Les Patriarches, Sélectionne
Camille (Late Harvest), Solitaires

Is this a winery or an animal park? There is something
of a circus atmosphere at La Bauge ("wild boar"), with a
range of caged and free-range animals and exotic birds
vying for the visitor's attention alongside the wines. After
forty years as a dairy farmer, Alcide Naud diversified into
raising wild boar, deer, wild sheep, stags, pheasant, and
exotic birds. The wild boar pâté and smoked venison
sausages you can purchase in the wine shop (and consume
at the picnic tables) are products of the farm's extensive
woodland acreage (you can buy a licence to hunt with a
crossbow on the property, if that's your taste, and they'll
even help prepare and transport your meat). The vineyard, a quick walk from the charming village of Brigham,
is situated on the south side of the Appalachian foothills
on land that was once the Champlain Sea. A tractor-
hauled covered wagon will take you through the vineyard
and the exotic animal reserve, where you will see Texas
longhorns, Peruvian llamas, Himalayan yaks, Australian
emus, European deer, South American nandous,
Japanese sikas, red deer, and the wild boar that give the
property its name.

Since 1996, Simon Naud, Alcide's son, has been in
charge of the winemaking and the vineyard. He has
made many experimental plantings to find the right
varieties for his soil. A visit here is a great experience for
the whole family.

Vignoble les Blancs Coteaux

1046, ROUTE 202 (RUE BRUCE), DUNHAM, QC J0E 1M0 (450) 295-3503
WWW.BLANCSCOTEAUX.COM

YEAR FOUNDED: 1989 **FOUNDERS:** Pierre Genesse and Marie-Claude
Lizotte **WINEMAKER:** Jacqueline Dubé **GRAPE VARIETIES:** (red)
Sabrevois, Frontenac; (white) Seyval **RECOMMENDED WINES:** La Taste
Vendange Sélectionnée, La Vieille Grange

The Dubé family purchased Les Blancs Coteaux with its
brightly painted red farmhouse and hundred-year-old barn
from Pierre Genesse, who had planted the original vineyard. The name was inspired by the flowering apple trees
that cover the slopes above the winery. The Dubés keep
not only the name but Genesse's product portfolio as well.
For the Dubés, farming 25 acres of vines is a true family
project, involving two brothers and two sisters and their

Stone chapel at Vignoble de la Chapelle Ste. Agnès.

spouses. In addition to making the wine and cider with
the help of a consultant, Jacqueline Dubé, a former nurse,
also does the bookkeeping. The shop, selling a range of gift
ideas, has a wonderfully rustic atmosphere and is well worth
a visit. Also available are gift and picnic baskets filled with
local food products. The statue in front of the winery—
Homage to Bacchus—is a favourite photo-op for visitors.

Vignoble le Cep d'Argent

1257, CHEMIN DE LA RIVIÈRE, MAGOG, QC J1X 3W5
(819) 864-4441; 1-877-864-4441 WWW.CEPDARGENT.COM

FOUNDERS: Denis Drouin, Gaston Dorval, Jacques C. Daniel, Marc
Daniel, and Jean-Paul and François Scieur **WINEMAKER:** Jean-Pierre
Bonville **GRAPE VARIETIES:** (red) Maréchal Foch, De Chaunac, Ste-
Croix; (white) Seyval Blanc, Geisenheim, Cayuga **RECOMMENDED**
WINES: Oak-aged Seyval, Fleur de Lys, Sélection des Mousquetaires

Le Cep d'Argent is the most northerly winery in the
Eastern Townships, located on the hills between Magog

Vignoble les Chants de Vigne

459, CHEMIN DE LA RIVIÈRE, MAGOG, QC J0E 1M0 (819) 847-8467
CHANTSDEVIGNE@QC.AIRA.COM

YEAR FOUNDED: 1996 **FOUNDER:** Jacques Daniel **WINEMAKER:** Marc
Daniel **GRAPE VARIETIES:** (red) Ste-Croix, Maréchal Foch; (white) Seyval
Blanc, Vandal-Cliche, Ortega, Cayuga **RECOMMENDED WINE:** L'Opéra

When Jacques Daniel sold his interest in Le Cep
d'Argent, he and his son, Marc, looked to start a smaller,
less commercial operation. Daniel bought a 10-acre site
nearby, planted the vineyard in 1996, and named the
winery "Songs of the Vine." The same sense of poetry is
carried over to the naming of the wines, each of which
bears a musical connotation (Le Jazz, Le Boléro, Le Kyrie).
L'Opéra is a Pineau des Charentes–style wine made with
Geisenheim juice fortified with spirit. The terrace at Les
Chants de Vigne, with its commanding view, is an ideal
spot to taste the wines. As well as making the wine, Marc
Daniel is an accomplished chef who takes his turn at the
stove for the winery's catered dinners.

Vignoble de la Chapelle Ste. Agnès

2565, CHEMIN SCENIC, SUTTON, QC J0E 2K0 (450) 538-0303
WWW.VINDEGLACE.COM

YEAR FOUNDED: 2002 **FOUNDER:** Henrietta Antony **WINEMAKERS:**
Christian Barthomeuf, with John Antony **GRAPE VARIETIES:** (red)
Frontenac; (white) Vidal, Geisenheim 332, Riesling, Gewurztraminer,
Muscat Ottonel, Swenson White **RECOMMENDED WINES:** Geisenheim,
Vidal Icewine, Vin de Paille

Henrietta Antony, who left South Moravia (now the Czech
Republic) in 1949 as a teenager, owns the largest fine
antiques store in Montreal. In 1959 she bought 14 acres of
land in Glen Sutton, near the American border, and each
time one of her neighbours sold she bought the property.
She invested millions of dollars to create a Rhône-style
terraced vineyard that descends down to an ornamental
lake and a three-storey stone cellar. But first she built a gem
of a Romanesque chapel consecrated to Sainte-Agnès, a
thirteenth-century Bohemian saint.

Antony flew back to the Czech Republic to ask
friends there how to recreate wine cellars worthy of her
project. They took her to the cellars of the Knights
Templar, dating back to 1258, and that's what she has
recreated here. She imported European stonemasons to
fashion the cathedral-like design, with its basket-weave
vaulted ceilings, medieval arches, and stone carvings. "It
was done with grey matter. It was done with heart," she
will tell you. The eighteen terraces of vines that lead up
from the artificial lake to the house took four years to
build. "I thought they deserved a château," she says, so

and Sherbrooke. The vineyard that slopes down to the
banks of Lake Magog was planted in 1985 by Denis Drouin
and his five original partners. His winemaker at that time,
Alain Bayon, introduced him to two brothers, Jean-Paul
and François Scieur, who became his partners in 1991.
The Scieur brothers, sixth-generation winemakers from
Champagne, were the first to produce a sparkling wine in
Quebec by the champagne method.

The original partnership broke up when Jacques Daniel
and his son, Marc, left to start their own winery at
Vignoble les Chants de Vigne. Denis Drouin and the
Scieur brothers now run the flourishing company that is
perhaps Quebec's most publicized winery and certainly one
of its largest. Since those early years, the vineyard holdings
have been expanded to more than 110 acres. Realizing
the importance of tourism to promote their wines, the
owners have created two function rooms for parties and
conventions—the Chevalier Room (accommodating 150)
and the Medieval Room (250). The Champagne connection continues, as both the current winemaker and the
vineyard manager are from that region.

The winery at Vignoble Clos Ste-Croix.

she had cellars dug into a hillside, on three floors, 42 feet deep. Each of the chambers is furnished with antiques from the seventeenth and eighteenth centuries.

At the time of writing, the building of the château has been discontinued in favour of more vineyard terraces, and Antony confesses to having lost money on the stock market. Her son John is the assistant winemaker to consultant Christian Barthomeuf, and together they produce the most costly wines in the province—a *vin de paille* for $66 a 200 millilitre bottle that rivals a fine Sauternes. "I wanted to do a place that would inspire people," says Antony. It does— and it's not to be missed for its spectacular architecture, historic artifacts, and sweet wines. A tour of this spell-binding winery, with its magnificent stone cellar, costs $25, including a tasting. It's worth the expense.

The winery's website, www.vindeglace.com, indicates the emphasis here: sweet dessert wines of international calibre. This is without question Quebec's most spectacular winery to visit, and the wines live up to its visual appeal.

Vignoble Clos Ste-Croix

3734, RUE PRINCIPALE, DUNHAM, QC J0E 1M0 (450) 295 3281
WWW.CLOSSTECROIX.CA

YEAR FOUNDED: 1991 **FOUNDER:** Pierre-Paul Jodoin
WINEMAKER: Jean-Paul Martin **GRAPE VARIETIES:** (red) Ste-Croix, Maréchal Foch; (white) Seyval Blanc **RECOMMENDED WINE:** Ste-Croix

In the heart on the village of Dunham, on its main street, you'll find this charming winery tucked away behind a beautiful red-brick Loyalist house. The winemaking facility, adjacent to the house, is located in a old, weathered barn dating back to 1902. French native Pierre-Paul Jodoin hobby-farms what he claims to be the smallest commercial winery in Quebec (he runs a car security business when he can tear himself away from the vineyard). Jodoin's grapes come from 5 acres of vines in his back garden planted mainly to Ste-Croix, the variety that gave the enterprise its name. The ornamental lake that creates a little warmth for the vines was once a swamp, which Jodoin drained and landscaped. He planted his first 100 vines in 1991 and, each year, planted more, until he had five thousand, two-thirds of which were in production in 2005.

Vignoble Clos Saragnat

100, CHEMIN RICHFORD, FRELIGHSBURG, QC J0J 1C0 (450) 298-1444
WWW.SARAGNAT.COM

YEAR FOUNDED: 2003 **FOUNDERS:** Louise Dupuis and Christian Barthomeuf **WINEMAKERS:** Christian Barthomeuf, Louise Dupuis **GRAPE VARIETIES:** (white) Geisenheim, Vidal, Muscat Ottonel, Gewurztraminer, Riesling **RECOMMENDED WINES:** Icewine; Ice Cider, Ice Pear

In 2003 Christian Barthomeuf and Louise Dupuis purchased a histroic 92-acre apple orchard on the slope of Mount Pinnacle, close to the Vermont border. Some of the trees were over seventy years old. The couple created a winery they called Clos Saragnat, after Barthomeuf's ancestral family name in his native Arles. The custom-built winery is a small structure faced with cedar shakes above a cellar. Here Barthomeuf makes his sweet wines—Vin de Paille, Ice Cider (a category of wine he created in 1989), and Ice Pear. Christian Barthomeuf, a pioneer of the Quebec wine industry and its most respected—if controversial—consultant, is a strong advocate of organic farming, and he rails against the pesticides being used extensively in Quebec's vineyards and orchards. Barthomeuf claims that pesticides are more concentrated in iced products. He will not even drive a tractor in his vineyard, using horses instead, for fear of compacting the soil and impeding drainage. Barthomeuf cellars his products for three years, without filtration, and he will not use pumps to move the juice or the finished wine, for fear of compromising their flavours. As a result, his wines show very clean, concentrated flavours.

Vignoble Coteau St-Paul

1595, ROUTE 112 (RUE PRINCIPALE), ST-PAUL-D'ABBOTSFORD, QC J0E 1A0
(450) 379-5069 HTTP://PAGES.GLOBETROTTER.NET/COTEAU.ST.PAUL

YEAR FOUNDED: 2004 **FOUNDER:** Jean Guy Gosselin
WINEMAKER: Jean Guy Gosselin **GRAPE VARIETIES:** (red) Chancellor, Sabrevois, Frontenac; (white) Prairie Star, Louise Swenson, Muscadet **RECOMMENDED WINES:** Sabrevois; Ice Cider

Jean Guy Gosselin was bitten by the grape when he toured Europe. Originally from northern Ontario, he confesses to being brought up on Baby Duck, but the European experience gave him a taste for fine wine. Gosselin's photogenic winery-cum-cidery on the southern slope of Mount Yamaska looks rather like a small wooden castle and is located right by the highway; he will tell you that its design was inspired by the architecture of a

CHRISTIAN BARTHOMEUF
PIONEER AND PROPHET

"When I started planting vines in Dunham in 1979 I started with a book in my hand. The same thing for wine. I can cook. The rest is feeling." French winemaker Christian Barthomeuf was born in Arles in 1951. He took a sabbatical from film-making in 1974, came to Quebec, bought a farm in Dunham, and stayed. That farm became Côte d'Ardoise, the winery he would eventually sell to Montreal plastic surgeon Jacques Papillon.

From that time, Barthomeuf began consulting to a variety of wineries and cideries, notable among them Pomelière in Dunham (where he first made Ice Cider), La Face Cachée, Domaine Pinnacle, and Chapelle Ste. Agnès. Twenty years ago, Barthomeuf will tell you, he believed he could make wine in Quebec, but now he confesses he is aiming at a higher level—"Not a regional business, not nationalistic, wine has to be international." That's why he's concentrating his efforts at Clos Saragnat and Chapelle Ste. Agnès on high-level products (read expensive) that will appeal to the international market—*vin de paille* and Iced Cider.

sixteenth-century Norman castle. Picnic tables are set out by the fruit stall, which is housed under the replica of an ancient market stall covered with a wooden roof. The vineyards you see from the road in front of the apple orchard are table grapes. Grapes for wine are grown farther up the mountain slope, where they get better exposure to the sun and better drainage. The property has 10 acres of vines (planted in 1999) and 20 acres of apple trees. Gosselin outlines the work that goes into growing both grapes and apples in a little museum in the reception and tasting rooms, a good stop for kids who get impatient with winery visits.

Domaine des Côtes d'Ardoise

879, ROUTE 202 (RUE BRUCE), DUNHAM, QC J0E 1M0 (450) 295-2020
WWW.COTESDARDOISE.COM

YEAR FOUNDED: 1980 **FOUNDER:** Christian Barthomeuf **WINEMAKER:**
David Cottineau **GRAPE VARIETIES:** (red) Gamay, Maréchal Foch, De
Chaunac, Lucie Kuhlmann; (white) Riesling, Seyval, Aurore
RECOMMENDED WINES: Seyval Carte d'Or, Côte d'Ardoise (Gamay and
Maréchal Foch)

"Ardoise" means slate and refers to the soil of Dr.
Jacques Papillon's horseshoe-shaped vineyard set in a
perfect natural amphitheatre. It was the first vineyard to be
planted in the modern era of Quebec wines (in 1980), and
it happens to be on the first hill you see as you drive south
from Montreal. Protected by trees, the vineyard rises
behind the weathered, ivy-covered old barn built in 1945,
where you can taste Côtes d'Ardoise's eleven wines.

Forty sculptures by Canadian artists are set around the
grounds and in the vineyard—with pride of place, at the
highest point, going to a huge monarch butterfly (it's
actually an old railway snowplough painted to resemble
a butterfly). The vineyard was originally planted by
Christian Barthomeuf. He bought the farm in 1977 and,
seven years later, sold it to Jacques Papillon, a Montreal
plastic surgeon. With its special microclimate ("I've never
had frost after May 2 in twenty years," claims Papillon),
the vineyard can support such tender vinifera varieties as
Riesling and Gamay. A visit here is worth a whole afternoon as you enjoy the art, taste the wines, and sample
the restaurant's food (or your own). There is also a covered terrace in the picnic area.

Domaine Félibre

740 CHEMIN BEAN, STANSTEAD, QC J0B 3E0 (819) 876-7900
WWW.DOMAINEFELIBRE.COM

YEAR FOUNDED: 1998 **FOUNDERS:** Gilles Desjardins and Catherine
Hébert **WINEMAKER:** Gilles Desjardins **GRAPE VARIETIES:** (white) Eona;
(fruit) apple, raspberry, blackcurrant, cherry **RECOMMENDED WINES:**
Cru des Vallons, Givré

When Montrealers Gilles Desjardins and Catherine
Hébert decided to forsake the big city in 1991, they bought
a 250-acre farm in a remote part of southeastern Quebec
near the American border. You may have difficulty finding
them, but don't give up. Their 5-acre vineyard and apple
and cherry orchards are gorgeously set in the surrounding
hills, and the welcome is warm. From the MacBarry
apples grown here, the couple produces a unique product
called Givré (apples picked after a frost). First they press
the juice and then freeze it, removing the ice before
fermenting what juice is left. It takes 5 kilos of apples to
make a half-bottle of this iced cider. They also produce

other fruit wines from their own harvest. The website
says their wine is on the wine list at the luxury George
V Hotel in Paris. It's worth checking out this winery, if
only for that.

Vignoble la Mission

1044, BOULEVARD PIERRE LAPORTE (ROUTE 241), BRIGHAM, QC J2K 4R3
(450) 263-1524 WWW.VIGNOBLE-LAMISSION.COM

YEAR FOUNDED: 1997 **FOUNDERS:** Marie-Josée Clusiau and Alejandro
Guerrero **WINEMAKER:** David Cottineau **GRAPE VARIETIES:** (red) Seyval
Noir, Chancellor, Maréchal Foch, Léon Millot; (white) St. Pepin, Muscat,
Seyval Blanc, Vidal, Geisenheim **RECOMMENDED WINES:** La Mission
White, Vidal Icewine, "Port"

Century-old sugar maples line the entrance to this
enchanting property with a magnificent view of the surrounding hills and wood lots. The best time to visit is when
the leaves are changing for a spectacular panorama of
colour. Marie-Josée Clusiau and Alejandro Guerrero
bought a 50-acre farm in 1997 and planted fifteen varieties

Vignoble l'Orpailleur.

in the 8-acre vineyard they created. They lived with their two teenage daughters above the winery and shop, in an old house that was formerly a maple syrup factory. In 2004 Jay Bassila and Jean-Christophe Hirsch purchased the winery. They make a much sought-after Ice Wine, as well as red, rosé, and white wine and a fortified port-style red.

Vignoble l'Orpailleur

1086, ROUTE 202 (RUE BRUCE), DUNHAM, QC J0E 1M0 (450) 295-2763
WWW.ORPAILLEUR.CA

YEAR FOUNDED: 1982 **FOUNDERS:** Hervé Durand, Charles-Henri de Coussergues, and Frank Furtado **WINEMAKER:** Charles-Henri de Coussergues **GRAPE VARIETIES:** (red) Seyval Noir; Maréchal Foch; De Chaunac, Chancellor; (white) Seyval, Vidal, Geisenheim 318
RECOMMENDED WINES: Icewine, L'Orpailleur Élevé en Fut de Chêne, L'Orpailleur Blanc, L'Apérid'Or

In 1982 two French winemakers, Hervé Durand and Charles-Henri de Coussergues, along with their Quebec associate, theatrical producer Frank Furtado, planted a vineyard in Dunham for a winery to be called Vignoble du Château Blanc, after the historic farmhouse on the property. Three years later they took in another partner, Pierre Rodrigue, and, thanks to a poem composed by Gilles Vigneault, in which he likened growing wine in Quebec to panning for gold, the enterprise was renamed L'Orpailleur ("the gold panner"). The original wood house has been expanded in colonial style to include a restaurant (formerly the shed for farm machinery and tools) and a wine shop. From its lookout tower on the second floor, you can see a commanding view of the surrounding vineyards. Inside the original house is an exhibition of wine culture through the ages, complete with a collection of antique corkscrews. If you visit only one winery in Dunham, this one will give you the complete Quebec wine experience and a history lesson to boot. The hour-long tour includes a video. In September, L'Orpailleur sets off fireworks to mark the beginning of the grape harvest—courtesy of Frank Furtado, who puts on firework displays across Canada.

Winemaker Charles-Henri de Coussergues was born near Nîmes in the south of France, where he studied oenology and worked in his family winery before immigrating to Quebec in 1982. His oak-aged Seyval Blanc is one of the best I've tasted.

Vignoble les Pervenches

150, CHEMIN BOULAIS, FARNHAM, QC J2N 2P9 (450) 293-8311
WWW.LESPERVENCHES.COM

YEAR FOUNDED: 1997 **FOUNDER:** Yves Monachon **WINEMAKER:** Michael Marler **GRAPE VARIETIES:** (red) Maréchal Foch; (white) Chardonnay, Seyval Blanc **RECOMMENDED WINES:** Seyval-Chardonnay, Seyval-Vidal, Cuvée de Montmollin

You'll find some of the best Quebec wines here at Les Pervenches. *Pervenche*, in English, means periwinkle, the native flower of Savoie. That is the former home of Yves Monachon, who planted the 8-acre vineyard in 1991 with vines imported from France. If you can't make it to the winery, you'll find Les Pervenches on the wine lists of the province's top restaurants (only 800 cases are made). The youthful Michael Marler, who took over the property in 2000 with his wife, Véronique Hupin, graduated in agriculture from McGill University and then studied winemaking in Toulouse. The spare, single-storey winery is set behind the house, adjacent to the vineyard. Marler is the only producer of Chardonnay in Quebec, a buttery, green-apple-flavoured wine that he barrel ferments in Burgundian style and blends with 20 percent Seyval. Curiously, Marler gives Seyval pride of place on the label.

You'll find Les Pervenches east of Farnham, at the beginning of the wine route. It's essential viewing for Chardonnay lovers and for all those interested in the way climate and soil can shape the taste of this popular grape.

Vignoble Domaine du Ridge

205, CHEMIN RIDGE, ST-ARMAND, QC J0J 1T0 (450) 248-3987
DOMRIDGE@SYMPATICO.CA

YEAR FOUNDED: 1999 **FOUNDER:** Denis Paradis **WINEMAKER:** Jean
Berthelot **GRAPE VARIETIES:** (red) Maréchal Foch, Baco Noir, De
Chaunac, Seyval Noir; (white) Seyval Blanc, Geisenheim, Vidal, Cayuga
RECOMMENDED WINE: Vent d'Ouest

Denis Paradis, a federal Liberal MP and former minister
of state (financial institutions), started planting his vineyard,
which now extends over 42 acres, in 1996. He will tell
you candidly that he knew nothing about wine production
until one of his neighbours convinced him to plant a
vineyard and offered to teach him how to make wine.

The Loyalist Victorian house on a sequestered side road
is now the winery office, while the heavy lifting is done
in a new barn designed to fit into its pastoral setting.

The time to visit this winery is during harvest, especially for an event Paradis calls Cuvée du Fouloir: he
invites twenty women to foot-crush his Seyval Blanc, to
the accompaniment of an accordion. The crushing tank
looks like an outdoor Portuguese port lagar—but it's
actually the base of an old silo that Paradis had restored
and remodelled with oak panelling. A walk through the
200-acre property under tree-lined paths is a delight in the
summer heat. But the foot-crushing of the Seyval Blanc
is the real show.

Vignoble de la Sablière

1050, CHEMIN DUTCH (ROUTE 235), ST-ARMAND, QC J0J 1T0 (450) 248-2634
LASABLIERE@ACBM.NET

YEAR FOUNDED: 1993 **FOUNDERS:** Irénée Belley and Sandra Moreau
WINEMAKER: Irénée Belley **GRAPE VARIETIES:** (red) Ste-Croix,
Maréchal Foch; (white) Seyval Blanc, Geisenheim **RECOMMENDED
WINE:** Seyval Blanc

La Sablière translates as "the sandbox." The property is so
named because of the sandy soil of this tiny winery (it
produces a mere 350 cases) set in the picturesque countryside near Bedford.

Founders Irénée Belley and Sandra Moreau escaped
from Montreal for the solitude of the country, where they
wanted to farm organically. Belley, a former set painter for
movies, is a talented artist, and her ironic cartoon-like
paintings grace the path to the winery. She also designed
La Sablière's colourful labels. The *cuverie* and the tasting
room are housed in an old stone farm building whose thick
walls maintain a cool temperature even in summer.

La Sablière's wines tend to be very dry, given the rigour
of their philosophy—no added sugar during fermentation
to boost alcohol. The result is a nervy Seyval Blanc that
resembles a *vinho verde* in its crisp, citric flavour.

Robert Brisebois at Les Trois Clochers.

Vignoble les Trois Clochers

341, RUE BRUCE, DUNHAM, QC J0E 1M0 (450) 295-2034
VIGNOBLELESTROISCLOCHERS@QC.AIRA.COM

YEAR FOUNDED: 1986 **FOUNDERS:** Claude Rhéaume and Réal
Normandeau **WINEMAKER:** Robert Brisebois **GRAPE VARIETIES:** (red)
Chancellor, Maréchal Foch; (white) Seyval, Vidal **RECOMMENDED
WINES:** Vidal Icewine, Les Trois Clochers Blanc

Robert Brisebois, a geologist and long-time home winemaker, and his wife, Nadège Marion, a schoolteacher,
purchased the winery in 1987. They operate this tiny
hands-on facility from an old stone farmhouse on a part-
time basis. The day I visited, Brisebois emerged from the
chai with his hands and arms purple to the elbow from
extracting the skins from the press. The bijou winemaking
area, packed to the rafters with equipment, is the size of a
small garage and is located under the tasting room, which
resembles a nineteenth-century schoolroom. From its deck,
you can see Dunham's three church bell towers that give
the winery its name. Set among rolling hills, the farm, in
addition to grape vines, supports geese and turkeys. The
7.5-acre vineyard gradually slopes away from the winery.
Picnic tables set out on the lawns afford a relaxing pastoral
setting, especially if accompanied by the fruity wine Les
Trois Clochers Rouge as the maples begin to turn.
Brisebois hand-bottles and labels all his wines. Buy his
Icewine if he has any available to sell.

Basses-Laurentides

For the wine lover who can't spend more than half a day in discovering Quebec wines, a thirty-minute drive (in off-peak hours) from downtown Montreal towards Mirabel Airport will take you to the vicinity of the three wineries in Basses-Laurentides. Mountains, forests, lakes, and valleys characterize this area—a favourite destination for hikers, bikers, and picnickers, with its labyrinth of quiet country roads. One of the most beautiful walking and biking areas is the 200 kilometre linear park that runs along a former railway bed from Saint-Jérôme northwest through the Laurentian Mountains to Mont-Laurier. Many of the stations along the route have been renovated as comfort stops, cafés, boutiques, exhibition spaces, and tourist kiosks.

The most spectacular of the three wineries in this region is La Roche des Brises at St-Joseph-du-Lac, with its fine restaurant (voted the second-best table in the Laurentians) and its five-star country inn with spa. In the foothills of the Laurentians, where La Roche des Brises is located, the soil is rocky and gravelly. Farther north at St-Benoît and the secluded Vignoble des Négondos, the soil gets even rockier. Towards the east on the plain, the soil is more workable, a mix of sandy clay and limestone that you'll find at Vignoble de la Rivière du Chêne in St-Eustache. Large bodies of water, such as the St. Lawrence and Lac des Deux Montagnes, and the protecting hills of the Basses-Laurentides provide the important microclimates that allow these northerly wineries to sustain their vineyards.

When you're touring through the town of St-Benoît de Mirabel, look for Intermiel, a company founded by Christian and Viviane Macle in 1976. They operate the largest apiary in Quebec, with 2,000 beehives. The store sells honey wine, honey, royal jelly, beeswax, and other bee byproducts as well as an intriguing sweet alcoholic drink called Geai Bleu, made from two Quebecois staples—wild blueberries and maple syrup.

TOURING WINERIES
in Basse-Laurentides

SINGLE DAY: You can visit all three wineries in this region in one day quite comfortably. Each one offers a different experience. If you want to travel first class, spend some time over a meal at La Roche des Brises. Or, for a more earthy experience, a picnic in the woods at Vignoble des Négondos is the call.
WEEKEND: Take a leisurely tour through all three wineries and spend some quality time with the bees at Intermiel.

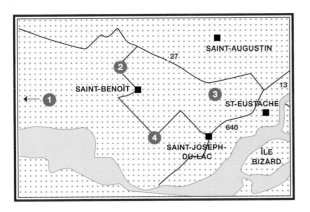

BASSES-LAURENTIDES WINERIES

1 VIGNOBLE DU CLOS BAILLIE
2 VIGNOBLE DES NÉGONDOS
3 VIGNOBLE DE LA RIVIÈRE DU CHÊNE
4 LA ROCHE DES BRISES

Vignoble du Clos Baillie

490, RUE BAILLIE, GATINEAU (AYLMER), QC J9J 3R5 (819) 827-3220
WWW.QUEBECVINO.COM

YEAR FOUNDED: 1999 **FOUNDER:** Raymond Huneault **WINEMAKER:**
Jean-Marc Major **GRAPE VARIETIES:** (red) Frontenac, Sabrevois;
(white) Vandal-Cliche, Seyval Blanc, Swenson **RECOMMENDED WINE:**
Kelly-Dot (red)

The name of the winery, "Baillie," recalls the Scottish
heritage of the original settlers on the land near Aylmer
rather than the French heritage of the current proprietor,
Raymond Huneault. Clos du Baillie's vineyard was planted in 1999 in the Gatineau Hills at the foot of Mount
King, behind Huneault's house.

A flooded quarry at the base of the vineyard created
a 15-acre lake, which in turn created a favourable microclimate for grape growing.

The winery is close enough to downtown Ottawa (ten
minutes by car) to be a destination for the capital's wine
lovers. In May 2000 a late frost threatened the vines, so
Huneault lit small fires around the vineyard. "I smoked
out the entire city of Aylmer," he wrote. "I had visitors
all night. They were curious and wanted to know what the
hell was going on."

Huneault claims it was a great advertisement for his
winery! He has also planted another vineyard called La
Rose des Neiges between Papineauville and Montebello.
His winemaker, Jean-Marc Major, is also a grower,
whose 2-acre vineyard, in Cumberland, is even closer to
downtown Ottawa.

Vignoble des Négondos

7100, RANG SAINT-VINCENT, ST-BENOÎT-DE-MIRABEL, QC J7N 3N1
(450) 258-2099; 1-877-309-2099 WWW.NEGONDOS.COM

YEAR FOUNDED: 1997 **FOUNDERS:** Carole Desrochers and Mario Plante
WINEMAKERS: Carole Desrochers, Mario Plante **GRAPE VARIETIES:** (red)
Maréchal Foch, De Chaunac (with experimental plantings of Ste-Croix,
Frontenac, and Louise Swenson); (white) Seyval, Cayuga, Geisenheim
318 and 322, Seyve Villard 23512, Vidal **RECOMMENDED WINES:** Orélie,
Rosois (rosé)

A red-clay dirt road separates the vineyards as you
approach the custom-built winery with its distinctive blue
roof. Mario Plante, a social worker, and Carole Desrochers,
a kindergarten teacher, are self-taught winemakers who
operate the only certified organic vineyard in Quebec. The
house and winery—carefully painted and fresh looking—
are surrounded by a species of maple tree that gave the
enterprise its name.

In 1996, when Plante and Desrochers planted their two
parcels of vines, 8 acres in all, they sent away more than
100 truckloads of rocks they had removed, with much
effort, from the site.

Vignoble de la Rivière du Chêne

807, RIVIÈRE DU NORD, ST-EUSTACHE, QC J7R 4K3 (450) 491-3997
WWW.VIGNOBLEDELARIVIEREDUCHENE.QC.CA

YEAR FOUNDED: 1998 **FOUNDERS:** Daniel Lalande and Isabelle Gonthier
WINEMAKERS: Jérémie d'Hauteville, Richard Bastien **GRAPE VARIETIES:**
(red) Marechal Foch, Baco Noir, Lucie Kuhlmann, Sabrevois, Frontenac,
Ste-Croix; (white) Vandal-Cliche, Geisenheim 318, Vidal, St. Pepin, Kay
Gray **RECOMMENDED WINES:** Cuvée William Blanc, L'Éraportéross

Jérémie d'Hauteville, an oenologist who trained at the
renowned French wine school in Montpellier, took over
this winery in 2002 from Daniel Lalande, whose family
farm produced maple syrup. Lalande blended the syrup
into the wines he made here, a practice continued by
d'Hauteville because of their popularity.

The attractive redwood winery and tasting room are
not the easiest to find along the country roads, but are
certainly worth the effort. The reception room resembles
a large maple-syrup cabin. In fact, Vignoble de la Rivière
du Chêne produces a delicious port-style fortified red wine
spiked with maple syrup. The winery also produces red,
white, and rosé wine, Late Harvest, and Icewine.

In September 2004, Richard Bastien, an oenologist
from Reims in Champagne, joined the team.

La Roche des Brises

2007, RUE PRINCIPALE, ST-JOSEPH-DU-LAC, QC J0N 1M0 (450) 472-2722
WWW.ROCHESDESBRISES.COM, RESTAURANT: L'AUBERGE DES BRISES,
(450) 472-3477

YEAR FOUNDED: 1993 **FOUNDER:** Jean-Pierre Bélisle **WINEMAKER:**
Jean-Paul Martin **GRAPE VARIETIES:** (red) Maréchal Foch,
Lucie Kuhlmann, Ste-Croix; (white) Geisenheim 318, Vandal-Cliche
RECOMMENDED WINES: Maribriand (Maréchal Foch/Lucie
Kuhlmann), Maréchal Foch, Saint Croix, Dernière Danse, Geisenheim
Vendange Tardive

When Jean-Pierre Bélisle, a lawyer and former deputy
house leader in the Quebec Assembly, purchased the
property in 1993, he had no intention of getting into the
wine business—let alone the hospitality trade. He was more
interested in enjoying the view of Montreal. And what a
view of mountains and forests! But now it's a full-time occupation, and he is also the president of the Association of
Quebec Vignerons. Adjacent to the contemporary winery
is the fine-dining restaurant, which boasts an extensive
international wine list. Across the road is the rustic and
charming seven-room country inn, complete with spa
facilities, called Auberge Roche des Brises.

In addition to the vineyards, Bélisle also farms 1,000
apple trees. "I chose this region," he says, "because there
were no rules. It was like cowboy country." Winemaker
Jean-Paul Martin also makes wines at Clos de la Montage
and Clos Ste-Croix.

Quebec City

If you've ever spent a winter in Quebec City, you're forgiven if you shake your head in disbelief that this region grows wine. Although it is the most recently exploited vineyard area in the province, its history dates back to the founding of French Canada. Ever since Jacques Cartier discovered an abundance of wild grapevines growing up the trees on the Île d'Orléans, the image has excited the imagination of Quebecois winegrowers. But past experiments were doomed to failure because early growers did not have the benefit of winter-hardy varieties that could withstand polar temperatures. It is only since 1979, when the first experimental vineyard was planted at Beauport and, two years later, at Charlesbourg (the location of Vignoble Bourg Royal in the suburbs of the city), that vines have flourished in this region. The St. Lawrence River makes it possible and, as long as the vines are planted within sight of the river, they can survive if the grower selects the right winter-hardy varieties. The river reflects sunlight back onto the vines and gives off stored heat in the winter.

Of all the wine regions in Quebec, this one is perhaps the least interesting in terms of overall quality but the most fascinating when it comes to agri-tourism. Simply put, this area is a tourist mecca: ancient stone houses with steeply raked roofs and wraparound balconies clustered along the Chemin Royal, Montmorency Falls, the working flour mill of Moulin du Petit Pré, the gorgeous church at St-Joachim, the bee museum with its delicious honey wine at Château-Richer, the bird sanctuary at Cap Tourmente, the summer theatres in Beauce and Lévis, and the fascinating streets of Quebec City. And if the wines of this region are somewhat astringent, their lack of richness is made up by the warmth of the welcome.

**TOURING WINERIES
in Quebec City**

SINGLE DAY: Spend the morning at the Moulin du Petit Pré and then head for Île d'Orléans and visit Vignoble de Sainte-Pétronille and Vignoble Isle de Bacchus.
WEEKEND: Follow the plan above on day one. Spend your second day in the historic town of Saint-Jean-Port-Joli and the Vignoble du Faubourg.

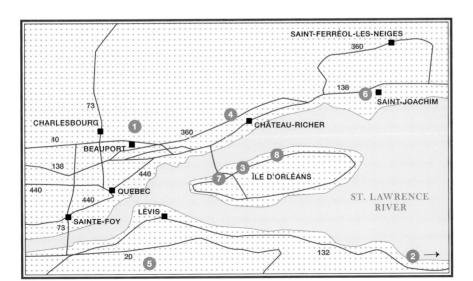

QUEBEC CITY WINERIES

1 VIGNOBLE BOURG ROYAL
2 VIGNOBLE DU FAUBOURG
3 VIGNOBLE ISLE DE BACCHUS
4 VIGNOBLE LE MOULIN DU PETIT PRÉ
5 VIGNOBLE LE NORDET
6 DOMAINE ROYARNOIS
7 VIGNOBLE DE SAINTE-PÉTRONILLE
8 DOMAINE DE LA SOURCE À MARGUERITE

Vignoble Bourg Royal

1910, RUE DES ÉRABLES, CHARLESBOURG, QC G2L 1R8
(418) 681-9119 WWW.VIGNOBLEBOURGROYAL.COM

YEAR FOUNDED: 1997 **FOUNDERS:** Corporation du Vignoble Communtaire de Bourg-Royal (a winery cooperative) **WINEMAKER:** Jorj Radu **GRAPE VARIETIES:** (red) Ste-Croix, Maréchal Foch, Michurinetz, Severnyi, Léon Millot; (white) Vandal-Cliche, Eona **RECOMMENDED WINES:** L'Esprit du Nord (Ice Cider), Larme Rosée

From the ebullient, extroverted Jorj (George) Radu's vineyard you can see the skyline of Quebec City. The winery is located in the city suburbs and surrounded by modern housing. Before immigrating to Canada, Jorj managed a state-owned vineyard in his native Romania. When he arrived in Canada, he started his own cidery in Quebec, and then, in 2002, he purchased the 20-acre vineyard, which had been left untouched since the original owners declared bankruptcy. The winery is utilitarian in appearance, but Radu will charm you with his self-confidence and occasionally outrageous statements about winemaking in Quebec. The walls of his restaurant-cum-party-room are decorated with stuffed animals—a bear, a fox, and a variety of game birds. Radu claims to have invented Ice Cider (his is excellent), but so does Christian Barthomeuf—

and with more justification. One product Radu can lay claim to is the world's first cranberry Icewine, which he calls L'âme de Dracula (Dracula's Soul).

Vignoble du Faubourg

479, RUE DES BOURGNAULTS, SAINT-JEAN-PORT-JOLI, QC G0R 3G0
(418) 598-6121 SYLVIEGAUVIN222@HOTMAIL.COM

YEAR FOUNDED: 2004 **FOUNDERS:** Richard Turmel and Marion Roy, Sébastien Vaillancourt and Sylvie Gauvin **WINEMAKERS:** Sébastien Vaillancourt, Sylvie Gauvin **GRAPE VARIETIES:** (red) Maréchal Foch, GR 7, Lucie Kulhmann, Sabrevois, Elmer Swenson 517, Ste-Croix; (white) Prairie Star, Delisle, St. Pepin, Kay Gray, Vandal-Cliche **RECOMMENDED WINE:** Vandal-Cliche

Diminutive, effusive Richard Turmell and his charming wife, Marion Roy, run an artisanal winery in a community of artisans. They have the distinction of owning the most northerly winery in Quebec and probably the coldest and the most windswept. Their contemporary, brightly painted, log-cabin-style facility, with imposing wood doors that once graced the entrance to a nunnery, faces the St. Lawrence River, about 2 kilometres away. The building is perched on a soft sandy-loam slope above the picturesque

Entrance at Vignoble Isle de Bacchus.

Vignoble Bourg Royal (ABOVE) and its winemaker and owner, Jorj Radu (RIGHT).

port town of Saint-Jean-Port-Joli—designated a "Culture Capital of Canada" in 2005. Along with the most prestigious woodcarving museum in North America, this town is home to numerous woodcarvers, weavers, potters, and model-boat builders.

Vignoble Isle de Bacchus

1071, CHEMIN ROYAL, ST-PIERRE, ÎLE D'ORLÉANS, QC G0A 1N0
(418) 828-9562 WWW.ISLEDEBACCHUS.COM
ACCOMMODATION: LA MAISON DU VIGNOBLE, (418) 828-9562

YEAR FOUNDED: 1998 **FOUNDERS:** Donald and Alexandre Bouchard, Lis Roy **WINEMAKERS:** Donald Bouchard, Alexandre Bouchard **GRAPE VARIETIES:** (red) Ste-Croix, Maréchal Foch, Michurinetz; (white) Vandal Blanc, Eona, Geisenheim **RECOMMENDED WINES:** Le 1535, Le Saint-Pierre

The island was originally named Isle de Bacchus in 1593 by Jacques Cartier because of the abundance of wild grapevines he found growing up the trees. Donald Bouchard, a retired lawyer who owns the property, planted the original vineyard in 1986, and it is now expanded to 5 acres. Nine years later Bouchard formed a partnership with Jean-Louis Crête and Pierre Lemieux, wine professionals who had experience in grape growing and wine marketing. The winery also draws grapes from 5 acres the partners planted at Bernières and Saint Nicholas. Both of these vineyards are located on the island's western slopes, which provide one of the province's longer growing seasons. The winery's *cuverie* is located in the cellar of a magnificent eighteenth-century stone house, and its tasting room was originally the kitchen below the main rooms. The living area of the house has maintained its historic integrity, with its stone walls, open fireplace, and old timbers. This historic home is licensed as a B&B, and it makes a wonderful base for touring.

Vignoble le Moulin du Petit Pré

7007, AVENUE ROYALE, CHÂTEAU-RICHER, QC G0A 1N0 (418) 824-7077
WWW.MOULIN-PETITPRE.COM

YEAR FOUNDED: 1995 **FOUNDERS:** Redmond Hayes, Julian Bédard, and Pierre Rousseau **WINEMAKER:** Pierre Rousseau **GRAPE VARIETIES:** (white) Vandal-Cliche **RECOMMENDED WINE:** Elixir de Meunier (raspberry liqueur)

Winding narrowly above the highway, the road to Château-Richer, Route de la Nouvelle-France, is the oldest road in North America. However, it's worth taking to see the old stone houses with their open verandahs, which date back to the seventeenth century. This winery— one of Quebec's leading tourist attractions—is not to be missed. It's located in a historic flour mill right on the avenue Royale (*pré* is an old French word for a hayfield). The vineyard, above the winery, is up a tortuously steep drive perched high above the St. Lawrence and, unless you're a picnicker, a photographer, or a viticulturist, you might want to spend the bulk of your time in the winery itself. Installed in North America's first industrial flour mill, built by Bishop François Montmorency de Laval in 1695, the water-driven mill is still in commercial use to make stone-ground organic flour. The miller and his wife, dressed in traditional clothes, will show you the milling operation.

The winery is located in the basement of the stone building and, surprisingly, you take an elevator to the cellar—a contemporary intrusion from the time when the mill was used by the Ministry of Cultural Affairs for office space. In 1995 Pierre Rousseau, a biochemist who ran a beekeeping business on the side and made mead for the Musée de l'Abeille, formed a partnership to rent the mill from a non-profit organization as a winery. In addition to 10 acres of vines, the group also grows raspberries, currants, and Saskatoon berries to make fruit wines. The shop offers a variety of gift ideas and wine-related paraphernalia. Make a stop to sample the crêpes on the restaurant's terrace as you watch the flow of the Petit Pré River. Every year the winery holds a harvest festival called Fête de Vendange—check the website for details.

Vignoble le Nordet

991, CHEMIN DES ÎLES, PINTENDRE, LÉVIS, QC G6C 1B5 (418) 833-7183
CBOURGET@WEBNET.QC.CA

YEAR FOUNDED: 2000 **FOUNDER:** Carl Bourget **WINEMAKER:** Pierre-Étienne Bourget **GRAPE VARIETIES:** (red) Sabrevois, Ste-Croix; (white) Delisle, Prairie Star, St. Pepin **RECOMMENDED WINE:** Iced Cider

Carl Bourget, his wife, Hélène Gonthier, and their three sons share a passion for their family winery. The family planted their vineyard on the banks of the Etchemin River in 1997 and had their first harvest two years later. The winery has been successful enough since its foundation for the family to double the size of the tasting room and the *cuverie*. Bourget's son, Pierre-Étienne, makes the red and

white wines as well as an Icewine engagingly named Winter Solstice and an award-winning Ice Cider. Also in the portfolio is Solagio, a semi-sparkling cider with cranberry, and Solagio with citrus juice, sold in four-packs. You can help harvest the grapes at Le Nordet if you call in the fall and reserve a place. But even if you don't volunteer to pick grapes, you'll get a warm family welcome here.

Domaine Royarnois

146, CHEMIN DU CAP-TOURMENTE, SAINT-JOACHIM, QC G0A 3X0
(418) 827-4465 WWW.ROYARNOIS.COM

YEAR FOUNDED: 1996 **FOUNDERS:** Roland Harnois and Camille Roy **WINEMAKER:** Roland Harnois **GRAPE VARIETIES:** (red) Sabrevois, Riparia varieties, Ste-Croix; (white) Vandal-Cliche **RECOMMENDED WINE:** Vin du Petit Cap

A forty-five-minute drive east of Quebec City will take you to a 600-acre dairy farm situated on the north shore of the St. Lawrence, one of the most northerly wineries in the province. The name of the winery is a combination of the owners—Camille Roy and Roland Harnois. Since

Conrad Brillant of Domaine de la Source à Marguerite.

1996 Roland, a chemical engineer with a passion for trees, has produced three white wines here from Vandal-Cliche and Ste-Croix grapes, which he doesn't bury in winter, but uniquely trains above ground on high trellises. The vines survive thanks to a special local microclimate. The winery itself is located in a huge dairy built in 1970 and, like many Canadian vintners, Roland uses milk tanks to ferment his wines. Behind the winery is the Laurentian Plateau leading up to the Laurentian Mountains, one of the oldest mountain chains in the world. The grand family home—a stone mansion with a gabled roof—is a replica of a Norman château. The winery was built to complement the wood-and-stone style of the house.

Camille Roy grows a variety of plants in the garden for aromatherapy and homeopathic medicines. The winery's labels depict snow geese, which you can spot at the nearby Cap Tourmente reserve along with other abundant wildlife. Also nearby is the charming village of Saint-Joachim, one of the oldest in North America, with a parish church dating back to 1779. If you are history buffs and wine lovers, this domaine is an excellent place to stop.

Vignoble de Sainte-Pétronille

1A, CHEMIN DE BOUT-DE-L'ÎLE, STE-PÉTRONILLE, QC G0A 4C0
(418) 828-9554 WWW.VIGNOBLEORLEANS.COM

YEAR FOUNDED: 1989 **FOUNDER:** Jean Larsen **WINEMAKER:** Jean Berthelot, Louis Denault **GRAPE VARIETIES:** (red) Ste-Croix; (white) Vandal-Cliche **RECOMMENDED WINE:** Cuvée Ste-Pétronille

Sainte-Pétronille sits high above the St. Lawrence at the western end of Île d'Orléans, with a magnificent view of the river, Montmorency Falls, and the graceful bridge to the island. It boasts the first commercial planting of the renowned grape breeder Joseph Vandal's newly developed crossing, Vandal-Cliche, the first hybrid that did not need winter protection. This grape is widely planted in the province and produces a white wine with a fruity, almost grapey character. If you want to witness some oenological history, make a beeline for Sainte-Pétronille to see where Jean Larsen planted the first commercial Vandal-Cliche vineyard in 1990.

The winery is in the basement of the elegant Norman-style house, with its green roof and large covered verandahs. The house looks as though it has been there for two centuries, but Louis Denault and Nathalie Lane built it in 1991. Winemaking is a parallel career for Denault, as he builds bridges as well as other major construction projects. He is currently building on a smaller scale at home—a shop and a tasting room on the property—and he plans a bistro for 2006. The couple make three wines here as well as mistelle (grape juice fortified with alcohol). The views from the vineyard alone are worth stopping for. It's a photographer's dream as you look towards Montmorency Falls.

Domaine de la Source à Marguerite

3788, CHEMIN ROYAL, STE-FAMILLE, ÎLE D'ORLEANS, QC G0A 3P0
(418) 952-6277 WWW.DOMAINEMARGUERITE.COM

YEAR FOUNDED: 2002 **FOUNDERS:** Diane Dion and Conrad Brillant **WINEMAKER:** Conrad Brillant **GRAPE VARIETIES:** (red) Maréchal Foch, Michurinetz, Sabrevois, Frontenac, Elmer Swenson 517, Elmer Swenson 4725 **RECOMMENDED WINE:** Ice Cider

Conrad Brillant, a retired banker, purchased this farm, with thirty-four varieties of apples, on Île d'Orléans in 2001. He decided to add wine to his flourishing cider business and, in 2002, planted a vineyard behind the orchard. Brillant also has an experimental plot of Gamay and Pinot Noir planted on a slope, with a great view of the Laurentian Mountains, that runs down to the river. You'll find the winery in a large renovated barn located right on the chemin Royal. In addition to the apple products, the farm grows pears and raspberries. You can buy the fresh fruit, juices, and jams along with the range of fermented products in the cider salesroom, an old wooden barn across the road from the winery. The tasting room, offering wines and a variety of ciders and mistelles, is currently located here as well. Given its scenic location, this winery is an ideal picnic spot.

ÎLE D'ORLÉANS

The perfect little island is perhaps better known for its cideries than its wineries. Located in the St. Lawrence River, the island is chock full of nineteenth-century churches, restaurants serving traditional Quebec dishes, roadside fruit stands, sugar bushes and orchards, chocolate factories, and cheese producers. Île d'Orléans, where the Vandal-Cliche grape was first propagated, also boasts the most northerly red oak stand on the continent, Canada's oldest golf course (1868), and its oldest chapel.

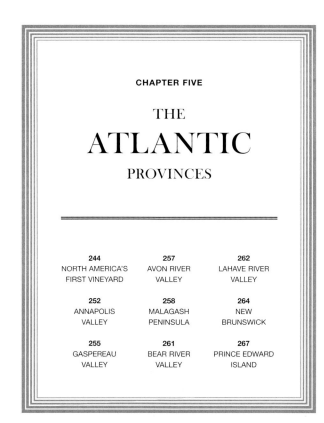

CHAPTER FIVE

THE

ATLANTIC

PROVINCES

The idea that you can grow grapes and make wine in the Maritimes might at first blush sound perverse or at best quixotic. Most people "from away" have an image of Canada's Atlantic provinces as the domain of icebergs, howling gales, raging seas, and pitiless snowbound winters. But nature has a way of compensating climate-challenged regions with oases of calm and relative tranquility. It may surprise you to learn that St. John's, Newfoundland, is Canada's third-warmest city in winter, ranking just below Victoria and Vancouver in mean temperature. Look at a map and you will see that most of the Maritime provinces are located farther south than British Columbia.

Glenda Baker's impending Dark Cove Winery at Gambo, which is 40 kilometres east of Gander, Newfoundland, has thirty-one grape varieties planted in the vineyard, including such tender vinifera varietals as Chardonnay, Gewurztraminer, and Pinot Noir. She will tell you that roses, irises, Saskatoon berries, blueberries, bilberries, cherry trees, and apple trees grow wild there. "From all indications, Gambo appears to be well suited for cool climate viticulture," says Baker, "in spite of the fact that it's on the same latitude as Paris and Volgograd."

Nor should we forget that in AD 1001, when Leif Ericsson set sail from Norway in a Viking longboat, he landed eventually at L'Anse aux Meadows in

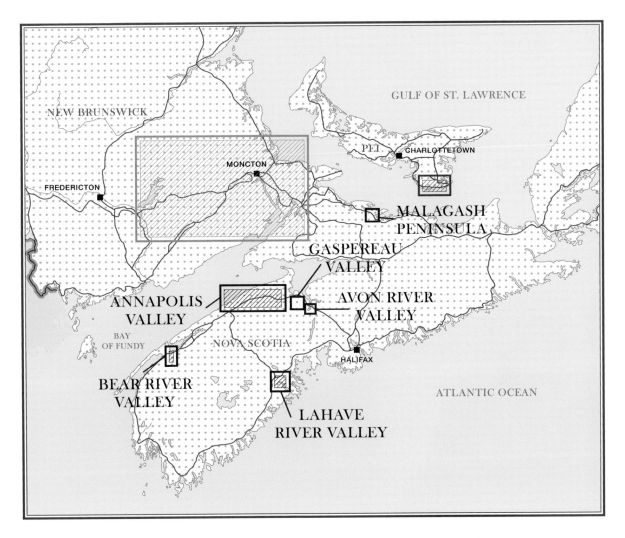

THE WINE REGIONS OF THE ATLANTIC PROVINCES

northern Newfoundland. Noting the proliferation of wild grapes, he named the place Vinland. This legend had its echoes over 500 years later when Jacques Cartier found an abundance of wild grapes growing on an island in the St. Lawrence and named it Isle de Bacchus.

The fact that there are not more wineries in the Maritimes should be the surprise, given that the urge to make wine has, over the past twenty years or so, become a passionate pursuit of many Canadians. Even armchair vintners dream of retiring to a grape-growing region and planting a vineyard. I expect

PREVIOUS SPREAD: Pictou Harbour, Northumberland Strait, Nova Scotia. OPPOSITE: 150-year-old Delaware vine in Miller Point Peace Park near Bridgewater, Nova Scotia.

we'll see more wineries in the Maritimes for the next edition of this atlas.

Midway between the equator and the North Pole, Nova Scotia is an unlikely winegrowing region. Apart from Prince Edward Island, this province has the smallest number of wineries of any established wine region in Canada, but it is fiercely proud of them. Wherever you go, you will find the local wines displayed on lists in hotels as elegant as the Blomidon Inn in Wolfville (a *Wine Spectator* magazine Grand Award winner) and in the smallest guest houses along the Evangeline Trail.

When I mention Nova Scotia wines, those who have never visited the province raise their eyebrows, yet, ironically, Nova Scotia has a legitimate claim to be the site of Canada's first vineyard. Marc Lescarbot, a French lawyer and historian, chronicled the year he spent at Port Royal in 1606–7 in his

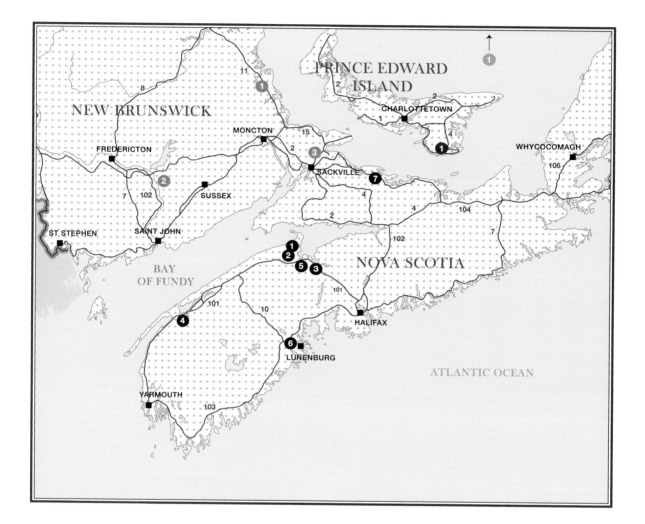

WINERIES OF THE ATLANTIC PROVINCES

Nova Scotia

ANNAPOLIS VALLEY
1 BLOMIDON RIDGE ESTATE WINERY
2 DOMAINE DE GRAND PRÉ

AVON RIVER VALLEY
3 SAINTE-FAMILLE WINES

BEAR RIVER VALLEY
4 BEAR RIVER VINEYARDS

GASPEREAU VALLEY
5 GASPEREAU VINEYARDS

LAHAVE RIVER VALLEY
6 PETITE RIVIÈRE VINEYARDS

MALAGASH PENINSULA
7 JOST VINEYARDS

New Brunswick

1 LA FERME MAURY: "LES VINS DE L'ACADIE"
2 GILLIS OF BELLEISLE WINERY
3 WINEGARDEN ESTATE WINERY

Prince Edward Island

1 ROSSIGNOL ESTATE WINERY

Newfoundland

1 DARK COVE COTTAGE FARM & WINERY

Chris Naugler, author of *The Tangled Vine*, and Sher Clain on their deer fence, Bridgewater, Nova Scotia.

History of New France. Lescarbot wanted to be Nova Scotia's first vigneron, but he was frustrated in this enterprise by a forgetful shipmate. He writes of his discovery of grapevines while exploring the coast near the Saint John River in New Brunswick with Jean de Biencourt, Seigneur de Poutrincourt: "The said M. de Poutrincourt seeing there such excellent grapes gave orders to his valet to tie up and put in the long-boat a bundle of vines they had taken. Master Louis Hébert, our apothecary, who wished to dwell in these parts, had rooted a large number of them, with the intention of planting them at Port Royal, where there are none, though the soil there is well fitted for vines; but this was stupidly forgotten and neglected to the great displeasure of the aforesaid gentleman and of us all."

The desire of the French settlers to plant vineyards was eventually satisfied in the spring of 1633 when the high-ranking naval officer Isaac de Razilly, chosen by Cardinal Richelieu to reclaim Acadia for France, set up the outpost Fort-Ste-Marie-de-Grace (now LaHave). In the following year de Razilly wrote to Marc Lescarbot, who had by then returned to France, "I have planted some vines as they do in Bordeaux which come along very well...Vines grow

MARBLE MOUNTAIN
CAPE BRETON

Although there are no wineries in Cape Breton, there is a thriving vineyard, and the scenery is so beautiful you shouldn't miss it. With its dramatic blend of steep hills and winding roads, the drive around these saltwater lakes—a magnet for boaters—through woodlands, farms, and villages is one of the most scenic in eastern Canada. The region is a major nesting area for bald eagles, and these impressive birds can often be seen in majestic flight or perched on shoreline trees. The sudden appearance of white-tailed deer, osprey, foxes, and raccoons can make driving an adventure. The Scottish heritage is much in evidence and is well captured at the Nova Scotia Highland Village Museum. The Marble Mountain Museum features a history of quarrying in the late 1800s.

The lone commercial vineyard overlooks the Bras d'Or Lakes and is the most easterly vineyard in Canada. John Pratt's 10-acre plot on limestone soil has the distinction of seeing the first rays of sun in North America. His is also the coolest region of Nova Scotia and, unless global warming has a profound effect on the province, other growers may not be tempted up the mountain to join him. Wine grapes are also grown in Lower Debert, Pictou County, and Antigonish.

here naturally. The wine made from these has been used to celebrate mass." Unfortunately, de Razilly never did get the opportunity to enjoy the fruit of the vineyard he cultivated, because he died suddenly in December 1635.

With the expulsion of the Acadians in 1755, grape growing for the production of wine in the province came to an end and would not be revived until the second half of the twentieth century. In *The Tangled Vine: Winegrowing in Nova Scotia*, Chris Naugler writes: "However, table grape growing was still a promising occupation. The first reference to viticulture by English settlers comes from the early 1800s when Charles Prescott imported and grew Isabella grapes on his farm at Starr's Point in the eastern Annapolis Valley."

By the mid-nineteenth century there was a thriving commercial production of table grapes on family farms in the Annapolis Valley and along the South Shore. Evidence of the fact still remains in the 150-year-old vine at the Miller Point Peace Park near Bridgewater. The province's first commercial winery to use locally grown grapes was created by Roger Dial, a political science professor at Dalhousie, in 1980. Dial, a Californian, had trained as a wine-maker at the David Bynum winery in Sonoma and had planted experimental vineyards in the Annapolis Valley as early as 1977. He called his enterprise

Grand Pré Wines. Among other hybrids in the vineyard that Dr. Norman Morse, Dial's partner in the winery, planted were two Russian red varieties, Michurinetz and Severnyi. These unusual grapes had arrived at the Agriculture Research Station in Kentville via a circuitous route.

On a visit to Halifax in 2003, I tasted the 1982 vintage of both of these wines. They came from the cellar of Dial's former store manager, John Stuart, now owner of one of four private wine shops in the city. When Dial sold a boxed set of the two wines twenty years ago, Stuart told me, he advised his customers to hold them for twenty-five years. Dial may have been right. The Severnyi was still holding its colour and showed a rich blackcurrant flavour with good acidity; the Michurinetz, marketed under the more pronounceable name of Cuvée d'Amur,

On the scenic Sunrise Trail, which runs from Wolfville, Nova Scotia, to the Malagash Peninsula.

was beginning to take on the prunelike notes of a red wine that had passed its prime.

Unfortunately, Dial's vision outstripped his finances and in 1987 he was forced to close his cottage winery. But after a lengthy reconstruction they would open again—under the proprietorship of a Swiss banker named Hanspeter Stutz—as the grandly named Domaine de Grand Pré.

At the time of writing, there are 350 acres of vineyard, six active grape wineries, and three fruit wineries in a province whose climate, during the growing season, is less hospitable than either Ontario's or British Columbia's. In accumulated heat units, the weather is more akin to that of Quebec.

The wines produced here, given that climate, are high in acidity. Chardonnay is a rare commodity in Nova Scotia, but the locally propagated L'Acadie Blanc can be made in Chablis style, as crisp and dry as a Granny Smith apple. Seyval Blanc, once an important white grape in Ontario and now out of favour, is widely planted here, delivering a crisp, citrusy wine with racy acidity. Another Nova Scotia specialty is New York Muscat, which, with its aromatic bouquet and flavours of orange blossom and cardamom, is ideal for spicy dishes. While efforts are being made by Chris Naugler and others to grow Pinot Noir, the most successful red variety is the hybrid Maréchal Foch, which makes a wine with a sour-cherry flavour not dissimilar to Beaujolais. Arguably, of all Canada's regions, Nova Scotia's wines are most in tune with the regional dishes, featuring fish and seafood, and the locally grown vegetables.

For all the difficulties it faces as a wine-producing region, the enthusiasm and confidence of the winemakers in the future of their enterprise are infectious. (Nearly everyone connected with the industry has a car licence plate that reads NS WINE.) An industry-developed study in 2002 projected that, by 2020, Nova Scotia will have twenty wineries. The authors describe the Annapolis Valley as similar to Germany's Rhine Valley, and the Gaspereau Valley as akin to the Mosel. If Ontario is like Bordeaux and Burgundy in its growing season, then this comparison is fairly apt.

L'ACADIE:
NOVA SCOTIA'S OWN GRAPE

Nova Scotia's most widely planted grape, L'Acadie, is unique to the province, apart from small plantings in New Brunswick. Although it was bred by O.A. Bradt in Ontario's Horticultural Research Institute at Vineland Station in 1953, it never caught on with Niagara growers. L'Acadie is a winter-hardy, early ripening grape that's perfect for short growing seasons. It's a cross of Cascade x SV14-287 and can survive in temperatures down to −31° Celsius.

When researchers abandoned work on the crossing, cuttings were sent to Dr. Don Craig at the Agriculture Research Station in Kentville, where it seemed to flourish. Easily identifiable in the vineyard by its upright growth and red canes, this mildew-resistant white grape was found to perform better than Seyval Blanc in Nova Scotia's short growing season.

In 1975 Roger Dial made the first wine from this variety, which until then had rejoiced in the unromantic name of V-53261. He called his wine L'Acadie Blanc. Like Austria's signature grape Grüner Veltliner, L'Acadie can be made in a range of wine styles from light and bone dry without oak to richly expressive fruit that has been aged on the lees (solid grape particles) in off-dry style buttressed with vanilla oak flavours.

Chris Naugler's vineyard at Bridgewater, Nova Scotia.
OPPOSITE: Historic church along the Sunrise Trail, Nova Scotia.

Given the number of wine growers who currently sell their grapes to the existing wineries—and a surprisingly high number of these growers are either doctors or dentists—the twenty-winery figure may well be reached before 2020. Grape growers usually get the itch to see their name on a wine label, and that means opening their own winery.

Since sparkling wines require grapes that are not as ripe as those needed for table wine, this region would be ideal to produce champagne-style bubblies—and that's exactly what Benjamin Bridge and L'Acadie Vineyards in the Gaspereau Valley have in mind.

Apart from such established wineries as Jost in Malagash and Grand Pré in the Annapolis Valley, where the investment is visible, the other operations are small and farm based, but the legendary Maritime hospitality is evident wherever you stop. If you are touring the wineries, you will find that they are well spread out and require at least three days, if you are to do justice to the once and future

wine region of Nova Scotia. The modern wine industry in Nova Scotia began here, and the valley currently supports the largest concentration of vineyards in the province. The most favoured vineyard sites are on the airy, well-drained, south-facing slopes of North Mountain, elevated above the frost pockets that occur on the valley floor. From the air, this area of gently rolling hills looks like a patchwork quilt of orchards, vineyards, and vegetable fields, with forests occupying the less favoured high ground. The presence of Acadia University in Wolfville has attracted a vibrant arts community, as well as a high-tech sector, that happily co-exists with the farming population. Long-time residents can trace their lineage back to the New England planters who came north to settle the land when the British drove out the Acadians in 1755. But the history goes even further back to 1605, when a small party of French explorers sailed into the Annapolis Basin and established the first European settlement in Canada at Port Royal. As a result, handsome heritage houses abound in this area.

Annapolis Valley (See map on page 246)

Running along the western spine of Nova Scotia, this verdant, fertile valley has been farmed for four centuries and is still one of the most important apple-growing regions in the country. This 135-kilometre-long valley was carved out originally through glacial activity and the erosion of its soft red-stone base. Dubbed "Canada's first breadbasket," the valley runs from Wolfville to Annapolis Royal between a rugged escarpment to the north (North Mountain, composed of basaltic rock) and a parallel range of mountains on the south (South Mountain, made up of soft sandstone, as is the valley floor). The two mountain ranges, separated by 10 kilometres, offer shelter from offshore winds. The region, whose official name is the Annapolis-Cornwallis Valley, has the warmest temperatures in the province and moderately low rainfall. The soils vary along its length from sandy loam to clay, to clay loam, and back to sandy loam. This combination makes them ideal terrain for planting vineyards.

With its abundance of lakes and rivers, this area is a paradise for canoers and kayakers. You can take time out from tasting to go whale watching or simply to marvel at the rising tide in the Minas Basin. The drive along the Evangeline Trail follows the Fundy Coast, taking you through fishing villages, rocky shore-lines, sandy beaches, and salt marshes replete with birdlife, past apple orchards, farms, and fortresses that date back four hundred years to the first European settlers in the area. A good time to visit is during the five-day Apple Blossom Festival (end of May) or the Harvest Wine Fest at Sainte-Famille Wines (in early October) in Falmouth, followed in mid-month by the Cranberry Harvest Festival.

TOURING WINERIES in the Annapolis Valley

You can take in four wineries in a day if you plan your trip from Wolfville, where there is an abundance of B&Bs and attractive inns.
SINGLE DAY: Check to see the time of the rising tide in the Bay of Fundy. Start in the morning at Blomidon Estate near the Bay of Fundy and cross the valley floor to Gaspereau Vineyards in the Gaspereau Valley. Then make your way to Domaine de Grand Pré for lunch. In the afternoon, drive east to Falmouth, where you'll find Sainte-Famille Wines.
WEEKEND: Spend one day at the wineries and the second visiting the national historic sites Annapolis Royal, Fort Anne, and Port-Royal. If time permits, take in the theatre at Wolfville.

Blomidon Estate Winery

10318 HIGHWAY 221, CANNING, NS B0P 1H0 (902) 582-7565
HADWINES@NS.SYMPATICO.CA

YEAR FOUNDED: 1997 **FOUNDERS:** Peter Jensen and Laura McCain Jensen **WINEMAKERS:** Wes Lowrey, Robert Power **GRAPE VARIETIES:** (red) Baco Noir, Shiraz; (white) L'Acadie, Chardonnay, Seyval Blanc **RECOMMENDED WINES:** L'Acadie Blanc, Baco Noir

In 2003 Blomidon had the distinction of marketing the first Nova Scotia Chardonnay since Roger Dial's Grand Pré vintages of 1984 and 1985. This Chardonnay, a light, lemony, very crisp wine, could be mistaken for a Petit Chablis and bodes well for the future. The original vineyard that slopes down from the winery building towards the Bay of Fundy was planted in 1986 under the name of Habitant Vineyards, and its first grapes were contracted to Dial at Grand Pré. The name was subsequently changed to Blomidon Estate in 1997. The enterprise, with its vineyard augmented to 20 acres, was purchased by Peter Jensen and Laura McCain Jensen, proprietors of

Creekside Estate and Paragon Vineyards wineries in Ontario. Blomidon's tasting room, with its mustard-coloured facade, and the winery at the back are in a modern barn-like construction with a view of the Bay of Fundy. Next door is Dr. Alan McIntyre's vineyard, where Jost sources some of its Pinot Noir.

Domaine de Grand Pré

11611 HIGHWAY 1, PO BOX 105, GRAND PRÉ, NS B0P 1M0
(902) 542-1753; 1-866-GP WINES (1-866-479-4637)
WWW.GRANDPREWINES.NS.CA
RESTAURANT: LE CAVEAU, (902) 542-7177

YEAR FOUNDED: 1978 **FOUNDER:** Roger Dial **WINEMAKER:** Jürg Stutz **GRAPE VARIETIES:** (red) Léon Millot, Maréchal Foch, Lucie Kuhlmann; (white) Seyval Blanc, L'Acadie, New York Muscat, Vidal Blanc, Ortega **RECOMMENDED WINES:** Maréchal Foch Reserve, Seyval Blanc, Vidal, New York Muscat Icewine (and a sweet cider called Pomme d'Or)

Hanspeter Stutz, a Swiss banker, bought Roger Dial's old Grand Pré Winery from the next owners, Jim Landry and

TOP: Cows grazing in the Annapolis Valley. ABOVE: Domaine de Grand Pré's restaurant sign.

THE KENTVILLE AGRICULTURE RESEARCH STATION

Since 1913, Agriculture Canada's experimental farm in Kentville has been testing fruits and vegetables for their ability to withstand local conditions. While its chief mandate has been fruit crops, it has also tested grapevines. Much of this work was done by Dr. Donald L. Craig, who, in his fifty-one-year career at Kentville, devoted much of his energies to finding suitable wine and table grape cultivars for the region.

In his quest for early ripening varieties, Dr. Craig visited the Summerland Research Station in British Columbia, where he found two Russian varieties from the Amur River Valley, Michurinetz and Severnyi. The strains had arrived in Canada as a result of a barter deal with the Soviet Union—Nova Scotia raspberries for Russian vines. The cuttings were planted at Summerland and some were traded to Dr. Craig for blueberries. He gave a few of the cuttings to Dr. Norman Morse, who planted them on an experimental basis. When Roger Dial started Grand Pré, he purchased the grapes from Morse and was so excited by the wines he made from them that he persuaded Morse to plant more. They would become the mainstay of Grand Pré's red wine production, along with Maréchal Foch. Dial suggested that these *amurensis* varieties "could be the Cabernet Sauvignon and Pinot Noir of Nova Scotia. They're very complex with lots of tannins, enormous colour, and big esters." The Russian varieties were widely planted in the 1980s, but they have now fallen out of favour among growers.

The original experimental site on the Reid farm in Bear River has come to life again since 1987, when it was purchased and replanted by Chris Hawes for his Bear River Vineyards.

ROGER DIAL

THE FATHER OF NOVA SCOTIA WINE

"Typical of all of us who were doing start-up wineries in the mid-1970s, we were full of the hope that we would create a European-style wine-as-food culture—that wine would find its way to the table of everyone, that it would be recognized as an agricultural venture." That's the way Roger Dial talks about his pioneering efforts to bring home-grown wine to Nova Scotia.

When I visited the winery to interview him in 1982, Grand Pré was the size of a four-car garage. It was the only game in town, but Dial told me: "In ten years the Gaspereau Valley is going to look like the Mosel." His prophecy is slowly coming true, as vineyards are replacing grazing land and orchards on the south-facing slopes of the Gaspereau Valley. Though he no longer makes wine commercially, other winemakers have taken up the torch to realize his vision.

Dial has spent more than thirty-seven years in ventures spanning virtually every aspect of wine culture. As an entrepreneur, he has owned and operated wineries in California and Nova Scotia, founded wine shipping and viticultural nursery enterprises, and developed media/communications ventures to promote everything vinous (from the minutiae of wine art to the grand sweep of "appellation consciousness").

As a winegrower, Dial has developed hundreds of acres of vineyards and championed high-quality cold-climate varietals (notably *Vitis amurensis* and L'Acadie—a French-American hybrid developed at Vineland, Ontario, as V-53261 and renamed L'Acadie in homage to his adopted home) against the cultural reductionism of the vinifera-only tide. As a winemaker, he has won gold medals in competitions from Bristol to New York and Toronto. As a writer, he has written extensively for the popular wine press, drafted wine legislation, and produced the occasional viticultural research report.

Roger Dial's most recent enterprise is a wine website, www.AppellationAmerica.com, where, with his son, Adam, his goal is to "reconfigure and expand the mindset of the North American wine culture." (Visit it—it's a magnificent site and a great research tool.) He believes that the future of Nova Scotia's wine industry lies in developing distinctive wines that reflect their terroir, in the same manner that Burgundy has, for generations, sold its wines to the world.

Jürg and Hanspeter Stutz of Domaine de Grand Pré.

Karen Avery, in 1996. Founded in 1978, the winery can claim to be the oldest in the province—except that Stutz closed it down for the next four years while he spent several million dollars replanting the vineyards and constructing a showplace winery and cellar. Part of the beautifully landscaped site, with cobblestoned walkways inlaid with giant grape leaves of granite, is an art gallery below the tasting room and a cottage-style restaurant that serves a Swiss menu. From the art gallery you have a view into the wine cellar. During the reconstruction, Stutz sent his son Jürg to the Waedenswil wine school in Switzerland to learn winemaking. Three years later, Jürg returned for his first crush in 1999. "We want to make wine with 100% Nova Scotia–grown fruit," he says. "Something I'm really aiming for is the clean, crisp wines you get in Switzerland."

Stutz reopened the dazzling complex as Domaine de Grand Pré in 2000 (it's like a small, very tidy, and elegant wine hamlet). Since then it has become a magnet for tourists. Though the winery is based on hybrid varieties, he has an experimental mother block with forty-four varietals. The Pergola is an ideal spot to sit with a glass of wine and take in the luxurious feeling of the place. Stutz also makes an excellent cider, and I get the feeling he is as proud of it as he is of the wines his son makes. The attractive art labels, the ultra-modern tasting-room bar, and the carved stone inlays in the cellar make this winery a distinctive one to visit.

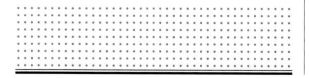

Gaspereau Valley (See map on page 246)

Those who are thinking of starting up a winery operation in Nova Scotia could do no better than look to this pastoral landscape as an ideal location for their vineyard. A tranquil way to enjoy the scenery here is to float down the winding river on an inner tube (as the kids do) and relish the bucolic sight of cows at pasture, apple orchards, hayfields, and the odd vineyard. Apple orchards have always flourished in this valley, south of Wolfville on the other side of South Mountain, and, given its potential as a grape-growing subregion, it's interesting that vineyard development started here only in the mid-1990s. You'll find that all of the vineyards in the Gaspereau Valley have been planted on the north side of the river, an area known locally as the Wolfville Ridge—a siting on south-facing slopes that ensures them the maximum hours of sunshine.

The Gaspereau is a comparatively small area of immense charm that runs east of the Annapolis Valley and offers an expanse of steep slopes. The soil is ideal for grape growing: sandy silt over clay. The summer sunshine ensures sufficient heat units during the growing season for the grapes to ripen well. In general, the soils are similar to those of the Annapolis-Cornwallis Valley, of which Gaspereau is an offshoot. It's narrower here than in the Annapolis Valley, so the slopes are more steeply raked and offer very good drainage. The Gaspereau River, which meanders along the valley floor, has a moderating influence on winter temperatures.

> **TOURING WINERIES**
> in the Gaspereau Valley
>
> Since only one winery is currently operating in the Gaspereau Valley, you will have time to explore the area before returning to the Annapolis Valley. By 2008, when Benjamin Bridge and L'Acadie Vineyards open, there should be a critical mass of wineries in this area.
> **SINGLE DAY:** Visit Gaspereau Vineyards.
> **WEEKEND:** You can take in all the wineries in the Annapolis Valley and the Gaspereau if you are a dedicated winery visitor.

Gaspereau Vineyards

2239 WHITE ROCK ROAD, GASPEREAU, NS B4P 2R1
(902) 542-1455 WWW.GASPEREAUWINE.COM

YEAR FOUNDED: 2003 **FOUNDERS:** Hans Christian and Karen Jost
WINEMAKER: David Gardner **GRAPE VARIETIES:** (red) Lucie Kuhlmann; (white) New York Muscat, L'Acadie, De Chaunac, Vidal, Ortega
RECOMMENDED WINES: De Chaunac, Lucie Kuhlmann, L'Acadie Blanc, Dry Muscat, Ortega Vidal Icewine

In addition to owning the largest winery in Nova Scotia in Malagash, Hans Christian Jost also operates the smallest winery in the province, in the Gaspereau Valley, an hour's drive from Halifax. It produces 2,000 cases a year. The reason he planted a 37-acre vineyard (1996) on a former apple orchard and built a small red barn of a winery here is because he believes that the Gaspereau Valley has the greatest potential of any area of Nova Scotia for growing grapes and marketing wine. And he may well be proved correct. The soil here varies markedly between the lower south-facing slope nearer the winery, consisting of loam (and planted to De Chaunac, L'Acadie, New York Muscat, and Lucie Kuhlmann), and the warmer upper part that is mainly clay loam and slate (good for Chardonnay, Ortega, Riesling, and Vidal). Frankly, I find these Gaspereau Vineyards wines more stylish and elegant in their pure fruit flavours than the more commercial offerings from the Malagash facility.

Jost vineyard in the Gaspereau Valley. FOLLOWING PAGE: The Gaspereau vineyard.

Avon River Valley (See map on page 246)

This area of gentle hillsides and flat alluvial plains boasts some of the best farmland in the province. Much of it was reclaimed from the salt marshes in the mid to late 1600s by the Acadians, who built dykes to drain the rich soil from the mud flats. Visitors can still see the old stone houses dating back to the seventeenth century, a testament to the determination and courage of the Acadian settlers who built them. And you can also see the wooden Fort Edward that housed the British troops who expelled them from the area. The town of Windsor, where you'll find the fort, at the eastern gate of the Annapolis Valley, is known as the "Birthplace of Hockey," as well as the home of giant pumpkins and the annual Sam Slick Days Festival (at the end of July).

The climate and rainfall here are similar to those of the Annapolis Valley. Because of the richness of the soil, grape growers have to be wary of "vigour"— too luxuriant a growth of foliage and wood in the vineyard will diminish the flavour concentration of the fruit. Pruning and leaf-thinning will direct the energy into the growth of the bunches of fruit, rather than foliage, and produce more intense flavours.

The geographic feature that defines this region, known as the Windsor Lowlands, is the extensive Avon River estuary. Tidal influxes from the Minas Basin to the north have carried deposits of red silt into the estuary, rendering its shoreline extraordinarily fertile. This tidal effect has created a soil base that is made up mainly of shale, with substantial amounts of limestone and gypsum. The southern end of the Avon River Valley has a harder base, consisting of the granite and slate rocks of the Atlantic Uplands. From the touring perspective, the Avon River is a rushing torrent in winter and spring, with spectacular rapids. During the summer and autumn months, the river dries up to become a series of pools in a bed of granite boulders and tea-tree thickets.

> **TOURING WINERIES**
> in the Avon River Valley
>
> **SINGLE DAY:** Only one winery is currently operating in this part of Nova Scotia, so you need a mere couple of hours to visit it. I recommend that you add Grand Pré to your itinerary.
> **WEEKEND:** Take in Sainte-Famille, and overnight at a B&B before heading to Malagash, where you can enjoy a winery visit in the morning and the beach in the afternoon.

Sainte-Famille Wines

11 DUDLEY PARK LANE, RR 2, FALMOUTH, NS B0P 1X0
(902) 798-9418; 1-800-565-0993 WWW.ST-FAMILLE.COM

YEAR FOUNDED: 1989 **FOUNDERS:** Suzanne and Doug Corkum **WINEMAKER:** Suzanne Corkum **GRAPE VARIETIES:** (red) Maréchal Foch, Baco Noir, Cabernet Franc; (white) Riesling, Seyval Blanc, L'Acadie, Vidal, Siegfried, Chardonnay **RECOMMENDED WINES:** Maréchal Foch Reserve, L'Acadie Blanc, Seyval Blanc

This homey winery is located on the site of an old Acadian village known as La Paroisse Sainte-Famille de Pisiquit, which was settled about 1685. Suzanne Corkum, born in Oregon's Willamette Valley (a great wine-producing region known for its Pinot Noir and Pinot Gris), first planted the vineyard in 1979. The only winery she could sell her grapes to in those days was Roger Dial's Grand Pré. When Grand Pré was forced into receivership, the Corkums had no market for their grapes. In 1989 they opened their own winery, naming it after the parish where they lived. The soils here on the flats are a mix of clay and sand on a base of limestone, producing wines with lots of flavour and sometimes startling acidity. There's a rustic, down-home look and feeling about the winery, with none of the glitz and professionalism you find in the other well-established names in the province. The wine shop promotes local products such as cheeses, jams, and crafts. This winery is especially worth visiting in the first week of October for the annual Harvest Wine Fest.

Malagash Peninsula (See map on page 246)

The Malagash Peninsula is a remote area on the coastal plain that runs from the Cumberland Basin to Pictou and Merigomish Island, one that's well worth the two-hour drive from Halifax to get there. This farming country has gently rolling fertile hills punctuated by forests of oak, spruce, birch, and alder, and sleepy villages along the coastal inlets with broad sandy beaches. The drive north from the capital is not inspiring until you begin to see the sparkling waters of the Northumberland Strait in the distance—the warmest salt waters north of the Carolinas. Here, the views are magnificent: from the rocky shoreline you can watch the abundant birdlife and, in May and June, the bobbing lobster boats. You can also see Prince Edward Island on the horizon. Given its favoured climate and tourist attractions such as Blue Sea Beach Park and the Malagash Museum, which interprets the history of Canada's first salt mine, among other things, it's ironic that only one winery, Jost, has so far chosen to situate here.

The soil inland is characterized by fine red sandstones and shales. The shallow basin of the Northumberland Strait ensures warm water temperatures during summer and fall, which reflect back on the vineyards—rather like Lake Erie in southwest Ontario. In late fall the warmth of the water inhibits frost, giving the grapes a few extra weeks to hang for better ripening. Malagash enjoys some of the lowest rainfall in Nova Scotia, with a yearly average of about 1,000 millimetres. This comparatively balmy climate allows Jost to ripen such cool-climate grapes as L'Acadie, New York Muscat, Lucie Kuhlmann, and Maréchal Foch.

TOURING THE WINERY
in the Malagash Peninsula

The summer months are the best time to visit this area. There is only one winery here—Jost Vineyards—and it's the largest in the province. No doubt there will be others in the near future as land prices in Gaspereau rise.
SINGLE DAY: Head for Jost Vineyards and spend the rest of the day in Blue Sea Beach Park.
WEEKEND: For your second day, you'll have time to visit the wineries in both the Annapolis and Gaspereau valleys.

Jost Vineyards

48 VINTAGE LANE, MALAGASH, NS B0K 1E0
(902) 257-2636; 1-800-565-4567 WWW.JOSTWINE.COM

YEAR FOUNDED: 1983 **FOUNDERS:** Hans Wilhelm Jost, Erna Jost, Ellen Jost, and Hans Christian Jost **WINEMAKERS:** David Beardsall, Hans Christian Jost **GRAPE VARIETIES:** (red) Baco Noir, Maréchal Foch, Léon Millot, Lucie Kuhlmann, Pinot Noir; (white) L'Acadie, New York Muscat, Vidal, Riesling, Chardonnay, Ortega, Seyval Blanc **RECOMMENDED WINES:** Eagle Tree New York Muscat, Léon Millot, Maréchal Foch Reserve, Muscat Icewine, Vidal Icewine

The province's biggest winery, Jost Vineyards, boasts a 35,000-case production, and you see the Jost label in virtually every restaurant, hotel, and licensed B&B in the province. Jost Vineyards markets thirty-eight different wines in all. It would take you five weeks at a bottle a night to try them all! Thanks to Hans Christian Jost's tireless efforts in promoting his products, he manages to sell them all and, at the same time, beat the drum for Nova Scotia wines.

Hans Christian, as everyone calls him, farms 45 acres of vines dating back to 1978, when his father, Hans Wilhelm, and his mother, Erna, established the vineyard on the Malagash Peninsula overlooking the Northumberland Strait. (Hans Christian is fond of saying you could fit the entire grape acreage of Ontario into the Malagash Peninsula and there would still be lots of vineyard land available.) Once he had completed a business diploma course, Hans Christian flew to Germany in 1985 to study viticulture and oenology under Professor Helmut Becker at the Geisenheim Research Institute. A year later, Jost

Hans Christian Jost of Jost Vineyards, Nova Scotia's largest winery.

Vineyard at Jost, looking north towards Prince Edward Island.

Vineyards received its farm winery licence. In 1988 Jost was thrust into the position of running the family winery at a young age following the death of his father. Since then he has become the unofficial leader of Nova Scotia's nascent wine industry. His colleague Chris Naugler says of him: "In his kind, soft-spoken way he has been a cheerleader for the whole industry here. Most important, he has been a strong advocate of single-vineyard bottlings, which has allowed us to begin examining the attributes of the different wine-growing regions." Jost is a selfless promoter of the wines of Nova Scotia, even taking time out of his business day to tour visitors around the wineries of his competitors. "I'd love to see a winery in every political riding in the province," he says. The Jost winery is a wood-panelled complex that sits at the foot of the vineyard within sight of the Northumberland Strait. In addition to the winery in Malagash, Jost has built another facility to crush the grapes he's growing in his Gaspereau Vineyards on 37 acres of land. Jost's enthusiasm for Nova Scotia wines is infectious—as you'll discover when you visit his winery.

Bear River Valley (See map on page 246)

While the Annapolis Valley and Malagash are well-known to Nova Scotia wine lovers, the Bear River Valley region at the southwestern end of the Annapolis Valley is virtually unknown. However, the pioneering efforts of Chris Hawes on the eastern side of the Bear River have proved that grapes can flourish in the slate-and-gravel soil and, without doubt, more vineyards will be planted here in the future. The Annapolis Basin, fed by the Bay of Fundy, provides an ameliorating effect on cool spring temperatures, rendering its climate milder than that of the Annapolis Valley itself. Here, too, the soil type is Wolfville sandy loam. Hawes calls this area "a maritime climate paradox. There is calm air, exceptional summer sun, and no fog." Visitors will enjoy the village of Bear River, some of whose stores and accommodation were built on stilts over the tidal flow that rises and falls close to 30 feet, twice a day, and empties 4 miles farther on towards the coast, into the Annapolis Basin. The churches and houses beyond the village centre seem to cling to the steep hillsides that rise from the river. In fact, it's a photographer's and naturalist's dream location. And don't miss the Bear River First Nation Heritage and Cultural Centre, which displays the cultural heritage of the Mi'kmaq people.

**TOURING THE WINERY
in the Bear River Valley**

Again, there is only one winery to visit here, so you may consider linking this region to your trip through the Gaspereau Valley.
SINGLE DAY: Visit Bear River Vineyards and explore the fascinating town of Bear River itself.
WEEKEND: After a day at the winery and the town below, head for the Gaspereau and Annapolis valleys.

Bear River Vineyards

133 CHUTE ROAD, BEAR RIVER, NS B0S 1B0 (902) 467-4156
WWW.NSWINE.COM

YEAR FOUNDED: 1992 **FOUNDER:** Chris Hawes **WINEMAKER:** Chris Hawes **GRAPE VARIETIES:** (red) Pinot Noir, Maréchal Foch, Baco Noir; (white) Riesling, Chardonnay, Pinot Gris **RECOMMENDED WINES:** not tasted

Chris Hawes grew up in the Niagara Peninsula and, as a teenager, worked in vineyards. He left Ontario for Nova Scotia in 1969, where he lived next door to Roger Dial at Grand Pré in Wolfville, an association that cemented his passion for wine. Although he himself didn't work for Dial, his son Nicholas did. In 1986 Hawes purchased the old experimental Bear River plot, which had been planted in 1963 by the Kentville Agriculture Research Station but was now part of the Reid farm and no longer under vines. The next year Hawes began to plant his own 5-acre vineyard on the steeply graded, south-facing slope. He is currently building a 3,600-square-foot gravity-feed winery based in the old barn on the property. The facility will be on three levels and, from it, you will be able to see the picturesque town of Bear River, with its buildings on stilts above the tidal flow.

The emphasis here is on education and environmental concerns. Hawes uses solar power, and his cars run on vegetable oil.

Maréchal Foch grapes.

LaHave River Valley (See map on page 246)

If you scratch the surface of the hills east of the LaHave River, you'll find a reddish earth known as Wolfville sandy loam. It's the same soil you find in the Annapolis Valley, and you can blame it on repeated glacial activity during the Quaternary Period (75,000 to 10,000 years ago), which carried the red Triassic sandstone south. The unique feature of this emerging wine region is the concentration of small, oval hills called drumlins that rise beyond both banks of the river. These hills offer spectacular drainage because they are made up of deep layers of sand, gravel, and broken slate. Their south slopes are ideal vineyard sites. The meagre soils force vines to put down deep roots in search of nutrients, picking up trace elements that make for more complex aromas and flavours. The minerals absorbed through the roots of the vine give the grapes an added flavour dimension—a taste of place, or what the French call terroir. There is a consistent minerally flintiness in the taste profile of the wines grown here. The reds show plum, raspberry, and spice, while the whites are crisp, with citrus and floral notes.

On the west side of the LaHave River, the drumlins are made up of Bridgewater loam, a soil that is grey rather than red in colour. The LaHave River Valley now has vineyards on the hills above both the LaHave River and the Petite Rivière. A geographic distinction between the two soils will probably be made in future to separate these two subregions.

The river's estuary, and beyond it the Atlantic Ocean, moderate temperatures here. Coastal towns such as Lunenburg and Liverpool are prone to fog, but at a distance of 5 to 20 kilometres inland the temperatures are warmer and the vineyard sites still benefit from the proximity of these large bodies of water. According to viticulturalists, this narrow zone, along with the Bear River Valley in Annapolis County, contains the mildest winegrowing areas east of the Niagara Peninsula and can best support the noble European grapes such as Chardonnay and Pinot Noir. As mentioned in the introduction to this region, the LaHave River Valley is rich in history and tradition. You need only take a dime from your pocket to see the best-known icon of Canadian shipbuilding—the schooner *Bluenose* under full press of sails. The maritime tradition extends back over 500 years, when the first European fishermen began visiting the area. The immediate impression of the towns and villages is of stately wooden houses, family farms, and white beaches. "The residents have always been self-reliant and somewhat suspicious of authority," writes Dr. Chris Naugler, a grape grower who will soon open his own winery, LaHave River Vineyards. "This possibly stems from Prohibition times when rum-running to the United States was a major business enterprise." The Nauglers and their winemaking colleagues the Wamboldts (Petite Rivière Vineyards), like many of the families who live in the LaHave River Valley, can trace their roots back ten generations or more.

TOURING THE WINERY in the LaHave River Valley

The towns along the shore, such as Lunenburg and Mahone Bay, are so inviting that you may forget you're here to taste wine!

SINGLE DAY: Take in Petite Rivière Vineyards and wander the streets of Lunenburg and Mahone Bay, where you'll find great shops.

WEEKEND: You can comfortably drive from this area to Wolfville to visit the wineries in the Annapolis Valley.

The LaHave River near Bridgewater.

Petite Rivière Vineyards

4300 ITALY CROSS ROAD, CROUSETOWN, NS B0J 1V0
(902) 688-2295 WWW.PETITERIVIEREWINES.CA

YEAR FOUNDED: vineyard 1993; winery 2002 **FOUNDERS:** Philip
Wamboldt and Carol Slack-Wamboldt **WINEMAKER:** Philip Wamboldt
GRAPE VARIETIES: (red) Léon Millot, Lucie Kuhlmann, Triomphe
d'Alsace, Baco Noir, Pinot Noir, Zweigelt; (white) Seyval Blanc, L'Acadie,
Chardonnay **RECOMMENDED WINES:** Bear Hills Vineyard Chardonnay,
Côte de LaHave sur Lie, Côte de LaHave Terres Rocheux

Philip Wamboldt comes from an old LaHave family
whose roots date back ten generations in the area. He is
a real estate appraiser turned vintner, although his interest
in wine predates his office job and he planted his first
vineyard when he was still in high school. Wamboldt has
been growing grapes commercially since 1994, the year
he planted the 7-acre Harmon's Hill Vineyard on sandy
loam soil. In 2000 he bought a second vineyard (St.
Mary's, with very dry, rocky soil) close by the first at
Harmon's Hill. On this sloping site close to the road he
and his wife, Carol, built their chapel-like winery themselves. The whitewashed building, with its steeply raked
roof, is two storeys and has the shop and stucco-walled
tasting room above, overlooking St. Mary's Vineyard.
The combination of the two vineyards, with their differ-
ing soil structures, gives the couple more complex
flavours in their grapes, allowing Wamboldt to make
some of the best wines in the province. Be sure to stop
by and taste.

New Brunswick (See map on page 246)

In 1998 New Brunswick's Department of Agriculture established a program with the province's fruit growers to allow the production of wines and distilled products. The following year the first winery, the Gagetown Cider Company, opened its doors. Since then, most of the subsequent wineries have been small, farm-based family affairs that have concentrated on the production of fruit wines, ciders, schnapps, and liqueurs. Gagetown and Belliveau Orchards make an appealing apple Ice Wine. The leader in this fruit wine and fruit distillates sector has been the Rosswog family at Winegarden Estate in Baie Verte, who not only vinted and distilled products for their competitors but also made grape wines. La Ferme Maury in St-Édouard-de-Kent also makes its red wine at Winegarden Estate. The newest winery in New Brunswick, Gillis of Belleisle, opened in 2003 and produces both a red and a white wine.

Now that three wineries in the province are making grape wines, this incipient critical mass will no doubt encourage other fruit growers to get into the vineyard business. And who knows? New Brunswick might rival Nova Scotia as a wine province.

**TOURING WINERIES
in New Brunswick**

SINGLE DAY: The Winegarden Estate Winery in Baie Verte will give you the most complete picture of winemaking in this province, whether grape wines, fruit wines, fruit distillates, or liqueurs. So make a beeline here and take time to enjoy the dunes along the sandy beach.
WEEKEND: If you enjoy camping, you can spend the night at La Ferme Maury after visiting Winegarden Estate. The next day take a leisurely drive to Gillis of Belleisle Winery in Springfield to enjoy the dessert wines.

La Ferme Maury
"Les vins de l'Acadie"

2021, ROUTE 475, ST-ÉDOUARD-DE-KENT, NB E4S 4W2
(506) 743-5347 WWW.FERMEMAURY.COM

YEAR FOUNDED: 1996 **FOUNDERS:** Serge Maury and Denise Boucher **WINEMAKER:** Winegarden Estate **GRAPE VARIETIES:** (red) Maréchal Foch, Lucie Kuhlmann, Léon Millot **RECOMMENDED WINE:** Cuvée St-Édouard

Don't be surprised to find chickens pecking around the motorhomes on the farm's campsite, a short distance from a fine sandy beach. Serge Maury, Parisian by birth, met Denise Boucher in Greece in 1985 when he was a naval officer. He followed her home to New Brunswick and married her. Maury planted his vineyard in 1996 on an old dairy farm facing the Northumberland Strait, not far from Shediac, the self-styled "Lobster Capital of the World." His grapes and fruits are vinified at Winegarden Estate in Baie Verte, making it the first co-op winery in New Brunswick. Ultimately, Maury plans to have his own facility. During the summer, visitors are invited to leave their names at the retail shop if they wish to participate as pickers in the fall harvest. For their efforts, they are rewarded with a hearty meal and are welcomed by artists or local musicians. Denise Maury operates the campsite

on the farm and, every night, Serge invites the newly arrived campers for a complimentary tasting of his wines. This winery is a delightful stop on your way to marvel at the Boutouche Dunes.

Gillis of Belleisle Winery

1826 ROUTE 124, SPRINGFIELD, NB E5T 2K2 (506) 485-8846
WWW.GILLISOFBELLEISLE.COM

YEAR FOUNDED: 2002 **FOUNDERS:** Rod and Judy Gillis
WINEMAKERS: Gillis family **GRAPE VARIETIES:** (red) Baco Noir, Frontenac; (white) Cayuga, L'Acadie Blanc **RECOMMENDED WINES:** L'Acadie Blanc, Frontenac, Raspberry dessert wine

This winery is a little piece of Tuscany transported to New Brunswick, exuding Old World charm. The style reminds me of a hilltop property you'd find in the Chianti Classico zone. You enter the winery through 5 metre arched doors into a spacious reception hall with bead-board walls and a copper ceiling. The winery is perched halfway up Judy's Hill (named for Rod Gillis's wife, who regularly hikes its numerous trails); it overlooks the

Winegarden's Steffen Rosswog, a fifth-generation distiller, with his column still.

Gürtne
Apparateba
W-7833 Endinge
Deutsch
Tel. 07642/343
Fax 07642/771

A vine mural at Winegarden Estate Winery & Distillery.
OPPOSITE: Lighthouse at Cape Bear, PEI.

Belleisle Valley in the lower Saint John River watershed. Gillis, a lawyer, started the enterprise as a hobby, and it just grew as he planted more and more vines. The Gillises, with their daughter Carey, who manages the facility, specialize in the production of unique red and white wine as well as seasonal fruit and dessert wines. The labels have a background of New Brunswick tartan, which speaks to the family's origins in the Isle of Skye.

You can play a game of bocce here, make the acquaintance of Eeyore the donkey in the paddock beside the vineyard, or just wander the apple orchard with glass in hand.

Winegarden Estate Winery & Distillery

(FORMERLY ROSSWOG FARM DISTILLERY)
851 ROUTE 970, BAIE VERTE, NB E4M 1Z7 (506) 538-7405
WWW.WINEGARDENESTATE.COM

YEAR FOUNDED: 1991 **FOUNDERS:** Werner and Roswitha Rosswog
WINEMAKERS: Steffen Rosswog **GRAPE VARIETIES:** (red) Maréchal Foch, Valiant, Severnyi; (white) Eona, L'Acadie Blanc, Minnesota 76, Edelweiss, Swenson **RECOMMENDED WINE:** L'Acadie Blanc

Werner Rosswog emigrated to Baie Verte in 1983 from Germany, where his family had been winemakers and distillers of eaux-de-vie since the 1860s. In 1991 he and Roswitha (herself a master distiller) created the first private fruit distillery in the Atlantic provinces with two pot stills imported from Germany. Rosswog's first product was Johnny Ziegler Apple Schnapps (named in honour of his ancestor Johann Ziegler, the family's first distiller). He received his farm winery licence in 1997 and extended his portfolio into wine and liqueurs as well as custom crushing for other New Brunswick wineries, both fruit and grape operations. Inside the white industrial building you'll find over fifty different products, including the first L'Acadie Blanc made in New Brunswick. The Rosswog family worked cooperatively with Gagetown Cider to produce the first apple wines, as well as providing the winemaking for Ferme Maury, Tierney Point Winery, and Tuddenham Farms. Werner and Roswitha's son Steffen is now the distiller and winemaker at Winegarden.

The annual Winegarden Fest, held every August, has become a popular open-air event for this region. It is a family outing with musical entertainment ranging from a brass band to bluegrass music—complete with sausages and wine tasting, of course.

Prince Edward Island (See map on page 246)

"Forty years ago," says winemaker John Rossignol, "there used to be some sixty farmers growing tobacco in Prince Edward Island. The industry is in decline and now there are only a half a dozen." But as Lake Erie North Shore has shown, where tobacco can flourish, so too can grapevines.

When John Rossignol planted his vineyard overlooking the Northumberland Strait in 1993, his neighbours thought he was crazy. But he's still there, the only vintner on the island, battling the elements and producing grape wines, fruit wines, cider, and mead. The unique feature of the winery used to be that the tender vinifera varieties—Cabernet Franc, Pinot Noir, and Chardonnay—were grown in abandoned greenhouses left over from the island's failed tobacco industry. Two acres of vines were planted under glass. Unfortunately, this brave venture ended after seven years, and Rossignol was forced to tear out the vines and abandon his greenhouse experiment. The vinifera vines experienced extreme stress owing to temperature fluctuations, in spite of being protected under glass from the harshest winter conditions. Undaunted, and convinced that there are microclimates on the island that can support vinifera in the open air, Rossignol is planting Pinot Noir in the northeast part of PEI, near Souris.

> **TOURING THE WINERY**
> **in Prince Edward Island**
>
> **SINGLE DAY:** Since there is only one winery on the island, your choice is simple. John Rossignol's facility is a unique experience in all senses of the word.
> **WEEKEND:** Tour PEI and enjoy the legendary islander hospitality.

OPPOSITE: Sunset at Cape Bear near Rossignol Estate Winery (ABOVE).

Rossignol Estate Winery

RR 4, MURRAY RIVER, PRINCE EDWARD ISLAND C0A 1W0 (902) 962-4193
WWW.ROSSIGNOLWINERY.COM

YEAR FOUNDED: 1994 **FOUNDER:** John Rossignol **WINEMAKER:** John
Rossignol **GRAPE VARIETIES:** (red) Pinot Noir, Maréchal Foch, Baco
Noir, Valiant; (white) L'Acadie Blanc, Seyval Blanc; (fruit wines) straw-
berry, rhubarb, apple, raspberry, cranberry, blueberry **RECOMMENDED
WINES:** Seyval Blanc, Baco Noir; Blueberry wine

Sheep graze on the rolling hills around the vineyard of
Prince Edward Island's first—and so far only—commercial
winery. John Rossignol's ocean-front farm, with its south-
facing slope, overlooks the Northumberland Strait towards
Pictou Island. In 1990 Rossignol sailed the ketch he built
himself from Ontario to PEI. There he built a house on
Little Sands Island that would become the Rossignol winery. While deciding on the direction of his career (he had
worked as a contractor in food and beverage processing
equipment), Rossignol planted a vineyard in 1993. The
following year he began to make wine from frozen fruit
and then from fresh grapes.

The winery's labels are original island artwork painted
by neighbouring folk artist Nancy Perkins and by John
Rossignol himself.

Rossignol's fruit wines include strawberry, strawberry-
rhubarb, apple, raspberry, cranberry, and blueberry, and
they also produce table wines, such as Pinot Cabernet
(Franc), Maréchal Foch, Seyval Blanc, and Chardonnay,
as well as barrel-aged Haneveldt Cider. It's a unique winery run by a multi-talented man. You can sample free of
charge if you make a donation.

APPENDIX

GLOSSARY

Certain wine terms may be unfamiliar to those with a casual interest in the subject. Some of these words are technical, while others are wine descriptors. Together this language is a form of shorthand in the industry, and, in the interests of brevity and narrative flow, I have not explained the individual terms in the text.

Wine experts use a special vocabulary among themselves to describe the bouquet, taste, style, and health of a wine. You may come across some of these descriptions of wines on wine lists. Or they may crop up on shelf-talkers and other promotional blurbs at your local liquor store. Don't be put off by the jargon; it's really only a shorthand to describe the wine.

Technical terms

ALEMBIC A pot used for distilling wine into brandy. The term derives from the Arabic word *al-anbiq*, meaning a still.

AMPELOGRAPHER Someone who studies grapevines.

BLEED The French call it *saigner*—to bleed off juice from the fermenting vats to intensify the colour of red wines. The bled-off juice is usually bottled as a rosé.

BRIX The measure of the sugar content of grape juice, usually between 19 and 25 in Canada, depending on ripeness. If you halve the Brix reading, it will give you a rough guide to the alcoholic strength of the wine when it has been fermented to dryness.

CANOPY MANAGEMENT Balancing the vines to produce more concentrated flavours in the grapes by various pruning techniques, including debudding, shoot positioning, and leaf removal.

CARBONIC MACERATION A technique first used in Beaujolais to make light, fruity red wines that can be consumed young. Whole uncrushed grape clusters are placed in a closed stainless-steel vat. The weight of the top grapes

eventually presses down on those at the bottom, breaking their skins and starting fermentation. The fermentation jumps in a chain reaction to each of the individual berries and occurs inside the skins. Very little tannin is extracted this way and, when the grapes are lightly pressed after a few days, the wine can be consumed within a matter of weeks. This is how Beaujolais Nouveau is made.

CHAI French term for a barrel cellar.

CLONAL SELECTION Selecting the best plants in a vineyard to propagate so as to improve the quality and yield of fruit from the vine.

COOPERAGE The place where barrels are made; also, the collective noun for barrels.

CUVERIE A French term for the place where the wine is made, most often underground in Europe or in a temperature-controlled building in contemporary facilities.

GRAVITY FLOW A term applied to wineries that use the force of gravity to transport their grapes and wine from one process to the next, instead of subjecting them to the pressure of pumping, which can compromise flavour. The grapes begin at the top of the winery and are fed by their own weight into the crusher; the juice then flows into the fermentation tanks below, and the wine finally moves on for aging in barrels or tanks before being fed by pipes to the lowest level for bottling.

PREVIOUS SPREAD: Wine secateurs at a Quebec grape harvest.

LAGAR A rectangular stone vat with metre-high walls, used for foot-treading grapes in Portugal's Douro region.

MERITAGE A term (rhymes with heritage) coined in California in 1981 by the winner of a competition in the *Los Angeles Times* to denote a Bordeaux-style blend. For reds, a blend of Cabernet Sauvignon, Merlot, and Cabernet Franc; for whites, a blend of Sauvignon Blanc and Semillon (sometimes also Muscadelle).

MUST Crushed grapes and juice before the fermentation process turns them into wine.

OIDIUM A fungus-like powdery mildew that attacks the vine.

REVERSE OSMOSIS An electronic process for the removal of alcohol or acetic acid from wine to bring it down to regulatory levels.

ROTARY FERMENTATION Fermentation tanks that rotate slowly to ensure maximum skin contact with juice in order to extract more colour for red wines, especially Pinot Noir.

TENTING A technique developed in cold growing regions during the winter and early spring to protect the vines by covering them with sheets of plastic secured over the lowest trellising wire.

TERROIR A French expression for the total environment in which a grapevine grows, giving the wine flavours a sense of place. It includes not only the soil and the microclimate but also exposure to sunlight, wind, and drainage.

VIN DE PAILLE A concentrated, sweet dessert wine made from dried grapes. Originally they were left to dry on straw mats (hence the name, "straw wine").

Wine-tasting terms

AROMA The smell of the grapes in freshly made wine— the recognizable perfume of a specific grape variety. Bouquet, in contrast, is the smell of wine after it has aged in the bottle.

AROMATIC The rich, spicy perfume that pervades the taste of the wine as well as its bouquet. Good examples are Gewurztraminer and Muscat.

ASTRINGENT A quality that is more of a tactile sensation than a taste. A wine that is high in tannin and acidity will leave a dry, scratchy feeling on the roof of the mouth and the insides of the cheeks. Red Bordeaux or Barolo can be very astringent.

AUSTERE A polite term for a wine that's really hard to drink because it lacks fruit and any other pleasurable qualities. It is usually applied to expensive wines that should taste better but, because you've paid a lot for them, you don't want to admit that you bought a dog. The opposite is "generous."

BACKWARD A wine that should have developed but hasn't. Slow to mature, it needs more time in the cellar.

BARREL AGING Winemakers can age the wine in stainless-steel vats or in oak barrels. Stainless steel is inert and retains the freshness of the fruit; oak, because of the presence of air, matures the wine and imparts certain flavours of vanilla, coconut, and toast. It is more expensive to age a wine in oak than in stainless steel, and this factor will be reflected in the price of the wine.

BAKED Grapes grown in hot climates can get "sunburnt," especially if there is little rainfall. The wines have a baked character, reflected in a roasted, earthy flavour.

BALANCE A wine is in balance when all of its components— fruit, alcohol, acidity, tannin, and oak—are harmonious. If one or more of these parts predominates, the wine will be out of balance.

BARNYARD A bouquet most characteristic of some red and white Burgundies, Pinot Noirs, and Chardonnays. If you have ever mucked out a stable, you will know this smell— slightly rotting hay with an overtone of manure. It sounds revolting, but in a wine it has an attractive quality and is a term of praise. Wine people are weird.

BEAUJOLAIS NOUVEAU A wine to drink young, lightly chilled. The new Beaujolais is released on the third Thursday in November (*see* carbonic maceration). Canada makes Gamay Nouveau (the same variety used in Beaujolais).

BITTER A taste that can result from tannin (bite into a grape pit or grape stalk to experience how bitter it is) or from underripe grapes or the grapes from young vines.

BLUSH A style of wine made usually from Zinfandel in California. The colour has a faint tinge of pink and a perceptible sweetness. It's produced in the same way as rosé—a few hours of skin contact with the juice to extract a little colour.

BODY A wine can be light-bodied, medium-bodied, or full-bodied—a direct result of the amount of alcohol in the wine and the extract from the grape. Body expresses itself as weight in the mouth.

BOTRYTIS A disease, whose full Latin name is *Botrytis cinerea*, that attacks the skins of ripened grapes in warm, humid conditions. This fungus-like growth pierces the skins and allows the water to evaporate, thus concentrating the sugars and the acids. The dried-out grapes look disgusting on the vine (rather like dead bats in an anatomy class), but they make wonderfully honeyed wines such as Sauternes and Beerenauslese wines.

BOTTLE AGE Wines, unlike spirits, mature in glass bottles. They change over the years, whereas Scotch or gin remains the same. Bottle age gives wine mellowness and a more intense bouquet. Eventually, a wine that has matured will begin to decline.

BOTTLE SICKNESS There will be a great difference in taste between a wine in the cask and one that has been newly bottled. The act of bottling introduces large quantities of oxygen into the wine that initially give sulphury off-flavours. The wine settles down after a few weeks and loses unpleasant odours and tastes.

BOUQUET The smell of wine that has aged in the bottle and become more complex. A mature wine, one that has aged for fifteen years (or more), may give off a bouquet that has nothing to do with fruits, flowers, or vegetables. It can be a mix of more organic smells such as leather, chocolate, and coffee beans. With practice, you can tell the condition of the wine as well as its taste from the smell of a wine when you pull the cork and pour some into a glass. That's why wine waiters give you a sample in your glass before pouring for the whole table.

BUTTERY A smell and a taste usually associated with oak-aged Chardonnay grown in warm climates, such as California and Australia.

CAT'S PEE A smell associated with Sauvignon Blanc wines, usually when the grapes get overripe. Self-explanatory.

CEDAR One of the smells of fine red Bordeaux wines, associated with the Cabernet Sauvignon grape. Sometimes it's called "cigar box."

CHOCOLATE A smell you can find in rich red wines, especially from warm growing regions.

CLEAN A wine without flaws, off-odours, or bad tastes.

COMPLEX A wine that has many levels of perfume and taste sensations—an interesting and very good wine.

CORKED A wine that has turned, usually because of oxidation, and smells and tastes of vinegar. It may have a brown hue in both whites and reds. It has nothing to do with the cork (*see* corky).

CORKY The smell of a bad cork in the wine. A cork that is infected can change the taste of the wine, while traces of the bleaching agent used to whiten it can add a chemical flavour.

CREAMY A sensation of the wine on the palate—an unctuous fruitiness and softness found in Chardonnays grown in warm conditions.

CRISP A description of white wines with perceptible acidity—wines that refresh the palate.

DEPTH A wine that has different levels of enjoyment, a richness of bouquet, and flavour that changes in the glass.

DRY A wine whose sugars have been fully fermented. There will be some residual sweetness from the fruit, but the acidity will give it a dry finish.

DUMB A wine that has nothing to say. An undeveloped, immature wine whose bouquet and flavours are locked in—the oenological equivalent of a taciturn adolescent.

DUSTY The aftertaste and feeling left in the mouth of maturing tannins in red wines.

EARTHY Tasting of the soil, a quality found in reds from hot growing regions.

ELEGANT A well-balanced wine of high quality. This term is used mainly when describing lighter wines. Rich, full-bodied wines would be termed robust, meaty, or some other graphic term.

EUCALYPTUS Certain Californian and Australian Cabernet Sauvignons have a bouquet of eucalyptus because the grapes are overripe. This quality can also appear as a bell-pepper smell.

EXTRACT Soluble solids from pressed grapes (other than their sugars) that give the wine body and weight.

FAT A weight-challenged wine, full of alcohol and extract, heavy on the palate and overly rich. It can be a compliment or a criticism, depending on the context.

FINESSE A synonym for elegance—a wine whose elements are perfectly in harmony.

FINISH The final taste of the wine—the sensory impression left in the mouth once you have swallowed it.

FIRM A wine that has structure, thanks to its acidity, as opposed to flabby.

FIRST GROWTH This term does not refer to anything that happens in the vineyard. Rather, it is a designation of quality for Bordeaux wines. In 1855 the wines of the Médoc and Graves were divided by price and quality into five growths (*crus*). The First Growths were the top wines.

FLABBY A wine that lacks acidity to give it structure and length of finish. Such a wine will taste sweet and soft on the palate and go nowhere.

FLAT A wine that lies on the palate and bores you to death—there's no flavour, no life in it. It also refers to a sparkling wine that has been left too long in the glass so that all the bubbles have disappeared.

FLINTY Certain wines, such as Sauvignon Blanc grown in cool climates, can have a bouquet reminiscent of struck flint, slightly smoky.

FLORAL Smelling of flowers. You find flower smells in Riesling (spring flowers), Gewurztraminer (roses), and some reds (lilac, iris).

FORWARD A young wine that is showing more maturity than its age suggests—an overachiever.

FOXY The smell of wines made from labrusca grapes—the native North American varieties (such as Concord and Niagara). An unpleasant aroma that puts you in mind of a dog that's been left out in the rain. The term derives from wild or "fox" grapes.

FRESH A wine whose bouquet starts your mouth watering and whose taste enlivens and cleanses the palate because of its crisp acidity.

FRUITY A wine with good extract that tastes of fruit—cherries, plums, gooseberries, melon, blackberries, black-currants, etc.

FULL-BODIED A high-alcohol wine that feels rich and weighty in the mouth.

GERANIUM One flower you do not want to smell in a wine. Its unpleasant odour indicates that a microbiological fault was induced in the wine during fermentation.

GRAPEY Certain wines taste exactly like the fresh grapes they were made from—Muscat and Muscatel are prime examples.

GREEN Wines that taste immature because the grapes were not ripe enough at harvest or the vines are still young.

GRIP A wine with a real presence, one that asserts itself with its tannins on the palate, has grip.

HARD A wine with excessive tannin, which will take several years of bottle age to soften up. Examples include Barolo, red Bordeaux.

HERBACEOUS Smelling of freshly cut grass and flowers. It's a description of young white wines, particularly Sauvignon Blanc.

HONEYED Sweet wines take on a honey-like bouquet with age. You can smell honey in Sauternes, old Late Harvest Rieslings, and Icewines.

LEGS When you swirl a glass, the alcohol in liquid form clings to the side of the glass and eventually falls back to the surface of the wine in tears or "legs." The Germans call this phenomenon "church windows," which they resemble. The thickness of the legs and the speed at which they move gives you an indication of the wine's alcoholic strength. The slower the pace, the higher the alcohol.

LENGTH The staying power of a wine's aftertaste. The longer you can taste it, the better the wine.

LIGHT A wine lacking body (alcohol) but not necessarily flavour. The wines of the Mosel in Germany are light but have wonderfully rich Riesling flavours.

LUSCIOUS A term used to describe dessert wines when the sweetness, creaminess, and softness are balanced with enough acidity not to let the wine cloy on the palate.

MADERIZED The term comes from the word *Madeira*. White wines when they get too old begin to turn brown and taste like Madeira—slightly oxidized, flat, and tinny.

MEDIUM-DRY A wine that has perceptible sweetness but finishes dry. Example: off-dry Riesling.

MEDIUM-SWEET One level above medium-dry in the sweetness scale. Example: Late Harvest Riesling.

MUST The juice of white grapes or the juice and skins of black grapes before fermentation.

MUSTY The smell of a dank cellar, usually associated with a bad cork or a dirty barrel.

NOBLE ROT An easier name for the benign disease *Botrytis cinerea*.

NOSE The smell of a wine—its bouquet or aroma.

OAKY The smell and the taste of oak in a wine, especially apparent when the oak is new. The smells and flavours can range from vanilla to coconut to smoky toast to spices such as nutmeg and cloves.

OFF-DRY A wine that has some residual sweetness but finishes dry.

OXIDIZED A wine that has been exposed to air, rendering it flat and prune-like in taste.

PETROL Yes, gasoline—the characteristic smell of aging Riesling, and very appealing, too.

PÉTILLANT A French word meaning slightly sparkling but not visibly so—a sensation of bubbles on the tongue.

PLONK A humorous description of a simple, everyday quaffing wine.

RACY A fresh, light white wine with stimulating acidity.

ROSÉ A pink wine, either dry or semi-sweet, made from red grapes. The newly pressed grape juice is left in contact with the skins for a matter of hours to extract the colour desired by the winemaker.

SHORT A wine whose flavour suddenly drops out—one with no discernible finish, usually as a result of rain during the harvest, which swells the grapes and dilutes the fruit and sugars.

SOFT A wine that has mellowed with age. Sweet wines will also have a softness because the sugar will mask the acidity in them.

SPICY An exotic spiciness like cardamom, found particularly in Gewurztraminer.

SPRITZIG A German word for prickling on the tongue from wines that have bound-in carbon dioxide (see *pétillant*).

STEMMY A green, bitter taste of grape stems causing excess tannin in the wine, usually from young vines.

SULPHUR This substance and its compounds are used to prevent oxidation and to kill off bacteria in wine. In France, barrels are cleaned by burning sulphur sticks inside them.

SULPHURY The smell of sulphur in wine that has been overly treated with sulphur products. At up to 30 parts per million, sulphur is barely detectable on the nose. If you exceed this proportion, you get a burnt match-head smell.

TANNIN An astringent, bitter-tasting compound that occurs naturally in the skins, stalks, and pits of grapes. Wood tannins are present in oak barrels, too. Tannin acts as a preservative, allowing a red wine to age gracefully. Eventually the tannin will precipitate out and fall to the bottom of the bottle as fine sediment.

TART A wine that is high in acidity, usually because of unripe grapes.

VANILLA The smell and taste of new French oak. American oak can have more of a coconut smell.

VARIETAL A single grape type whose name will appear on the label. Examples: Chardonnay, Merlot, Pinot Gris.

VINEGAR If a wine smells of vinegar, send it back. It's over the hill.

VOLATILE ACIDITY Too much, and the wine begins to smell like nail polish and to taste like balsamic vinegar. All wines contain some volatile acidity, but, when excessive, it shows that the wine is starting to become vinegar.

WEIGHT A term to describe how the wine feels in the mouth. The heavier on the palate, the more alcohol. Weightier wines come from the hotter growing regions, where sunshine can build up grape sugars.

WOODY A wine that has been kept too long in oak, imparting a woody flavour.

CANADA'S FUTURE WINERIES

The process of creating a wine atlas of necessity means that you will never be up to date with all the wineries that are about to open their doors. Wineries are springing up like mushrooms across Canada and I look forward in a future edition to giving more information on the following enterprises, which are about to do their first crush following the 2006 harvest or will do so in a year or two.

BRITISH COLUMBIA

OLIVER TWIST ESTATE WINERY
RR 1, S46, C14
OLIVER, BC V0H 1J0
(250) 485-0227

STONEBOAT WINERY
S-56, C-6, RR 1
OLIVER, BC
(250) 498-4714
LANNY_MARTINIUK@TELUS.NET.

WHY? WHY NOT WINERY
2273 OLIVER RANCH ROAD
OKANAGAN FALLS, BC
(250) 497-8197
WHY-WHYNOTWINERY@SHAW.CA

ONTARIO

CALAMUS ESTATE WINERY
3100–6TH AVENUE
JORDAN, ON L0R 1S0
1-888-225-9866
WWW.CALAMUSWINES.COM

COLDWATER WINE COMPANY
10 TRUMPOUR ROAD
HILLIER, ON K0K 2T0
COLDWATER@MAGNMA.CA

DOMAINE CALCAIRE
8554 DANFORTH ROAD
HILLIER, ON K0K 2J0
(613) 476-5339
CALCAIRE@KOS.NET

FIELDSTONE ESTATE
565 BAKKER ROAD
HILLIER, ON K0K 2L0
(613) 399-1176

MARIANNE HILL VINEYARDS
3953 HIXON STREET
BEAMSVILLE, ON L0R 1B7
(905) 563-5144
MARIANNEHILL@CANADA.COM

**RAVINE VINEYARD
ESTATE WINERY**
1366 YORK ROAD
ST. DAVIDS, ON L0S 1P0
WWW.RAVINEWINES.COM

**ROBERT THOMAS
ESTATE WINERY**
784 COUNTRY ROAD 18, RR 1
CHERRY VALLEY, ON K0K 1P0
DEBRA.MARSHALL@KOS.NET

QUEBEC

**DOMAINE L'ANGE GARDIEN,
VIGNOBLES ET VERGERS**
6869, AVENUE ROYALE (ROUTE DE
LA NOUVELLE-FRANCE)
L'ANGE-GARDIEN, QC G0A 2K0
(418) 877-6678
JLCRETE@SYMPATICO.CA

**VIGNOBLE DOMAINE
LES BROMES**
285, CHEMIN BROME
LAC BROME (BROME LAKE),
QC J0E 1S0
(450) 243-0266
WWW.DOMAINELESBROMES.COM

CÔTE DES LIMOUSINS
1980, BOULEVARD DAVID
BOUCHARD ROAD
GRANBY, QC J2G 8C7
(450) 375-1680

VIGNOBLE DU MITAN
4034, CHEMIN ROYALE
STE-FAMILLE, ÎLE D'ORLÉANS,
QC G0A 3P0
(418) 828-2649
MERCELIN@VIDEOTRON

VIGNOBLE ORLÉANS
2212, CHEMIN ROYALE
ST-PIERRE, ÎLE D'ORLÉANS,
QC G0A 40E
(418) 660-7412
FAMILE-BILODEAU@VIDEOTRON.CA

DOMAINE VINGT DYEU
23, CHEMIN DES VINGTS
ST-BASILE-LE-GRANDE, QC J3N 1M2
(514) 754-1020
RCHAMPAGNE@XPLORNET.COM

NOVA SCOTIA

L'ACADIE VINEYARDS
310 SLAYTER ROAD, RR 1
WOLFVILLE, NS B4P 2R1
(902) 542-3034
WWW.LACADIEVINEYARDS.CA

BENJAMIN BRIDGE VINEYARDS
1842 WHITE ROCK ROAD
WOLFVILLE, NS B0P 1X0
(902) 542-4407
GMCCONNELL@ETRUSCAN.COM

LAHAVE RIVER VINEYARDS
PO BOX 89
BRIDGEWATER, NS B4V 2W6
(902) 543-4700

NEW BRUNSWICK

LA CAVE À VIN BOUDREAU
110 RUE PRINCIPALE
MEMRAMCOOK, NB E4K 1A9
(506) 871-6553 OR (506) 871-7553

NEWFOUNDLAND

**DARK COVE COTTAGE
FARM & WINERY**
220 J.R. SMALLWOOD BOULEVARD
GAMBO, NL A0G 1T0
(709) 674-4545
WWW.DCCW.CA

CANADA'S FRUIT WINERIES

There are approximately 16,000 fruit growers in Canada. Mercifully, not all of them make wine from their orchards and berry patches. But the number of farmers who are turning their tree fruit and berries into fruit wines is growing; and so too is the demand for their products.

According to the Fruit Wine Growers of Canada, fruit wine sales across the country have doubled since 1998 and are projected to grow at an annual rate of 30 percent as consumers discover the freshness and authentic, recognizable flavours of these wines. The bulk of Canada's fruit wineries are found in Ontario and the Atlantic provinces, with British Columbia beginning to emerge as a player in this market. Quebec has always been famous for its ciders and iced apple wine and still is, deservedly so.

Ontario is the most organized of the provinces in this area. It has established its own association, Fruit Wines of Ontario (www.fruitwinesofontario.com), which includes some fifteen wineries dedicated to producing fruit wines only, as well as some well-established grape wineries, such as Southbrook, Magnotta, Hernder, and Ocala, that produce fruit wines, too. The organization has developed its own quality assurance system, based on the same concept as the VQA for Ontario-grown grape wines. Its symbol is QC (Quality Certified), a system of control that's regulated by the national body, Fruit Wines of Canada, and taste tested and analyzed by the LCBO laboratory.

Fruit wines are made much the same way as grape wines. The stalks and pits of the fruit are removed mechanically, and some fruits (except for berries) are washed. (Unlike grape wines, the fruit or its juice can be stored frozen for later fermentation.) The fruit is processed by spinning in a drum, to extract the juice centrifugally, or in an inflatable bladder press, to separate the juice from the skins or peels. The resulting liquid is poured into a fermentation vat, usually stainless steel, and yeast is added if necessary. The juice then undergoes fermentation, converting the sugars into alcohol. The resulting wine is ready for consumption in one month to three months. Most fruit wines are made to replicate the flavour of the original fruit, although some producers are trying to recreate the flavour of Cabernet Sauvignon from blueberries, for example, to give the perception of more complexity.

Most fruit wines benefit from being chilled to accentuate their freshness, whether they are dry, off-dry, or sweet. As with grape wines, the mark of a good fruit wine is balance and harmony: the acidity and the sweetness should create a delicious tension in the flavour that lingers on the palate. And, of course, it should taste like the fruit from which it is made, as if you've just plucked it off the tree or bush.

British Columbia Fruit Wineries

British Columbia's wine industry did not start with grapes but with other fruit—loganberries, to be exact—which grew in abundance on the Saanich Peninsula of Vancouver Island. Loganberry wine was produced by the Growers' Wine Company, which was subsequently taken over by Jordan Winery in 1928 and absorbed into Brights in 1986. The tradition of fruit-wine production in BC is much older than the grape-wine industry and has continued to thrive ever since—if not as spectacularly as the grape wine. Currently there are seventeen operating cideries and fruit or honey wineries in the province, producing wines from apples, berries, pears, stone fruits, rhubarb, quinces, kiwis, and honey. Westham Island Estate even makes pumpkin wine.

Some operations, such as Cherry Point Blossom Winery in Richmond and Marley Farm Winery in Saanichton, make both grape wines and fruit wines. These fruit-based products range in style from bone dry to very sweet (Elephant Island makes an Iced Cider). While most of the fruit wines come from farmed operations, some—Honeymoon Bay Blackberry Winery and Cherry Point Vineyards on Vancouver Island, for instance—rely on the blackberries that grow wild around them for their raw material.

Fruit wineries do not have to meet strict windows for harvesting and making their wines (they can freeze their fruit for later use), so they have the luxury of producing wines when they need them. Unlike grape wines, fruit wines, once they have been fermented, can be bottled a few weeks after production and will be ready for sale and consumption.

BLOSSOM WINERY
5941 MINORU BOULEVARD
RICHMOND, BC V6X 2B1
(604) 232-9839
WWW.BLOSSOMWINERY.COM

BLUE HERON FRUIT WINERY
18539 DEWDNEY TRUNK ROAD
PITT MEADOWS, BC V3Y 2R9
(604) 465-5563
WWW.BLUEHERONWINERY.CA

BONAPARTE BEND WINERY
HIGHWAY 97
CACHE CREEK, BC V0K 1H0
(250) 457-6667
BBWINERY@COPPERCREEK.BC.CA

EAST KELOWNA CIDERY CO.
2981 EAST KELOWNA ROAD
KELOWNA, BC V1W 4A6
(250) 860-8118

**ELEPHANT ISLAND
ORCHARD WINES**
2730 AIKENS LOOP
NARAMATA, BC VOH INO
(250) 496-5522
WWW.ELEPHANTISLANDWINE.COM

FORBIDDEN FRUIT WINERY
620 SUMAC ROAD
CAWSTON, BC V0X 1C0
(250) 499-2649
EKCIDER@SHAW.CA

THE FORT WINE COMPANY
26151–84TH AVENUE
LANGLEY, BC V1M 1M6
(604) 857-1101; 1-866-921-9463
WWW.THEFORTWINECO.COM

**HONEYMOON BAY
BLACKBERRY WINERY**
9940 SOUTH SHORE ROAD
HONEYMOON BAY, BC V0R 1T0
(250) 749-6094
MIRNAMOFFAT@DSHAW.CA

HORNBY ISLAND WINERY
7000 ANDERSON DRIVE
HORNBY ISLAND, BC V0R 1Z0
(250) 335-3019
WWW.HORNBYWINE.COM

MARLEY FARM WINERY
1831D MOUNT NEWTON
CROSS ROAD
SAANICHTON, BC V8M 1L1
(250) 652-8667
WWW.MARLEYFARM.CA

MERRIDALE CIDERWORKS
1230 MERRIDALE ROAD
COBBLE HILL, BC V0R 1L0
(250) 743-4293; 1-800-998-9908
WWW.MERRIDALECIDER.COM

MIDDLE MOUNTAIN MEAD
3505 EUSTON ROAD
HORNBY ISLAND, BC V0R 1Z0
(250) 335-1397
WWW.MIDDLEMOUNTAINMEAD.COM

RAVEN RIDGE CIDERY
3003 DUNSTER ROAD
KELOWNA, BC V1W 4A6
(250) 763-1091
WWW.K-L-O.COM

SPILLER ESTATE WINERY
475 UPPER BENCH ROAD NORTH
PENTICTON, BC V2A 8T4
(250) 490-4162; 1-800-610-3794
WWW.SPILLERESTATES.COM

**TUGWELL CREEK HONEY
FARM AND MEADERY**
8750 WEST COAST ROAD
SOOKE, BC V0S 1N0
(250) 642-1956
WWW.TUGWELLCREEKFARM.COM

WELLBROOK WINERY
4626–88TH STREET
DELTA, BC V4K 3N3
(604) 946-1868
WWW.WELLBROOKWINERY.COM

**WESTHAM ISLAND
ESTATE WINERY**
2170 WESTHAM ISLAND ROAD
DELTA, BC V4K 2N2
(604) 946-7471
WWW.WESTHAMISLANDWINERY.COM

Ontario Fruit Wineries

Jim Warren, consulting winemaker and teacher, has a long history of making both grape and fruit wines in Ontario. Three times Ontario Amateur Winemaker Champion, three times Canadian Amateur Winemaker Champion, Warren has gone on in his professional years to help a plethora of wineries to distinguish themselves with their products. He has consulted to Angels Gate Winery, Daniel Lenko Estate Winery, EastDell Estates, Kacaba Vineyards, Legends Estates Winery, Muskoka Lakes, and Trillium Hill, among others. In 1996 he won seven gold medals at the Ontario Wine Awards and was voted Winemaker of the Year. Since then, Warren has gone on to collect many other awards and accolades for his wines.

But his interest is not only in grape wines. Warren, a dedicated and compulsive winemaker who loves to experiment, is also a consummate producer of fruit wines. In this capacity he was instrumental in setting up the Fruit Wines of Ontario association and in framing the regulations that govern fruit winemaking across Canada. Fruit wines tend to be considered the poor cousin of grape wines, but not for Jim Warren.

"The advantage of fruit wines is that you don't have to make your fruit wine all at once. You can freeze your fruit and go back to it when you need it. Most fruit wineries are small players and, when they sell out, they can make another batch. They can control their overhead a little better that way. From my overall experience—I'm a grape winemaker foremost—I have to tell you that fruit winemaking can be even more fun than making grape wine. It can be more creative. Everything lends itself to more versions—you can have a dry, an off-dry, medium-sweet, sweet, or even iced fruit wine. You can't do that with many grapes, except perhaps Riesling and Vidal, which are more adaptable. And if things go wrong, you have a little more leeway to repair damage.

"Fruit winemaking is more challenging from the issue of acidity because most fruits are way out of whack with too much acid. The winemaker has to bring it down. That's why for the longest time fruit wines were so sweet—they were just masking the acidity with sugar. But that doesn't work all the time. You also have the issue of amelioration (addition of water to bring down acidity), and I'm suggesting that instead of water because it gives a nicer character."

APPLEWOOD WINERY
12442 MCCOWAN ROAD
STOUFFVILLE, ON L4A 7X5
(905) 642-4720
WWW.APPLEWOOD
FARMWINERY.COM

**ARCHIBALD ORCHARDS
& ESTATE WINERY**
6275 LIBERTY STREET NORTH, RR 5
BOWMANVILLE, ON L1C 3K6
(905) 263-2396
WWW.ARCHIBALDS-
ESTATEWINERY.ON.CA

**BELLAMERE COUNTRY MARKET
& WINERY**
1260 GAINSBOROUGH ROAD
LONDON, ON N6H 5K8
(519) 473-2273
WWW.BELLAMERE.COM

BIRTCH FARMS ESTATES WINES
RR 7
WOODSTOCK, ON N4S 7W2
(519) 469-3040
WWW.BIRTCHFARMS.COM

BRUS' ORCHARDS & WINERY
KING'S HIGHWAY NO. 19
TILLSONBURG, ON N4G 4H1
(519) 842-2262
WWW.EXECULINK.COM/~BRUS/

THE COUNTY CIDER COMPANY
RR 4
PICTON, ON K0K 2T0
(613) 476-1022
WWW.COUNTYCIDER.COM

COX CREEK CELLARS
7687 WELLINGTON ROAD 22, RR 5
GUELPH, ON N1H 6J2
(519) 767-3253
WWW.COXCREEKCELLARS.ON.CA

DOWNEY'S FARM MARKET
13682 HEART LAKE ROAD
INGLEWOOD, ON L0N 1K0
(905) 838-2990
WWW.DOWNEYSFARM.ON.CA

KAWARTHA COUNTRY WINES
2275 COUNTRY ROAD 36
BUCKHORN, ON K0L 2J0
(705) 657-9916

LEASKDALE WINERY
12699 DURHAM ROAD 1
UXBRIDGE, ON
(905) 852-0185

LEGENDS ESTATES
4888 ONTARIO STREET NORTH
BEAMSVILLE, ON L0R 1B3
(905) 563-6500
WWW.LEGENDSESTATES.COM

**MAGNOTTA WINERY
CORPORATION**
271 CHRISLEA ROAD
VAUGHAN, ON L4L 8N6
(905) 738-9463; 1-800-461-9463
WWW.MAGNOTTA.COM

MUNRO HONEY & MEADERY
3115 RIVER STREET
ALVISTON, ON N0N 1A0
(519) 847-5333
WWW.MUNROHONEY.COM

MUSKOKA LAKES WINERY
1074 CRANBERRY ROAD
BALA, ON P0C 1A0
(705) 762-3203
WWW.CRANBERRY.CA

NORFOLK ESTATE WINERY
RR 1
ST. WILLIAMS, ON N0E 1P0
(519) 586-2237
NEWINE@KWIC.COM

**PINE FARMS CYDER AND
FRUIT WINERY**
KING CITY, ON L7B 1A3
(905) 833-5459
WWW.PINEFARMSORCHARD.COM

RUSH CREEK WINES (KOSHER)
RR 2
AYLMER, ON N5H 2R2
(519) 773-5432
WWW.RUSHCREEKWINES.COM

**SCOTCH BLOCK COUNTRY
WINERY**
9365–10TH SIDEROAD, RR 5
MILTON, ON L9T 2X9
(905) 878-5807
WWW.SCOTCHBLOCK.COM

SOUTHBROOK WINERY
1061 MAJOR MACKENZIE DRIVE
RICHMOND HILL, ON L4C 1R9
(905) 832-2548
WWW.SOUTHBROOK.COM

STONEY RIDGE ESTATE WINERY
3201 KING STREET
VINELAND, ON L0R 2C0
(905) 562-1324
WWW.STONEYRIDGE.COM

**SUNNYBROOK FARM ESTATE
WINERY**
1425 LAKESHORE ROAD, RR 3
NIAGARA-ON-THE-LAKE,
ON L0S 1J0
(905) 468-1122
WWW.SUNNYBROOKFARMWINERY
.COM

WAGNER ESTATE WINERY
1222–8TH CONCESSION
MAIDSTONE, ON N0R 1K0
(519) 723-4807
CATS6DR@AOL.COM

Quebec Fruit Wineries

Cider has been made in Quebec since the middle of the seventeenth century, a tradition that has been unbroken since then. Fruit wines and mead (honey wine) are recent developments, ones that many grape wineries undertake to protect themselves against the loss of their grape crops. Most of the Quebec wineries featured in this book will also produce wines made from apples, stone fruit, or berries. Those dedicated to fruit alone are listed here.

ABBAYE CISTERCIENNE
471, RUE PRINCIPALE
ROUGEMONT, QC J0L 1M0
(450) 469-2880

AU PAVILLON DE LA POMME
1130, BOULEVARD LAURIER
MONT-ST-HILAIRE, QC J3G 4S6
(450) 464-2654
WWW.PAVILLONDELAPOMME.COM

**CIDRERIE DE L'ABBAYE
SAINT-BENOÎT**
CHEMIN DE L'ABBAYE
ST-BENOÎT-DU-LAC, QC J0B 2M0
(819) 843-4080
WWW.ST-BENOIT-DU-LAC.COM

CIDRERIE VERGER BILODEAU
2200, CHEMIN ROYAL
ST-PIERRE, ÎLE D'ORLÉANS,
QC G0A 4E0
(418) 828-9316
WWW.CIDRERIEBILODEAU.QC.CA

CIDRERIE DU BOUT DE L'ÎLE
20, CHEMIN DU BOUT DE L'ÎLE
STE-PÉTRONILLE, ÎLE D'ORLÉANS,
QC G0A 4C0
(418) 828-9603
WWW.POLYCULTUREPLANTE.COM

CIDRERIE DR. ALIX
169, RANG DE LA MONTAGNE
ROUGEMONT, QC J0L 1M0
(450) 469-3004

**CIDRERIE FLEURS DE
POMMIERS**
1047, ROUTE 202
DUNHAM, QC J0E 1M0
(450) 295-2223

CIDRERIE DU VERGER GASTON
1074, CHEMIN DE LA MONTAGNE
MONT-ST-HILAIRE, QC J3G 4S6

**CIDRERIE ET VERGER DENIS
CHARBONNEAU**
575, RANG DE LA MONTAGNE
MONT-ST-GRÉGOIRE, QC J0J 1K0
(514) 347-9184

**CIDERY LA FACE CACHÉE
DE LA POMME**
617, ROUTE 202
HEMMINGFORD, QC J0L 1H0
(450) 247-2899
WWW.APPLEICEWINE.COM

CIDRERIE VERGER LAMARCHE
175, MONTÉE DU VILLAGE
ST-JOSEPH-DU-LAC, QC J0N 1MO
(450) 623-0695
WWW.VERGERLAMARCHE.COM

CIDRERIE MICHEL JODOIN
1130, PETITE CAROLINE
ROUGEMONT, QC J0L 1MO
(450) 469-2676
WWW.CIDRERIE-MICHEL-
JODOIN.QC.CA

CIDRERIE DU MINOT
376, COVEY HILL ROAD
HEMMINGFORD, QC J0L 1HO
(450) 247-3111
WWW.DUMINOT.COM

**CIDRERIE LA POMME DU
ST-LAURENT**
505, CHEMIN BELLEVUE OUEST
CAP ST-IGNACE, QC G0R 1H0
(418) 246-5957

**CIDRERIES ET VERGERS
SAINT-ANTOINE**
3101, ROUTE 132 (MARIE-VICTORIN)
SAINT-ANTOINE-DE-TILLY,
QC G0S 2C0
(418) 886-2375
WWW.MEDIOM.COM/~EMILEAUB

CIDRERIE ST-NICOLAS
2068, ROUTE 132 (MARIE-VICTORIN)
SAINT-ANTOINE-DE-TILLY,
QC G0S 2C0
(418) 836-5505

LA CIDRERIE DU VILLAGE
509, RUE PRINCIPALE
ROUGEMONT, QC J0E 1S0
(450) 469-3945
WWW.LACIDRERIEDUVILLAGE.
QC.CA

CIDERIE LA VIRGINIE
485, ROUTE 277
STE-GERMAINE, QC G0R 1S0
(418) 625-3456
WWW.CIDRERIEVIRGINIE.QC.CA

DOMAINE LEDUC-PIEDIMONTE
30, CHEMIN DE MARIEVILLE
ROUGEMONT, QC J0L 1M0
(450) 469-1469
WWW.LEDUC-PIEDIMONTE.COM

DOMAINE STEINBACH
2205, CHEMIN ROYAL
ST-PIERRE, ÎLE D'ORLÉANS, QC
G0A 4E0
(418) 828-0000
WWW.DOMAINESTEINBACH.COM

ECONOMUSÉE DE LA POMME
1074, CHEMIN DE LA MONTAGNE
MONT-ST-HILAIRE, QC J3G 4S6

FERME HUBERT SAUVÉ
140, RANGE DU MILIEU
SALABERRY-DE-VALLEYFIELD,
QC J6S 0E7
(450) 373-2979

FERME QUINN
2495, BOULEVARD PERROT
NOTRE-DAME-DE-L'ÎLE-PERROT,
QC J7V 8P4

IRDA–VERGER DU PARC
PARC NATIONAL DU MONT-ST-BRUNO
330, CHEMIN DES VINGT-CINQ EST
ST-BRUNO, QC J3V 4P6

**PEPINIÈRE ET VERGERS
PEDNEAULT ET FRÈRES**
45, RUE ROYALE EST
ÎLE-AUX-COUDRES, QC G0A 3J0
(418) 438-2365

**VERGER ET VIGNOBLE
CASA BRETON**
270, CHEMIN JEAN-GUÉRIN OUEST
ST-HENRI-DE-LÉVIS, QC G0R 3E0
(418) 882-2929
WWW.CASABRETON.COM

LES VERGERS DE LA COLLINE
5, ROUTE 137 NORTH
STE-CÉCILE-DE-MILTON, QC J0E 2C0
(450) 777-2442
WWW.LESVERGERS
DELACOLLINE.COM

**VERGERS ET CIDRERIE DENIS
CHARBONNEAU**
575, RANG DE LA MONTAGNE
MONT-ST-GRÉGOIRE, QC J0J 1K0
(450) 347-9184
WWW.VERGERSDC.QC.CA

VERGER ÉMILIE
1372, RUE PRINCIPALE
ROUGEMONT, QC J0L 1M0
(450) 469-2813

VERGER HENRYVILLE
660, ROUTE 133
HENRYVILLE, QC J0J 1E0
(450) 299-2733
WWW.VERGERHENRYVILLE.COM

VERGER JEAN-GUY BISSON
925, RUE PRINCIPALE
ROUGEMONT, QC J0L 1M0
(514) 469-1309

VERGER CIDRERIE LARIVIÈRE
1188, RANG 8
ST-THÉODORE D'ACTON, QC J0H 1Z0
(450) 546-3411
WWW.CLEMENTLARIVIERE.COM

**VERGER ET CIDRERIE
LÉO BOUTIN**
710, RANG DE LA MONTAGNE
MONT-ST-GRÉGOIRE, QC J0J 1K0
(514) 346-3326
WWW.VERGERBOUTIN.COM

VERGER MADO
342, HAUT CORBIN
ST-DAMASE, QC J0H 1J0
(514) 797-3637

**VERGERS ÉCOLOGIQUES
MARCHAND**
790, CHEMIN DE LA MONTAGNE
MONT-ST-HILAIRE, QC J3G 4S6
(514) 467-8197

LES VERGERS LAFRANCE
1473, CHEMIN PRINCIPAL
ST-JOSEPH-DU-LAC, QC J0N 1M0
(450) 491-7859

VERGER DE LA MONTAGNE
118, CHEMIN DU SOUS-BOIS
MONT-ST-GRÉGOIRE, QC J0J 1K0
(514) 460-2858

**VERGERS ÉCOLOGIQUES
NATURE PLUS**
990, CHEMIN DE LA MONTAGNE
MONT-ST-HILAIRE, QC J3G 4S6
(514) 446-3154

LES VERGERS NICOLET
5760, RUE PRINCIPALE
GRAND ST-ESPRIT, QC J0G 1B0
(819) 289-2101

VERGER TOTEM
150, RANG DE LA MONTAGNE
ROUGEMONT, QC J0L 1M0
(450) 469-2521

Atlantic Provinces Fruit Wineries

The first winery to open in the Atlantic provinces was, in fact, a fruit winery: in the 1930s Chipman Wines made an apple cider called Golden Glow at a facility near Kentville in the heart of the Annapolis Valley. The enterprise lasted until 1983, and in its latter years it became a bottling plant for imported grape wines. The Chipman brands were acquired by Andrés in 1984.

Since the mid-1990s, more and more farmers are seeing the economic value of turning their fruit and berries into beverage alcohol products. There is more security for them in dealing with fruit than with combatting the challenges of trying to keep grapevines alive through the winter months.

NOVA SCOTIA FRUIT WINERIES

ELDERKIN'S FARM MARKET & U-PICK
198 GREENWICH, RR 2
WOLFVILLE, NS B0P 1X0
(902) 542-7198
WWW.ELDERKINSAPPLES.COM

LUNENBURG COUNTY WINERY
813 WALBURNE ROAD, RR 3
MAHONE BAY, NS B0J 2E0
(902) 644-2415
WWW.CANADA-WINE.COM

TELDER BERRY FARM AND WINERY
1251 ENFIELD ROAD
NINE MILE RIVER, NS B3S 2T7
(902) 883-8433
WWW.TELDERBERRYWINES.COM

WILLIAMSDALE WINERY LTD.
1330 COLLINGWOOD ROAD
WILLIAMSDALE, NS B0M 1E0
(902) 686-3117
DCARTER@CA.INTER.NET

NEW BRUNSWICK FRUIT WINERIES

FERME BOURGEOIS FARMS AND BELLIVEAU ORCHARD PRÉ-D'EN-HAUT
1209, RUE PRINCIPALE STREET
MEMRAMCOOK, NB E4K 2S6
(506) 758-0295

FERME BOURGEOIS FARMS
(506) 758-2325 (BELLIVEAU ORCHARD)
WWW.FERMEBOURGEOISFARMS

GAGETOWN CIDER COMPANY
16 FOX ROAD
GAGETOWN, NB E5M 1W6
(506) 488-2147
APPLEMAN@NB.SYMPATICO.CA

TIERNEY POINT WINERY
69 ROUTE 785
PENNFIELD, NB E5H 1W4
(506) 755-6942

TUDDENHAM FARMS
ROUTE 1
OAK BAY, NB E3L 2X1
(506) 466-1840
TIERNEYPT@NBNET.NB.CA

NEWFOUNDLAND FRUIT WINERIES

NOTRE DAME WINES
29 DURRELL STREET
TWILLINGATE, NL A0G 1Y0
(709) 884-2707
WWW3.NF.SYMPATICO.CA/
WEILWINERY

RODRIGUES WINERY
(OFF TRANS-CANADA HIGHWAY ON ROUTE 81)
WHITBOURNE, NL A0B 3K0
(709) 759-3003
WWW.RODRIGUESWINERY.COM

Prairie Provinces Fruit Wineries

The Prairie provinces may not be able to grow grapes for wine because of the extremes of summer and winter temperatures, but they can grow fruit. And where there's fruit there are always those impassioned vintners who want to turn berries and orchard fruit into wine.

MANITOBA

D.D. LEOBARD
133 DEBAETS STREET
WINNIPEG, MB R2J 3R9
(204) 661-9007
WWW.DDLEOBARDWINERY.COM/
DDLEOBARD@MTS.NET

RIGBY ORCHARDS LTD.
BOX 163
KILLARNEY, MB R0K 1G0
(204) 523-8879
WWW.ROAMINGRIVER.CA/
WINE.HTML

SASKATCHEWAN

ASPEN GROVE WINERY
PO BOX 218
WHITE CITY, SK S0G 5B0
(306) 771-2921
WWW.ASPENGROVEWINERY.COM

BANACH WINERY
341–22ND STREET WEST
BATTLEFORD, SK S0M 0E0
(306) 445-9463

ALBERTA

FIELDSTONE FRUIT WINES
BOX 19, SITE 6, RR 1
STRATHMORE, AB T1P 1J6
(403) 934-2749
FIELDSTONE@DIRECWAY.COM

BIBLIOGRAPHY

Aspler, Tony. *Wine Lover's Companion*. 3rd ed. Toronto: McGraw-Hill Ryerson, 1988.

Cass, Bruce, editor, with Jancis Robinson, consultant editor. *The Oxford Companion to the Wines of North America*. New York: Oxford University Press, 2000.

Dubois, Jean-Marie, and Laurent Deshaies. *Guide des vignobles du Québec*. St. Laurent, Quebec: Les Presses de l'Université Laval, 1997.

Ejbich, Konrad. *A Pocket Guide to Ontario: Wines, Wineries, Vineyards & Vines*. Toronto: McClelland & Stewart, 2005.

Galet, Pierre. *A Practical Ampelography: Grapevine Identification*. Ithaca, NY: Cornell University Press, 1979.

Naugler, Chris, Bruce Wright, and Robert Murray. *The Tangled Vine: Winegrowing in Nova Scotia*. Bridgewater, NS: blue frog, 2003.

Plocher, Tom, and Bob Parke. *Northern Winework: Growing Grapes and Making Wine in Cold Climates*. Hugo, Minn.: Northern Winework, 2001.

Robinson, Jancis. *Vines, Grapes and Wines*. New York: Alfred A. Knopf, 1986.

Schreiner, John. *British Columbia Wine Country*. Photography by Kevin Miller. Vancouver: Whitecap, 2003.

Schreiner, John. *Icewine: The Complete Story*. Toronto: Warwick Publishing, 2001.

Schreiner, John. *The Wineries of British Columbia*. Victoria: Orca Book Publishers, 1994.

Schreiner, John. *The Wines of Canada*. London: Mitchell Beazley, 2005.

Sloan-McIntosh, Kathleen. *A Year in Niagara: The People and Food of Wine Country*. North Vancouver: Whitecap, 2002.

Tiessen, Ron. *The Vinedressers: A History of Grape Farming & Wineries on Pelee Island*. 2nd ed. Pelee Island, Ontario: Heritage Centre, 1997.

Waters, Chris, and Walter Sendzik. *Vines Buyers' Guide to Canadian Wines*. St. Catharines: Vines Publishing, 2005.

INDEX

Note: Page references **in bold type** indicate the subject of a sidebar or, in the case of wineries that have more than one reference, the main entry for that winery. Wineries in French-speaking regions whose names contain the terms "Clos" or "Vignoble" (vineyard) or "Domaine" (estate) are indexed under their descriptive names (e.g., Vignoble les Blancs Coteaux is listed as "Blancs Coteaux, Vignoble les"). Wineries in English-speaking areas that use these terms are listed under "Domaine" or "Clos."

The Wine Atlas of Canada was produced by Angel Editions under the editorial and art direction of Sara Angel.

Editor: Sarah Davies
Design and maps: Underline Studio
Copy editor: Rosemary Shipton
Assistant editor: Amy Hick
Index: Gillian Watts
Research assistance: Amber Austin

A NOTE ABOUT THE TYPE

The Wine Atlas of Canada was set using three typefaces. Baskerville was designed by John Baskerville in the 1750s. Giza was designed by David Berlow, based on an 1845 specimen by Vincent Figgins. In 1983, Linotype released the Helvetica Neue typeface, based on Helvetica, which was designed by Max Miedinger in 1957.